SELECTED WRITINGS

THE
OTHER VOICE
IN
EARLY MODERN
EUROPE

A Series Edited by Margaret L. King and Albert Rabil Jr.

RECENT BOOKS IN THE SERIES

Marguerite de Navarre

SELECTED WRITINGS

A Bilingual Edition

⁓

Edited and Translated by
Rouben Cholakian and Mary Skemp
with an Introduction by
Rouben Cholakian

THE UNIVERSITY OF CHICAGO PRESS
Chicago & London

Marguerite de Navarre, 1492–1549

Rouben Cholakian is Burgess Professor of Romance Languages Emeritus at Hamilton College. He is the author of numerous publications, most recently of *The Bayeux Tapestry and the Ethos of War*, and, with his late wife, Patricia Cholakian, a biography of Marguerite de Navarre.

Mary Skemp is an independent scholar who lives and teaches in Madison, Wisconsin.

The University of Chicago Press, Chicago 60637
The University of Chicago Press, Ltd., London
© 2008 by The University of Chicago
All rights reserved. Published 2008
Printed in the United States of America

17 16 15 14 13 12 11 10 09 08   1 2 3 4 5

The University of Chicago Press gratefully acknowledges the generous support of James E. Rabil, in memory of Scottie W. Rabil, toward the publication of this book.

ISBN-13: 978-0-226-14270-8 (cloth)
ISBN-13: 978-0-226-14272-2 (paper)
ISBN-10: 0-226-14270-1 (cloth)
ISBN-10: 0-226-14272-8 (paper)

Library of Congress Cataloging-in-Publication Data
Marguerite, Queen, consort of Henry II, King of Navarre, 1492–1549.
[Selections. English & French. 2008]
Selected writings : a bilingual edition / Marguerite de Navarre ; edited and translated by Rouben Cholakian and Mary Skemp ; with an introduction by Rouben Cholakian.
p. cm. — (The other voice in early modern Europe)
Includes bibliographical references and index.
ISBN-13: 978-0-226-14270-8 (cloth : alk. paper)
ISBN-13: 978-0-226-14272-2 (pbk. : alk. paper)
ISBN-10: 0-226-14270-1 (cloth : alk. paper)
ISBN-10: 0-226-14272-8 (pbk. : alk. paper)
I. Cholakian, Rouben Charles, 1932– II. Skemp, Mary. III. Title.
PQ1631.A23 2008
848'.308—dc22   2008011665

CONTENTS

ACKNOWLEDGMENTS

Writers invariably have an invisible army of moral supporters and research aides who help to transform an idea into a reality. This anthology is no exception. We would like therefore to express here our thanks to Jana Brill, Amanda Chism, Megan Goin, Corona Machemer, Mark Pitsch, Timothy Robinson, Giovanna Suhl, and Britanny Thomas. We are particularly grateful to series editors Margaret King and Albert Rabil whose vision has made possible the publications of so many early women writers, otherwise unknown to a larger reading public.

Rouben Cholakian and Mary Skemp

THE OTHER VOICE IN EARLY MODERN EUROPE: INTRODUCTION TO THE SERIES

Margaret L. King and Albert Rabil Jr.

THE OLD VOICE AND THE OTHER VOICE

In western Europe and the United States, women are nearing equality in the professions, in business, and in politics. Most enjoy access to education, reproductive rights, and autonomy in financial affairs. Issues vital to women are on the public agenda: equal pay, child care, domestic abuse, breast cancer research, and curricular revision with an eye to the inclusion of women.

These recent achievements have their origins in things women (and some male supporters) said for the first time about six hundred years ago. Theirs is the "other voice," in contradistinction to the "first voice," the voice of the educated men who created Western culture. Coincident with a general reshaping of European culture in the period 1300–1700 (called the Renaissance or early modern period), questions of female equality and opportunity were raised that still resound and are still unresolved.

The other voice emerged against the backdrop of a three-thousand-year history of the derogation of women rooted in the civilizations related to Western culture: Hebrew, Greek, Roman, and Christian. Negative attitudes toward women inherited from these traditions pervaded the intellectual, medical, legal, religious, and social systems that developed during the European Middle Ages.

The following pages describe the traditional, overwhelmingly male views of women's nature inherited by early modern Europeans and the new tradition that the "other voice" called into being to begin to challenge reigning assumptions. This review should serve as a framework for understanding the texts published in the series The Other Voice in Early Modern Europe. Introductions specific to each text and author follow this essay in all the volumes of the series.

TRADITIONAL VIEWS OF WOMEN, 500 B.C.E.–1500 C.E.

Embedded in the philosophical and medical theories of the ancient Greeks were perceptions of the female as inferior to the male in both mind and body. Similarly, the structure of civil legislation inherited from the ancient Romans was biased against women, and the views on women developed by Christian thinkers out of the Hebrew Bible and the Christian New Testament were negative and disabling. Literary works composed in the vernacular of ordinary people, and widely recited or read, conveyed these negative assumptions. The social networks within which most women lived—those of the family and the institutions of the Roman Catholic Church—were shaped by this negative tradition and sharply limited the areas in which women might act in and upon the world.

GREEK PHILOSOPHY AND FEMALE NATURE. Greek biology assumed that women were inferior to men and defined them as merely childbearers and housekeepers. This view was authoritatively expressed in the works of the philosopher Aristotle.

Aristotle thought in dualities. He considered action superior to inaction, form (the inner design or structure of any object) superior to matter, completion to incompletion, possession to deprivation. In each of these dualities, he associated the male principle with the superior quality and the female with the inferior. "The male principle in nature," he argued, "is associated with active, formative and perfected characteristics, while the female is passive, material and deprived, desiring the male in order to become complete."[1] Men are always identified with virile qualities, such as judgment, courage, and stamina, and women with their opposites—irrationality, cowardice, and weakness.

The masculine principle was considered superior even in the womb. The man's semen, Aristotle believed, created the form of a new human creature, while the female body contributed only matter. (The existence of the ovum, and with it the other facts of human embryology, was not established until the seventeenth century.) Although the later Greek physician Galen believed there was a female component in generation, contributed by "female semen," the followers of both Aristotle and Galen saw the male role in human generation as more active and more important.

In the Aristotelian view, the male principle sought always to reproduce

---

1. Aristotle, *Physics* 1.9.192a20–24, in *The Complete Works of Aristotle*, ed. Jonathan Barnes, rev. Oxford trans., 2 vols. (Princeton, 1984), 1:328.

itself. The creation of a female was always a mistake, therefore, resulting from an imperfect act of generation. Every female born was considered a "defective" or "mutilated" male (as Aristotle's terminology has variously been translated), a "monstrosity" of nature.[2]

For Greek theorists, the biology of males and females was the key to their psychology. The female was softer and more docile, more apt to be despondent, querulous, and deceitful. Being incomplete, moreover, she craved sexual fulfillment in intercourse with a male. The male was intellectual, active, and in control of his passions.

These psychological polarities derived from the theory that the universe consisted of four elements (earth, fire, air, and water), expressed in human bodies as four "humors" (black bile, yellow bile, blood, and phlegm) considered, respectively, dry, hot, damp, and cold and corresponding to mental states ("melancholic," "choleric," "sanguine," "phlegmatic"). In this scheme the male, sharing the principles of earth and fire, was dry and hot; the female, sharing the principles of air and water, was cold and damp.

Female psychology was further affected by her dominant organ, the uterus (womb), *hystera* in Greek. The passions generated by the womb made women lustful, deceitful, talkative, irrational, indeed—when these affects were in excess—"hysterical."

Aristotle's biology also had social and political consequences. If the male principle was superior and the female inferior, then in the household, as in the state, men should rule and women must be subordinate. That hierarchy did not rule out the companionship of husband and wife, whose cooperation was necessary for the welfare of children and the preservation of property. Such mutuality supported male preeminence.

Aristotle's teacher Plato suggested a different possibility: that men and women might possess the same virtues. The setting for this proposal is the imaginary and ideal Republic that Plato sketches in a dialogue of that name. Here, for a privileged elite capable of leading wisely, all distinctions of class and wealth dissolve, as, consequently, do those of gender. Without households or property, as Plato constructs his ideal society, there is no need for the subordination of women. Women may therefore be educated to the same level as men to assume leadership. Plato's Republic remained imaginary, however. In real societies, the subordination of women remained the norm and the prescription.

The views of women inherited from the Greek philosophical tradition became the basis for medieval thought. In the thirteenth century, the su-

---

2. Aristotle, *Generation of Animals* 2.3.737a27–28, in *The Complete Works*, 1: 1144.

preme Scholastic philosopher Thomas Aquinas, among others, still echoed Aristotle's views of human reproduction, of male and female personalities, and of the preeminent male role in the social hierarchy.

ROMAN LAW AND THE FEMALE CONDITION. Roman law, like Greek philosophy, underlay medieval thought and shaped medieval society. The ancient belief that adult property-owning men should administer households and make decisions affecting the community at large is the very fulcrum of Roman law.

About 450 B.C.E., during Rome's republican era, the community's customary law was recorded (legendarily) on twelve tablets erected in the city's central forum. It was later elaborated by professional jurists whose activity increased in the imperial era, when much new legislation was passed, especially on issues affecting family and inheritance. This growing, changing body of laws was eventually codified in the *Corpus of Civil Law* under the direction of the emperor Justinian, generations after the empire ceased to be ruled from Rome. That *Corpus*, read and commented on by medieval scholars from the eleventh century on, inspired the legal systems of most of the cities and kingdoms of Europe.

Laws regarding dowries, divorce, and inheritance pertain primarily to women. Since those laws aimed to maintain and preserve property, the women concerned were those from the property-owning minority. Their subordination to male family members points to the even greater subordination of lower-class and slave women, about whom the laws speak little.

In the early republic, the *paterfamilias*, or "father of the family," possessed *patria potestas*, "paternal power." The term *pater*, "father," in both these cases does not necessarily mean biological father but denotes the head of a household. The father was the person who owned the household's property and, indeed, its human members. The *paterfamilias* had absolute power—including the power, rarely exercised, of life or death—over his wife, his children, and his slaves, as much as his cattle.

Male children could be "emancipated," an act that granted legal autonomy and the right to own property. Those over fourteen could be emancipated by a special grant from the father or automatically by their father's death. But females could never be emancipated; instead, they passed from the authority of their father to that of a husband or, if widowed or orphaned while still unmarried, to a guardian or tutor.

Marriage in its traditional form placed the woman under her husband's authority, or *manus*. He could divorce her on grounds of adultery, drinking wine, or stealing from the household, but she could not divorce him. She could neither possess property in her own right nor bequeath any to her children upon her death. When her husband died, the household property passed not to her but to his male heirs. And when her father died, she had no claim to any family inheritance, which was directed to her brothers or more remote male relatives. The effect of these laws was to exclude women from civil society, itself based on property ownership.

In the later republican and imperial periods, these rules were significantly modified. Women rarely married according to the traditional form. The practice of "free" marriage allowed a woman to remain under her father's authority, to possess property given her by her father (most frequently the "dowry," recoverable from the husband's household on his death), and to inherit from her father. She could also bequeath property to her own children and divorce her husband, just as he could divorce her.

Despite this greater freedom, women still suffered enormous disability under Roman law. Heirs could belong only to the father's side, never the mother's. Moreover, although she could bequeath her property to her children, she could not establish a line of succession in doing so. A woman was "the beginning and end of her own family," said the jurist Ulpian. Moreover, women could play no public role. They could not hold public office, represent anyone in a legal case, or even witness a will. Women had only a private existence and no public personality.

The dowry system, the guardian, women's limited ability to transmit wealth, and total political disability are all features of Roman law adopted by the medieval communities of western Europe, although modified according to local customary laws.

CHRISTIAN DOCTRINE AND WOMEN'S PLACE. The Hebrew Bible and the Christian New Testament authorized later writers to limit women to the realm of the family and to burden them with the guilt of original sin. The passages most fruitful for this purpose were the creation narratives in Genesis and sentences from the Epistles defining women's role within the Christian family and community.

Each of the first two chapters of Genesis contains a creation narrative. In the first "God created man in his own image, in the image of God he created him; male and female he created them" (Gn 1:27). In the second, God created Eve from Adam's rib (2:21–23). Christian theologians relied principally on Genesis 2 for their understanding of the relation between man and woman, interpreting the creation of Eve from Adam as proof of her subordination to him.

The creation story in Genesis 2 leads to that of the temptations in Genesis 3: of Eve by the wily serpent and of Adam by Eve. As read by Christian theologians from Tertullian to Thomas Aquinas, the narrative made Eve responsible for the Fall and its consequences. She instigated the act; she deceived her husband; she suffered the greater punishment. Her disobedience made it necessary for Jesus to be incarnated and to die on the cross. From the pulpit, moralists and preachers for centuries conveyed to women the guilt that they bore for original sin.

The Epistles offered advice to early Christians on building communities of the faithful. Among the matters to be regulated was the place of women. Paul offered views favorable to women in Galatians 3:28: "There is neither Jew nor Greek, there is neither slave nor free, there is neither male nor female; for you are all one in Christ Jesus." Paul also referred to women as his coworkers and placed them on a par with himself and his male coworkers (Phlm 4:2–3; Rom 16:1–3; 1 Cor 16:19). Elsewhere, Paul limited women's possibilities: "But I want you to understand that the head of every man is Christ, the head of a woman is her husband, and the head of Christ is God" (1 Cor 11:3).

Biblical passages by later writers (although attributed to Paul) enjoined women to forgo jewels, expensive clothes, and elaborate coiffures; and they forbade women to "teach or have authority over men," telling them to "learn in silence with all submissiveness" as is proper for one responsible for sin, consoling them, however, with the thought that they will be saved through childbearing (1 Tm 2:9–15). Other texts among the later Epistles defined women as the weaker sex and emphasized their subordination to their husbands (1 Pt 3:7; Col 3:18; Eph 5:22–23).

These passages from the New Testament became the arsenal employed by theologians of the early church to transmit negative attitudes toward women to medieval Christian culture—above all, Tertullian (*On the Apparel of Women*), Jerome (*Against Jovinian*), and Augustine (*The Literal Meaning of Genesis*).

THE IMAGE OF WOMEN IN MEDIEVAL LITERATURE. The philosophical, legal, and religious traditions born in antiquity formed the basis of the medieval intellectual synthesis wrought by trained thinkers, mostly clerics, writing in Latin and based largely in universities. The vernacular literary tradition that developed alongside the learned tradition also spoke about female nature and women's roles. Medieval stories, poems, and epics also portrayed women negatively—as lustful and deceitful—while praising good housekeepers and loyal wives as replicas of the Virgin Mary or the female saints and martyrs.

There is an exception in the movement of "courtly love" that evolved in southern France from the twelfth century. Courtly love was the erotic love between a nobleman and noblewoman, the latter usually superior in social rank. It was always adulterous. From the conventions of courtly love derive modern Western notions of romantic love. The tradition has had an impact disproportionate to its size, for it affected only a tiny elite, and very few women. The exaltation of the female lover probably does not reflect a higher evaluation of women or a step toward their sexual liberation. More likely it gives expression to the social and sexual tensions besetting the knightly class at a specific historical juncture.

The literary fashion of courtly love was on the wane by the thirteenth century, when the widely read *Romance of the Rose* was composed in French by two authors of significantly different dispositions. Guillaume de Lorris composed the initial four thousand verses about 1235, and Jean de Meun added about seventeen thousand verses—more than four times the original—about 1265.

The fragment composed by Guillaume de Lorris stands squarely in the tradition of courtly love. Here the poet, in a dream, is admitted into a walled garden where he finds a magic fountain in which a rosebush is reflected. He longs to pick one rose, but the thorns prevent his doing so, even as he is wounded by arrows from the god of love, whose commands he agrees to obey. The rest of this part of the poem recounts the poet's unsuccessful efforts to pluck the rose.

The longer part of the *Romance* by Jean de Meun also describes a dream. But here allegorical characters give long didactic speeches, providing a social satire on a variety of themes, some pertaining to women. Love is an anxious and tormented state, the poem explains: women are greedy and manipulative, marriage is miserable, beautiful women are lustful, ugly ones cease to please, and a chaste woman is as rare as a black swan.

Shortly after Jean de Meun completed *The Romance of the Rose*, Mathéolus penned his *Lamentations*, a long Latin diatribe against marriage translated into French about a century later. The *Lamentations* sum up medieval attitudes toward women and provoked the important response by Christine de Pizan in her *Book of the City of Ladies*.

In 1355, Giovanni Boccaccio wrote *Il Corbaccio*, another antifeminist manifesto, although ironically by an author whose other works pioneered new directions in Renaissance thought. The former husband of his lover appears to Boccaccio, condemning his unmoderated lust and detailing the defects of women. Boccaccio concedes at the end "how much men naturally surpass women in nobility" and is cured of his desires.[3]

---

3. Giovanni Boccaccio, *The Corbaccio, or The Labyrinth of Love*, trans. and ed. Anthony K. Cassell, rev. ed. (Binghamton, N.Y., 1993), 71.

WOMEN'S ROLES: THE FAMILY. The negative perceptions of women expressed in the intellectual tradition are also implicit in the actual roles that women played in European society. Assigned to subordinate positions in the household and the church, they were barred from significant participation in public life.

Medieval European households, like those in antiquity and in non-Western civilizations, were headed by males. It was the male serf (or peasant), feudal lord, town merchant, or citizen who was polled or taxed or succeeded to an inheritance or had any acknowledged public role, although his wife or widow could stand as a temporary surrogate. From about 1100, the position of property-holding males was further enhanced: inheritance was confined to the male, or agnate, line—with depressing consequences for women.

A wife never fully belonged to her husband's family, nor was she a daughter to her father's family. She left her father's house young to marry whomever her parents chose. Her dowry was managed by her husband, and at her death it normally passed to her children by him.

A married woman's life was occupied nearly constantly with cycles of pregnancy, childbearing, and lactation. Women bore children through all the years of their fertility, and many died in childbirth. They were also responsible for raising young children up to six or seven. In the propertied classes that responsibility was shared, since it was common for a wet nurse to take over breast-feeding and for servants to perform other chores.

Women trained their daughters in the household duties appropriate to their status, nearly always tasks associated with textiles: spinning, weaving, sewing, embroidering. Their sons were sent out of the house as apprentices or students, or their training was assumed by fathers in later childhood and adolescence. On the death of her husband, a woman's children became the responsibility of his family. She generally did not take "his" children with her to a new marriage or back to her father's house, except sometimes in the artisan classes.

Women also worked. Rural peasants performed farm chores, merchant wives often practiced their husbands' trades, the unmarried daughters of the urban poor worked as servants or prostitutes. All wives produced or embellished textiles and did the housekeeping, while wealthy ones managed servants. These labors were unpaid or poorly paid but often contributed substantially to family wealth.

WOMEN'S ROLES: THE CHURCH. Membership in a household, whether a father's or a husband's, meant for women a lifelong subordination to others.

In western Europe, the Roman Catholic Church offered an alternative to the career of wife and mother. A woman could enter a convent, parallel in function to the monasteries for men that evolved in the early Christian centuries.

In the convent, a woman pledged herself to a celibate life, lived according to strict community rules, and worshiped daily. Often the convent offered training in Latin, allowing some women to become considerable scholars and authors as well as scribes, artists, and musicians. For women who chose the conventual life, the benefits could be enormous, but for numerous others placed in convents by paternal choice, the life could be restrictive and burdensome.

The conventual life declined as an alternative for women as the modern age approached. Reformed monastic institutions resisted responsibility for related female orders. The church increasingly restricted female institutional life by insisting on closer male supervision.

Women often sought other options. Some joined the communities of laywomen that sprang up spontaneously in the thirteenth century in the urban zones of western Europe, especially in Flanders and Italy. Some joined the heretical movements that flourished in late medieval Christendom, whose anticlerical and often antifamily positions particularly appealed to women. In these communities, some women were acclaimed as "holy women" or "saints," whereas others often were condemned as frauds or heretics.

In all, although the options offered to women by the church were sometimes less than satisfactory, they were sometimes richly rewarding. After 1520, the convent remained an option only in Roman Catholic territories. Protestantism engendered an ideal of marriage as a heroic endeavor and appeared to place husband and wife on a more equal footing. Sermons and treatises, however, still called for female subordination and obedience.

THE OTHER VOICE, 1300–1700

When the modern era opened, European culture was so firmly structured by a framework of negative attitudes toward women that to dismantle it was a monumental labor. The process began as part of a larger cultural movement that entailed the critical reexamination of ideas inherited from the ancient and medieval past. The humanists launched that critical reexamination.

THE HUMANIST FOUNDATION. Originating in Italy in the fourteenth century, humanism quickly became the dominant intellectual movement in

Europe. Spreading in the sixteenth century from Italy to the rest of Europe, it fueled the literary, scientific, and philosophical movements of the era and laid the basis for the eighteenth-century Enlightenment.

Humanists regarded the Scholastic philosophy of medieval universities as out of touch with the realities of urban life. They found in the rhetorical discourse of classical Rome a language adapted to civic life and public speech. They learned to read, speak, and write classical Latin and, eventually, classical Greek. They founded schools to teach others to do so, establishing the pattern for elementary and secondary education for the next three hundred years.

In the service of complex government bureaucracies, humanists employed their skills to write eloquent letters, deliver public orations, and formulate public policy. They developed new scripts for copying manuscripts and used the new printing press to disseminate texts, for which they created methods of critical editing.

Humanism was a movement led by males who accepted the evaluation of women in ancient texts and generally shared the misogynist perceptions of their culture. (Female humanists, as we will see, did not.) Yet humanism also opened the door to a reevaluation of the nature and capacity of women. By calling authors, texts, and ideas into question, it made possible the fundamental rereading of the whole intellectual tradition that was required in order to free women from cultural prejudice and social subordination.

A DIFFERENT CITY. The other voice first appeared when, after so many centuries, the accumulation of misogynist concepts evoked a response from a capable female defender: Christine de Pizan (1365–1431). Introducing her *Book of the City of Ladies* (1405), she described how she was affected by reading Mathéolus's *Lamentations*: "Just the sight of this book . . . made me wonder how it happened that so many different men . . . are so inclined to express both in speaking and in their treatises and writings so many wicked insults about women and their behavior."[4] These statements impelled her to detest herself "and the entire feminine sex, as though we were monstrosities in nature."[5]

The rest of *The Book of the City of Ladies* presents a justification of the female sex and a vision of an ideal community of women. A pioneer, she has received the message of female inferiority and rejected it. From the four-

4. Christine de Pizan, *The Book of the City of Ladies*, trans. Earl Jeffrey Richards, foreword by Marina Warner (New York, 1982), 1.1.1, pp. 3–4.

5. Ibid., 1.1.1–2, p. 5.

teenth to the seventeenth century, a huge body of literature accumulated that responded to the dominant tradition.

The result was a literary explosion consisting of works by both men and women, in Latin and in the vernaculars: works enumerating the achievements of notable women; works rebutting the main accusations made against women; works arguing for the equal education of men and women; works defining and redefining women's proper role in the family, at court, in public; works describing women's lives and experiences. Recent monographs and articles have begun to hint at the great range of this movement, involving probably several thousand titles. The protofeminism of these "other voices" constitutes a significant fraction of the literary product of the early modern era.

THE CATALOGS. About 1365, the same Boccaccio whose *Corbaccio* rehearses the usual charges against female nature wrote another work, *Concerning Famous Women*. A humanist treatise drawing on classical texts, it praised 106 notable women: ninety-eight of them from pagan Greek and Roman antiquity, one (Eve) from the Bible, and seven from the medieval religious and cultural tradition; his book helped make all readers aware of a sex normally condemned or forgotten. Boccaccio's outlook nevertheless was unfriendly to women, for it singled out for praise those women who possessed the traditional virtues of chastity, silence, and obedience. Women who were active in the public realm—for example, rulers and warriors—were depicted as usually being lascivious and as suffering terrible punishments for entering the masculine sphere. Women were his subject, but Boccaccio's standard remained male.

Christine de Pizan's *Book of the City of Ladies* contains a second catalog, one responding specifically to Boccaccio's. Whereas Boccaccio portrays female virtue as exceptional, she depicts it as universal. Many women in history were leaders, or remained chaste despite the lascivious approaches of men, or were visionaries and brave martyrs.

The work of Boccaccio inspired a series of catalogs of illustrious women of the biblical, classical, Christian, and local pasts, among them Filippo da Bergamo's *Of Illustrious Women*, Pierre de Brantôme's *Lives of Illustrious Women*, Pierre Le Moyne's *Gallerie of Heroic Women*, and Pietro Paolo de Ribera's *Immortal Triumphs and Heroic Enterprises of 845 Women*. Whatever their embedded prejudices, these works drove home to the public the possibility of female excellence.

THE DEBATE. At the same time, many questions remained: Could a woman be virtuous? Could she perform noteworthy deeds? Was she even, strictly speaking, of the same human species as men? These questions were debated over four centuries, in French, German, Italian, Spanish, and English, by authors male and female, among Catholics, Protestants, and Jews, in ponderous volumes and breezy pamphlets. The whole literary genre has been called the *querelle des femmes*, the "woman question."

The opening volley of this battle occurred in the first years of the fifteenth century, in a literary debate sparked by Christine de Pizan. She exchanged letters critical of Jean de Meun's contribution to *The Romance of the Rose* with two French royal secretaries, Jean de Montreuil and Gontier Col. When the matter became public, Jean Gerson, one of Europe's leading theologians, supported de Pizan's arguments against de Meun, for the moment silencing the opposition.

The debate resurfaced repeatedly over the next two hundred years. *The Triumph of Women* (1438) by Juan Rodríguez de la Camara (or Juan Rodríguez del Padron) struck a new note by presenting arguments for the superiority of women to men. *The Champion of Women* (1440–42) by Martin Le Franc addresses once again the negative views of women presented in *The Romance of the Rose* and offers counterevidence of female virtue and achievement.

A cameo of the debate on women is included in *The Courtier*, one of the most widely read books of the era, published by the Italian Baldassare Castiglione in 1528 and immediately translated into other European vernaculars. *The Courtier* depicts a series of evenings at the court of the duke of Urbino in which many men and some women of the highest social stratum amuse themselves by discussing a range of literary and social issues. The "woman question" is a pervasive theme throughout, and the third of its four books is devoted entirely to that issue.

In a verbal duel, Gasparo Pallavicino and Giuliano de' Medici present the main claims of the two traditions. Gasparo argues the innate inferiority of women and their inclination to vice. Only in bearing children do they profit the world. Giuliano counters that women share the same spiritual and mental capacities as men and may excel in wisdom and action. Men and women are of the same essence: just as no stone can be more perfectly a stone than another, so no human being can be more perfectly human than others, whether male or female. It was an astonishing assertion, boldly made to an audience as large as all Europe.

THE TREATISES. Humanism provided the materials for a positive counterconcept to the misogyny embedded in Scholastic philosophy and law and inherited from the Greek, Roman, and Christian pasts. A series of humanist treatises on marriage and family, on education and deportment, and on the nature of women helped construct these new perspectives.

The works by Francesco Barbaro and Leon Battista Alberti—*On Marriage* (1415) and *On the Family* (1434–37)—far from defending female equality, reasserted women's responsibility for rearing children and managing the housekeeping while being obedient, chaste, and silent. Nevertheless, they served the cause of reexamining the issue of women's nature by placing domestic issues at the center of scholarly concern and reopening the pertinent classical texts. In addition, Barbaro emphasized the companionate nature of marriage and the importance of a wife's spiritual and mental qualities for the well-being of the family.

These themes reappear in later humanist works on marriage and the education of women by Juan Luis Vives and Erasmus. Both were moderately sympathetic to the condition of women without reaching beyond the usual masculine prescriptions for female behavior.

An outlook more favorable to women characterizes the nearly unknown work *In Praise of Women* (ca. 1487) by the Italian humanist Bartolommeo Goggio. In addition to providing a catalog of illustrious women, Goggio argued that male and female are the same in essence, but that women (reworking the Adam and Eve narrative from quite a new angle) are actually superior. In the same vein, the Italian humanist Mario Equicola asserted the spiritual equality of men and women in *On Women* (1501). In 1525, Galeazzo Flavio Capra (or Capella) published his work *On the Excellence and Dignity of Women.* This humanist tradition of treatises defending the worthiness of women culminates in the work of Henricus Cornelius Agrippa *On the Nobility and Preeminence of the Female Sex.* No work by a male humanist more succinctly or explicitly presents the case for female dignity.

THE WITCH BOOKS. While humanists grappled with the issues pertaining to women and family, other learned men turned their attention to what they perceived as a very great problem: witches. Witch-hunting manuals, explorations of the witch phenomenon, and even defenses of witches are not at first glance pertinent to the tradition of the other voice. But they do relate in this way: most accused witches were women. The hostility aroused by supposed witch activity is comparable to the hostility aroused by women. The evil deeds the victims of the hunt were charged with were exaggerations of the vices to which, many believed, all women were prone.

The connection between the witch accusation and the hatred of women is explicit in the notorious witch-hunting manual *The Hammer of Witches* (1486) by two Dominican inquisitors, Heinrich Krämer and Jacob Sprenger. Here the inconstancy, deceitfulness, and lustfulness traditionally associated with women are depicted in exaggerated form as the core features of witch behavior. These traits inclined women to make a bargain with the devil—

sealed by sexual intercourse—by which they acquired unholy powers. Such bizarre claims, far from being rejected by rational men, were broadcast by intellectuals. The German Ulrich Molitur, the Frenchman Nicolas Rémy, and the Italian Stefano Guazzo all coolly informed the public of sinister orgies and midnight pacts with the devil. The celebrated French jurist, historian, and political philosopher Jean Bodin argued that because women were especially prone to diabolism, regular legal procedures could properly be suspended in order to try those accused of this "exceptional crime."

A few experts such as the physician Johann Weyer, a student of Agrippa's, raised their voices in protest. In 1563, he explained the witch phenomenon thus, without discarding belief in diabolism: the devil deluded foolish old women afflicted by melancholia, causing them to believe they had magical powers. Weyer's rational skepticism, which had good credibility in the community of the learned, worked to revise the conventional views of women and witchcraft.

WOMEN'S WORKS. To the many categories of works produced on the question of women's worth must be added nearly all works written by women. A woman writing was in herself a statement of women's claim to dignity.

Only a few women wrote anything before the dawn of the modern era, for three reasons. First, they rarely received the education that would enable them to write. Second, they were not admitted to the public roles— as administrator, bureaucrat, lawyer or notary, or university professor—in which they might gain knowledge of the kinds of things the literate public thought worth writing about. Third, the culture imposed silence on women, considering speaking out a form of unchastity. Given these conditions, it is remarkable that any women wrote. Those who did before the fourteenth century were almost always nuns or religious women whose isolation made their pronouncements more acceptable.

From the fourteenth century on, the volume of women's writings rose. Women continued to write devotional literature, although not always as cloistered nuns. They also wrote diaries, often intended as keepsakes for their children; books of advice to their sons and daughters; letters to family members and friends; and family memoirs, in a few cases elaborate enough to be considered histories.

A few women wrote works directly concerning the "woman question," and some of these, such as the humanists Isotta Nogarola, Cassandra Fedele, Laura Cereta, and Olympia Morata, were highly trained. A few were professional writers, living by the income of their pens; the very first among them was Christine de Pizan, noteworthy in this context as in so many others. In addition to *The Book of the City of Ladies* and her critiques of *The Romance of the Rose*, she wrote *The Treasure of the City of Ladies* (a guide to social decorum for women), an advice book for her son, much courtly verse, and a full-scale history of the reign of King Charles V of France.

WOMEN PATRONS. Women who did not themselves write but encouraged others to do so boosted the development of an alternative tradition. Highly placed women patrons supported authors, artists, musicians, poets, and learned men. Such patrons, drawn mostly from the Italian elites and the courts of northern Europe, figure disproportionately as the dedicatees of the important works of early feminism.

For a start, it might be noted that the catalogs of Boccaccio and Alvaro de Luna were dedicated to the Florentine noblewoman Andrea Acciaiuoli and to Doña María, first wife of King Juan II of Castile, while the French translation of Boccaccio's work was commissioned by Anne of Brittany, wife of King Charles VIII of France. The humanist treatises of Goggio, Equicola, Vives, and Agrippa were dedicated, respectively, to Eleanora of Aragon, wife of Ercole I d'Este, duke of Ferrara; to Margherita Cantelma of Mantua; to Catherine of Aragon, wife of King Henry VIII of England; and to Margaret, Duchess of Austria and regent of the Netherlands. As late as 1696, Mary Astell's *Serious Proposal to the Ladies, for the Advancement of Their True and Greatest Interest* was dedicated to Princess Anne of Denmark.

These authors presumed that their efforts would be welcome to female patrons, or they may have written at the bidding of those patrons. Silent themselves, perhaps even unresponsive, these loftily placed women helped shape the tradition of the other voice.

THE ISSUES. The literary forms and patterns in which the tradition of the other voice presented itself have now been sketched. It remains to highlight the major issues around which this tradition crystallizes. In brief, there are four problems to which our authors return again and again, in plays and catalogs, in verse and letters, in treatises and dialogues, in every language: the problem of chastity, the problem of power, the problem of speech, and the problem of knowledge. Of these the greatest, preconditioning the others, is the problem of chastity.

THE PROBLEM OF CHASTITY. In traditional European culture, as in those of antiquity and others around the globe, chastity was perceived as woman's quintessential virtue—in contrast to courage, or generosity, or leadership, or rationality, seen as virtues characteristic of men. Opponents of women charged them with insatiable lust. Women themselves and their defenders—without disputing the validity of the standard—responded that women were capable of chastity.

The requirement of chastity kept women at home, silenced them, isolated them, left them in ignorance. It was the source of all other impediments. Why was it so important to the society of men, of whom chastity was not required, and who more often than not considered it their right to violate the chastity of any woman they encountered?

Female chastity ensured the continuity of the male-headed household. If a man's wife was not chaste, he could not be sure of the legitimacy of his offspring. If they were not his and they acquired his property, it was not his household, but some other man's, that had endured. If his daughter was not chaste, she could not be transferred to another man's household as his wife, and he was dishonored.

The whole system of the integrity of the household and the transmission of property was bound up in female chastity. Such a requirement pertained only to property-owning classes, of course. Poor women could not expect to maintain their chastity, least of all if they were in contact with high-status men to whom all women but those of their own household were prey.

In Catholic Europe, the requirement of chastity was further buttressed by moral and religious imperatives. Original sin was inextricably linked with the sexual act. Virginity was seen as heroic virtue, far more impressive than, say, the avoidance of idleness or greed. Monasticism, the cultural institution that dominated medieval Europe for centuries, was grounded in the renunciation of the flesh. The Catholic reform of the eleventh century imposed a similar standard on all the clergy and a heightened awareness of sexual requirements on all the laity. Although men were asked to be chaste, female unchastity was much worse: it led to the devil, as Eve had led mankind to sin.

To such requirements, women and their defenders protested their innocence. Furthermore, following the example of holy women who had escaped the requirements of family and sought the religious life, some women began to conceive of female communities as alternatives both to family and to the cloister. Christine de Pizan's city of ladies was such a community. Moderata Fonte and Mary Astell envisioned others. The luxurious salons of the French *précieuses* of the seventeenth century, or the comfortable English drawing rooms of the next, may have been born of the same impulse. Here women not only might escape, if briefly, the subordinate position that life in the family entailed but might also make claims to power, exercise their capacity for speech, and display their knowledge.

THE PROBLEM OF POWER. Women were excluded from power: the whole cultural tradition insisted on it. Only men were citizens, only men bore arms, only men could be chiefs or lords or kings. There were exceptions that did not disprove the rule, when wives or widows or mothers took the place of men, awaiting their return or the maturation of a male heir. A woman who attempted to rule in her own right was perceived as an anomaly, a monster, at once a deformed woman and an insufficient male, sexually confused and consequently unsafe.

The association of such images with women who held or sought power explains some otherwise odd features of early modern culture. Queen Elizabeth I of England, one of the few women to hold full regal authority in European history, played with such male/female images—positive ones, of course—in representing herself to her subjects. She was a prince, and manly, even though she was female. She was also (she claimed) virginal, a condition absolutely essential if she was to avoid the attacks of her opponents. Catherine de' Medici, who ruled France as widow and regent for her sons, also adopted such imagery in defining her position. She chose as one symbol the figure of Artemisia, an androgynous ancient warrior-heroine who combined a female persona with masculine powers.

Power in a woman, without such sexual imagery, seems to have been indigestible by the culture. A rare note was struck by the Englishman Sir Thomas Elyot in his *Defence of Good Women* (1540), justifying both women's participation in civic life and their prowess in arms. The old tune was sung by the Scots reformer John Knox in his *First Blast of the Trumpet against the Monstrous Regiment of Women* (1558); for him rule by women, defects in nature, was a hideous contradiction in terms.

The confused sexuality of the imagery of female potency was not reserved for rulers. Any woman who excelled was likely to be called an Amazon, recalling the self-mutilated warrior women of antiquity who repudiated all men, gave up their sons, and raised only their daughters. She was often said to have "exceeded her sex" or to have possessed "masculine virtue"—as the very fact of conspicuous excellence conferred masculinity even on the female subject. The catalogs of notable women often showed those female heroes dressed in armor, armed to the teeth, like men. Amazonian heroines romp through the epics of the age—Ariosto's *Orlando Furioso* (1532) and Spenser's *Faerie Queene* (1590–1609). Excellence in a woman was perceived as a claim for power, and power was reserved for the masculine realm. A woman who possessed either one was masculinized and lost title to her own female identity.

THE PROBLEM OF SPEECH. Just as power had a sexual dimension when it was claimed by women, so did speech. A good woman spoke little. Excessive speech was an indication of unchastity. By speech, women seduced men. Eve had lured Adam into sin by her speech. Accused witches were commonly accused of having spoken abusively, or irrationally, or simply too much. As enlightened a figure as Francesco Barbaro insisted on silence in a woman, which he linked to her perfect unanimity with her husband's will and her unblemished virtue (her chastity). Another Italian humanist, Leonardo Bruni, in advising a noblewoman on her studies, barred her not from speech but from public speaking. That was reserved for men.

Related to the problem of speech was that of costume—another, if silent, form of self-expression. Assigned the task of pleasing men as their primary occupation, elite women often tended toward elaborate costume, hairdressing, and the use of cosmetics. Clergy and secular moralists alike condemned these practices. The appropriate function of costume and adornment was to announce the status of a woman's husband or father. Any further indulgence in adornment was akin to unchastity.

THE PROBLEM OF KNOWLEDGE. When the Italian noblewoman Isotta Nogarola had begun to attain a reputation as a humanist, she was accused of incest—a telling instance of the association of learning in women with unchastity. That chilling association inclined any woman who was educated to deny that she was or to make exaggerated claims of heroic chastity.

If educated women were pursued with suspicions of sexual misconduct, women seeking an education faced an even more daunting obstacle: the assumption that women were by nature incapable of learning, that reasoning was a particularly masculine ability. Just as they proclaimed their chastity, women and their defenders insisted on their capacity for learning. The major work by a male writer on female education—that by Juan Luis Vives, *On the Education of a Christian Woman* (1523)—granted female capacity for intellection but still argued that a woman's whole education was to be shaped around the requirement of chastity and a future within the household. Female writers of the following generations—Marie de Gournay in France, Anna Maria van Schurman in Holland, and Mary Astell in England—began to envision other possibilities.

The pioneers of female education were the Italian women humanists who managed to attain a literacy in Latin and a knowledge of classical and Christian literature equivalent to that of prominent men. Their works implicitly and explicitly raise questions about women's social roles, defining problems that beset women attempting to break out of the cultural limits that had bound them. Like Christine de Pizan, who achieved an advanced education through her father's tutoring and her own devices, their bold questioning makes clear the importance of training. Only when women were educated to the same standard as male leaders would they be able to raise that other voice and insist on their dignity as human beings morally, intellectually, and legally equal to men.

THE OTHER VOICE. The other voice, a voice of protest, was mostly female, but it was also male. It spoke in the vernaculars and in Latin, in treatises and dialogues, in plays and poetry, in letters and diaries, and in pamphlets. It battered at the wall of prejudice that encircled women and raised a banner announcing its claims. The female was equal (or even superior) to the male in essential nature—moral, spiritual, and intellectual. Women were capable of higher education, of holding positions of power and influence in the public realm, and of speaking and writing persuasively. The last bastion of masculine supremacy, centered on the notions of a woman's primary domestic responsibility and the requirement of female chastity, was not as yet assaulted—although visions of productive female communities as alternatives to the family indicated an awareness of the problem.

During the period 1300–1700, the other voice remained only a voice, and one only dimly heard. It did not result—yet—in an alteration of social patterns. Indeed, to this day they have not entirely been altered. Yet the call for justice issued as long as six centuries ago by those writing in the tradition of the other voice must be recognized as the source and origin of the mature feminist tradition and of the realignment of social institutions accomplished in the modern age.

We thank the volume editors in this series, who responded with many suggestions to an earlier draft of this introduction, making it a collaborative enterprise. Many of their suggestions and criticisms have resulted in revisions of this introduction, although we remain responsible for the final product.

PROJECTED TITLES IN THE SERIES

Emilie du Châtelet, *Selected Writings,* edited with an introduction by Judith P. Zinsser, translated by Isabelle Bour and Judith P. Zinsser

Helisenne de Crenne, *Complete Works,* edited and translated by Timothy Reiss

Christine de Pizan, *Debate over the "Romance of the Rose,"* edited and translated by David F. Hult

Christine de Pizan, *Early Defense of Women Poems,* edited and translated by Thelma Fenster

Christine de Pizan, *Life of Charles V,* edited and translated by Nadia Margolis

Christine de Pizan, *The Long Road of Learning*, edited and translated by Andrea Tarnowski

Isabella d'Este, *Selected Letters*, edited and translated by Deanna Shemek

Catharina Regina von Greiffenberg, *Meditations on the Incarnation, Passion, and Death of Jesus Christ*, edited and translated by Lynne Tatlock

Pernette du Guillet, *Complete Poems*, edited with an introduction by Karen James, translated by Marta Finch Koslowsky

Sister Margaret of the Mother of God, *Autobiography*, edited with an introduction by Cordula van Wyhe, translated by Susan Smith

Marguerite de Navarre, *The Heptameron*, edited by Mary B. McKinley, translated by Rouben Cholakian

Lucrezia Marinella, *Enrico, or Byzantium Conquered*, edited and translated by Maria Galli Stampino

Ana de Mendoza, *Selected Letters*, edited and translated by Helen H. Reed

Valeria Miani, *Celinda: A Tragedy*, edited with an introduction by Valeria Finucci, translated by Julia Kisacky

Sister Giustina Niccolini, *Chronicle of Le Murate*, edited and translated by Saundra Weddle

Antonia Tanini Pulci, *Saints' Lives and Biblical Stories for the State (1483–1492)*, edited by Elissa Weaver, translated by James Cook (a revised edition of *Florentine Drama for Convent and Festival*, published in the series in 1997)

Oliva Sabuco, *The True Medicine*, edited and translated by Gianna Pomata

Gaspara Stampa, *Complete Poems*, edited and translated by Jane Tylus

Gabrielle Suchon, *On Philosophy and On Mortality*, edited and translated by Domna Stanton and Rebecca Wilkin

Sarra Copia Sullam, *Jewish Poet and Intellectual in Early Seventeenth-Century Venice*, edited and translated by Don Harrán

Maria de Zayas y Sotomayor, *Exemplary Tales of Love and Tales of Disillusion*, edited and translated by Margaret R. Greer and Elizabeth Rhodes

VOLUME EDITOR'S INTRODUCTION

THE OTHER VOICE

If she had been author of only the extraordinary collection of tales known as the *Heptameron*, Marguerite de Navarre would most assuredly deserve a place in the pantheon of Renaissance writers. But this remarkable woman is now slowly emerging as a person of many skills and a singular talent of her time.[1]

She was sister to a king and wife to another, an ardent reformist,[2] a generous patron,[3] an astute politician, and a diligent humanist. But as the years passed and the glitter of court life waned, Marguerite de Navarre recognized her true vocation: she was—uniquely for a queen—a writer.

A prominent player in the political arena, Marguerite nevertheless not only found time to devote to what she lovingly called her *doulce escrip-*

---

1. For the biography of Marguerite, readers of French should consult Pierre Jourda, *Marguerite d'Angoulême, Duchesse d'Alençon, reine de Navarre (1492–1549): Etude biographique et littéraire*, 2 vols. (1930; reprint, Geneva: Slatkine, 1978). Readers of English should consult Patricia Cholakian and Rouben Cholakian, *Marguerite de Navarre: Mother of the Renaissance* (New York: Columbia University Press, 2006). As for the ever-increasing number of essays and books about Marguerite, one should first see H. P. Clive, *Marguerite de Navarre: An Annotated Bibliography* (London: Grant & Cutler, 1983). Of course much has been written about her since, and students of the queen of Navarre will need to examine the bibliographical listings published annually by the Modern Language Association (MLA).

2. In order to distinguish this brand of reformists from others—perhaps more political or social in nature—one might better think of Marguerite as an "evangelical" reformist. The French term for the Gospels is *l'évangile*, where this group of critics of the church expected to find the essential source for their religious inspiration. Their goal was not to break away from the church but to "reform" from within.

3. Marguerite has to have been one of the most influential and generous patrons of her time. She was, it seems, forever granting annual stipends to various *secrétaires*, who included such notables as Bonaventure des Périers (1510?–1544?), and the quick-witted and iconoclastic poet Clément Marot (1496–1544), the enfant terrible of her literary entourage.

ture (sweet writings) but astounds us with the rich variety and scope of her œuvre. Beside the *Heptameron*, her collected works include mystical poetry, plays, and philosophical and narrative verse. There is also an immense body of letters[4]—well over a thousand survive—sent to relatives, friends, and prominent figures over the years.

From across the years, the "voice" we hear in these pages is frequently a voice of self-conscious distress, a call to arms. Marguerite's acute awareness of her identity as a woman alerts readers to not only her desperate sense of difference but her passionate commitment to redressing the blatant gender imbalance. When her brother the king goes off to war, she bewails her fragile feminine body that prevents her from standing with the other combatants. Her outspoken fictional alter ego, Parlamente, in the *Heptameron*, never misses an opportunity to point an accusatory finger at abusive and disloyal husbands and lustful men of the cloth. At the time of her namesake niece's marriage, she composes for her an allegorical poem whose essential message is a warning against the sexual aggressiveness of men. In *The Coach (La coche)*, the three ladies who tell their tales of love gone wrong ultimately bond in friendship rather than compete for pity.

Whether we call her a feminist or a protofeminist, this voice rings true, one of the earliest to proclaim a space for the woman writer. Marguerite's determined championing of women's causes makes this sixteenth-century author/queen an indispensable part of any history in search of that "other voice."

HISTORICAL CONTEXT

Marguerite was witness to and protagonist in one of the watershed moments in European history. At the heart of these dramatic changes was a cultural phenomenon that has come to be known as the Renaissance, its prime movers the humanists. Instead of attempting, however, to define these complicated terms—experts have devoted their careers to that project[5]—we shall instead concentrate on providing a quick overview of the world in which

---

4. In 1841 and 1842, respectively, F. Génin published two volumes, one general and one of letters to her brother the king, Francis I. In 1930, Marguerite's French biographer Pierre Jourda published an important annotated inventory of whatever correspondence had been discovered to that date. Several other scholars since, notably V.-L. Saulnier, have uncovered a number of additional letters, and of course one can never know for sure how many are yet to be located. For insight into some of the political implications in Marguerite's correspondence, one might consult the recent study by Barbara Stephenson, *The Power and Patronage of Marguerite de Navarre* (Burlington, VT: Ashgate, 2004).

5. A good place to begin is the recent readable study by Margaret L. King, *The Renaissance in Europe* (New York: McGraw-Hill, 2003).

Marguerite was born, specifically focusing on the areas of religion, politics, and culture.

Religion

One cannot speak of the humanist movement without speaking of the Reformation, its intellectual and spiritual cousin. The causes and major characteristics of the Reformation have been examined at great length by many specialists in the field.[6] We shall limit ourselves to a few essential observations. What in fact were these evangelical reformists after? What precisely in the church did they disapprove of?

By far the most explosive issue was clerical abuse, which took two forms. On the one hand, clergy had become too worldly, too inclined to think about wealth for themselves and for Mother Church. Bishops and priests did not often present sterling examples of spiritual self-denial. With full papal sanction, they preyed on believers who thought they could buy their way into paradise by the purchase of indulgences, remission of punishment for their sins.[7] The other point of conflict was over scriptural interpretation; humanists, inspired by the new critical spirit, challenged clerical supremacy in that area and thus brought about an increased interest in learning Greek and Hebrew, the languages in which the earliest versions of the Bible were written. Their motto became *ad fontes* (back to the sources), and their pedagogical ambitions were made concrete by the invention of movable type and the growth of the printing industry, leading to publications in both classical and vernacular languages.

Several authors responsible for this development deserve to be singled out here. One of the most inspired of humanist writers was undoubtedly the learned Dutch theologian Desiderius Erasmus (1466?–1536), whose interest in the classics made him a central figure in the reform movement. As early as the 1440s Lorenzo Valla had composed important commentaries on the New Testament, which, in 1503, Erasmus discovered in their original manuscript form. This find may very likely have been what led him to publish his own bilingual Greek and Latin edition of the New Testament in 1516, his

---

6. For serious students who already have some knowledge about the Reformation, there are any number of thoroughgoing analyses by experts. But for those who want a quick summary, see Mark Greengrass, *The French Reformation* (London: Edward Arnold, 1987), or Norman Davies, *A History of Europe* (Oxford: Oxford University Press, 1996), chap. 7.

7. The practice dates back to medieval times when sinners had to endure public penance for their misdeeds, but was not formalized until the creation of the so-called Treasury of Merit. It was in good measure this money-making activity which fired up Martin Luther. Luther eventually left the church in 1521 (i.e., he was excommunicated), but not without also leaving his mark. In 1562 the Council of Trent outlawed the buying and selling of indulgences.

Latin translation being the first since the Vulgate rendering by Saint Jerome (c. 347–420). Erasmus also included critical annotations to the Greek text of the New Testament, which quickly earned the critical ire of some Catholic theologians. Nevertheless, there was such a thirst among educated readers for this kind of scholarly reading that Erasmus's work went through four subsequent editions (1519, 1522, 1527, 1536), each much expanded over its predecessor.

He was also responsible for an unusual publication of skillfully turned and easily understandable paraphrases of the books of the New Testament (the Book of Revelation excepted), to say nothing of numerous editions of the Church Fathers, whose writings represented an indispensable part of Christian tradition. But above all he is known for his witty satire *Praise of Folly*, a cutting and highly amusing brief in behalf of Christian reform. Erasmus hits home with his acerbic irony when he contrasts church leaders in their small-minded foolishness with those who are genuine "fools for Christ" (1 Cor. 4: 10).

While Erasmus never broke from the church, his tempestuous contemporary, Martin Luther (1483–1545), fought a vigorous battle with papal authority until he was excommunicated in 1521. In his "Three Treatises" of 1520[8] he declared (1) that all Christians are equal in status before God (i.e., that there is no distinction in standing between clergy and laity, celibate and married), and (2) that the authority for all Christian doctrine and belief is the Bible and not the papacy, from which it follows (a) that the sacraments were not seven but only two, Baptism and the Eucharist and (b) that we are saved by faith in the grace of God alone and not by works of the law (which do not save but only condemn us). This latter notion, "saved by grace alone," brought Erasmus into conflict with Luther; Erasmus was less inclined to subordinate the role of human responsibility. Like his younger contemporary John Calvin, Luther remained closer to the Augustinian notion of predestination, but in his case it seemed to have more to do with the psychology of faith (the "freedom" of not being responsible for a "goodness" of which all of us are incapable) than with any metaphysical predisposition. It is hardly surprising that given the centrality of Scripture in his view of Christian belief and practice, Luther spent ten years translating both testaments of the Christian Bible from Hebrew and Greek into German.[9]

---

8. The three treatises were "An Open Letter to the Christian Nobility of the German Nation," "The Babylonian Captivity of the Church," and "The Freedom of a Christian." Their themes are summarized in the text above.

9. Marguerite certainly kept abreast of Luther's religious revolt in Germany and probably knew of, if she did not actually read anything from, his voluminous production. There is some correspondence between her and Erasmus, but nothing has ever been unearthed between her and Luther.

The third and last significant figure to be discussed here was in fact a personal friend to Marguerite, the brilliant pedagogue and reformist theologian Jacques Lefèvre d'Etaples (c. 1455–1536), who in 1512 published a commentary on Romans, where he put forward a theory of biblical exegesis that emphasized the spiritual rather than the merely literal meaning of the text. Under the leadership of Guillaume Briçonnet, bishop of Meaux after 1521, Lefèvre eventually headed a team of translators in Meaux, which produced a French version of the New Testament in 1523 and of the Old Testament in 1530. These important translations were authorized by Francis I. It is entirely possible that his sister Marguerite prompted him to do so.

To conclude, then, many revolutionary changes in religious belief and practice were taking place during the queen of Navarre's lifetime, and humanistic interest in classical learning and religious reform often went hand in hand with the intellectual restlessness that was altering old ways of thinking. Marguerite was very aware and generally supportive of all this religious renewal. She nurtured and protected the reformers at Meaux. She offered shelter to the aging Lefèvre d'Étaples, who, it is reported, died in her arms. On a number of occasions she came to the defense of important leaders in the movement, notably Guillaume Farel and even the eminent John Calvin.[10] Though she never became a Protestant, her role in these earliest attempts to correct the abuses within the church hierarchy has to be seen as vital, and any history of that period must consider her as one of the prominent players in the changes that were taking place in the religious world of the sixteenth century.

Politics

Political thought also underwent some significant developments during this period, though political practice remained largely unaffected for some generations. Two "new" views of political order excited much interest in the early sixteenth century. The first was Thomas More's (1478–1535) *Utopia* (1516). The title comes from the Greek roots *ou topia* (no place) or *eu topia* (the place where things are well). Book 1 is a critique of contemporary England, book 2 an attempt to describe a society that could overcome its shortcomings. The greatest of these was private property, which promotes selfishness (and widespread poverty) rather than social virtue. Given this problem, the solu-

---

10. Unfortunately, however, during Marguerite's closing years, the Genevan spiritual leader turned against her for siding with a brand of mysticism he uncompromisingly disapproved of. In a letter to her he accused the queen of Navarre of having "assaulted God's truth" (see his *L'excuse aux Nicodémites* [Justification of the Nicodemians]). The two were never again reconciled.

tion was to do away with private property in favor of communal property and institute a form of education that enforced individual virtue through a system of social and intellectual constraints, within which the pursuit of pleasure and virtue both became possible. This new genre of literature reflected an emerging capitalist world, and the fact that it has remained popular since More's time suggests that we live in that same world, perhaps even more exaggeratedly so. Niccolò Machiavelli wrote a political tract, *The Prince* (1532), that has had a history as long and influential as More's; this treatise does not propose a new kind of social and political order but focuses on *power* as the bedrock notion of all politics. Based on his experience as a kind of secretary of state for the city of Florence in the first decade of the 1500s, Machiavelli argues that politics is about gaining and keeping power and that while the goal of politics is moral (social order and peace), its means are not necessarily moral, maybe even, from a Christian point of view, impossibly immoral. In one respect More and Machiavelli share the same terrain: both accept the Christian view of humans as imperfect (sinful) and seek ways in which to fence in that imperfection in the interest of public order and peace, which are the preconditions for individual virtue and achievement.

It is not clear whether Marguerite would have known of the writings of either of these seminal thinkers, but it has to be said she was, as sister to a king, profoundly involved in her brother's political career. At the same time that she stood behind his steady march toward absolute authority, she did not take lightly her reformist leanings and worked steadily to keep the king from forgetting his own religious education. But alas, war and territorial greed were integral parts of kingship, and while some fought with words, others took to the battlefield.

During Marguerite's life four powerful rulers struggled with one another for European hegemony: Henry VIII of England (1509–47), her own brother Francis I (1515–47), the Holy Roman Emperor Charles V (1519–56),[11] and whichever pope at any given time sat on Peter's throne. Depending upon the political climate, each formed alliances, sometimes with one, sometimes with another. The most formidable and consistent enemies, however, were Charles V and Francis I, equally ambitious, equally unyielding, and each eager to undo the other.[12] Theirs was a constantly turbulent relationship

---

11. The Holy Roman Empire was in some sense the sequel to the original Roman Empire that collapsed in the fourth century. It comprised a huge area, including Spain, Austria, southern Italy, Holland, Belgium, eastern France, and most of modern Germany.

12. In one of the letters written during her difficult and painful negotiations with Spain to obtain her brother's release after his capture by Charles's forces at Pavia in 1525, Marguerite

often contested on the battlefield in wars that cost enormously in lives and revenues. By far the worst of these military confrontations, and surely the most embarrassing for French pride, was the battle of Pavia (1525), where the French king and many of his top officers were captured by imperial forces and led into Spain.[13]

Francis I may well have devoted far too much of his country's monies to his political campaigns, draining the national treasury for territorial gain, but in the process of war making he forged a nation and created a sense of national pride. His sister, Marguerite, meanwhile, though no warrior, stood close by him in his determination to turn a series of provinces into a unified country. Her numerous admiring and sympathetic letters to Francis lend intimacy to this pivotal chapter in European political history.[14]

Culture

Although the contradictions in Renaissance society were reflected in the writings of Luther, More, and Machiavelli, the humanists by and large identified with the upper classes of society, the older aristocracy, and the emergent and increasingly powerful upper bourgeoisie.[15] But even the upper bourgeoisie suffered ideologically at the hands of the older aristocracy, whose ideals looked to the social past rather than to the emerging economic future. The best indicator is Baldassare Castiglione's highly influential *Book of the Courtier* (1528), a series of four conversations in which noble men and women discuss what it means to be an ideal courtier for an ideal prince.[16]

---

bluntly refers to the emperor's "mortal hatred" of the French king and how this makes her suspicious of all the people she has to deal with there. *Nouvelles lettres de la reine de Navarre à son frère le roi François Ier*, ed. F. Génin (Paris: Renouard, 1842), 127.

13. The shock of hearing of their king's imprisonment left a terrible mark on the French psyche. Rabelais mournfully recalls the dreadful event a decade later in his giant tale *Gargantua* (chap. 39).

14. Génin's second volume of letters includes only letters to the king. See also the examples given in Elizabeth Goldsmith and Colette Winn, eds., *Lettres de femmes: textes inédits et oubliés du XVe au XVIIIe siècle* (Paris: Champion, 2005), 3–32.

15. Some historians speak of a "boom" time: "Indeed, the sixteenth century was an age of economic expansion all over Europe." John A. Garraty and Peter Gay, *The Columbia History of the World* (Newton, MA: Dorset Press, 1984), 488. But, in fact, whatever measurable improvements can be identified applied more to the bourgeoisie than to poor peasants. There was not as yet much sensitivity to the causes of poverty. We recall that in 1524, when the German peasants rose in arms against their oppressive landlords in what has come to be called the Peasants' Revolt, even Luther spoke against them. In his tract *Against the Robbing and Murdering Hordes of Peasants* (1525), he urged nobles to smite the "devilish rebels."

16. For a good summary, see King, *Renaissance in Europe*, 234–38.

The text suggests a kind of unwritten contract between a generous patron and his sophisticated court companions, an ideal which Marguerite and Francis lived out in their own lives as magnanimous guardians of the arts.

The decidedly more independent-minded Marguerite, however, would have taken issue with some aspects of the definition of the courtly lady presented by Castiglione. While she would certainly have approved of the Neoplatonic concept of love (book 4), she would have been less sanguine about the portrait of a demure woman, expected to please by her good looks and "womanly sweetness" (book 3).

Marguerite followed closely the literary debate in her own country known as the *querelle des femmes*. A number of French authors took up the profeminist cause, and she knew them personally. One was Charles Fontaine, whose *Against the Courtly Lady* (*Contre amye de court*, 1543) is a poetic diatribe in response to an earlier antifeminist tract by Bertrand de La Borderie, *The Court Lady* (*Amye de court*, 1541). Another was one of Marguerite's own writers-in-residence,[17] Antoine Héroët, whose *The Perfect Friend*[18] (*La parfaicte amye*, 1542) draws heavily on Neoplatonism and essentially desexualizes love.[19]

It is not always easy to determine whether the social status of aristocratic women encouraged this kind of writing. For certain, however, the queen of Navarre, as patron and author, allied herself with the feminist cause by encouraging authors who shared her views and by contributing to significant profeminist writings herself. She was also an exemplar of the new woman: educated, sophisticated, brilliant in conversation, and a fervent devotee of art, music, and literature.

---

17. Marguerite was patron to a large number of *secrétaires*, who, like Héroët, were on her payroll and often followed her around as part of her regular staff.

18. The term *parfait*, used in this context, is difficult to render in English. Some scholars have translated it as "honest," in itself an ambiguous term which reappears in the "precious" (*précieux*) terminology of the following century. The best one can say is that it stands in for the type of courtly/Neoplatonic love that is chaste, pure, unselfish, and, in the end, the gateway to divine love. To this idea must be added the expression *serviteur* (literally, servant), which in this special amorous vocabulary suggests the "perfect" lover.

19. It would be too complicated to introduce here the other influential cultural strands which were part of the discussion of love. There is the Christianizing Platonism made popular by the Italian philosopher Marsilio Ficino (1433–99), and the idea of "courtly love" favored by the twelfth-century troubadours, different and yet the same. In the simplest terms, the troubadours had fashioned a way of looking at the love partner which deflected and disguised more than it subordinated erotic feelings. See Rouben C. Cholakian, *The Troubadour Lyric: A Psychocritical Reading* (Manchester, England: University Press, 1990).

MARGUERITE'S LIFE AND WORKS

Born in 1492, two years before her brother Francis, Marguerite lived most of her early life in the shadow of this younger sibling, who was groomed for kingship. Though there is little question that the chief preoccupation of their mother, the formidable Louise of Savoy, countess of Angoulême, was her adored "césar," who mounted the French throne in 1515, she gave both her children the same educational opportunities. It was this important fact that allowed Marguerite to grow into her own person, obsessively obsequious to the monarch perhaps, but by no means a shrinking violet.[20]

When Francis became king, Marguerite, by then in her early twenties, made ample use of her exceptional social skills and lively intelligence. With her ready wit and winning charm, she fascinated both foreign ambassadors and contemporary artists, helping to turn her brother's court into one of the most attractive in all Europe.

In 1509 she had been married off to a dull-witted aristocrat, Charles, duke of Alençon. It was a childless marriage and has been deemed a loveless one by most of Marguerite's biographers, though that assessment may be overstated. Inserted in *Les prisons* (Prisons), for example, we find a description of this first husband's death, admittedly composed in imitation of a stylized deathbed form known as an "agony," but nevertheless suggesting genuine sentiments of affection.[21] Indeed, when Charles fell fatally ill, shortly after the disastrous battle of Pavia in 1525, Marguerite lovingly nursed him until his last breath.

That military scuffle for hegemony over the duchy of Milan[22] was a

20. For a few years, Louise kept a journal. When against all odds Francis did in fact become king—his two immediate predecessors had no surviving sons and only males could accede to the French throne—Louise wrote, somewhat peevishly, in her journal: "On the day of the Conversion of Saint Paul, 1515, my son was anointed and blessed in the church at Reims. For this I am dutifully thankful to divine mercy, through which I have been fully repaid for all the adversities and distresses I had to endure in my earliest years, in the flower of my youth." Louise de Savoie, *Journal*, ed. M. Petitot (Paris: Foucault, 1826–27), 16: 397.

21. Marguerite depicts her husband as a devoted Christian and a man of honor in "war and peace." The latter reference was no doubt introduced by Marguerite to counteract rumors of Charles's supposed cowardice at the battle of Pavia. *Les Prisons*, ed. Simone Glasson (Geneva: Droz, 1978), 211–12. If there was a serious rift in the marriage it may have been caused by the inability to produce an heir. Marguerite frequently speaks of her "sterility" in her letters to the bishop of Meaux. See, for example, *Guillaume Briçonnet/Marguerite d'Angoulême: Correspondance*, ed. Christine Martineau, Michel Veissière, and Henry Heller, 2 vols (Paris: Lahure, 1975–79), 2: 170–71.

22. The justification for the so-called Italian Wars—fought intermittently from the close of the fourteenth century through the better part of the sixteenth—goes back to a claim based

Figure 1. Anon., *Louise de Savoie.* Picture Collection, The Branch Libraries, The New York Public Library, Astor, Lenox and Tilden Foundations.

Figure 2. Anon., *François I.* The State Hermitage Museum, St. Petersburg, Russia. Photograph © The State Hermitage Museum.

disaster for France, an embarrassment for Francis, who was captured by the forces of the Holy Roman Emperor Charles V, and a singularly important moment in the life of Marguerite. While her mother, named regent, remained in Paris to govern the nation, Marguerite was sent to negotiate her brother's release in Spain, where she proved to be a hard-nosed diplomat.[23] Undaunted by the dishonest maneuverings of the emperor, who knew he had a great prize in his grip, Marguerite worked vigorously for the honor of her country and her king. And if in the end Francis had to give up his two sons as hostages in order to gain release, he would never accuse his sister of having been anything but stalwart and unflinching in her efforts. He certainly never forgot that when she arrived in Madrid he was at death's door and that it was probably she who saved his life.[24]

France was a Catholic country, yet Marguerite was not only a witness to but also a participant in the earliest rumblings of religious reform there. Already by June 1521, she had begun a lengthy correspondence with one of the most important leaders of the movement, Guillaume Briçonnet, bishop of Meaux.[25] For nearly four years, they exchanged letters in which Marguerite prompted the bishop to teach and to explain. And the erudite bishop willingly complied, offering elaborate interpretations of biblical passages. Marguerite happily discovered in Briçonnet's extraordinary exegetical skills the answers to her spiritual uneasiness. But while the two were in many ways like-minded, they were also very different. If a common religious project of reform brought them together, political and social status would ultimately

---

on the marriage in 1387 of Francis's great-grandfather, Louis de Valois, to Valentina Visconti. The Visconti family ruled the duchy of Milan until 1447. Their successors, the Sforzas, were not allies of France.

23. From the very start, Marguerite understood that her task would not be an easy one. In one of her numerous letters to her brother from this period, she writes: "I believe by continuing to be adamant, we will force them to speak another language. . . . We will deliver you, with God's help, but I beseech you, since they are going about it in such an infamous way, do not be impatient if it takes time to get them to the point we desire." *Poésie du roi François Ier, de Louise de Savoie, duchesse d'Angoulême, de Marguerite de Navarre,* ed. Aimé Champollion-Figeac (Geneva: Slatkine, 1970), 358–59.

24. It was the court gossip Pierre de Bourdeille, seigneur de Brantôme (1540–1614), who, speaking of Francis's grave condition while captive, wrote: "And thus the king often said that had it not been for her [Marguerite], he would be dead." *Recueil des dames,* ed. Etienne Vaucheret (Paris: Gallimard, 1991), 179.

25. Marguerite already knew Briçonnet (1470?–1533) when he was abbot at St.-Germain-des-Prés in Paris. But the correspondence between them probably began only after he was appointed bishop at Meaux, where he quickly surrounded himself with priests who shared his reformist views. Among these were Gérard Roussel, Guillaume Farel, and the noted humanist Jacques Lefèvre d'Étaples, all of whom became intimates of Marguerite as well.

separate them. When the religious establishment began aggressively to pursue those who espoused ideas deemed heretical, she was able to find refuge in a powerful brother's protection, while Briçonnet was made to recant before unyielding canonical judges.

But so long as the exchange lasted, Marguerite found enormous comfort in unburdening herself. From the very start, she enthusiastically revealed the spiritual and psychological tempests that were buffeting her and spoke openly of her deep feelings of inadequacy. She refers to herself as a "lost sheep" (7),[26] "blind, deaf, unknowing, and paralytic" (29), trapped in a crown of thorns (33). She longs for the "true radiance of sunshine" the bishop can supply so as to "shed light" on her interior darkness (63). She signs her letters "the enfeebled Marguerite" (12), or the "Marguerite who forgets herself" (35). Like a famished child she aches for the sustenance her confessor can give her and is willing to gather up the generous "crumbs of bread" he makes available to her (69).

We feel her struggling with her faith and wanting to come to terms with death, not her own but the deaths of those whom she loves and who are taken from her. Marguerite was especially grief-stricken by the loss of her eight-year-old niece Charlotte (117, 119). That terrible death in 1524 led her to compose her first theological poem, *Dialogue in the Form of a Nocturnal Vision (Dialogue en forme de vision nocturne)*, although it was not published until later (1533). Interestingly, it is not Marguerite who gives wise counsel in the poem but the deceased girl. The resurrected Charlotte tells her distressed aunt that she hopes "you will believe what you cannot see and taste what you long for" (124). These encouraging words are meant to remind Marguerite that the genuine Christian sees death not as a threat but as a blessing.

The Briçonnet correspondence comes to an abrupt halt in November 1524. Was this because of the distracting rumblings of war as Francis plotted his invasion of Italy? Or have some of the letters simply been lost? In any event, Briçonnet seems to diminish as a significant figure in Marguerite's life, though she continues to write many letters, to her brother, to her mother, and most especially to Anne de Montmorency, an important personage in the royal court.[27] One cannot underestimate the significance

26. The references here represent the numbering of the letters in *Guillaume Briçonnet/Marguerite d'Angoulême: Correspondance.*

27. Anne de Montmorency (1493–1567) was not only a prominent figure in Francis's court but a longtime family friend. Although Marguerite's relationship with him was not always a smooth one (he was a religious conservative), Montmorency was one of her favored correspondents, and her letters to him are a vital source of information.

Figure 3. François Clouet, *The Connétable Anne de Montmorency*. Photograph: R. G. Ojeda. Photograph © Réunion des Musées Nationaux / Art Resource, New York.

of this letter writing, both as it provides insights into the writer's personal life and as a place where Marguerite learns the intellectual satisfactions of putting words on paper.

Her first husband barely dead and buried, Marguerite was again seen as a valuable political pawn. This time the choice of husband fell upon Henri d'Albret, king of Navarre.[28] Quite exceptionally, royal matchmakers and bride saw eye to eye. Henry was virile, clever, an accomplished warrior, young—ten years Marguerite's junior—and by all standards, a lot more attractive than his uninspired predecessor. So on January 30, 1527, in elaborate festivities that lasted eight days, the thirty-year-old widow became Queen Consort of Henry of Navarre. It was probably a much more successful marriage than the first, and certainly more important to political history, because in November of the next year, Marguerite gave birth to the mother of the future Henry IV, Jeanne d'Albret.[29]

As protesting turned into Protestantism in the German states between 1517 and the 1520s, tensions in France between reformists and religious conservatives grew unremittingly. Prompted by Francis's long absence during his Spanish captivity, the Faculty of Theology at the University of Paris, with the collaboration of the Paris Parlement, began tracking down dissident Catholics in earnest, bringing them to trial—often in a peremptory manner—and burning many at the stake.

Hardly recovered from her ordeal in Spain, Marguerite found that she had her hands full shielding reformists from the aggressive behavior of conservative leaders, eager not only to defend the true faith but to safeguard their own hegemony. They found a formidable opponent in the king's sister, not easily intimidated and ready, at least in her own territories where she held political sway, to use her political clout to come to the rescue of

28. If the arrangement appealed to Marguerite for personal reasons, it won court favor for political ones. The kingdom of Navarre, located near the Pyrenees, was seen by Francis as a valuable buffer between France and Spain. In the end, Marguerite also came to appreciate her political jurisdiction in these new territories, where she could exercise her will as a reformist, far from the interfering constraints of the conservative Paris Parlement.

29. See Nancy L. Roelker, *Queen of Navarre: Jeanne d'Albret, 1528–1572* (Cambridge: Harvard University Press, 1968), for interesting insights into this complicated mother/daughter relationship. History has not always been fair in assessing Marguerite's "maternal" instincts. Not only are we unjustly inclined to impose our different modern standards on what such a relationship ought to be, but we have not always interpreted the events with proper care. Marguerite, for example, worked tirelessly to undo Jeanne's marriage to Guillaume de Cleves, which she correctly saw as a bad choice, both politically and psychologically. For an attempt to redress some critical misreadings of Marguerite's relationship with her daughter, see Cholakian and Cholakian, *Marguerite de Navarre*, 14–15, 32–37, 109–11, in which the authors take issue with Roelker's harsher assessment of Marguerite as a mother.

Figure 4. François Clouet, *Henri d'Albret, King of Navarre*. Musée Condé, Chantilly, France. Photograph by Harry Bréjat. Photograph © Réunion des Musées Nationaux / Art Resource, New York.

Figure 5. Anon., *Jeanne d'Albret*. Photograph courtesy Bibliothèque publique et universitaire, Genève.

besieged reformists. In his study on the Reformation, Mark Greengrass has noted: "Whenever we see those of evangelical opinions surviving in France in the 1530s, it is to Marguerite de Navarre that we are tempted to look first to explain how and why."[30]

Though it is highly probable that Marguerite had been putting her ideas on paper for a long time, it was not until 1531 that she published any of her formal writings. The first, titled *The Mirror of the Sinful Soul (Le miroir de l'âme pécheresse)*, was a poetic manifesto of reformist doctrine that caused an explosion of disapproval among French religious authorities.[31] The irate theologians of Paris saw to it that Marguerite's poem was placed among the list of books to be officially censored. Their embarrassing public disapprobation finally forced the king himself to intercede on Marguerite's behalf.

Then, in 1534, a band of dissenters plastered offensive anti-Catholic posters in a number of places, including the door of the king's bedchamber.[32] Francis, until now for the most part willing to tolerate religious dissent, had to take a more aggressive stance. He could hardly do otherwise, beholden as he was to all those, including bishops, who were heavily taxed to pay for his expensive war making. The decision, nonetheless, had to be difficult, because the king was well aware of his sister's firm devotion to the reformist agenda. She, on the other hand, recognizing her current unpopularity and the embarrassment to the king, found it the better part of valor to avoid the royal court for a time and retire to her estates in the south until things calmed down a bit.

Perhaps this was the excuse she needed, for the 1530s was a particularly productive time in Marguerite's literary life. Interestingly, she turned to an entirely new genre for her, the theater.[33] Her work is still quite far from

---

30. Greengrass, *French Reformation*, 25. She was not always successful. An unhappy example is the case of the outspoken and unruly dissenter Louis de Berquin, whom Marguerite tried to protect, but to no avail. In April 1528, Berquin, along with his books, was made into a fiery spectacle on the Place de Grève, a dire warning to all future "Lutherans."

31. It was actually not the 1531 publication which caused the rumpus but the subsequent edition of 1533, which also reproduced a French translation of psalm 6 by her favorite protégé Clément Marot. The church fathers considered vernacular translations of biblical texts a serious threat to their authority. The fact remains that Marguerite's reformist poem enjoyed enormous success, going into several editions during her own lifetime. A Geneva press put out an astounding—for the time—two thousand copies.

32. Robert J. Knecht, *Renaissance Warrior and Patron: The Reign of Francis I* (Cambridge: Cambridge University Press, 1994), chap. 15, offers a good summary of the facts of this explosive event, which has come to be known as the *affaire des placards*.

33. For further information on Marguerite's place in the theater, one should consult the bibliography in Régine Reynolds-Cornell's recent translation and edition of the secular plays of Marguerite: *Théâtre profane* (Ottawa: Dovehouse, 1992).

those majestic achievements of the French classical theater, but any study of the early stage in France has to take into account Marguerite's contributions. Not surprisingly her first plays were biblical in inspiration, written very much in imitation of morality plays from the late Middle Ages. Were it not for interludes where the dramatist puts reformist preaching into the mouths of her characters, these first theater works, written in near-doggerel verse, would hold no interest for us at all.[34]

But the queen of Navarre came to appreciate the dialogic possibilities of the theater as an avenue of expression, and when she did, she began to create some of her best writings. If the insubstantial *The Patient (Le mallade)*, though at moments amusing enough,[35] fizzles out in a preachy and predictable denouement, *The Inquisitor (L'inquisiteur)* shows real promise in its clever turns of phrase and charming confrontation between a pompous "inquisitor" and his innocent adversaries "les enfants," who ultimately outwit him. Honest faith from the heart triumphs over skillful reasoning from the mind, an idea which neatly fits in with the dramatist's religious message.

Toward the close of the decade, Marguerite, very much interested in the emerging Neoplatonist movement, fostered a veritable "Plato project," engaging contemporary writers and humanists like Bonaventure des Périers, Etienne Dolet, and Antoine Héroët to prepare, for the very first time, French editions of texts by and about the Greek philosopher.[36] We know too that Marguerite herself made extensive use of the theme of platonic love in the *Heptameron*.

The queen of Navarre was never reticent in the face of injustice, but the injustice which left those of her gender sorry victims of male sexual aggression made her especially unhappy and thus turned her into a staunch defender of women's rights. She recognized all too well that the problem lay with a public that hypocritically condoned male behavior, while it fiercely censured female misconduct in matters of sex. Not able to confront the issue

34. As Barbara Marczuk notes: "In a period of transition, the Queen sought out the form most likely to allow expression of the ideas which haunted her so as to articulate her own religious feelings and concerns." Marguerite de Navarre, *Les comédies bibliques*, ed. Marczuk (Geneva: Droz, 2000), 27.

35. At one moment, in a manner that suggests Molière's satirical humor, the patient's wife is made to caution her husband against consulting doctors: "You're always running after them: But their paws are dangerous. Just the other day they killed the lawyer's daughter." Marguerite de Navarre, "Le Mallade," in *Théâtre profane*, 15.

36. For example, the humanist poet Bonaventure des Périers, one of several writers in Marguerite's paid entourage, was prompted to translate from the Greek Plato's dialogue *Lysis*. It is easy to see how that work, dealing with friendship and the idea of unselfish devotion, would have been highly interesting to Marguerite.

Figure 6. Anon., *Marguerite and François*. Photograph courtesy Bibliothèque nationale de France.

directly, she found redress in many of the antimasculinist tales and comments of the *Heptameron*.[37]

Two tales in particular, however, suggest more than a theoretical discussion. Her deeply felt resentment stemmed, it seems most likely, from a terrible personal experience, which Marguerite describes in novellas 4 and 10 of the *Heptameron*.[38] The seducer, barely disguised in these two fictionalized episodes of attempted rape, was almost certainly Guillaume Gouffier, seigneur de Bonnivet, admiral of France, and longtime friend of the Angoulême family.

In the discussions which follow each story, Parlamente/Marguerite takes several opportunities to define Neoplatonic love as a purifying agent and antidote to male aggression. In novella 19, for example, she speaks of "perfect love" thus: "One will never love God perfectly without first perfectly loving a creature of this world." It is obvious how this amorous ideal and Marguerite's religious convictions converge. But it would be a serious error in interpretation to see this comment as a defense of the courtly love model, which tended to remove the woman from the physical world of desires and pleasures. Marguerite was too much of a realist and too much of a dedicated spokesperson for gender equality to go that route. Her apology for Neoplatonic love is less a wholesale endorsement of the idealized female than an energetic plea for honoring woman's own emotional needs.

In later years, Marguerite spent less and less time at the court, in part because she felt herself excluded from the decision making, in part because she found the religious mode oppressively conservative, and in part because she simply had a greater need to be alone. Whatever energies she may once have expended on the intrigues of court life, she now increasingly devoted to her literary works. And as the years went by and her health began to fail, she became more conscious of herself as a writer. She worked continually on her collection of stories, composing the interesting prologue for the *Heptameron*.[39]

---

37. Over and again in the discussions which follow each of the stories, Marguerite's outspoken mouthpiece, Parlamente, lambastes male misbehavior. She depicts men as essentially driven by violence and lust (*L'Heptaméron*, ed. Michel François [Paris: Garnier, 1960], 301), in a quest for recognition and honor that meant "killing other men in war" (ibid., 175).

38. Patricia Cholakian argues that this personal tragedy was the essential generative source of the pervasive rape theme in the *Heptameron*: "By 'generative,' I mean that it was the traumatic experience of near-rape, fictionalized in novella 4, that originally compelled Marguerite de Navarre to collect and write stories about sexual assault." *Rape and Writing in the* Heptameron *of Marguerite de Navarre* (Carbondale: Southern Illinois University Press, 1991), 216. See also in this regard Cholakian and Cholakian, *Marguerite de Navarre*, chap. 2.

39. Like her predecessor Boccaccio, she invents a disaster frame, a pretext for her ten *devisants* (literally, conversationalists) to while away the time of their confinement by exchanging sto-

Figure 7. Jean Clouet, *Guillaume Gouffier, seigneur de Bonnivet*. Musée Condé, Chantilly, France. Photograph by R. G. Ojeda. Photograph © Réunion des Musées Nationaux / Art Resource, New York.

In the spring of 1547, she learned that the brother who had been so central to her life had died. Distraught at not having been with him, she poured out her sorrow in a series of moving *Spiritual Songs (Chansons spirituelles)*, in an allegorical play fraught with philosophical speculations on death, *The Death of the King (Le trepas du roi)*, and in a long, dirge-like poem, *The Ship (Le navire)*.

Her terrible grief was not an obstacle to creativity, but rather an inspiration; the last years of her life were indeed marked by extraordinary productivity and by some of her best works, including her masterpiece, the *Heptameron*. It was as if she were impatient to leave her lasting mark on the world. In 1548, she composed her *Comedy of Mont-de-Marsan (La comédie de Mont-de-Marsan)*, which gives us an intimate sense of her frame of mind as the time of her own death inevitably approached. And during these years, she completed *The Prisons (Les prisons)*, by far the longest piece she ever wrote, nearly six thousand decasyllabic couplets.

The Prisons is, for many, Marguerite's greatest poetic achievement, "the crowning glory of her spiritual journey as well as of her literary evolution."[40] The narrating voice is that of a man who describes his escape from the grips of love, earthly ambition, and science, until at last he finds peace in God's embrace. Though some have seen as its fundamental inspiration Dante's *Divine Comedy* and/or the French medieval allegory *The Romance of the Rose (Le Roman de la rose, 1230–80)*, it is quintessential Marguerite, the sometimes wistful, sometimes heartening culmination of more than thirty years of meditation on her immortal soul.

Only someone with a very strong sense of herself as a writer would have done what Marguerite did next. No doubt feeling her death close at hand, she spent her last months seeing to the publication of an anthology of her literary creations. In two volumes, one devoted to religious and one to secular texts, Marguerite worked to leave as a final statement to posterity what she deemed the most significant of her writings. Punning on her own name, she called her compendium *Pearls from the Pearl of Princesses (marguerites de la Marguerite des princesses)*. The work has been puzzling to historians, however. Since Marguerite leaves out some works, they invariably wonder what her criteria for selection were.

Another complication has to be added to that inquiry. Nearly four centuries after Marguerite's death, the eminent Renaissance scholar Abel Le-

---

ries. They are trapped by a devastating flood in the town of Cauterets in the Pyrenees, a spa that Marguerite frequently visited.

40. *Les Prisons*, 9.

franc discovered a stash of unpublished works that included *The Ship* and *The Prisons*, the two above-mentioned plays, and a precious group of verse letters exchanged between Marguerite and her daughter Jeanne d'Albret. How is it that none of these appeared in her anthology? Were they deliberately set aside, and if so, for what reason? Lefranc argues that it was most likely Jeanne who carefully put them away, so carefully that they were not uncovered for centuries. But having said that much, he is unable to offer an explanation of Jeanne's motivations.[41] Nor does he clarify how it was that Marguerite did not include any of these important works in her self-directed compendium. The most reasonable hypothesis would seem to be that although she was getting on in years and ailing, the queen of Navarre still hoped to add to her two-volume anthology one additional book for the works left out and another for the completed collection of tales.[42]

When Marguerite died on December 21, 1549, surrounded by her devoted staff, she was able to leave this world with a real sense of accomplishment. She had played a noteworthy role in her brother's royal court. Though a Catholic to the end, she had been an energetic defender of the reformist cause. She had spoken out against the sexual aggressiveness of men and made people think twice about what an equitable love relationship ought to be. Finally, she had contributed importantly to the literature of the period.

Some will certainly want to remember her most for her role as a reformer. If in fact she herself never converted, it had to have been her strong influence as a mother that caused Jeanne, some time after both her parents were dead, to become a full-fledged Protestant. The chain of influence continued, for this same daughter gave birth to another Protestant—true to his religion until forced to surrender his beliefs in order to become king and bring to an end the civil wars and persecutions that wracked France in the latter half of the sixteenth century.[43]

---

41. *Les dernières poesies*, ed. Abel Lefranc (Paris: Colin, 1896), 1: ii.

42. It is important at this juncture to recall that the posthumously published *Heptameron*—with only the seventy-two tales we know of—was in fact modeled on Boccaccio's *Decameron*, suggesting that its author planned on an even hundred stories. In an early manuscript copy of the *Heptameron*, put together by Adrien de Thou, the editor in fact leaves room for the yet to be added—as if the insertions were imminent—twenty-eight remaining stories. Brantôme always refers to the collection as Marguerite's "cent nouvelles." In short, it is only reasonable to believe that Marguerite hoped time would allow her to bring the project to a happy conclusion. In any event, it was not until 1559, two years after Pierre Boaistuau put out a truncated and totally inadequate edition in 1557 that Claude Gruget prepared the first reliable edition of the extant stories, respecting their probable order and providing the book with the title that has stuck to this day, the *Heptameron*.

43. Everyone recalls Henry of Navarre's clever quip when crowned Henry IV: "Paris is worth a Mass."

But is that how Marguerite would have chosen to be remembered? Though she would not by any means have denigrated her participation in religious reform, her growing commitment to writing suggests that the stalwart reformer sought first and foremost to carve out a place for herself as a literary woman.

When her eulogist, Charles de Sainte Marthe, said of his erstwhile patron that "one has never seen a more perfect woman," he certainly realized that he was speaking to an audience of friends and family members. But time and the feminist movement have proven him right. Slowly Marguerite's extensive work is being rediscovered and published, slowly but assuredly she is finding her place next to the "giants" of French sixteenth-century literature—Rabelais, Ronsard, and Montaigne.

ANALYSIS

If Molière's fatuous M. Jourdain in *The Would-Be Gentleman* (*Le bourgeois gentilhomme*, 1671) was amazed to learn that he was speaking "prose," so was his audience. Until rather recent times, if you had something worthy to say, you invariably chose to put it into verse. Prose was generally reserved for commercial and political communications, not literature. So instinctive was this to an aristocratic and educated mind like Marguerite's that—with the significant exception of her *Heptameron*—virtually all of her creations are in verse, even many of the letters she sent off to her brother and her mother.

She composed dozens of such verse letters (*Epîtres*), a few of which appear here as examples. These hastily written works are admittedly often filled with banalities and prone to doggerel, but they are not without autobiographical interest. More ambitious are her long theological verse essay *The Mirror of the Sinful Soul* (*Le miroir de l'âme pécheresse*); her teaching allegory about male sexual behavior, *The Fable of False Pride* (*La fable du faux cuyder*); her theatrical-like dialogue about love, *The Coach* (*La coche*); and her profoundly searching play about human values, *The Comedy of Mont-de-Marsan* (*La comédie de Mont-de-Marsan*), all of which are part of this anthology. Let us take a closer look at each to understand better what the queen of Navarre was trying to communicate to her sixteenth-century readership.

The Mirror of the Sinful Soul

If women writers were scarce in Marguerite's time, women theologians were unheard of. The queen of Navarre had no formal theological education, but from her earliest years she had been well versed in biblical literature, and her lengthy correspondence with her spiritual advisor, Briçonnet, sharpened her ideas and at the same time taught her much about the language of the mystic. It is therefore predictable that her first publication was a poetic treatment of her religious views.

The Mirror of the Sinful Soul (1531) is an excellent model of a mystic's voyage of the soul. Beginning with a vigorous self-denigration, which portrays in gloomy detail the sinner's dismal "world of darkness," the narrator/confessor turns to "sweet Jesus" to intercede on her behalf. Like all the "sons of Adam," she sees herself as marked from birth by failure because of Augustinian "original sin." Moreover, like a true reformist she can hope for salvation only through faith, not works, and the "generous gift of grace."[44]

Marguerite's confessional examination introduces a complex set of metaphors—biblical for the most part—to define the sinner's desperate search for peace and love and her difficult relationship with her God. She is the prodigal child who, after a tempestuous search for self-gratification, returns groveling home to a forgiving father. She is the mother in the Solomon story, unwilling to have her child/soul divided. She is Moses who marries an outsider. She is the unfaithful wife in Jeremiah who deserves condemnation. She is the ritualist who plays at a game of sham religiosity.

But divine love comes unconditionally to her rescue, and this sinner who has experienced rebirth through baptism no longer falters or weakens. Now she is the sought-after beloved, the Shulamite woman in *The Song of Songs*. She is a courageous pilgrim on a spiritual voyage toward union with her God. Not even the "sting of death" will cause her to hesitate. Like Saint Paul she will welcome it: "O sweet Death, in the name of his love, come to me and lead me to my God." And like the apostle too, who is stunned into awed silence, she will end her prayer in the tacit knowledge that through God's love she has undeservedly won the promise of eternal life.

Because of the interweaving of Catholic doctrine, reformist theology, and the language of the mystic, it is not always easy to separate out the several strands here. Often the theological distinctions are a matter more of degree than of kind. Since the thirteenth century, the practice of private confession (in contrast with the monastic practice of public confession) had been an essential Catholic experience. As the poem's title would suggest, *Mirror* is first and foremost a confession. But if the recognition of one's multiple failings is standard confessional speech, the exaggerated pounding of

---

44. Christian grace is a thorny issue. There is "natural grace," which is simply God's gift of human existence, and "supernatural grace," by which although one is born sinful, one is redeemed through the beneficence of a celestial father who promises eternal life. But there are nuances of theological thought. Jansenists, for example, believe that grace is given only to those who confess adherence to the one true church, and Calvinists deem that it is granted to a predetermined few.

the breast here owes much to the new thinking. The insistence upon human nothingness (*rien*) compared with God's perfection (*tout*) is an integral part of reformist logic. Recognition of one's fallen nature is the required first step toward redemption. And so the text abounds with repetitious professions of sinfulness.[45]

It is not as if lay Catholics knew nothing about the Bible, but the reformists' emphasis on personal devotion and regular biblical readings turned Christians like Marguerite into specialists who could and did cite religious texts with astounding confidence and ease. *Mirror*, rich in references to both the Hebrew and the Christian Bibles, makes its author an admirable example of what the new religion hoped for—people not only conversant with biblical literature but prepared to interpret on their own.

The debate over whether works or faith was the ultimate means to salvation was the major sticking point in all the theological discussions of the period. If traditionalist Catholics preached salvation through good works, Protestants saw it as the inevitable and munificent reward of faith alone. Marguerite notes that it is faith that allows her to receive the sacred word and faith that makes possible her comprehension of the mystery of the incarnation. It is "unpretentious faith" and "simple faith" that bring her ultimate satisfaction and the assurance of a happy afterlife; for hers, she vigorously proclaims, is a "mighty God of faith!"

In brief then, *Mirror* has to be appreciated as a remarkable confluence of the old and the new religion. And if at moments the words seem too effusive to our modern ears, that is because we have, by and large, lost the taste for this kind of numinous writing. Yet if one wishes to have an intimate understanding of Marguerite's spiritual life, *The Mirror of the Sinful Soul* is indisputably the place to begin.

The Fable of False Pride

Marguerite's first serious biographer, Pierre Jourda, would like us to believe that when the queen of Navarre decided to write a narrative poem for her soon-to-marry namesake niece, her only ambition was to moralize on the theme of human pride. To be certain, *The Fable of False Pride* (*La fable du faux cuyder*, 1543), is about that most subtle of human failings, pridefulness. It is also indisputable that as a reformist thinker Marguerite wanted to impress her readers once again with the inescapable need for salvation through

---

45. "Although Marguerite's poems tend to culminate in the experience of *illuminatio,* they often open in darkness and fear." Robert Cottrell, *Grammar of Silence* (Washington, DC: Catholic University Press, 1986), 103.

God's unrestricted gift of grace. In that important theological sense, this is the same author who penned *The Mirror of the Sinful Soul*, heavily preoccupied with the Augustinian notion of the fallen creature who can be redeemed only through divine intervention. But Jourda fails to see the other significant, nonreligious, themes which feed into the story.

Before that discussion, however, let us first take a moment to review the essentials of the narrative. Marguerite is among the first French writers to follow the lead of Italian pastoralists like Jacopo Sannazaro (1456–1530) and set her tale in a bucolic locale, with classical mythology as her basic frame. We are in a never-never land of nymphs, Satyrs, and miraculous happenings. Diana, goddess of childbirth and special patroness of women—the choice is not without significance in defining the profane themes in the poem—is surrounded by her adoring and adored nymphs. Five of them, awakened by the sounds of music, rise from a noonday nap to seek out its source. The music is coming from a nearby field where Satyrs are merrily singing and dancing, as Satyrs are wont to do. The nymphs, in their *prideful* naiveté and ignorance, do not realize that a trap has been set for them and rush in to participate in the festivities. When assaulted by the Satyrs, they cry desperately for help in what is one of several long harangues that interrupt the flow of the narrative. Another occurs as Diana makes ready to come to their rescue while she expostulates on the sin of pride. At every turn, Marguerite internalizes the problems facing her characters, and in a manner that presages the classical monologues of Racine and Corneille, she thus enters into the thoughts of her fictional actors. In the end, Diana rescues her insubordinate "children," but only to turn them into weeping willows. At the same time, she watches with a mother's satisfaction while the helpless and frustrated Satyrs have only the bark of unyielding trees to embrace.

One cannot fully understand Marguerite's intentions without taking into account two key features of the plot. The theme of maternalism comes up far too often to be considered merely incidental and secondary to the poem's development. Nor is it a theme which lacks psychological subtleties. When her children are endangered, this mother, like any protective mother, promises to "fight to the end" to save her own. Even at her most irate, she acknowledges her maternal duty: "I would have done an injustice to their cry for sympathy, if I did not respond to their appeal." At the same time, this is not an altogether unselfish love that is being described. Diana, who worships her children and who inspires that love reciprocally—witnessed in the beautiful apologetic plea of the five lost sheep—insists upon her primacy. It is she who "furnished them with worth," and she who deserves and expects their unwavering obedience. The unforgiving crime of those who strayed from her authority was foolishly to believe "themselves to be of value without me."

It is equally noteworthy that if the five nymphs are punished for their pride, the description of the Satyrs is an unmitigated portrait of nasty male sexual behavior. From the very start of her didactic enterprise the narrator tells her audience—incidentally only women[46]—that she aims to "impart the malevolence of men." When the Satyrs discuss their strategy of seduction, they speak of it as "the one thing without which all the rest means nothing." They are seen as "evil creatures," with "grasping" and "terrifying" hands. They are "corrupted by lust," rank hypocrites who boast of winning over their victims while actually hoodwinking them to the point where they "mistook bad for good." Worse still, they are remorseless. To the very end they arrogantly claim: "If we did not have our fill of these women, it was not from not trying."

Taking into account the queen of Navarre's own sad tale of victimization at the hands of a family friend, Bonnivet, whose attempted rape of the young Marguerite is twice memorialized in the *Heptameron*, one quickly understands that *The Fable of False Pride*, while it certainly speaks of pride as "the worst of all sins," is not just a theological allegory. In counseling a niece she loved, Marguerite, at one and the same time, plays both the maternal and the abused woman. To miss that point is to miss a good deal of what this poem is all about.

The Coach

Among her secular works, *The Coach* (*La coche*, 1543) is certainly one of Marguerite's most innovative and intriguing. A narrative poem, it nonetheless has very definite theatrical aspects. The whole is set up like a series of scenes, each with its description of the decor as well as the dress and gestures of the characters involved. Although the references to the outdoor settings are sketchy, any concern at all for describing the settings is far from commonplace in the literature of the period. The work is also striking for the unusual way in which Marguerite, the author, creates a fictional Marguerite in the story's action. The third-person narrator outside the text proper and the first-person character within the text proper are one and the same. This allows Marguerite to self-reflect as if she were a made-up character like the others.

By reinventing herself in the poem, she seems to gain an emotional

---

46. Early into the story, Marguerite identifies her audience when she says, "As you shall see, ladies-in-waiting . . ."

distance which allows her to speak more openly and personally. Marguerite comments not only on her mystical inner life; she thinks about the passage of time and about her own aging. Toward the end of the poem, she sadly writes:

> My fifty years of life, my failing strength,
> demand that I forget the past
> in order to better think of my approaching death,
> without memory of or remorse over
> whether I had pain or joy in love.

With that she confesses to two crucial losses, which she significantly places side by side: the loss of love (she cannot recover "the name, the words, and the deeds of that blind conqueror [Cupid]," even to the point of being unable to empathize, "because a heart that contains no pleasure is pained to see it in others") and the loss of "the power, the glory, and the sweet pleasure of writing." One of these sources of anguish is more real than the other, however. Age may have dampened her enthusiasm for the pleasures of love and caused her to come face to face with her own death. But as this astonishing poem reveals, she has experienced no measurable diminution in her writing skills in spite of protestations to the contrary.[47]

In *The Coach* Marguerite borrows from an old literary format, the courtly debate in which women compete for the honor of being the ones who suffer most in the search for love.[48] Though she significantly strays from the traditional genre by presenting the rivals as mutual and self-supporting friends, she never entirely abandons the basic debate structure. The last contestant asks: "Do you contend that you are in greater torment. . . . Where is there a martyred spirit like my own? . . . What small sorrow this is compared with my great sacrifice." The comments are ironic since this woman has given up a worthy lover to bond with her two suffering companions. In short, by implication, contestant number three is paradoxically the winner.

This is the exceedingly clever and imaginative way in which Marguerite brings together the essential theme of her narrative, substituting for the inadequacies and frustrations of a self-serving erotic love between man and

---

47. For a more general plot summary, see the short introduction preceding the translation.

48. The genre has a complicated history. French medieval writers early on invented debate poems—*jeu parti* and *tenson*—in which two poets offered opposing views on some given subject, usually on a theme of love. Later, the poet Alain Chartier (1385–1433) turned the form into a debate among women who compete for honors in their tales of amorous woe.

woman (*eros*) the self-sacrificing love among friends (*agape*). That is why, when convention and good politics require that one of the ladies make the king the final arbiter of the contest, and Marguerite professes herself too ashamed to "present my scribbling before the eyes of such a perfect mind," it is decided in the spirit of compromise that the text should be left in the hands of the duchess of Étampes, who will present it to his majesty. The duchess was the king's longtime mistress, but more significant to this pro-feminist plot, she was also Marguerite's closest ally and friend at court. The poet thus manages to flatter the king her brother, all the while underscoring the theme of female relationships.

The Comedy of Mont-de-Marsan

The Comedy of Mont-de-Marsan may very well be the best of the nearly dozen plays that Marguerite wrote. And to think that had it not been for Abel Lefranc's lucky find, we might never have known about it! It is by far the most playable of all her theater pieces, rich in comic repartees and singing parts and packed with enough ideas to keep an audience seriously engaged until its very inconclusive denouement. In short, *The Comedy of Mont-de-Marsan* is probably the one play from the queen of Navarre's repertoire able to entertain and amuse a modern audience. Though it is not exactly action-packed, four allegorical figures come very much alive in a debate that searches for a philosophy of life, offering no easy solution, but giving a clever summary of some if its creator's favorite themes. What are these?

At the heart of the matter would seem to be the metaphysical issue of ultimate reality. Are we material substance or immaterial spirit? The Worldly Woman declares from the start that she "cannot touch [her soul]" and that what finally counts for her is what she can see and feel, namely, her body. The Superstitious Woman, by contrast, argues that her physical self is of no consequence and that what uniquely interests her is the part of her being which, after death, will gloriously transcend this world to become part of the only meaningful reality above: "You place too high a value on your fleshly body," she tells her rival philosopher. "Take up pain and doubt as true pleasure, forgetting your body in favor of your soul. As for my own body, I kill it every day; for I struggle hard to gain paradise." At that juncture the third allegorical figure, the Wise Woman, arrives on the scene, and the debaters turn to her to arbitrate. This is how she replies: "The body without a soul is nothing more than a mass of earth that lasts only a short time." In philosophical terms, neither monism is valid. The truth about reality is a metaphysical dualism which defines us as both body and soul. Marguerite has learned her lessons well, but she does more than present a philosophical discussion; as far as she is concerned, the argument about the nature of reality serves only as a point of departure for the larger theological issue of love.[49]

Thus, like so much of Marguerite's writing, *The Comedy of Mont-de-Marsan* is yet another examination of the meaning of love, profane versus divine. When the Worldly Woman proudly announces that she loves her body, the Wise Woman responds that this is a "beastly love" which can only bring about madness. When the Superstitious Woman boasts of loving only her soul, the Wise Woman's reply remains the same. In either case, she argues, the only true love is the love of God and that cannot come about until one learns to humble oneself. Otherwise the Superstitious Woman's "mumblings are useless." Thus, in addition to the pride of the body we must also beware of the pride of the soul. In this fashion, the scene has been set for the arrival of what is implied to be the highest form of love, allegorized in the person of the Shepherdess, who, like the children in the play *The Inquisitor* (1543), represents a simple, unquestioning devotion, and who sings rather than reasons.

One is tempted, because of this theatrical progression, to assume that the Shepherdess sums up Marguerite's own concept of love. But that would be an oversimplification of the complexities presented in this play. Marguerite was no anti-intellectual. She may, in a part of her being, have identified with that kind of mystical transport, as evidenced in her *Mirror of the Sinful Soul*. But she also thought out her beliefs, reasoned like the Wise Woman, and was not ready to surrender her rational self to her devotions. In brief, what makes this play so fascinating is what so often characterized Marguerite's mind. She thinks in dialogic terms, so that she is not likely to reduce her subject to a categorical answer that precludes argument.[50]

One cannot leave this analysis without asserting as well that there is a less obvious but important feminist element in this plot. As in *The Coach*,[51] the world of the *Comedy of Mont-de-Marsan* is exclusively a woman's world.

---

49. There seems little doubt that the queen knew well, either firsthand or through the many commentaries of the period, the platonic ideas popularized by Ficino (Jourda, *Marguerite d'Angoulême*, 1: 505–8, 1: 510–14, 2: 757). In 1536–37, she herself encouraged translations of Plato's *Symposium* and *Crito*.

50. It has always been a temptation to oversimplify meaning in Marguerite. Abel Lefranc, who has his own theological axe to grind and wanted to prove Marguerite a "Protestant," holds out for a debate here between Catholicism and Protestantism.

51. There is, we remember, a strange exchange at the beginning of *The Coach*, where the narrator, Marguerite, speaks sympathetically to a peasant. Is this a nod in the direction of the pastoral or a political statement on her part?

There are no men here, and the question of love is deliberately seen from a woman's point of view. The stylish, self-loving Worldly Woman and the presumptuous and ritual-loving Superstitious Woman are two parts of the same feminine mystique. Marguerite herself would not have wished to conceal her womanhood or her sexual needs. She could and did love. Though she was no ritualist who favored a nonthinking devotion to God, she was devoted in her own way. As a reformist she denied the validity of empty-headed ceremony, but she was not about to give up the Catholic Mass with its glorious liturgy. And as for the two other characters represented, the Wise Woman and the Shepherdess, she assimilated these opposites within her own persona. Her mind in no way subjugated her heart, or vice versa.

As in *The Coach* these debating women also bond. The Wise Woman persuades the first two to come around to her way of reasoning, and though the Shepherdess's annoying indifference to their pleadings for the name of her lover is a comical tit for tat that goes on a bit too long, they identify with her sentiments without knowing who exactly she is talking about. And before the Shepherdess sings her final love song, the Superstitious Woman offers to pray to God to forgive her intemperance, to which the Wise Woman responds that they were all young once. In the end they go off together: "Let us withdraw, for it is late," amicably suggests the Wise Woman, as if speaking to old friends.

The Heptameron

No one surely is going to argue that *The Heptameron* is not Marguerite's masterpiece. It is an extraordinary accomplishment, not only in what it says, but in the way it says it. The queen of Navarre spent years gathering her tales together and doubtless would have reached the desired one hundred if health and time had allowed. But if that did not come to pass, we can nonetheless be grateful for what is there.

In her prologue, Marguerite is amazingly precise about the genesis of her collection. To the nine other characters stranded by a flood in the Pyrenean town of Cauterets, her alter ego Parlamente suggests that they exchange tales to pass the time. She goes on to confess that the idea is far from original and is in fact inspired by Boccaccio's *Decameron*, which had recently been translated into French.[52] What is more, she confesses that at one time it was the objective of several court figures, including Francis I, the Dauphin

---

52. This was the second translation. Marguerite, who had read the original Italian, had herself commissioned this new translation in 1544, giving the task to one of her own protégés, Antoine Le Maçon.

and Dauphine, and "Madame Marguerite," to follow Boccaccio's example, except in one important respect. *Their* tales would be "truthful." So strongly did they feel about this exception that they even decided never to call upon professional writers, who, by dint of their "rhetorical" devices, might "falsify the truth." As it happened, events prevented the realization of the joint project. But now, Parlamente tells her newfound companions, the ideal moment has presented itself to undertake that aborted mission.

If Marguerite makes such a point of this "exception," the remark invites examination. Is her storytelling true to life? Do we have a realistic sense of place and people? In a word, are we to see her collection as an important link in the narrative evolution that eventually led to nineteenth-century writers like Balzac and Dickens? Using the four tales represented in this anthology, let us put her literary ambition to the test.

As to plots, the storytellers remind us over and again of their sources.[53] At the close of novella 4, for example, Nomerfide announces to her listeners that she is about to tell a tale (novella 5) which she "personally knows." More than that, she has actually "checked into it on the very site where it took place."

The text of the prologue to each story often specifically identifies the geographical location where the action is to transpire, thus concretely situating it in a real world that readers will promptly recognize.[54] Novella 4, we are told, is set in Flanders. Novella 11 takes us to a small town in western France, called Thouars. Marguerite situates novella 69 in her own residence at Odos. And finally novella 72 brings us to a city she knew very well from her many travels there, the prosperous intellectual mecca of Lyons.

Although Marguerite's descriptions of exteriors and interiors are succinct, she usually says enough to conjure up an image. The chateau that the brother and sister visit in novella 4 is "sumptuous and beautifully maintained," and the room the sister is given is "handsomely appointed with full-length tapestries" and a floor that is "thickly carpeted." Before he attacks the princess, the seducer/host admires himself in a "candle-lit mirror." On occasion, a comical euphemism replaces the common term, as for example when the latrine in novella 11 becomes "that place where you cannot send a servant in your stead."

---

53. Including two of the tales represented here, novellas 4 and 69, in many instances the narrating characters themselves assure their audience that the story they are about to relate is true: 5, 9, 11, 14, 15, 21, 23, 31, 35, 42, 43, 47, 51, 53, 61, 63.

54. "She takes great pains to give to her tales an air of truth, to locate them clearly in cities and countries which she names with a certain precision." Jourda, *Marguerite d'Angoulême*, 2: 792.

When defining the characters in the *Heptameron*, we have to keep in mind that throughout there are two sets of dramatis personae, those who tell the tales and those who are in the tales.[55] The people who frequent the stories themselves represent a wide social range: aristocrats, clergy, merchants, servants, and even peasants.[56] Sometimes they have names and sometimes they are even historical figures. Though the names have been left out of novella 4, it is conventional scholarly wisdom that the brother and sister mentioned here are no other than Francis I and Marguerite and that the would-be rapist is, as noted above, Guillaume Gouffier, seigneur de Bonnivet, a friend of the family.[57] On occasion scholars have simply not been able to find any models for named characters. Neither the person called La Mothe nor Madame de la Tremoïlle in novella 11 has been identified, and as for Ronsex (round sex), Marguerite is obviously just having fun. In novella 72, however, she actually names herself.[58]

Typical of the novella tradition, the characters in the tales themselves require little more than the most superficial and perfunctory of depictions to conjure up an image.[59] When Ronsex in novella 11 is caught in unclothed disarray, we are simply informed that the men who are looking on in amazement see her "bare-assed." The phrase is succinct but quite adequate. The author gives an aura of authenticity to novella 69 when she refers to the maid's *sarot,* "a smocklike hood which went on her head and down upon her shoulders—a style peculiar to that region." Marguerite, with the keen eye of a writer, must have seen these headpieces in the country near Odos where she spent so much of her time.

By far Marguerite's most successful technique in making her characters

---

55. While it would be inaccurate to say that Marguerite wrote a roman à clef, many of her characters do grow out of personal relationships. Over the years critics have tried to put historical names especially on the storytellers themselves. Jourda offers a summary of these theories in his *Marguerite d'Angouleme,* 2: 762–66. But much of his own assessment borrows from the earlier study by Félix Frank in the introduction to his three-volume edition of the *Heptameron* (Paris: Lisieux, 1879).

56. "There is no social class which is not represented by at least one character in this panoramic view of sixteenth-century society." Jourda, *Marguerite d'Angoulême,* 2: 825.

57. It is Brantôme who twice confirms that Marguerite is the *Heptameron*'s victim and that her aggressor is Guillaume Gouffier (1488–1525) (*Recueil des dames,* 553–54, 670). If scholars have not challenged his identifications, it is because both Brantôme's grandmother and his mother were ladies-in-waiting in Marguerite's entourage and most likely well aware of all that was going on in their employer's personal life.

58. Besides stories in which brother and sister play a confirmed role, their names come up at least twenty different times throughout the collection.

59. "There are numbers of brief descriptions—too brief for our modern tastes—that reveal Marguerite to be an accomplished observer of the world she lived in" (Jourda, *Marguerite d'Angoulême,* 2: 821).

seem palpitatingly real is her adroit use of dialogue. This is especially true of the storytellers or *devisants*, who, at the close of each tale, comment amusingly on the just-completed narrative. Their remarks to one another grow out of their personalities, such that, before long, one can nearly predict what they will say at any given moment.

At the close of novella 4, the character named Hircan, generally believed to be Marguerite's own womanizing second husband, Henri d'Albret, ungenerously remarks: "It seems to me that the wonderful gentleman of your story lacked courage." If he had "killed the old lady," the young one would have had to surrender to his advances.

Inevitably, when the tale of the lady's maid, Ronsex, comes to an end, all the participants turn to Oisille, known to be something of a prude. She disappoints them and shows that this was an age when everyone, even old fuddy-duddies, could enjoy a good joke: "Albeit this is a dirty story," she says, "how I would have loved to see La Mothe's face and the face of the woman to whom she had brought such questionable help."

There are often friendly but biting remarks exchanged among the storytellers, suggesting that in spite of the invented narrative circumstance, they all knew each other. When in novella 69, Simontault is teased by Parlamente for sexual misconduct, he responds rather sharply: "You'd do well to dwell on your own household without interfering with mine."

Marguerite is careful to match up stories with their storytellers.[60] The character Dagoucin was probably an old friend of hers and like her a Platonist. As such, in the heated *querelle des femmes*, he would have readily aligned himself with the profeminist forces. It is altogether fitting therefore that it is he who relates the last tale in the collection, dealing with an abused nun. In fact, when he finishes he reminds his audience that he was told the story by the duchess herself, that is, Marguerite, when she was still married to the duke of Alençon. Altogether on the other side of the fence, however, is the anticlerical and outspokenly antifeminist Saffredent, who, not surprisingly, says about this tale: "The only bad thing here that I see was that the unfortunate nun could not keep herself from lamenting."

In short, although we do not find here any of the exhaustive descriptions which would become the hallmark of the nineteenth-century novel, Marguerite's sensitivity to the well-chosen detail, her catholic range of subject matter, and her remarkable ear for accurate speech unequivocally put her in the path toward the realistic narrative.

---

60. For that reason, among others, Jourda considers Marguerite an "astute psychologist" (*Marguerite d'Angoulême*, 2: 886). See in this regard B. J. Davis, *The Storytellers in Marguerite de Navarre's "Heptameron"* (Lexington, KY: French Forum, 1978).

But realism is by no means the only reason to read these wonderful stories. As Marguerite convincingly explores a particular world, she also gives evidence of remarkable narrative skills, made up of wit, irony, and a keen sense of suspense, drama, and humor. She is by any standards a gifted storyteller, and it is no wonder that for four hundred years she has not only captured the imagination of readers but fascinated critics who continue to examine what it is that makes her narrative work. The scholarly commentary on the *Heptameron* is rich and astounding, and the spirited and plucky student who wants to examine that vast critical literature will be faced with a truly formidable task.[61]

Notwithstanding the *Heptameron's* significance in the history of prose fiction, success has unfortunately not carried over to the rest of Marguerite's writings. The queen of Navarre's contributions to other genres—the theater, verse narratives, and valuable theological essays composed in poetic language—have been generally ignored; critics and readers have by and large chosen to see Marguerite as a one-book author. Proper recognition of the varied extent of her substantial œuvre is long overdue.

At its very best, Marguerite's theater displays skill in clever dialogue, humor, and philosophical analysis. In both *The Coach* and *The Fable of False Pride*, she takes two old forms and, in an innovative and groundbreaking way, makes them vehicles for exploring original ideas on womanhood. Certainly no other woman writer before her manages as she does to bring to paper the essentials of the new theology. And in spite of the enormous distance in time and rank that separate us from the queen of Navarre, her extensive correspondence gives us an unexpected glimpse into this royal woman's opinions, judgments, beliefs, and feelings. In short, this "other voice" not only renders our knowledge of the French Renaissance more accurate and more complete but introduces us to a world-class author.

NOTE ON TRANSLATIONS

If one wishes to experience the subtleties of Marguerite's style and mind, one should of course read the originals. But that alas is easier said than done, not only because of the difficulty of many of these texts, but because much of

---

61. The gamut of methodologies inevitably includes historical and sociological techniques, as well as—consistent with modern-day practices—both psychological and feminist approaches. Numerous critics have done valuable work in search of analogues for individual novellas. Our own limited bibliography offers a good head start, but the ambitious student will want to consult the latest MLA listings, where, it immediately becomes apparent, of the more than two hundred publications listed on Marguerite—since the 1980s alone—better than half are devoted exclusively to her collection of stories.

what the queen of Navarre put to paper—with the reception of the *Heptam-eron*—is quite simply not readily available in French, let alone in English. It has thus been the goal of this current project to bring to an English-speaking readership a representative selection of this important sixteenth-century au-thor's works, along with their originals, in an easy-to-read bilingual format.

Anyone who has waded through the troubled waters of translating from a foreign tongue realizes all the possible pitfalls and challenges, especially when, as here, that language is in serious flux. We have dealt with particular issues of vocabulary and syntax either in the short introductions to the texts or in notes.

The invitation to stumble and fall is even greater when attempting to recapture the idiosyncratic technique of a poet's verse. Not being poets our-selves, we dared not take up that gauntlet. Instead, our philosophy through-out has been to offer prose translations, which, if they tell us nothing about rhyme, rhythm, and creative skills, at least communicate something of the writer's meaning. The value of a bilingual edition such as this one is to per-mit the more industrious reader to compare and evaluate.

Mary L. Skemp is responsible for the translations of and introductions to *The Coach* and *The Comedy of Mont-de-Marsan*, Rouben C. Cholakian for the remainder.

Rouben Cholakian

VOLUME EDITOR'S BIBLIOGRAPHY

PRIMARY SOURCES

Brantôme, Pierre de Bourdeilles, seigneur de. *Recueil des dames.* Ed. Etienne Vaucheret. Paris: Gallimard, 1991.

Calvin, Jean. *Treatises against the Anabaptists and against the Libertines.* Trans. and ed. Benjamin Wirt Farley. Grand Rapids, MI: Baker Book House, 1982.

Chartier, Alain. *La belle dame sans mercy; et les poésies lyriques.* Ed. Arthur Piaget. Paris: Droz, 1945.

Christine de Pizan. *Le livre des trois jugements.* In *The Love Debate Poems of Christine de Pizan,* ed. Barbara Altmann. Gainesville: University of Florida Press, 1998.

———. *Le livre du dit de Poissy.* Ed. Barbara Altmann. Toronto: University of Toronto Press, 1988.

Cicero. *L'Amitié.* Ed. and trans. Louis Laurand. Paris: Les Belles Lettres, 1928.

———. *De senectute, De amicitia, De divinatione.* Trans. William A. Falconer. Cambridge: Harvard University Press, 1964.

Goldsmith, Elizabeth, and Colette Winn, eds. *Lettres de femmes: textes inédits et oubliés du XVe au XVIIIe siècle.* Paris: Champion, 2005.

Heroët, Antoine; Bertrand de La Borderie; and Charles Fontaine. *Opuscules d'amour: Poèmes qui constituent l'essentiel de la Querelle des Amyes (1547).* Intro. M. A. Screech. New York: S. R. Publishing, 1970.

Louise de Savoie. *Journal.* In *Collection complète des mémoires relatifs à l'histoire de France,* ed. M. Petitot. Vol. 16. Paris: Foucault, 1826–27.

Machaut, Guillaume de. *Le jugement dou roy de Behaigne.* Ed. William Kibler and James Wimsatt. Athens: University of Georgia Press, 1988.

Marguerite de Navarre. *Chansons spirituelles: Marguerite de Navarre.* Ed. Georges Dottin. Geneva: Droz, 1971.

———. *The Coach and the Triumph of the Lamb.* Trans. Hilda Dale. Exeter: Elm Bank, 1999.

———. *La coche.* Ed. Robert Marichal. Geneva: Droz, 1971.

———. *La comédie de Mont-de-Marsan.* In *Théâtre profane,* ed. V. L. Saulnier.

———. *Les comédies bibliques.* Ed. Barbara Marczuk. Geneva: Droz, 2000.

———. *Les dernières poesies.* Ed. Abel Lefranc. Paris: Colin, 1896.

———. *Guillaume Briçonnet/Marguerite d'Angoulême: Correspondance.* Ed. Christine Martineau, Michel Veissière, and Henry Heller. 2 vols. Paris: Lahure, 1975–79.

————. *Heptaméron.* Ed. Félix Frank. 3 vols. Paris: Lisieux, 1879.

————. *L'Heptaméron.* Ed. Michel François. Paris: Garnier, 1960.

————. *The Heptameron.* Ed. and trans. P. A. Chilton. New York: Penguin Classics, 1984.

————. *L'Heptaméron.* Ed. Renja Salminen. Geneva: Droz, 1999.

————. *Lettres de Marguerite d'Angoulême.* Ed. F. Génin. Paris: Renouard, 1841.

————. *Les marguerites de la Marguerite des princesses.* Ed. Félix Frank. Paris: Cabinet du Bibliophile, 1873.

————. *Le miroir de l'âme pécheresse.* Ed. Joseph L. Allaire. Munich. Wilhelm Fink, 1972.

————. *Nouvelles lettres de la reine de Navarre à son frère le roi François Ier.* Ed. F. Génin. Paris: Renouard, 1842.

————. *Œuvres choisies: Marguerite de Navarre.* Vol. 1: *Poèmes.* Ed. H. P. Clive. New York: Appleton-Century-Crofts, 1968.

————. *Poésie du roi François Ier, de Louise de Savoie, duchesse d'Angoulême, de Marguerite de Navarre.* Ed. Aimé Champollion-Figeac. 1847. Reprint, Geneva: Slatkine, 1970.

————. *Les prisons.* Ed. Simone Glasson. Geneva: Droz, 1978.

————. *Théâtre profane.* Ed. V. L. Saulnier. Geneva: Droz, 1963. Ed. and trans. Régine Reynolds-Cornelle. Ottawa: Dovehouse, 1992.

Plato. *Lysis.* Trans. David Bolotin. Ithaca: Cornell University Press, 1979.

————. *Phaedrus.* Trans. R. Hackforth. Indianapolis: Bobbs-Merrill, 1952.

Rabelais. *Gargantua and Pantagruel.* Trans. J. M. Cohen. Baltimore: Penguin Books, 1955.

SECONDARY SOURCES

Ambrière, Francis. *Le favori de François Ier, Gouffier de Bonnivet, amiral de France.* Paris: Hachette, 1936.

Baider, Fabienne. "Plaisir du discours, discours sur le plaisir dans l'Heptaméron de Marguerite de Navarre." *Women in French* 11 (2003): 11–24.

Becker, Philippe Augustus. "Marguerite, duchesse d'Angoulême, et Guillaume Briçonnet, évêque de Meaux, d'après leur correspondance manuscrite." *Bulletin de la Société de l'histoire du protestantisme français* 49 (1900): 393–477.

Berriot-Salvadore, Evelyn. *Les femmes dans la société de la Renaissance.* Paris: Droz, 1990.

Bertrand, Dominique, ed. *Lire L'Heptaméron de Marguerite de Navarre.* Clermont-Ferrand: Presse Universitaire Blaise Pascal, 2005.

Cazauran, Nicole, ed. *L'Heptaméron de Marguerite de Navarre.* Paris: SEDES, 1976, 1991.

Champollion-Figeac, Aimé. *Captivité du roi François 1er.* Paris, 1874.

Cholakian, Patricia Francis. *Rape and Writing in the Heptaméron of Marguerite de Navarre.* Carbondale: Southern Illinois University Press, 1991.

Cholakian, Patricia Francis, and Rouben C. Cholakian. *Marguerite de Navarre: Mother of the Renaissance.* New York: Columbia University Press, 2006.

Cholakian, Rouben. *The Troubadour Lyric: A Psychocritical Reading.* Manchester, England: University Press, 1990.

Clive, H. P. *Marguerite de Navarre: An Annotated Bibliography.* London: Grant & Cutler, 1983.

Conley, Tom. "Inklines and Lifelines: About La Coche (1547) by Marguerite de Navarre." *Parallax* 6, no. 1 (2000): 92–110.

Cottrell, Robert. *The Grammar of Silence.* Washington, DC: Catholic University Press, 1986.

Davis, B. J. *The Storytellers in Marguerite de Navarre's "Heptameron."* Lexington, KY: French Forum, 1978.

Davis, Natalie Zemon. *Fiction in the Archives: Pardon Tales and Their Tellers in Sixteenth-Century France.* Palo Alto: Stanford University Press, 1987.

———. *Society and Culture in Early Modern France.* Palo Alto: Stanford University Press, 1975.

Davis, Natalie Zemon, and Arlette Farge, eds. *Histoire des femmes,* vol. 3: *XVIe–XVIIIe siècles.* Paris: Plon, 1991.

Duhl, Olga Anna, ed. *Quêtes spirituelles et actualités contemporaines dans le théâtre de Marguerite de Navarre. Renaissance and Reformation/Renaissance et Réforme* 26, no. 4 (2002).

Ferguson, Gary. *Mirroring Belief: Marguerite de Navarre's Devotional Poetry.* Edinburgh: Edinburgh University Press, 1992.

Ferguson, Margaret. "Recreating the Rules of the Game." In *Creative Imitation: New Essays on Renaissance Literature in Honor of Thomas M. Greene,* ed. Margaret Ferguson, David Quint, G. W. Pigman III, and Wayne Rebhorn. Binghamton, NY: Medieval and Renaissance Texts and Studies, 1992. 53–87.

Festugière, Jean. *La philosophie de Marsile Ficin et son influence sur la littérature française.* Paris: J. Vrin, 1941.

Freccero, Carla. "Queer Nation, Female Nation: Marguerite de Navarre, Incest, and the State in Early Modern France." *Modern Language Quarterly: A Journal of Literary History* 65, no. 1 (2000): 29–47.

Freer, Martha Walker. *The Life of Marguerite d'Angoulême, Queen of Navarre, Duchesse d'Alençon and de Berry.* 2 vols. London: Hurst and Blackett, 1895.

Garraty, John Arthur, and Peter Gay. *The Columbia History of the World.* Newton, MA: Dorset Press, 1984.

Greengrass, Mark. *The French Reformation.* London: Edward Arnold, 1952.

Jourda, Pierre. *Marguerite d'Angoulême, Duchesse d'Alençon, reine de Navarre (1492–1549): Etude biographique et littéraire.* 2 vols. 1930; Reprint, Geneva: Slatkine, 1978.

King, Margaret L. *The Renaissance in Europe.* London: Laurence King, 2003.

Knecht, Robert J. *Renaissance Warrior and Patron: The Reign of Francis I.* Cambridge: Cambridge University Press, 1994.

Koopmans, Jelle. "L'allégorie théâtrale au début du XVIe siècle: Le cas des pièces 'profanes' de Marguerite de Navarre." *Renaissance and Reformation/Renaissance et Réforme* 26, no. 4 (2002): 65–89.

Larsen, Anne, and Colette Winn, eds. *Renaissance Women Writers: French Texts/American Contexts.* Detroit: Wayne State University Press, 1994.

Lecoq, Anne-Marie. *François 1er imaginaire: symbolique et politique à l'aube de la Renaissance française.* Paris: Macula, 1987.

Lefranc, Abel. *Les idées religieuses de Marguerite de Navarre.* 1898; Geneva: Slatkine, 1969.

Leushuis, Reinier. "Mariage et 'honnête amitié' dans l'Heptaméron de Marguerite de Navarre: Des idéaux ecclésiastique et aristocratique à l'agapè du dialogue humaniste." *French Forum* 28, no. 1 (2003): 29–56.

Lyons, John D., and Mary B. McKinley, eds. *Critical Tales: New Studies of the Heptaméron and Early Modern Culture.* Philadelphia: University of Pennsylvania Press, 1993.

Mathieu-Castellani, Gisèle. *La conversation conteuse: Les nouvelles de Marguerite de Navarre.* Paris: Presses Universitaires de France, 1992.

Middlebrook, Leah. "'Tout mon office': Body Politics and Family Dynamics in the Verse Epitres of Marguerite de Navarre." *Renaissance Quarterly* 54, no. 4 (2001): 1108–41.

Polachek, Dora, E, ed. *Heroic Virtue, Comic Infidelity: Reassessing Marguerite de Navarre's Heptaméron.* Amherst, MA: Hestia Press, 1993.

———. "Scatology, Sexuality and the Logic of Laughter in Marguerite de Navarre's Heptameron." *Medieval Feminist Forum* 33 (2002): 30–42.

Reynolds-Cornell, Régine, ed. *International Colloquium Celebrating the 500th Anniversary of the Birth of Marguerite de Navarre.* Birmingham, AL: Summa, 1995.

Roelker, Nancy L. *Queen of Navarre: Jean d'Albret, 1528–1572.* Cambridge: Harvard University Press, 1968.

Saulnier, V. L. "Etudes critiques sur les comédies profanes de Marguerite de Navarre." *Bibliothèque d'humanisme et Renaissance* 9 (1949): 36–77.

Skemp, Mary. "Reading a Woman's Story in Marguerite de Navarre's La Coche." *Explorations in Renaissance Culture* 31, no. 2 (Winter 2005): 279–303.

Skenazi, Cynthia. "Les annotations en marge du Miroir de l'âme pécheresse." *Bibliothèque d'humanisme et Renaissance* (1993): 255–70.

Sommers, Paula. *Celestial Ladders: Readings in Marguerite de Navarre's Devotional Poetry of Spiritual Ascent.* Geneva: Droz, 1989.

———. "Marguerite de Navarre as Reader of Christine de Pizan." In *The Reception of Christine de Pizan from the Fifteenth to the Nineteenth Centuries: Visitors to the City,* ed. Glenda McLeod. Lewiston, NY: Mellon, 1991. 71–82.

Stephenson, Barbara. *The Power and Patronage of Marguerite de Navarre.* Burlington, VT: Ashgate, 2004.

Telle, Émile. *L'Oeuvre de Marguerite d'Angoulême, Reine de Navarrre, et la querelle des femmes.* Toulouse: Toulousaine Lion et Fils, 1937.

Tetel, Marcel. *Marguerite de Navarre's "Heptameron": Themes, Language, and Structure.* Durham: Duke University Press, 1973.

Thompson, Stith. *Motif-Index of Folk Literature.* 6 vols. Copenhagen: Rosenkilder and Begger, 1955–58.

Thysell, Carol. *The Pleasure of Discernment: Marguerite de Navarre as Theologian.* Oxford: Oxford University Press, 2000.

Winn, Colette. "Aux origines du discours féminin sur l'amitié . . . Marguerite de Navarre, La Coche." *Women in French Studies* 7 (1999): 9–24.

I

EPÎTRES / VERSE LETTERS

EDITOR'S INTRODUCTION

It is difficult to say when Marguerite composed her first verse letter or for that matter how many in her lifetime she wrote. It is probable that some have been lost to us.[1] In any event, it would seem that from the earliest years, the Angoulêmes, mother and children, exchanged such verse letters, composing them with the same ease and facility as if they were writing prose.

At her worst, Marguerite was capable of mere doggerel;[2] at her best, she could be both witty and charming, sometimes even dramatic and moving. The first letter here, composed at Blois in the summer of 1530, is addressed to Marguerite's mother, Louise of Savoy, who had gone to the south of France to meet her two grandchildren just returned from four grueling years as hostages in Spain.[3] Because of her pregnancy, Marguerite could not

1. The earliest preserved *épître* from Marguerite's hand is probably the one she sent to Francis during his captivity in Spain (1525). See Aimé Champollion-Figeac, *Captivité du roi François 1er* (Paris, 1847), 100–102.

2. As Leah Middlebrook notes, they were mostly written spontaneously. "'Tout mon office': Body Politics and Family Dynamics in the Verse *épîtres* of Marguerite de Navarre." *Renaissance Quarterly* 54, no. 4 (2001): 1110.

3. When, in 1526, due in good measure to the negotiating skills of his sister, Francis was finally released from captivity by the Emperor Charles V, it was with the sad understanding he would need to surrender his two male children, as proof of his good intentions to abide by the stipulations of the Treaty of Madrid. Once released, however, Francis, with the support of the Paris Parlement, did not give over the duchy of Burgundy as indicated in the agreement. He was able to get away with this disavowal because many European powers shared in his indignation at having to act under duress. On the other hand, perhaps through spite, Charles held onto the two boys, Henry, then only seven year old, and Charles, still younger, for nearly four years. Charles died under rather mysterious circumstances in 1545, while his brother, who eventually became king of France in 1547, seems never to have forgiven his father. The resentment understandably went very deep.

attend, and she barely hides her disappointment. The second, dating from January of 1544, enthusiastically praises her brother, who had just become a grandfather.[4] The third, composed in the fall of 1547, at the popular Pyrenees spa of Cauterets,[5] is, to our knowledge, the only surviving letter to Henri d'Albret, Marguerite's second husband. The final letter reproduced here, dating from the spring of 1549, is part of a unique epistolary exchange between Marguerite and her daughter, Jeanne, discovered only in 1895 by the eminent scholar Abel Lefranc.[6] It is thus one of the last examples of Marguerite's use of this interesting literary form.

4. The event loomed large because Henry II and Catherine de' Medici had failed to produce any children for the first ten years of their marriage. This Francis, named after his very happy grandfather, reigned as Francis II for only two years, from 1559 to 1560.

5. This mountain retreat plays a significant role in the life history of Marguerite because she chose to situate her collection of tales, the *Heptameron*, at Cauterets.

6. It became an important part of his edition of Marguerite's poems: *Les dernières poésies*.

EPÎTRES

Il m'est advis, Madame, que je offense
Le vray rapport de vostre conscience,
De vous escripre à present le plaisir
Que ceste foiz a vaincu mon desir,
Après que ay eue asseurance parfaicte,   5
Par l'union d'amytié immortelle,
De pitié vraye à bonté maternelle.
Ce que je sens vous faict assez congnoistre
Et mon grant bien au vostre recongnoistre.
Qu'est-il besoing doncques que vous escripve   10
Ce que savez par ceste amour naïfve?
Que me sert-il en ma lettre toucher
Ce que partez escript en vostre chair?
Que dis-je escript? Mais gravé sur les tables
De vostre cueur, à tout jamais durables.   15
Certes de peu, si ce n'estoit, madame,
Que la fumée yssant de la grant flamme
De ceste joye, où tout mon cueur se allume,
Par le tuyau d'une petite plume
Est or contraincte à prandre son passaige   20
Pour vous porter du grant feu tesmoignage:
Ce qui en sort n'est que seulle fumée,
Laquelle au vent est bientost consumée.
Le feu estant en l'esprit franc et libre
Me faict par vous, en vous et pour vous vivre.   25

Ce que je dis est clair et magnifeste,
Et l'indicible en mon sentiment reste;

VERSE LETTERS

It is my feeling, Madame,[7]
after you have given me fervent assurances
of the sincerity of your maternal kindness
and of our eternal bonds of affection,
that I am violating your true intent   5
when writing to you at present
of the pleasure that has conquered my desire.[8]
You know what I am feeling
and that I have subordinated my own well-being to yours.
So what need is there to write to you   10
about this innocent love with which you are familiar?
What point is there in telling you
what is written in your flesh?
Written? Say rather indelibly engraved
on the tablets of you heart.   15
Surely, very little, Madame,
if it wasn't that the smoke that issues from this great flame
of joy, entirely consuming me,
in order to find its just expression,
had to work its way   20
through the narrow passage of this pen.
What emerges is but smoke,
quickly dissipated by the wind.
But the fire, pure and unlimited,
allows me to live through you, in you, and for you.[9]   25

What I write is clear and transparent;
the inexpressible remains within me.

Le plus que escriptz, soit en rime ou en prose,
N'est pas le moins de l'heur où je repose;
Qu'il soit ainsi, on le scet par raison,   30
Et sans user d'aultre comparaison,
Chascun congnoist que au monde n'a personne
Qui plus que moy de juste droict sens donne,
Ayant ouy par la joyeuse voix,
Desjà commune en ce chasteau de Bloys,   35
Que vous avez la chose recouverte
Sans que tout gaing vous n'estimez que perte;
Que vous avez maintenant à voz yeulx
L'obgect plaisant qui les contante myeulx;
Que vous avez la veue au lieu ancrée   40
Qui de tous pleurs et larmes la recrée;
Que vous tenez en vos briez estenduz
Les desirez et les tient attenduz;
Que vous tenez de vos mains delicates
Le pris qui rend leurs peines non ingrates;   45
Que vous tenez à seure delivrance
Le bien et l'heur et delice de France,
Ceulx qui seront le support charitable
De la vieillesse honneste et venerable
De leurs amys, et le vray fort robuste   50
Pour les garder de toute injure injuste;
Que vous tenez, après divers alarmes,
En bonne paix voz filz de tant de larmes,
Qui vous feront, maulgré fortune amere,
Nommer partout très heureuse grant mere.   55
Mere, je diz, qu'on a veu tant souffrir
Pour saine vie à ses enfans offrir;
Qui, delivrez de prison et destresse,
Luy font du tout oublier sa tristesse.
Chascun me dict, pour plus me resjouyr,   60
La joye et l'heur dont vous pouvez joyr;
Qui sont si grans maintenent, que la preuve
En vostre face et parolle s'en treuve.
Mays c'est le moins: car la pure liqueur
De seure joye est tousjours près du cueur: 65
De quoy je sens le vostre si très yvre,
Que par nulle autre il n'en sera delivre.

Whatever finds expression in poetry or prose
can only dimly represent my truest happiness.
All reasonable people comprehend that.   30
Putting aside other comparisons,
everyone knows that there is no one in the world
who more willingly gives expression to the truth than I.
Throughout the castle of Blois,
it is being said in one common voice   35
that you have achieved the ultimate goal
without which all gain is but loss:
That you now have before your very eyes
the wonderful object which can best please them,
that you have your sights focused on the one thing   40
which can invoke tears and weeping,
that you hold in your outstretched arms
your long-awaited loved ones,
that you have in your hands,
the price which makes their pain worthwhile,   45
that you have in sure custody
the wealth, the joy, and the delight of France,
those who will generously support their friends
in their mature and venerable old age,
those who will have the necessary vigor   50
to protect them from every injustice.
After many anxieties, you safely hold
the sons, cause of so much grief,
who, in spite of their countless misfortunes,
will have you declared everywhere a fortunate grandmother.   55
The mother, I repeat, whom we saw endure great pain
in order to assure the safety of her children,
and the children who, delivered from pain and prison,
make her forget her sorrows.
To give me pleasure, everyone speaks   60
of the gladness and delight which you can now enjoy
and which are so apparent
that the proof is plain
both in your words and on your face.
But that is the least of it, for the pure liquor   65
of sure and certain joy lies close to the heart,
of which I sense yours to be so full

Cent foiz le jour je vous contemple et pense
Que vous avez maintenant la presence
De voz troys filz et d'une dame aussi   70
Que nommeray vostre fille Sanssi,
Je n'ay dit royne, estant bien asseurée
Que de ce nom se tient fort honnorée,
Et vous, madame, en estes si très aise
Que de ce mot force est vous complaise.
A tous propoz et toute heure il me semble
Que voy le Roy et Elle et vous ensemble   75
Au cabinet compter de voz fortunes,
Que vraye amour faict à vous troys communes.
C'est, sans mentir, ung singulier plaisir
Ramentevoir entre amys, à loisir,
Par passe-temps les fortunes passées,   80
Lorsqu'elles sont de bonheur compansées;
Et m'est advis, ainsi je le veulx croire
Pour mon grant bien, qu'avez de moy memoire,
Me souhaictant en vostre compagnie,
Dont je ne puys d'esprit estre bannye.   85
En y pensant, à bon droict, j'en souspire,
Et, d'un desir très ardant, je desire
De povoir estre, en quelque coing et angle,
Ung petit point de ce parfaict triangle.

Las! Quant je pense à la saison passée,   90
Tousjours malheur m'a très fort avancée
Aux lieux de dueil plains de telle souffrance,
Que mort estoit ma joye et esperance;
Cinq ans y a que vous vyz en ce lieu,
N'ayant secours ne medecin que Dieu,   95
En maladie, helas! si très extreme,
Que d'y penser j'en deviens pasle et blesme.
Ung an après, pour heureux avantaige,
Je fiz d'Espaigne en travail le voyaige,
Où me faillut comme en poste courir;   100
Et là trouver sur le poinct de mourir
Celluy qui seul, au temps de la misere,
M'estoit mary, pere et très aymé frere

that nothing will deliver it from drunkenness.
A hundred times a day I envision and think of you
having before your eyes now   70
three sons and the lady
whom I shall call your incomparable daughter.
I did not say queen, for I am sure
that she is very honored with the other title,
and you, madame, are so comfortable with it   75
that we must conform to your wishes in this matter.
At every moment and on every occasion,
I envision you, the king, and her,
sitting in your private quarters counting the fortune
that true love makes you share in common.   80
It is undoubtedly a singular pleasure
for good friends to take time in their leisure
to recall past hardships
when they are compensated by happiness.
And it is my feeling, and so I wish to believe   85
for my great good, that you remember me,
wishing me in your company
from which I cannot be banished in spirit.
Meditating on this, I quite understandably sigh,
and with a heavy heart, long   90
to be in some corner or angle,
a small part of that perfect triangle.[10]

Alas, recalling that earlier time,
I think how misfortune tormented me
with such great sadness,   95
that death was my only joy and hope.
Five years have passed since I last laid eyes on you there.[11]
You were so ill, and without medicine or help save for God,
that remembering it now,
I grow pale and blanch.   100
With happy results, a year later,
rushing by rapid post,
I made the difficult journey to Spain.
And there I found, at the point of death,
the one who was my only husband,   105
father, and beloved brother.

Et maintenant que la fortune adverse
Ne vous peult plus donner nulle traverse,   105
Par voz vertuz se sentant surmontée,
Elle s'en vient vers moy toute eshontée
Pour s'en vanger, me faisant reculler
Du lieu où plus je veulx et doy aller!
Et pour garder que je n'en face approche,   110
Un seul enfant m'a faict telle escarmouche,
Qu'il a fallu, à moy et à ma bande,
Gangner ce fort, qui n'est pas gloire grande.
Je n'ay point craint la mer et ses nauffraiges,   115
Des ennemys les effortz et oultraiges:
Las! maintenant me fault-il rendre ainsi
A ung enfant et toute à sa mercy?
C'est grand ennuy, certes, à ung bon cueur,
Qui a esté immuable vainqueur,   120
Quant est forcé à la fin qu'ung enfant
Soit de sa gloire et de luy triumphant.
Helas! madame, où puis-je avoir recours,
Sinon à vous, mon seul et seur secours,
Qui ne vouldriez pour rien laisser deffaire   125
Ce qui tant cher vous a cousté à faire.
Mesmes congnu que tout vostre exercice
Est en tous lieux faire de mere office.
Vous l'avez fait si bien sur la Garonne,
Que toute France en a seureté bonne;   130
Faictes aussi que le fleuve de Loyre
En donne foy d'eternelle memoire.
Puisqu'il est temps, humblement je supplie
Vostre bonté, de toute grace emplie,
Daigner pour moy prendre à cueur la matiere   135
Et vous en faire opportune priere:
Dont bon effect attent sans son merite.

༃

Le serviteur, fidele renommé,
Des anciens Pere de Foy nommé,
Avant qu'il eust de son obeïssance
Donné à tous exemple et congnoissance,

And now that adverse fortune
can no longer bring you harm,
conquered by your many virtues,
she shamelessly advances toward me   110
to take her revenge, by holding me back
from that place where I desire to be and ought to be.
And in order that I should not proceed,
a mere child made such a diversion
that it was necessary for me and my party   115
to gain this fort, which is no great glory.
I feared neither sea nor wreckage,
neither the advances nor the assaults of the enemy;
and yet, am I obliged to surrender
and put myself at the mercy of a child?[12]   120
It is surely a tremendous embarrassment for a great heart,
for one who has been a great conqueror,
in the end to have one's glory
trampled upon by a child.
Alas, Madame, where can I seek comfort   125
if not from you, my only solace,
you who would never wish to undo
what it has cost you so much to do?
It is well known that you have everywhere
performed your duties as a mother ought.   130
You performed them so well on the Garonne
that all of France enjoys complete safety.[13]
See to it that the Loire River marks the occasion
with an eternal remembrance.[14]
And as it is now time, I humbly ask   135
your goodness, full of grace,
to deign to take to heart what I say,
and to submit my petition at an opportune moment,
so that, though I do not deserve it, it has its good effect.

The servant, renowned for his faithfulness,[15]
called by the ancients the Father of Faith,
before giving an example and lesson
to all of his obedience,

Trois hommes vit, et un seul adora;   5
Car Dieu en tous congnut et honora,
Croyant pour vray son Dieu trespuissant estre
De l'Ange et l'homme la substance et l'estre.
Avant ces deux grans effectz de sa Foy,
Dieu le tira à luy et hors de soy,   10
En luy monstrant du Ciel les choses belles,
Luy commandant de nombrer les estoilles,
S'il luy estoit possible de ce faire.
Mais sachant bien que c'estoit un affaire
Où l'œil et sens de l'homme est impuissant,   15
Il luy jura, non que par mille ou cent
Multipliroit sur terre sa semence,
Mais par sa grande et puissance et clemence
Aux estoilles que l'on peult au Ciel voir,
Et dont le nombre nully ne peult sçavoir,   20
Feroit ainsi sa semence semblable,
Et comme aux grains du petit menu sable
Qui est aux bortz de ceste Mer tant grande.
Abraam lors, sans luy faire demande
Comme se peult faire chose impossible   25
N'y concevoir ce qui est insensible,
Creut fermement à sa seule parole,
Par vive Foy, qui n'est vaine ny fole,
Et il luy feut reputé à justice.
Par cest Foy feit à Dieu sacrifice   30
Non de son filz, de son corps, de ses biens,
Mais de son cœur, mettant du tout à riens
Sa volonté, son sçavoir, sa raison,
Les captivant soubs divine prison,
Sacrifiant Cuyder, desir, envie,   35
Ne congnoissant avoir Estre ne vie,
Sinon Dieu seul, lequel, en se voyant
Image vif dens le cœur du croyant,
Dit et promit qu'il vouloit estre amy
De ses amys, et aussi ennemy   40
Des ennemys de luy et de sa race,
Qu'il avoit prins en son amour et grace;
Et beniroit ceux qui le beniroient,
Et maudiroit ceux qui le maudiroient;

saw three men, but adored only one.[16]   5
For he recognized and honored the Divinity,
believing that his all-powerful God was in a real way
the substance and being of angel and man.
Witnessing these two wondrous manifestations of faith,
God drew him toward him, leaving his self behind.   10
Pointing to the beauties of the sky,
he asked if he could count
the number of stars in the heavens.
Knowing perfectly well that it was a matter
in which man's eye and senses were inadequate,   15
he promised him that he would increase his race,
not by a hundred or a thousand but,
through his great mercy and power,
by an amount equal to the innumerable stars
one could see above   20
and to the tiny grains of sand
that bordered the mighty sea
he would multiply his seed.
Then Abraham, questioning
neither how such an impossible feat could be,   25
nor how one could imagine what is unimaginable,
believed on the basis of this word alone,
by active faith that is neither vain nor foolish,
and God reckoned it to him as righteousness.
In this fashion he sacrificed to God,   30
not his son, nor his body nor his wealth,
but his heart, considering all else of no importance.
Surrendering pride, desire, and yearnings,
he made his will, knowledge, and reason
captives of the divine prison.   35
He recognized no other reality or existence
save in God alone, who, seeing his own image
engraved in the believer's heart,
made a promise that his friends and the friends
of his race would be his friends, his enemies   40
and the enemies of his race, his enemies,
for he had granted him his love and grace.
He would bless those who blessed him
and would curse those who cursed him.

Mettant à riens les ennemys par guerre,   45
Luy donneroit leur desirable terre.
Voila l'accord du puissant Createur
Avec un bon fidele serviteur,
Que je lisois dedens mon Hermitage,
Pensant en moy le bien et l'avantage   50
Qui par la Foy est donné au croyant.
Puis d'autrepart, en mon Esprit voyant
De mon Seigneur et mon Roy la Foy vive,
Envers son Dieu sa charité naïve,
Me sembla voir le second Abraam,   55
Qui vray David s'estoit monstré l'autre an,
Executant les batailles de Dieu,
Et Dieu pour luy bataillant en tout lieu;
En maduissant par ruine et par honte
Ses ennemis, tant que nul n'en tient compte.   60
Ce que l'on voit par le compte Guillaume,
Lequel servant le Roy et son Royaume
S'estoit fait riche, craint et fort estimé;
Mais maintenant fuitif, povre et blasmé,
Peult bien penser dont son honneur venoit,   65
Qui riche, heureux et craint le maintenoit.
Voila comment du Dieu de Paradis
Les ennemis du Roy sont tous mauditz;
Dessus lesquelz il luy donne puissance,
Et de leurs biens et terre jouissance.   70
Que ses amys sont beneis! je pensois,
Qui ce peult veoir? veu que les Escossois
Contre un tel Roy que le Roy d'Angleterre
Ont eu povoir de soustenir la guerre,
Et sont unis tous soubz l'obeïssance   75
De celle là qu'est venue de France,
Congnoissans bien qu'estans au Roy uniz,
Seront de Dieu et gardez et beneiz.
Puis je faisois par ce Royaume un tour,
Pensant à ceux qui ont au Roy amour;   80
A ceux aussi qui, par ingratitude,
A bien l'aymer n'ont mise leur estude.
Les uns voyois contens, sans cesser rire,
Autres crever d'ennuy, d'envie et d'ire:

Destroying his foes in war,   45
he would offer him their valuable land.
And thus was established the covenant
between the Almighty and his faithful servant,
about which I was reading in my Hermitage,[17]
while reflecting upon the benefits   50
accrued to the true believer.
Picturing at the same time in my mind's eye
the pure love of my lord and king
for his God and his fervent faith,
he seemed to me a second Abraham,   55
a true David who, a year past,
fought God's battle,
with God at his side.
God brought shame and ruin upon the king's enemies,
such that all are aware of it.   60
There is, for example, the tale of Guillaume,
who, serving the king and his kingdom,
made himself rich, feared, and much admired.
But now he is scared, poor, and accused,
and can readily appreciate whence his honors came,   65
and who made him wealthy, esteemed, and happy.[18]
And thus are the king's enemies
all punished by the God of paradise.
He gives him dominion over them
and disposal of their wealth and lands.   70
I thought to myself: How blessed are his friends.
This can easily be seen in the fact
that the people of Scotland were able
to take up arms against a king
like the king of England   75
and united under the banner of the French lady,
knowing that by allying themselves with our king,
they would be protected and blessed by God.[19]
I have made a tour of the country,
thinking of all those who love the king,   80
thinking too of those ungrateful people
who have not made it their priority to love him.
Some that I saw were happy, forever laughing,
others, full of jealousy, anguish, and anger.

Qui me feit lors juger pour tout certain   85
Que vous, mon Roy et Seigneur souverain,
Estiez de Dieu le Christ, l'aymé, l'eslu,
Comme Abraam et David, que j'ay leu.
Je m'arrestay contemplant ce passage;
Mais tout soudain viz venir un message   90
Qui confirma ma contemplation,
Me declarant la consolation
De vous, de nous, du royaume et de tous,
Par nouveau fruit tant desiré de nous.
Soudainement autre chose ne fiz   95
Que vostre lettre ouvrir, et quant un Filz
Je viz escrit, je convertis le lire
A louer Dieu, à plourer et à rire.
Un Filz, un Filz! ô nom dont sur tous noms
Tresobligez à Dieu nous nous tenons,   100
Le Filz du Filz du Pere tresheureux,
Enfant qui rend les ennemy paoureux,
Filz qui apporte en France un double cœur,
Pour estre Filz du Filz du grand Vaincqueur,
Filz beaucoup plus desiré qu'esperé,   105
Le reconfort du cœur desesperé;
Felicité du grand Pere qui voit
Filz de son Filz, que desiré avoit;
Filz apportant au grand Pere jeunesse,
En retardant par joye sa vieillesse: 110
Car aussi tost que devant ses yeux vint,
Ses quarante ans retournerent à vingt.
O Filz heureux, joye du jeune Pere,
Souverain bien de la contente Mere;
Heureuse Foy qui, après longue attente,   115
Leur as donné le fruit de leur pretente;
Filz en noz cœurs receu et embrassé,
Dont l'œil de Corps et d'Esprit n'est lassé
Te regarder en ce monde naissant.
Filz que chacun François va benissant,   120
Le bien venu tu es, car tu apporte
A nostre Roy le bien qui le conforte
Des grans ennuis qu'il a euz plus qu'assez,
Qu'en te voyant il tient pour tout passez,

All of which made me believe that you, 85
my king and sovereign lord,
are God's beloved and chosen Christ,
very much like Abraham and David about whom I was reading.[20]
I was lingering over this passage,
when suddenly came the message 90
which was to confirm my thoughts,
announcing the birth of our new and longed-for progeny,
our happiness, everyone's happiness,
the happiness of the kingdom.
I thought only of opening your letter.[21] 95
And upon seeing the word *Son*,
I went from reading to praising God,
to weeping and laughing.
A Son, a Son, a word that makes us all
turn with thanks toward God. 100
The Son of the Son of the most joyous Father,
a child that causes our enemies to tremble,
a Son who brings France double courage
as the Son of the Son of a great conqueror,
a Son, more hoped for than expected, 105
the comfort of a disheartened heart,
the joy of a grandfather who looks upon
the Son of the Son he so longed for,
a Son who rejuvenates a grandfather,
who happily postpones his old age. 110
No sooner did he lay eyes on him
that forty turned into twenty.
O happy Son, delight of a young father,
pleasure of a contented mother;
blissful faith which, after so long a wait, 115
has given them the fulfillment of their dreams;
Son received and embraced in our hearts,
neither soul nor body ceases to admire
the sight of your arrival into this world.
Son whom every French person blesses, 120
you are welcome, for you bring our king
the gladness which consoles him
in his excessive distress.
This gift from God is so wondrous

Car sy grand est ce don de Dieu donné,   125
Que tout ennuy doit estre abandonné.
Et quant à moy, Monseigneur, en voyant
Vostre escriture et vostre voix oyant,
Qui me promet que parfait le tenez
Quant à beauté, et qu'il ha bien grand nés,   130
J'ay tel plaisir et telle aise receue,
Que si plus grande en le voyant j'eusse eue,
La vie m'eust failly à ce besoing,
Dont mon malheur m'est heur d'en estre loing.
Si de beauté et du nés vous ressemble,   135
Si fera il de voz vertus ensemble;
Et sera tel, qu'en vivant vostre vie
Allongera: et quand, par sainte envie,
Après cent ans donnerez vostre esprit
A l'union de Dieu par JESUS CHRIST,   140
Dedens ce Filz tout fait à votre image
Demourrez vif, vivant vostre lignage;
Et Dieu vivant en vous, qu'il aymera,
Dieu de Françoys tousjours se nommera,
Dieu de Henry et Dieu du petit Tiers,   145
Lequel Françoys nommerez volontiers:
Car vostre Foy en leurs deux cœurs emprainte
Fera leur ame à vostre exemple sainte.
Ce Dieu tout bon de sa condition,
Multiplira sa benediction   150
En accroissant par sa grande clemence
En peu de temps sy fort vostre semence,
Que seulement le Royaume de France
N'en sera plein, comme j'ay esperance,
Mais en sera toute terre couverte,   155
Et par leurs mains la Sainte recouverte.
Alors sera la Foy par tout plantée,
Et sainte Eglise saintement augmentée;
Un seul Pasteur et seule bergerie
Sera lors veu en vraye confairie.   160
Le Seigneur Dieu, qui ainsy l'ha promis,
Y a desja bon commencement mis.
En vous il a commencé l'edifice,
Et ne fera aux vostres moindre office.

that seeing you he forgets all that has passed   125
and he leaves behind him all sorrows.
And as for me, my lord,
reading your writing and hearing your voice,
I envision him as perfection in physical beauty.
I take great pleasure and joy   130
in hearing of his generous nose.[22]
I might have expired if I had had to witness
in person his extraordinary good looks,
and so my grief in being far turns into a blessing.
If in nose and handsomeness he resembles you,   135
he will resemble you too in your virtues.
And thus his life will prolong yours.
And when with holy intent,
after a hundred years, you surrender in Christ
your soul to God,   140
in this Son, your exact image,
who continues the family line, you will survive.
And since God, whom he will love, is living in you,
he will be called the God of Francis,
the God of Henry, and the God of the little Third Party,[23]   145
and you will gladly name him Francis.
Your faith, imprinted upon their two hearts,
will by your example render their souls holy.
This God of innate goodness,
will in his infinite kindness   150
multiply his blessings upon you
by generously increasing your fecundity.
It is my hope that they will not only
fill the kingdom of France,
but the entire earth, and that by their efforts   155
the Holy Land will be recaptured.[24]
And thus will the faith take hold, and thus,
the holiness of Holy Church spread everywhere.
And so shall there be one Shepherd of one sheepfold,
united in one true community.   160
Our Lord God, who made us that promise,
has already put his plan in motion.
In you he has begun to construct his building
and your offspring will play no less role.[25]

Assez peuvent juger tous bons espritz,   165
Veu que par vous a tel fondement pris
Qu'aussi de vous, voire infaliblement,
Rendra parfait son tressaint bastiment,
Auquel il veult à jamais regner Roy,
Ainsi qu'il fait en vostre cœur par Foy.   170
Et s'il vous plaist, Monseigneur, de sçavoir
Plus largement il vous plaira de voir
Et d'escouter celuy qui le m'a dit,
En luy donnant, si'il vous plaist, tout credit.
Il estoit Roy ainsy comme vous estes,   175
Fidele à Dieu, plein de vertuz honnestes;
Il vous fera present de seize Estoilles,
Vous assurant que seize enfans fideles
De vostre chair sailliront sy luysans
Et par la Foy à leur Dieu si plaisans   180
Que leur vertu gouvernera le monde,
En commandant sur Terre et Mer profonde.
Il vous dira les secretz de son maistre,
Et en quel lieu à la fin promet mettre
Celuy qui ha en luy sa confiance.   185
Il en a fait tresseure esperance.
Pour le laisser parler je me tairay,
Mais par grand joye encores ne lairray
Dire: ô Seigneur, tout bon et tout puissant,
Ce povre esprit en vieil corps languissant,   190
Laisse l'aller maintenant en ta paix,
Car de tel bien et grace me repais
Qu'il me suffist; et de toy suis contente
De voir mon Roy grand Pere, et moy grand tante.
Rien plus ça bas ne veux, ne n'ay envie,   195
Fors de sa bonne, heureuse et longue vie.

ॐ

Celle qui pour eslongner vostre veüe
N'est point de vous (j'en suis seure) incongnue
Mais par esprit à vostre esprit presente
Ce triste escrit pour parole presente,
Doublement triste (il fault que je le die)   5

All those who are clearheaded can judge for themselves,   165
seeing that you are part of the foundation,
that through your perfection, indeed infallibility,
he will make his edifice most saintly
in which he will reign as king
as he does by faith in your heart.   170
And if it pleases you, my sovereign lord,
to know more, then recognize and take heed
of the source of my comments,
and give him full credit.
Like you, he was king,   175
true to God and full of virtue.
He will make you a gift of sixteen stars,[26]
assuring you that sixteen children,
will be the fruit of your flesh,
so brilliant and so pleasing to God because of their faith   180
that their virtue will govern the world
and command the land and the deep seas.
He will reveal to you the secrets of his master,
and in what place he finally promises to place
him who is obedient to him.   185
He has had sure experience of this.
And so to allow him to speak to you, I shall keep silent.
Yet in one last burst of joy I will permit myself to say:
O Lord, most gracious and powerful,
grant that this sad soul languishing in an old body   190
may find peace in you,
for to be nourished by such grace and riches
is enough for me. I give thanks to you
for the sight of my king a grandfather and myself a great-aunt.
And I seek nothing further here in this world   195
than that he should have a good, happy, and long life.

She who although far from you[27]
is not (I am sure) unknown to you,
but remains present in your thoughts,
presents this sad missive instead of words,[28]
doubly distressed (it must be said)   5

En vous laissant fasché de maladie.
Croire povez que assez m'estoit des yeux
L'eslongnement pour un temps ennuyeux,
Sans le sçavoir que j'ay de la douleur,
Qui le repoz vous oste et la couleur.   10
O quel ennuy d'estre de vous bannie,
Et vous laisser en telle compagnie
D'extreme mal et de douleur cruelle!
Et moy qui suis je puis bien dire celle
Qui plus voudroit de cœur et corps courir   15
Au seur moyen qui vous peust secourir,
Las! je m'en vois. Et si l'on dit: Qui est ce
Qui au besoing ainsi son amy laisse?
Un ignorant respondroit sus ce poinct:
C'est celle là qui l'ayme peu ou point.   20
Quand il est sain, ilz font grand chere ensemble;
Quand il a mal, elle s'en va; il semble
Que c'est mal fait de vraye amour l'office,
D'user de fuyte en lieu de bon service.
Ne croyez pas, ô amy tresparfait,   25
Cest ignorant qui se prend à l'effect;
Voyez le cœur de celle qui s'en va,
Que maugré soy de la terre enleva
Pour la jetter dens sa noire litiere,
Dont elle n'eut, fors de plourer, matiere.   30
Si les regretz des propos et deviz
Que nous tenons quand sommes viz à viz,
Tant vertueux, sans vice ny folie,
Nombrer je sceusse, et la melancolie
Qui cause en moy le triste souvenir,   35
Ma foible main ne pourroit soustenir
Sy grand labeur, ny aussi peu vostre œil,
Sans qu'il unist ses larmes à mon dueil.
Donques de peur que la triste escriture
Rende vostre œil triste par la lecture,   40
Je laisseray, mais que je vous revoye,
A vous compter mon ennuy; mais la joye
Qu'en peu de temps j'espere recevoir,
Je ne crains point le vous faire sçavoir.
Soyez certain que ces povres villages   45

to have left you troubled by illness.
To have to be away from you
for a spell was difficult enough,
without knowing of the suffering
that deprives you of rest and makes you pale.[29]   10
Oh, what a terrible anguish
to be banished and to see you
visited by great pain and cruel torment.[30]
I who am, it may well be said, the one
most eager to give body and soul   15
to find you a remedy.
But alas, I must go. And if one were to ask: Who is it
who in such need would abandon her companion,
an unknowing person might readily respond
to his question: "She who cares little or not at all.   20
When he is well, they make merry,
and when he is not, she departs."
This seems a sorry example of true love,
to choose leaving over helping.
But do not, O most perfect friend,[31]   25
give any credence to this simpleton who judges by appearance.
Look into the heart of the voyager, who
unhesitatingly took some earth
and threw it into her black litter
where it was washed away in her tears.   30
If I were to make a list of all the times
I have regretted words exchanged between us,
in seeming good faith and without evil intent,
the recollection of which saddens me
and causes me melancholy,   35
my enfeebled hand could not manage such a task
nor withstand your gaze
without joining your tears to my grief.
So for fear that my cheerless words
might bring sadness to your eyes,   40
I shall take leave, with the hope, however,
of seeing you again to speak of my concerns.
I do not hesitate to tell you how pleased
I am at the thought of our reuniting.
Be assured that these unfortunate towns,   45

Qui sont subjetz au martyre et pillages,
Quand on leur dit: Le Roy vient regarder
Voz povretez, et gensdarmes garder
De vous piller et faire nulz outrages,
N'ont tels plaisir ny joye en leurs courages   50
Comme j'auray quand quelqu'une courra
Hastivement, et en riant dira:
Pantagruel a bien prophetisé,
Car j'ay desja les Muletz advisé
De cestuy là qui vous avoit promis   55
D'estre en trois jours en sa santé remis.
Si je seray preste de me lever
Pour vous aller, où que soyez, trouver,
N'en doutez point; mais entendez qu'autant
Que mon cœur feut, vous laissant, malcontent,   60
Autant aura de joye et de plaisir
A vous revoir, et compter à loisir
Le bien, le mal que je pourray entendre,
En vous priant ne faire pas attendre
A voz amys longuement des nouvelles,   65
Que je requiers à Dieu nous donner telles
Que de bon cœur luy demandons en foy,
Et nous l'aurons dens trois jours, je le croy;
Et vous verrons en santé si parfaite,
Que nous dirons: Le Medecin a faite   70
La cure ainsi comme il nous avoit dit.
Pensez un peu s'il aura bon credit.
Et à celuy qui donne la santé
Sera de cœur un Te Deum chanté,
Le suppliant à vous et nous donner   75
Grace, et santé pour plus n'abandonner
Celle qui veult (mesmes en Paradis)
Estre avec vous; et plus ne vous en dis.

Cuydant au soir en repoz sommeiller,
Amour me vient tout soudain esveiller
Disant: «Escriptz et prens la plume en main,
Sans t'excuser ny attendre à demain.

victims of martyrdom and pillage,
when told that the king is coming
to inspect their misery and to offer police help
against plundering and evil deeds,[32]
will feel nothing of the joy and pleasure   50
that I will experience when some rapid courier
shall tell me with a smile
that Pantagruel prophesied accurately.[33]
I already envision the mules
of the one who promised   55
your recovery in three days times.
When I say that I shall be ready
to come to you wherever you might be,
do not doubt it, but understand that
unhappy as I was to leave you,   60
so much joy and pleasure will I have
to see you again and to reckon up at leisure
the good and bad that I will hear.
I beg you not to keep
your admirers waiting long for news   65
which I implore God to give us of such sort
that we ask him for in good faith
and which I trust we will have in three days' time.
Seeing you back in perfect good health,
we shall say: the doctor has accomplished   70
what he had promised.
Think of what this will do for his reputation.
And he who restores health
will have sung for him a Te Deum,
asking that he give us and you grace,   75
and health so that you will no more abandon
her who wishes to be with you even unto Paradise.
No more than this shall I say.

Hoping one evening that I might sleep in peace,[34]
Love came suddenly and awoke me saying:
"With no further ado or postponing till tomorrow,
take up your pen and write.

Prendre ne peult ta fille en passience   5
Ceste trop longue et facheuse sillence. »
Je luy respondz quasi tout en dormant:
« J'ay tant escript que je n'ay argument
Pour bien escrire. » Il me respond: « Ne cesse
Jusques à ce que la pauvre princesse   10
Soit jointe au bien que tant elle desire;
Alors ta main reposera d'escripre.
Mais jusques là ta fille n'abandonne,
Et par escript quelques escriptz nous donne. »
Je me levay estant par luy pressée,   15
Du papier pris et ma plume ay dressée,
Et en l'allée auprès de ma fenestre
Me promenay, pour plus à mon ayse estre.
Puis je m'assis et me prins à penser
Par quel endroit je pourrais commencer.   20
J'attendis peu, lorsque j'ouys ung bruict
D'un vent sortant et de feuille et de fruict,
Qui doulcement portoit à mon oreille
Ung son piteux qui me donna merveille.
Je me tournay et deça et delà   25
Pour mieux sçavoir le lieu d'où vient cela.
Mais je ne vis arbre, branche ny feuille,
Qui doulcement d'un accord ne se dueille.
Et à leur son les petites fontaines
Ont respondu comme esgalles en peines,   30
Avecques eulx la voix de la riviere,
Qui s'eslevoit par si doulce maniere,
Que j'ouy bien son amoureuse voix;
Mais ung seul mot entendre ne sçavois.
Mon couvre-chef je prins à destacher   35
Et mon oreille ouvrir et approcher.
Là j'entendis ung mot piteux et bas
De toutes ces voix redisant: « Helas!
Helas! Helas! or, l'avons nous perdue?
Las! dessus nous ne torne plus sa veue   40
Ceste beaulté qui nous embellissoit,
Ceste vertu qui nous resjouyssoit,
Ceste doulceur adoulcissant nos fruictz;
Or, sommes nous sans elle tous destruictz. »

Your daughter cannot cope   5
with this long and worrisome silence."³⁵
As if half asleep, I answered:
"I have written so much
I don't have anything more to say." And he replies: "Do not stop
until the unfortunate princess   10
reaches the happy destination³⁶ she longs for.
Then you may rest your writing hand.
But until that moment do not abandon your daughter,
and continue to give us of your writings."
Urged on by him, I got up,   15
took paper and pen, and,
looking for a pleasant spot,
went out onto the path near my window.
Then I sat down and wondered
how best to begin.   20
It wasn't long before I heard the rustling
of the wind through fruits and leaves,
sweetly carrying to my ears
a melancholic and wondrous sound.
I turned from side to side   25
to see where it was coming from.
There was neither tree, nor branch, nor leaf
that did not in one common voice sing out.
And the small fountains responded
to their lament in kind.   30
And with these the river's voice
which arose and joined in with such gentle tones
that I could hear its amorous voice.
And yet I was not able to decipher a single word.
To uncover my ears I pulled away   35
my scarf, and moved closer.
Then I heard in a soft and sad manner
the words that all these voices were intoning:
"Alas, alas, alas, have we lost her?
She no longer turns her gaze on us,   40
that beauteous creature who once embellished us,
that virtue which gave us pleasure,
that sweetness that made our fruits sweeter still.
and now, without her, we are all distraught."³⁷

Si je senty de toute creature   45
Un tel helas, croyez que ma nature
Ne peust souffrir d'oyr le demourant.
Mais n'en revins en ma chambre courant,
Avecques eulx criant: « Helas! mon Dieu
Ramene tost en ce desolé lieu   50
Celle que tant ciel et terre regrette,
Et que revoir incessamment souhaitte. »

Hearing this "alas," you can be sure   45
that my emotions could not bear
to listen to the rest.
I ran back into my room,
crying out with them: "Alas, my God,
quickly return to this desolate place   50
the one whom earth and sky lament
and incessantly beg to see again."

II

LE MIROIR DE L'ÂME PÉCHERESSE / THE
MIRROR OF THE SINFUL SOUL

EDITOR'S INTRODUCTION

L e miroir de l'âme pécheresse (1531), a verse exposition of Marguerite's religious convictions, was most likely not her first attempt at serious writing. That would probably have been her *Dialogue en forme de vision nocturne*, composed shortly after the death of her niece, Charlotte. Indeed it was the remarkable success of *Le miroir*, Marguerite's first real publication, that no doubt inspired her to add the earlier work to a second edition of it in 1533. Marguerite was dangerously audacious in publishing a theological work, exclusive domain of male clerics, and predictably it brought down upon her the violent wrath of the doctors of theology at the University of Paris.[1]

If one wished to examine Marguerite's evangelical beliefs, this would be an excellent place to begin. In addition to the obvious intimate familiarity with biblical literature, the poem follows closely the reformist views Marguerite learned from her mentor/confessor, Guillaume Briçonnet.[2] Here we find all the essential earmarks of the *devotio moderna*, with its heavy emphasis on personal piety, exaggerated self-deprecation, preoccupation with death, and total dependence on divine grace for salvation. Here too we can discover some of the more conspicuous characteristics of the language of the mystic: paradoxes, heavy-handed allegory, a highly personal relationship

---

1.   It was in fact the second, 1533 edition which caused Marguerite's book to be censured by the Faculty of Theology, so that she had to draw upon her prestige as sister to the king to come to her rescue. In the end, Nicolas Cop, the university's rector, unwilling to confront royal authority, sent his apologies for a decision he had not sanctioned.

2.   One cannot overstate the importance of this man's role in helping to shape Marguerite's theology. Briçonnet (1470?–1534), who descended from a long line of church leaders, was for several crucial years as bishop of Meaux a strong advocate for reform, and thus a likely candidate to become Marguerite's spiritual advisor. The lengthy correspondence between them reveals just how much the bishop influenced her thinking. See *Guillaume Briçonnet/Marguerite d'Angoulême: Correspondance.*

with the divine, in which one becomes child, spouse, and parent all at once, and finally a poignant love message to Jesus.

Scholars are sorely tempted to look for precedents for Marguerite's religious verse essay, and one can certainly point to countless uses of the mirror metaphor in medieval literature. Vincent de Beauvais's *Speculum* as well as his *Miroir historial* uses the image for philosophical reasons, and Claude Bouton's *Mirouer des dames et des demoiselles* for moralizing ones. But we come closer to the mark with works like Marguerite de Porete's *Miroir des âmes simples*, which Marguerite actually mentions in *Les prisons*, and the anonymous fifteenth-century *Mirouer de l'ame pecheresse tres utile et profitable*. But as Pierre Jourda rightly points out, if one is looking for sources, the best place to look is the Bible.[3] Marguerite's marginal citations—taken from both Hebrew and Christian texts—tell us all we need to know about her essential inspiration.[4]

This is a complex work, and one wonders if there is an inherent logic that defines the poem's sometimes meandering progression. Marguerite is not beyond digressions, but the general theme, one that compellingly moves the introspective analysis forward, is the relentless scrutiny of a devout Christian, who begins by vigorously chastising herself, the better in the end to find peace and solace in the salvation of a redemptive God.[5]

---

3. Jourda, *Marguerite d'Angoulême*, 1: 254–93.

4. It is significant that the penitent places at the opening of her soul-searching a citation from Psalm 50, which describes the inescapable day of divine judgment. For an in-depth analysis of all the marginal notes in the poem, see Cynthia Skenazi, "Les annotations en marge du *Miroir de l'ame pecheresse*," *Bibliothèque d'humanism et Renaissance* (1993): 255–70.

5. Gary Ferguson draws attention to the important fact—merely implied in Marguerite's analysis—that redemption is necessarily of the next world, and not of this one: "Within time, however, man remains imperfect," he writes in "Now in a Glass Darkly: The Textual Status of the 'je parlant' in the 'Miroirs' of Marguerite de Navarre," *Renaissance Studies* (1991): 410.

LE MIROIR DE L'ÂME PÉCHERESSE

Pseau. 50   *Seigneur DIEU cree en moy cueur net.*
Où est l'enfer remply entierement
De tout malheur, travail, peine, et torment?
Où est le puitz de malediction
Dont sans fin sort deseseperation?
Est il de mal nul si profond abisme   5
Qui suffisant fust pour punir la disme
De mes pechez? qui sont en si grand nombre
Qu'infinitude rend si obscure l'ombre
Que les compter ne bien veoir je ne puys,
Car trop avant avecques eulx je suis.   10
Et qui pis est, je n'ay pas la puissance
D'avoir d'ung seul, au vray, la congnoissance.
Bien sens en moy que j'en ay la racine,
Et au dehors ne voy effect ne signe
Qui ne soit tout branche, fleur, fueille, et fruict,   15
Que tout autour de moy elle produict.
    Si je cuyde regarder pour le mieulx,
Une branche me vient fermer les yeulx;
En ma bouche tombe, quant vueil parler,
Le fruict par trop amer à avaller.   20
Si pour ouyr, mon esperit se reveille,
Force fueilles entrent en mon aureille;
Aussi mon naiz est tout bousché de fleurs.
Voilà comment en peine, criz, et pleurs
En terre gist sans clarté ni lumiere   25
Ma paovre ame, esclave, et prisonniere,

THE MIRROR OF THE SINFUL SOUL

A clean heart create for me, God.   Psalm 50
Where is that hell fraught with misery,[6]
suffering, pain, and torment?
Where the pit of maledictions
out of which emerges endless despair?
Is there an abyss torturous and cruel enough   5
to punish one tenth of my sins?
So great in number are they
that the vastness blurs my vision
so that I cannot see well enough to count them.
I am overwhelmed.   10
Worse still, I am too incompetent
to deal with the least of them.
I sense they are deeply rooted in my being,
and all around me I see no effect, no sign
which is not a branch, a flower,   15
a leaf or a fruit generated by them.
        The moment I think I see better,
a branch comes and covers my eyes.
And when I try to speak, a fruit
too bitter to swallow fills my mouth.   20
If I am prone to listen,
countless leaves block my ears.
My nose is obstructed by flowers.
And so it is that in pain, shrieking, and weeping,
my unfortunate soul inhabits this world   25
of darkness and obscurity, a slave and a prisoner.

Les piedz liez par sa concupiscence
Et les deux bras par son acoustumance.
En moy ne gist le povoir du remede;
Force je n'ay pour bien crier à l'ayde.   30
        Brief, à jamais, à ce que je puis veoir,
Esperance de fin ne doy avoir;
Mais la grace que ne puis meriter
Qui poeut de mort chascun ressusciter
Par sa clarté ma tenebre illumine,   35
Et ma faulte sa vertu examine;
Rompant du tout le voile d'ignorance
Me donne, au vray, bien claire intelligence
Que c'est de moy, et qui en moy demeure,
Et où je suis, et pourquoy je labeure,   40
Qui est celluy lequel j'ay offensé
Auquel si peu de servir j'ay pensé.
Parquoy il fault que mon orgueil rabaisse
Et qu'humblement en plorant je confesse
Que, quant à moy, je suis trop moins que riens: 45
Iob. 10   Avant la vie boue, et après fyens,
et Gene. 8   Ung corps remply de toute promptitude
A mal faire, sans voulour aultre estude:
Subjecte à mal, ennuy, douleur, et peine,
Iob. 14   Vie briefve, et la fin incertaine,   50
Rom. 5, 7.   Qui soubz peché par Adam est vendu
1 Cor. 15.   Et de la loy jugé d'estre pendu.
Ps. 31.   Car d'observer ung seul commandement
Il ne m'advint en ma vie vrayement.
Rom. 7.   En moy je sens la force de peché,   55
Dont moindre n'est mon mal d'estre caché:
Tant plus dehors se cele et dissimule
Plus dans le cueur s'assemble et accumule.
Rom. 7.   Ce que Dieu veult, je ne le puys vouloir;
Ce qu'il ne veult, souvent desire avoir: 60
Qui me contrainct par ennuy importable
De ce fascheux corps de mort miserable
Desirer veoir la fin tant desiree
Par la vie rompue et dessiree.
        Qui sera ce qui me delivrera,   65
Et qui tel bien pour moy recouvrera?

My feet bound by longings,
my arms by cravings,
I am bereft of either power or remedy.
I do not even have the strength to cry out.   30
    In short, as far in the future as I can see,
no hope of relief is in sight.
But grace, which I do not merit,
and which can raise us all from the clutches of death,
by its bright light illuminates my darkness,   35
and by its great goodness looks upon my flaws.
Lifting the veil of ignorance,
it gives me the clear and proper vision
to see who and what I am,
where I am and why I strive,   40
who is the one I have injured,
whom I have hardly thought to serve.
And so it is that my pride must lessen
and I must humbly confess that, as for me,
I am less than nothing: 45
before life, dirt, and after, dung,
a body all too quick to do harm
with no further ado,
a slave to evil, pain, suffering and distress,
a brief existence, an uncertain end   50
which, through Adam's sin has been forfeited
and by the law⁷ sentenced to be hanged.
    For it has never truly occurred to me
to obey any of the commandments.
I feel within me sinful inclinations,   55
not the least of which is my tendency to deceive.
The more I conceal and hide,
the more my sins gather and grow in my heart.
What God wishes, I am unable to wish,
and what he does not want, I want.   60
And so this unbearable distress drives me
to desire for this miserable and mortal flesh
a longed-for end
to a broken and shattered life.
    Who will it be who delivers me?   65
And who will recover my happiness for me?

Las! ce ne poeut estre un homme mortel,
Car leur povoir et sçavoir n'est pas tel;
Mais ce sera la seule bonne grace
Du tout puissant, qui jamais ne se lasse,   70
Rom. 5. Par Jesuchrist, duquel il se recorde
Nous prevenir par sa misericorde.

    Las, quel maistre! sans avoir desservy
Nul bien de luy, mais l'ayant mal servy
Et sans cesser offensé chascun jour,   75
A mon secours ne faict pas long sesjour.
Il voit le mal que j'ay, quel, et combien,
Hiere. 10 Et, que de moy, je ne puys faire bien,
Mais cueur, et corps, si enclin au contraire,
Que nul povoir ne sens que de mal faire.   80

    Il n'attend pas qu'humblement je le prie,
Ne que, voiant mon enfer, à luy crye;
Rom. 8. Par son esperit faict ung gemissement
Dans mon cueur, grand inenarrablement,
Qui postule le don, dont le sçavoir   85
Est incongnu à mon foible povoir.
Et à l'heure cest ignoré souspir
Me rapporte ung tout nouveau desir,
En me monstrant le bien que j'ay perdu
Par mon peché, lequel bien m'est rendu   90
Et redonné par sa grace et bonté,
Qui tout peché a vaincu et dompté.

    O Monseigneur, et quelle est celle grace,
Quel est ce bien qui tant de maulx efface?
Vous estes bien remply de toute amour   95
De me faire ung si honneste tour.

    Helas! mon Dieu, je ne vous chercheoie pas;
Mais vous fuyoye en courant le grand pas;
Jean 3. Et vous ça bas à moy estes venu,
A moy, qui suis ver de terre tout nud.   100

    Que dis je, ver? je luy fais trop d'injure:
A moy qui suis tant infame et perjure,
D'orgueil remply par mondaine raison
De falsité, malice, et trahison.

Ps. 118   La promesse que mes amys ont faicte   105
Au baptesme, que depuis j'ay refaicte

For sure, no mortal being,
for human power and wisdom are not up to it.
It can come only from the infinite grace
of the Almighty, who never tires,
through the intercession of Jesus Christ,   70
who saves us by his mercy.
    Ah, what a Lord! Without having merited
any consideration from him, but having served him badly
and daily abused him,   75
I am not made to wait endlessly for his help.
He sees my shortcomings, each one and at every turn;
he sees that I am incapable of doing good on my own,
that body and soul are so inclined to do the opposite
that I have no will but to commit sins.   80
    He does not wait for me to beg mercy,
nor, seeing the hell I inhabit, wait for me to call upon him.
By his own will, he makes an ache
in my heart so unbearable
that it postulates the gift whose very meaning   85
is well beyond my understanding.
And at present this mysterious uneasiness
produces a new longing,
and reveals the riches I had forsaken
for my transgressions, given   90
and bestowed upon me once again through grace and compassion
which conquers and subdues all sin.
    And what, my Lord, is this grace,
this munificence which wipes away so much wickedness?
You are bursting with love   95
to have sought to favor me so.
    Alas, Lord, I was not seeking you out.
But instead I fled from you in great haste.
And you came down to me,
little more than a naked worm.   100
    Why do I say worm? I do it an injustice,
I, who am so debased and deceitful
and by worldly values made prideful,
false, malicious, and traitorous.
    The promise made by my friends at my baptism   105
and which I have since renewed[8]

Rom. 6	(Qui est sans fin de vostre passion
Ps. 43.	Sentir en moy mortification
	Estre tousjours avec vous en croix,
	Où vous avez pendu, comme je crois, 110
Rom. 6.	Et rendu mort la mort, et tout peché,
	Que souvent j'ay reprins et detaché).
	Rompue l'ay, denyee et faulsee,
	Ayant sy fort ma volunté haulsee,
	Par ung orgueil plein d'indiscretion 115
	Que mon debvoir et obligation
	Estoit du tout oublié par parresse.
Marc 16.	Et qui, plus est, le bien de la promesse
	Que j'euz de vous le jour de mon baptesme,
	Et vostre amour, j'en ay faict tout de mesme. 120
	Que diray je? encores que souvent
Apoca. 3.	De mon malheur vous vinsiez au devant
	En me donnant tant d'advertissementz
	Par parolle, par foy, par sacrementz,
	M'admonnestant par predication, 125
	Me consolant par la reception
	De vostre corps très digne et sacré sang,
	Me promettant de me remettre au reng
	Des bien eureux en parfaicte innocence.
	J'ay tous ces biens remys en oubliance; 130
	Ma promesse souvent vous ay rompue,
	Car trop estoit ma paovre ame repue
	De maulvais pain et damnable doctrine,
	En deprisant secours et medicine.
	Et quand aussi l'eusse voulu querir, 135
	Nul ne congnois qu'eusse peu requerir,
	Car il n'y a homme, ny sainct, ny ange
	Pour qui le cueur jamais du pecheur change.
	Las! bon Jesus, voiant ma cecité,
	Et que secours en ma necessité 140
Actes 4.	Ne puys avoir d'aulcune creature,
	De mon salut avez faict l'ouverture.
	Quelle bonté! mais quelle grand doulceur!
	Est il pere à fille, ou frere à soeur
	Qui ung tel tour jamais eust voulu faire? 145
	Tant fust il doulx, piteux, et debonnaire:

(which is endlessly to feel in myself
the mortification of your passion,
to be always with you on the cross,
on which you were hanged, I believe,   110
putting an end to death and all sin,
which often I have taken up and discarded).
    I have broken, denied, and falsified it,
having through my indiscreet pride
given so much importance to my will,   115
that through inattentiveness I have altogether
neglected duty and responsibility.
Worse yet, I have squandered
the promised benefits offered by you
at the time of my baptism.   120
    What should I say? although often
you have come to my rescue,
giving me countless warnings
by words, faith, and sacraments,
cautioning me through homily,   125
consoling me by giving me
your most worthy body and sacred blood,
promising to place me in the ranks
of the blessed of perfect innocence,
I have forsaken all these riches.   130
I have not kept my vows,
for my miserable soul has too often
fed upon harmful bread and bad doctrines,
disdaining help and medicine.
And even if I had tried,   135
I do not know whether I would have succeeded,
for there is neither man, nor saint, nor angel
who could ever change the heart of a sinner.[9]
    But sweet Jesus, seeing my blindness,
and seeing that no mortal   140
could help me in my dire need,
you came to my deliverance.[10]
What tenderness! And what incomparable gentleness!
Is there father to a daughter, brother to a sister,
who at any time would have done as much?   145
So kind, mild, compassionate, and noble:

1 Jean 4.   Venir d'enfer mon ame secourir
       Où contre vous elle vouloit perir.
       Sans aymer, las! vous l'avez aymee.
       O Charité ardente et entflammee,   150
       Vous n'estes pas d'aymer froid ne remys,
Roma. 5.   Qui aymez tous, voire voz ennemys;
       Non seulement leur voulant pardonner
       Leur offense, mais vous mesmes donner
       Pour leur salut, liberté, delivrance   155
       A mort, et croix, travail, peine, et suffrance.
          Quant je pense qui est l'occasion
Ephe. 2. Dont vous m'aymez, riens que dilection
       Je n'y puis veoir, qui vous mesmes incite
       A me donner ce que je ne merite.   160
          Donques, mon Dieu, à ce que je puis veoir,
1 Tim. 1. De mon salut le gré ne doib sçavoir
       Fors à vous seul: à qui j'en doib l'honneur,
       Comme à mon Dieu, saulveur, et createur.
       Mais qu'est cecy? pour moy faictes vous tant,   165
       Et encores vous n'estes pas content
       De m'avoir faict de mes pechez pardon,
Ephe. 2. Et de grace le très gratieux don.
          Bien suffiroit, saillant de tel danger,
       De me traicter ainsi qu'ung estranger,   170
       Mais mon ame traictez (si dire l'ouze)
       Comme mere, fille, soeur, et espouse.
Luc 15.   Moy, Monseigneur, moy, qui digne ne suis
       Pour demander du pain, approcher l'huys
       Du lieu très hault où est vostre demeure!   175
       Et qu'est cecy? tout soubdain en ceste heure
       Daigner tirer mon ame en telle haultesse
       Qu'elle se sent de mon corps la maistresse!
       Elle paovre, ignorante, impotente,
Philip. 4. Se sent en vous riche, sage, et puissante   180
       Pour luy avoir au cueur escript le rolle
       De vostre esperit et sacree parolle,
       En luy donnant foy pour la recepvoir,
       Qui luy a faict vostre filz concepvoir:
       En le croiant homme, Dieu, et saulveur,   185
Rom. 5.   De tout peché le vray restaurateur.

To come and save my soul from the hell
where, in denial of you, it wished to perish.
Unloved, you loved it.
Oh, passionate and fervent generosity!   150
You are never too cold or uncaring to love,
you who love all, even your enemies,
not only pardoning their offenses,
but offering up yourself as a sacrifice
for their salvation, freedom, and deliverance   155
from death, the cross, labor, pain, and suffering.
     When I think of what inspires
you to love me, charity is all
I see, which incites you
to give me what I do not deserve.   160
     Thus my Lord, as far as I can see,
I must attribute my salvation
to you alone, whom I must honor
as my God, creator, and savior.
But what is this? You do so much for me,   165
and still you are not satisfied
to have pardoned my sins
and granted me the generous gift of grace.
     It would have been understandable, enduring such danger,
that you should treat me like an outsider.   170
But, if I may say so, you treat my soul
like that of a mother, daughter, sister, and wife.[11]
     I, my Lord, who am unworthy
to ask for bread, to come to the door
where, in a lofty place, you have your dwelling!   175
And what is this? Suddenly at this moment
to deign to raise my soul to such heights
that it finds itself mistress of my body!
My soul, poor, ignorant, impotent,
feels rich, wise, and powerful in you,   180
by dint of your having written on her heart
the message of your spirit and your sacred word,
providing her with the faith to receive that spirit
which made her conceive your son:
believing him to be man, God, savior,   185
redeemer of all sins.

Parquoy daignez l'asseurer qu'elle est mere
De vostre filz, dont vous estes seul pere.
    Et encores, mon Dieu, voicy grand cas,
De bien faire vous ne vous lassez pas;   190
Mais luy monstrant que la divinité

Philip. 2. A prins le corps de nostre humainité,
Et s'est meslé avecques nostre cendre:
Ce que sans foy nul ne pourroit entendre,
Et par amour de nous tant approcher   195
Qu'il s'est uny avecques nostre chair;
Le regardant (comme soy) nommé homme
Se dit sa soeur et frere elle le nomme.
Bien doibt avoir le cueur ferme et asseur
Qui de son Dieu se poeut dire la soeur.   200
Après, venez par grand dilection
Luy declairer que sa creation
N'est seulement que par le bon vouloir
Qu'il vous a pleu tousjours à elle avoir,

Ephe. 1. En l'asseurant qu'avant son premier jour,   205
La prevoiant, y avez eu amour.
    Par celle amour engendree l'avez,
Comme vous seul bien faire le sçavez;
Et puis après dans ce corps l'avez mise,
Non pour dormir, ne pour estre remise,   210
Mais pour tous deux n'avoir aultre exercice
Que de penser à vous faire service.
Alors luy faict bien sentir verité
Qu'en vous y a vraye paternité.
    O quel honneur, quel bien, et quelle gloire   215
A ceste ame qui tousjours ha memoire
Qu'elle est de vous fille! et vous nommant
Pere, elle faict vostre commandement.
Qui a il plus? est ce tout? helas! non.
Il vous plaist bien luy donner aultre nom: 220
Vostre espouse la nommez, et de vous,
Vous appeller son mary et espoux;

Osee. 2. Luy declairant comme d'ung franc courage
Avez d'elle juré le mariage.
Par le baptesme luy avez faict promesse   225
De luy donner vostre bien et richesse.

You deign thus to assure my soul that she is mother
of your son and you the father.
        Moreover, my Lord, and here is a case in point,
you never tire of doing good,   190
but remind my soul that the divine
has assumed our humanity
and has mingled with our dust,
something one could never comprehend without faith.[12]
And through the loving desire to be closer to us,   195
he has become flesh like us.
Seeing him as human like herself,
my soul calls him brother while he names my soul sister.
Whoever wishes to be sister to God
must be firm and assured in her conviction.   200
Then with great love you came
and declared that my soul existed
only through the goodwill
it pleased you to bear toward her,
assuring her that even before her birth,   205
you had foreseen her and loved her.
        Through love you have begotten her,
as only you can,
and have placed her in this body,
not to lie dormant or inactive,   210
but so that both should have no greater concern
than to serve you.
And so my soul realizes
that in you lies her true paternity.
        What honor, what prosperity, what glory   215
for my soul to have to keep in mind
that she is your child. And in naming you father,
she does your bidding.
Is there any more? Is that all? Alas, no.
It pleases you to give her another name: 220
you christen her your spouse
and identify yourself as her husband and partner.
Speaking from an earnest heart,
you promise marriage.
Through baptism, you assure her   225
of your wealth and assets.

Ses maulx prenez, car riens que peché n'ha,
Lequel Adam son pere luy donna.
    Doncques ne sont ses tresors que pechez,

Lesquelz sur vous vous avez attachez; 230
Entierement avez payé sa debte,
Et de vos biens et très grande recepte,
L'avez si bien enrichie et douee
Que se sentant de vous femme advouee,
Se tient quicte de tout ce qu'elle doibt, 235
Peu estimant ce que ça bas ell'voit.
Son vieulx pere, et tous les biens qu'il donne
Pour son espoux de bon cueur habandonne.
    Vrayement mon Dieu, mon ame est bien gastee
Estre par vous de tel bien appastee, 240
Et delaissant le plaisir de la terre
Pour l'infiny, où est vraye paix sans guerre.
Je m'esbahis que tout soubdainement
Elle ne sort de son entendement.
Je m'esbahis qu'elle ne devient folle, 245
En perdant sens, contenance, et parolle.
    Pere, pere, las! que puis je penser?
Osera bien mon esperit s'avancer
De vous nomme Pere? ouy, et nostre,

Ainsi l'avez dit en la Paternostre. 250
    Or bien pere, mais vostre fille, quoy?
L'avez vous dit? mon Dieu, dictes le moy.
Helas! ouy, quant par grande doulceur

Distes: fille prestez moy vostre cueur.
O mon pere, en lieu d'en faire prest, 255
De soy donner à vous du tout est prest.
Recepvez le et ne vueillez permettre
Que loing de vous nully le puisse mettre.
Et qu'a jamais en fermeté loyale
Je vous ayme d'ung amour filiale. 260
    Mais, Monseigneur, si vous estes mon pere,
Puis je penser que je suis vostre mere?
Vous engendrer? vous par qui je suis faicte?
C'est bien ung cas, dont ne sçay la defaicte.
Mais la raison à ma doubte bien mistes, 265
Quant en preschant, estendant vos bras, distes:

You wipe away her transgressions, for she has nothing but sins,
given her by Adam, her progenitor.
    The only dowry of my soul is the sins
which you have taken upon yourself.   230
You have completely redeemed her debt,
and with your goodness and boundless merit
you have so richly endowed her,
that she considers herself to be your devoted spouse.
Valuing little of whatever she sees below,   235
she imagines herself free from liability.
Her old father, with all that he has provided,
she abandons in the name of her husband.
    Truly, Lord, my soul is spoiled
to be so generously nourished by you,   240
exchanging the pleasures of this world
for an eternity of peace without strife.
I am astounded that she does not suddenly
lose her reason,
astounded that she does not go mad,   245
surrendering all understanding, control, and speech.
    Father, O father, what must I think?
Will my spirit be so bold
as to name you father? Indeed, our father,
as you have designated in the Lord's Prayer.   250
    So much for father, but what about daughter?
Have you so authorized? Tell me, my Lord.
Ah, yes, when in wonderful benevolence
you say: daughter, lend me your heart.
O father, instead of just lending,   255
it is prepared to yield to you entirely.
Take my soul and never allow it
to be placed far from you.
May I love you in unwavering faithfulness
and filial love forever.   260
    But, Lord, if you are my father,
may I think of myself as your mother,
give birth to you, you by whom I am created?
It is an enigma I know not how to make sense of.
But you put an end to my quandary   265
when preaching with extended arms you said:

Matt. 12.   Ceulx qui feront le vouloir de mon pere
Mes freres sont, et ma soeur, et ma mere.
          Je croy doncques qu'en oyant ou lisant
La parolle que vous estes disant,   270
Et qu'avez dicte par vos sainctz et prophetes,
Et qu'encores par vos bons prescheurs faictes,
En la croiant, desirant fermement
De la complir du tout entierement,
Que par amour je vous ay engendré;   275
Dont sans crainte nom de mere prendray.
          Mere de Dieu, doulce vierge Marie,
Ne soyez pas de ce tiltre marrie.
Nul larroncin ne fais, ny sacrilege,
Riens ne pretendz sur vostre privilege,   280
Car vous seule avez sur toute femme
Receu de luy l'honneur si grand, ma dame,
Que nul esperit de soy ne poeut comprendre,
Comme en vous a voulu nostre chair prendre.
          Mere et vierge estes parfaictement,   285
Avant, apres, et en l'enfantement,
En vostre sainct ventre l'avez porté,
Nourry, servy, allaicté, conforté,
Suivy avez ses predications,
L'accompaignant en tribulations.   290
Brief, vous avez de Dieu trouvé la grace,
Que l'ennemy par malice et falace
Avoit du tout faict perdre en verité
Au paouvre Adam, et sa posterité.
          Par Eve et luy, nous l'avons tous perdue,   295
Par vostre filz elle nous est rendue.
Vous en avez esté pleine nommee
Dont n'en est pas faulse la renommée,
Car de grace, de vertuz, et de dons
N'avez faulte: puys que le bon des bons   300
Et la source de bonté et puissance,
Qui vous a faicte en si pure innocence,
Que de vertuz à tous estes exemple,
A faict de vous sa demeure et son temple.
En vous il est par amour confermee,   305
Et vous en luy ravye et transformee.

those who do the will of my father
are my brothers, sisters, and mothers.
    I think therefore when listening to or reading
the words which you have spoken,   270
and which you have pronounced through your prophets and saints,
and again through the mouths of your fine preachers,
in believing and wishing
that they may be fully realized,
I have given birth to you because of love.   275
Therefore without fear I will take the name mother.[13]
    Mother of God, sweet Virgin Mary,
do not take offense at this title.
I am not guilty of thievery or sacrilege.
I take nothing from your status,   280
for you alone among all women
have received God's immense honor, my lady,
an honor no one else can understand,
how he wished to become flesh in you.
    You are altogether mother and virgin,   285
before, after, and in childbirth.
You bore God's son in your holy person,
fed, cared for, nursed, and comforted him.
You abided by his prophecies
and stayed with him in his troubles.   290
In short, you earned God's grace
which the malicious and deceptive enemy
stole from unhappy Adam
and his posterity.
    Through him and through Eve we all lost it,   295
but through your son we regained it.[14]
You have been called "full of grace,"
and the designation is not false,
for in grace, virtue, and qualities,
you lack nothing. Ultimate goodness,   300
the source of all that is fine and commanding,
which has created you so completely pure
that you are an example to all,
makes you its dwelling place and temple.
Through love, Jesus is your sacrament of confirmation,   305
and through him you are transformed and granted ecstasy.[15]

De vous cuider mieulx louer, c'est blaspheme,
Car vous louant, on le loue luy mesme.
    Foy avez eu si très ferme et constante,
Que par grace elle a esté puissante   310
De vous faire du tout deifier.
Parquoy ne veulx cuyder edifier
Louenge à vous plus grande que l'honneur
Que vous a faict le souverain seigneur,
Car vous estes sa mere corporelle,   315
Et sa mere par foy spirituelle;
Mais en suyvant vostre foy humblement
Mere je suis spirituellement.
    Mais mon saulveur, de la fraternité
Qu'avez à moy par vostre humilité   320
M'appellant soeur, en avez vous riens dit?
Helas! ouy, car du pere mauldit
Avez rompu la filiation
En me nommant fille d'adoption.
    Or doncques, puis que nous n'avons qu'ung pere   325
Je ne craindray de vous nommer mon frere.
Vous l'avez dit en lieu bien autentique
Par Salomon en vostre doulx cantique,
Cantique 4.   Disant: Ma soeur tu as navré mon cueur,
Tu as navré mon cueur par la doulceur   330
D'ung de tes yeulx, et d'ung de tes cheveulx.
Las! mon frere, aultre bien je ne veulx
Que vous navrant navrée me sentir;
Par vostre amour bien m'y veulx consentir.
    Pareillement espouse me clamez,   335
En ce lieu là monstrant que vous m'aymez;
Et m'appellez par vraye amour jalouse:
Cantique 2.   Ma colombe, lieve toy mon espouse.
Parquoy diray par amoureuse foy
Qu'à vous je suis, et vous estes à moy.   340
Vous me nommez amye, espouse, et belle.
Si je le suis, vous m'avez faicte telle.
Las! vous plaist il telz noms me departir?
Ilz sont dignes de faire ung cueur partir,
Mourir, brusler, par amour importable,   345
Pensant l'honneur trop plus que raisonnable.

It would be blasphemous to presume to praise you more
since to praise you is to praise him.
    Your faith is so unshakable and true
that by grace it was compelling enough   310
in the eyes of all to deify you.
Therefore I do not wish to offer you
more admiration than the honor bestowed
upon you by our sovereign Lord,
for you are his corporal mother   315
and his mother in faith and spirit.
Humbly following your example in faith, however,
I become a spiritual mother.
    But, my savior, by naming me sister
through your fraternal humility,   320
have you intended anything further?
Alas, yes. For in adopting me as daughter,
you have severed the filial ties
to an imperfect father.
    Therefore, since we have but one father,   325
I do not hesitate to call you brother.
You have stated as much in a reliable source
which is your sweet Song of Solomon,
saying: Dear sister, you have broken my heart.
By the sweetness in but one of your eyes,   330
in but one hair, you have smitten me to the quick.
Dear brother, I seek no other joy
than that in breaking your heart, I should break my own.
Because of your love, I gladly submit.[16]
    In the same manner you call me wife,   335
proving thus your affection for me.
And because of true love, you call me jealous:
My dove and wife, arise.
And so in loving faith, I say
I am yours, and you mine.   340
You call me friend, wife, and beautiful one.
If I am all these, it is because you made me so.
Does it please you to give me such names?
They are enough to make a heart flee,
burn, and expire from intolerable longing,   345
thinking the honor beyond reason.

Mere, mere, mais de quel enfant?
C'est d'ung tel filz, que tout le cueur m'en fend.
Mon filz, mon Dieu, Jesus, o quel langaige!
Pere, fille, o bieneureux lignaige!   350
Que de doulceur, que de suavité
Vient de ceste doulce paternité!
Mais quel amour doibs je avoir? filiale.
Quelle crainte? bien reverentiale.
Mon pere, quoy? voire mon createur,   355

Ps. 26, 30 Mon protecteur et mon conservateur.
Vostre soeur? las! voicy grand amytié.
Or, fendez vous mon cueur par la moitié;
Faictes place à ce frere tant doulx;
Et que luy seul soit enfermé en vous,   360
Sans qu'ung aultre jamais y prenne lieu,
Fors Jesus seul, mon frere, filz de Dieu.
A nul aultre ne vueil rendre la place
Pour basture ou myne qu'on me face.
    Gardez mon cueur, mon frere et mon amy,   365
Et ny laissez entrer vostre ennemy.
O mon frere, pere, enfant, et espoux,
Les mains joinctes, humblement à genoulx,
Graces vous rendz, mercy, gloire et louenge,
Dont il vous plaist moy terre, cendre, et fange,   370
Mon cueur à tourner et convertir;
Et de grace si bien me revestir,
Et me couvrir, que mes maulx et pechez
Ne voiez plus, tant les avez cachez,
Si que de vous semblent en oubly mys,   375
Voire et de moy qui les ay tous commis,
Foy et amour m'en donnent oubliance,
Mettant du tout en vous seul ma fiance.
Jaques 3.   Donques, pere, où gist amour non feincte,
Dequoy puis je en mon cueur avoir crainte?   380
Je confesse avoir faict tous les maulx
Que faire on poeut, et que riens je ne vaulx,
Et que vous ay comme l'enfant prodigue
Habandonné, suyvant la folle ligue,
Où despendu j'ay toute ma substance,   385
Et tous voz biens receuz en habondance,

Mother, mother, but of what child?
It is of such a son that my heart is cut in two.
My son, my God, Jesus, oh, such terms!
Father, daughter, oh, blessed lineage.   350
What sweetness, what delight
is born of this gracious paternity!
But what kind of love is this? Filial.
What kind of fear? Reverential.
Father? Say rather creator,   355
protector, guardian.
Sister? Such an extraordinary affiliation.
So, my heart, break in two,
and make a place for this ever-so-gentle brother.
And let him alone be enclosed in you,   360
without ever anyone else settling in,
shelter for Jesus alone, my brother, the son of God.
However much they campaign or do battle against me,
to no other surrender any space.
　　Keep watch over my heart, my brother and my friend,   365
and let no enemy come in.
O brother, father, child, and husband,
with hands joined, humbly on my knees,
I, dirt, ashes, filth, give thanks,
praise, glory, and honor,   370
for which it pleases you to transform and convert my heart.
You wrap me so well in grace
that all the sins and errors of which I am guilty
you cannot see, for you have hidden them so well.
You hide them such that they seem forgotten by you   375
and by me, who have committed them.
May faith and love help me to forget
and may I place in you alone all my hopes.
　　So, father, where lies honest love?
What in my heart ought I to fear?   380
I confess myself guilty of all the wrongdoings
one can commit. I am worth nothing,
and like the prodigal child I abandoned you,
following the misguided pack
and giving it all my allegiance,   385
and I have received your goodness in abundance.

Mais paovreté m'a seiché comme fein,
Et mon esperit rendu tout mort de faim,
Cercheant manger le relief des pourceaulx;
Mais peu de goust trouvoie en telz morceaulx.   390

Dont en voiant mon cas mal attourné,
Jean 6.   A vous, mon pere, par vous suis retourné.
Luc 15.   Las! j'ay peché au ciel et devant vous;
Digne ne suis, je le dy devant tous,
Me dire enfant; mais, pere debonnaire,   395
Ne me faictes pis qu'à ung mercenaire.

Las! qu'est cecy? pas n'avez attendu
Ma priere, mais avez estendu
Vostre dextre, me venant recepvoir
Quant ne pensoye que me diagneissez veoir.   400

En lieu d'avoir par vous punition,
Vous m'asseurez de ma salvation.
Où est celluy donc, qui me condemnera
Quand mon pere mon peché luy nyera?
Il n'est juge qui puisse condemner,   405
Nul, puis que Dieu ne le veult point damner.
Je n'ay doubte d'avoir faulte de biens,
Puis que mon Dieu pour mon pere je tiens.
Mon ennemy nul mal ne me fera,
Car mon pere sa force deffera.   410
Si je doib riens, il payra tout pour moy;
Si j'ay gaigné la mort, luy, comme roy,
Me donnera grace et misericorde,
Me dilivrant de prison et de corde.

Mais voicy pis: quelle mere ay je esté   415
Apres avoir par foy et seureté
Receu le nom de vraye et bonne mere?
Trop je vous ay esté rude et amere,
Car vous ayant conceu et enfanté,
Laissant raison subjecte à volunté,   420
3. des Roys Sans vous garder je me suis endormye;
Et donné lieu à ma grande ennemye,
Qui est la mort d'ignorance, en dormant
Vous a robbé près de moy; finement
En vostre lieu m'a mys le sien tout mort.   425
Perdu vous ay, qui m'est ung dur remord.

Poverty dried me out like straw
and rendered my soul dead from hunger,
seeking food among the pigs,
where, however, I did not find satisfaction.[17]   390
    Seeing thus how badly things had turned out for me,
I came back to you, my father.
Alas, I have sinned against you and heaven.
I confess before all that I am not worthy
to be called your child. But you, O generous father,   395
do not treat me worse than a beggar.
    What! Without waiting to hear my prayer,
you reached out to me
your right hand, taking me in,
even when I thought you would not deign to see me.   400
    Instead of punishing me,
you have assured me of my salvation.
Where is he who would condemn me
when my father takes up my cause against him?
There is no judge who can rebuke me   405
so long as my God chooses not to.
I fear no lack of comfort
since God is my father.
My enemy can do me no harm,
since my father will undo him.   410
If I am in debt, he will pay.
If I am condemned to die, he as my ruler
will grant me grace and pardon me,
delivering me from prison and the cord.
    But there is worse still. Having by faith and promise   415
been given the name of true and loyal mother,
what sort of a mother have I been?
I have been too rude and sharp toward you,
for having conceived you and given life to you,
by surrendering my better judgment to willfulness,   420
I have failed to watch over you.
I have opened the door to my greatest enemy,
fatal negligence, which, as I slept,
took you from me. Stealthily,
in your stead, he substituted his own dead child.   425
I have lost you, a source of painful remorse for me.

Perdu vous ay, par ma faulte, mon filz,
Car trop de vous maulvaise garde feiz.
    Ma voisine, ma sensualité
En mon dormir de bestialité   430
M'a privee de vous, par son envye,
En me donnant ung aultre enfant sans vie,
Qui est peché, duquel je ne vueil point.
Je le quicte du tout: voilà le poinct.
Elle m'a dit qu'il est myen; c'est à elle,   435
Car aussi tost que vins à la chandelle
De la grace, que vous m'avez donnee,
Je congnuz bien ma gloire estre tournee,
Voiant le mort, n'estre myen; car le vif
Qu'elle avoit prins estoit le myen neïf.   440
Entre Jesus et peché, est le change
Trop apparent; mais voicy cas estrange:
Ceste vieille me faict le mort tenir
Qu'elle dit myen et le veult maintenir.
    O vray juge, Salomon veritable,   445
Ouy avez le proces lamentable
Et ordonné, contentant les parties,
Que mon enfant fust mys en deux parties.
La traistresse sy est bien accordee;
Mais quant me suys de mon filz recordee,   450
Plus tost en veulx souffrir privation
Que de son corps la separation;
Car vraye amour bien parfaicte et ardente
De la moitié jamais ne se contente.
J'ayme trop mieulx du tout plorer ma perte   455
Que de l'avoir à demy recouverte.
Peu satisfait auroye à mon envye
Si la moitié de luy avois sans vie.
Las! donnez luy plus tost l'enfant vivant.
Bien meilleur m'est que je meure devant   460
Que de souffrir Jesuchrist divisé.
Mais, mon seigneur, mieulx avez advisé,
Car en voiant mon mal en tout endroict,
Et que plus tost renonçoys à mon droit
Que de souffrir faire si grand rudesse,   465
3. des Roys   Distes de moy: ceste la vraye mere est ce,

I have lost you, by my own fault, my son,
for I was a bad guardian.
   My neighbor, my self-indulgence,
during my bestial slumber   430
deprived me of you out of envy,
and left me in your place a lifeless child,
who is sin, which I want no part of,
which I utterly reject. That is the issue.
She told me it was mine, but it was hers,   435
for no sooner had I come close to the light
of grace given to me by you,
than I realized my glory had returned.
I recognized that the dead one was not mine.
The living one she had stolen was my true one.   440
Between Jesus and sin, the switch is too obvious,
but here is the strangeness of the case:
this crone makes me hold the dead child
which she claims and insists is mine.
   O noble judge, true Solomon,   445
you have heard and passed judgment
on the sad tale and, giving satisfaction to the two parties,
ordered the child to be cut in two.[18]
The treacherous woman has agreed with this.
But when I think about my son,   450
I would rather suffer deprivation
than be separated from his body.
For true, ardent, and perfect love
can never be content with only half.
I would far rather weep for my loss   455
than rescue only half of it.
I would be little satisfied
if all I had were the lifeless half.
Thus, give her the living child.
I would rather die   460
than accept a divided Jesus.
But, my Lord, you have judged better.
Seeing at every turn my suffering,
that I would rather renounce my rights
than endure so great a trial,   465
you say of me: this is the true mother.

En me faisant mon enfant rebailler,
Pour qui voiez mon cueur tant travailler.
   O doulx Jesus, vous ay je retrouvé
Après avoir par ennuy esprouvé   470
Si vous aymoie? moy qui vous ay perdu
A moy mesmes vous vous estes rendu.
Las! daignez vous à celle revenir
Qui par peché ne vous a peu tenir?
Mon doulx enfant, mon filz, ma nourriture,   475
Duquel je suis très humble creature,
Ne permettez que jamais je vous laisse,
Car du passé me repens en confesse.
   Or venez donc, ma sensualité,
Venez pechez de toute qualité;   480
Vous n'avez pas povoir par nul effort
De me faire recepvoir l'enfant mort.

Pseau. 23. Celluy que j'ay est fort pour me deffendre,
Car luy mesme ne se laisra plus prendre.
Desjà est grand et plus fort que nul homme,   485
Parquoy je puis dormir et prendre somme
Auprès de luy, car tout bien regardé,
Me gardera mieulx que ne l'ay gardé.
Bien reposer me puis donc, ce me semble.
O quel repos de mere et filz ensemble!   490
Mon doulx enfant, mon Dieu, honneur et gloire
Soit à vous seul et à chascun notoire,
De ce qu'il plaist à vostre humilité,
Moy, moins que riens, toute nichilité,
Nommer mere; plus est le cas estrange   495
Et plus en ha vostre bonté louenge.
Plus que jamais à vous me sens tenue,
Dont il vous plaist soeur m'avoir retenue.
Soeur je vous suis, mais c'est soeur si maulvaise,
Que mieux pour moy vault que ce nom je taise,   500
Car oublyant le nom du parentage,
L'adoption de si noble lignage,
Vostre tant doulx et fraternel recueil,
Montee suis contre vous en orgueil.
De mes faultes ne me suis recordee;   505
Mais m'eslongnant de vous suis accordee

And recognizing my troubled heart,
you restore my child to me.
    O sweet Jesus, have I found you once again
after having had to learn painfully   470
how much I love you? I having forsaken you,
it was you who came after me.
Do you deign to seek out the one
who sinfully held you in so low esteem?
My sweet child, my son, my source of sustenance,   475
whose humble creation I am,
see to it that I never abandon you,
for I repent and confess my past.
    So come to me, my self-indulgence;
commit all sorts of sin.   480
You no longer have the power
to make me accept the lifeless child.
The one I possess is strong enough to defend me,
for he will no longer allow himself to be taken.
He is already full-grown and as robust as any man.   485
Thus I can sleep and take my repose
next to him, for most likely
he will take better care of me than I did of him.
I can, it seems to me, rest in peace.
Oh, what a peace between mother and son.   490
My docile child, my God, honor and glory
be to you alone. And may all take note that
in your humility it pleased you
to call me, who am less than nothing, a total nonentity,
mother. The more exceptional the circumstances,   495
the more praiseworthy your benevolence.
More than ever I feel myself beholden to you,
who treat me as sister.
I am your sister, but so undeserving
that it is better I not mention the word.   500
For forgetting my family ties,
the adoption of so noble a lineage
and your so kind and fraternal welcome,
make me rise up against you in my pride,
overlooking my shortcomings.   505
But distancing myself from you, I joined

Nomb. 12. Avec Aaron mon frere en trahison,
Voulant donner à voz oeuvres raison.
En murmurant de vous tout en secret
Dont en mon cueur doib porter grand regret.   510
    Helas! mon Dieu, mon frere et vray Moyse,
Debonnaire et très doulx, sans feintise
Qui tout faictes en bonté et justice,
J'ay estimé voz oeuvres estre vice,
Osant dire par façon trop legiere: 515
Pourquoy a'vous espousé l'estrangiere?
Vous nous donnez loy et punition,
Sans y vouloir avoir subjection.
Vous nous faictes de mal faire deffense,
Et pareil mal faictes, sans conscience.   520
Vous deffendez de ne tuer aulcun,
Mais pour ung jour bien plus de vingt et ung
Exod. 32. En tuastes et les feistes deffaire.
Commandement Dieu par vous nous feit faire
De n'espouser fille de l'estranger,   525
Mais vostre espouse en prinstes sans danger.
    Las! mon frere, tant de telles parolles,
Que je congnois et sçay bien estre folles,
De vous ay dit: dont le regret j'en sens,
Car en cela j'estois loing de bon sens.   530
Mais par grace la vive voix de Dieu
Bien me reprint, avant partir du lieu.
Que feistes vous alors de mon peché?
Las! mon frere, vous feustes empesché,
Nomb. 12 Non pour prier pour ma punition;   535
Mais pour mon bien et ma remission,
En demandant par très grand benefice
Qu'il pleust à Dieu mitiger sa justice.
Ce que du tout ne peustes obtenir,
Car ladresse me convint devenir,   540
A celle fin que voiant mon visage
Chascun congneust que n'avois esté sage.
    Ainsi je feuz mise comme ladresse
Hors des tentes du peuple et de la presse,
Car mieulx ne poeut une ame estre punye,   545
Que d'eslongner la saincte compagnie

with my treasonous brother Aaron, [19]
in wanting to justify your works.
Secretly and softly murmuring against you,
I should in my heart feel a great remorse.   510
     Alas, my God, my brother and true Moses,
noble and gentle, without dissembling,
whose every act is just and kind.
I thought your works to be wicked.
And I dared frivolously to ask: 515
Why did you marry the outsider?[20]
You dispense law and order
without wanting to be subject to it.
You forbid us to do evil
and without conscience you commit the same evils.   520
You prohibit killing
and yet in the course of one day more than twenty-one
you undo and slaughter.
By God's command you forbid
our marrying outsiders   525
and yet without reprimand you did just that.
     Alas, my brother, I have spoken so many words to you
that I know to be foolish,
and which I regret,
for I was not in my right mind.   530
But before faltering, I was saved
through the grace of God's true voice.
And how did you respond to my transgression?
Dear brother, you devoted yourself
not to asking for my punishment   535
but for my welfare and forgiveness.
You generously asked on my behalf
God's mitigation of his justice,
which you were not able to achieve.
For it was agreed that I should become a leper,   540
so that, looking upon my countenance,
everyone could see that I had not behaved well.[21]
     Thus like a leper I was removed
from the tent and the congregation,
for there is no more effective punishment   545
than separation from the saintly and faithful assembly

Des fidelles vertueux, bons, et sainctz,
Qui ne sont ladres par peché mais sont sains.
Qu'avez vous faict voiant ma repentence?
Vous avez mis fin à ma penitence;   550
Par vray amour, en vous non sesjournee,
Avez prié, et je suis retournee.
          O quel frere! qui en lieu de punir
Sa folle soeur, la veult à luy unir;
Pour injure, murmure, ou grande offense,   555
Grace et amour luy donne en recompense.
C'est trop, c'est trop! helas! c'est trop, mon frere:
A moy paovre ne debvez tel bien faire.
J'ay faict le mal, et vous me rendez le bien;
Vostre je suis, et vous vous dictes myen;   560
Vostre je suis, et vostre doublement,
Et veulx estre vostre eternellement.
Plus je ne crains d'Aaron la grand folye,
Nul ne sera qui de vous me deslye.
          Puis que frere et soeur ensemble sommes,   565
Il me chault peu de tous les aultres hommes.
Pseau. 26.   Vostre terre est mon vray heritage;
Ne faisons plus, s'il vous plaist, qu'ung mesnage.
          Puis qu'il vous plaist tant vous humilier
Que vostre cueur avec le myen lyer,   570
En vous faisant homme neïfvement,
Je vous en randz graces très humblement.
Comme je doib n'est pas en ma puissance;
Prenez mon cueur, excusez l'ignorance.
Puis que je suis de si bonne maison   575
Et vostre soeur, mon Dieu, j'ay bien raison
De vous louer, aymer, servir sans feindre,
Et riens fors vous ne desirer, ne craindre.
Gardez moy donc; à vous me recommande;
Aultre frere, ny amy ne demande.   580
Si pere a eu de son enfant mercy,
Si mere a eu de son enfant soucy,
Si frere à soeur a couvert le peché,
Je n'ay point veu, ou il est bien caché,
Que nul mary, pour à luy retourner   585
A sa femme ayt voulu pardonner.

which are virtuous, good, holy, fit,
and not sinful lepers but healthy.
And what did you do upon witnessing my contrition?
You brought an end to my penitence;   550
with the strength of true love that dwells in you,
you prayed, and I returned.
      Oh, what a sibling is this, who, instead of punishing
his wayward sister, seeks to reunite with her.
For insults, complaints, and abuse,   555
he rewards her with grace and love.
It's too much, my brother, far too much.
You should not be so generous to an unworthy creature like me
by repaying my misbehavior with kindness.
I am yours and you say you are mine.   560
I am yours, doubly yours,
and wish to be yours forever.
I am no longer afraid of Aaron's sin
and no one can separate me from you.
      And since brother and sister are as one,   565
the rest of the world leaves me indifferent.
It is your country that is my true heritage.
Let us therefore make together but a single family.
      Since you humble yourself
to join your heart to mine   570
by becoming an ordinary mortal,
I humble myself to give you thanks.
But since to thank you properly is not in my power,
take my heart and pardon my inadequacies.
Since, God, I am of such good lineage   575
and your sister, it is right
that I should earnestly serve, love, and praise you,
fearing and desiring no other.
Protect me then; I put myself in your hands.
I ask for no other friend or brother.   580
If a father has taken pity on a child,
if a mother has cared for a child,
if a brother has forgiven a sister's sins,
I have not seen it, or it is well hidden.
For no husband has wished to forgive a wife   585
in order to bring her back.

Assez en est, qui pour venger leur tort,
Par les juges les ont faict mettre à mort.
Aultres, voiantz leur peché tout soubdain
A les tuer n'ont espargné leur main.   590
Aultres, voiantz leurs maulx trop apparentz,
Renvoiees les ont chez leurs parentz.
Aultres, cuydantz punir leur maulvais tour,
Enfermees les ont dans une tour.
Bref, regardez toutes complexions,   595
La fin n'en tend qu'à grandz punitions.
Et le moins mal que j'en ay peu sçavoir
C'est que jamais ilz ne les veulent veoir.
Plustost ferez tourner le firmament
Que d'ung mary faire l'appoinctement   600
Avecques sa femme, pour ung mal quel a faict,
Quant il a veue ou prinse en son meffaict.
     Parquoy, mon Dieu, nulle comparaison
Ne puis trouver en nul temps ne saison;
Mais par amour qui est en vous si ample,   605
Icy estes seul et parfaict exemple.
     Doncques, mon Dieu, plus que jamais confesse,
Que je vous ay faulsé foy et promesse,
Osee 2.   Car espouse m'aviez constituee,
Et en l'estat d'honneur instituee.   610
Mais quel honneur! d'estre au lieu de l'espouse
Qui doulcement près de vous se repouse,
De tous voz biens reyne, maistresse, et dame,
En seureté de corps, d'honneur, et d'ame.
     Moy, villaine, point ne fault que j'oublye   615
Par vous, très noble, noblement anoblye.
Brief, plus de biens qu'on ne poeut desirer
Avois de vous; dont sans fin souspirer
Doibt bien mon cueur, jusqu'à partir du corps,
Pseau. 94. Et par plorer mes yeulx saillir dehors.   620
Trop ne pourroit ma bouche faire criz,
Veu que nouveaulx ne anciens escriptz
N'ont jamais faict si piteux cas entendre,
Comme celluy dont compte je veulx rendre.
Le diray je? l'oseray je annoncer?   625
Le pourray je sans honte prononcer?

But there are enough who, to avenge their wrongs,
have had them condemned to death by the courts.
Others, suddenly seeing their sins,
have not held back their hand to kill them.   590
Others still, recognizing their too apparent flaws,
have sent them back to their parents.
And still others, wishing to punish their evil ways,
have had them locked away in towers.
So whatever the particular circumstances,   595
they inevitably lead to serious chastisement.
At the very least, from what I have witnessed,
they wish no longer to see them.
You are more likely to turn the skies upside down
than to find a husband who is ready to make peace   600
with a wife guilty of a misdeed
he has caught her in.[22]
    So, my Lord, in no time or season
can I discover a comparable situation.
The abundant love which is in you   605
constitutes a perfect and unique example.
    So, my Lord, with even greater fervor I confess
that I have broken our covenant.
For you have made me your wife,
and returned me to honor.   610
And what an honor this: to be a diffident spouse
at the side of her husband, queen, lady,
mistress of all his goods,
secure in body, honor, and soul.
    Nor must I forget that, unworthy as I am,   615
you have nobly ennobled me.
In short, I have more riches than I could possibly desire,
for which I should ceaselessly pour out my heart
until it departs from my body,
weep until my eyes pop out.   620
My mouth cannot exclaim enough
at the thought of the tale I wish to relate,
more piteous than any writing,
new or ancient that has ever been heard.
Shall I speak it? Dare I tell it?   625
Can I narrate it without shame?

Ezech. 36.   Helas! ouy, car ma confusion
Est pour monstrer la grand dilection
De mon espoux, par quoy je ne fais compte,
Pour son honneur, de declairer ma honte.   630

    O mon saulveur, pour moy mort crucifix,
Ce faict n'est tel que de laisser ung filz,
Ny comme enfant, son bon pere offenser,
Ny comme soeur, murmurer ou tenser.

    Las! c'est bien pis, car plus grand est l'offense   635
Où plus y a d'amour et congnoissance,
Plus on reçoit de son Dieu privauté,
Plus luy faillir est grand desloyaulté.

    Moy, qui estoie nommee espouse et femme,
De vous aymee comme vostre propre ame,   640
En diray je la verité? ouy.
Laissé vous ay, oublyé et fouy.
Laissé vous ay, pour suyvir mon plaisir.
Laissé vous ay, pour ung maulvais choisir.
Laissé vous ay, source de tout mon bien.   645
Laissé vous ay en rompant le lien
De vray amour et loyaulté promise.
Laissé vous ay; mais où me suis je mise?
Au lieu où n'a que malediction.
Laissé vous ay, l'amy sans fiction,   650
L'amy de tous digne d'estre estimé,
L'amy, aymant premier que d'estre aymé.
Laissé vous ay, o source de bonté,
Par ma seule maulvaise volunté.
Laissé vous ay, le beau, le bon, le saige,   655
Le fort de braz, et le doulx de couraige.

Deuter. 32.   Laissé vous ay, et pour mieulx me retraire
De vostre amour ay prins vostre contraire.
C'est l'ennemy et le monde et la chair,
Qui sur la croix vous ont cousté si cher,   660

Galat. 4.   Pour les vaincre et mettre en liberté
Moy, qui par eulx longtemps avoie esté
Prisonniere, esclave, et tant liee
Que ne povoie plus estre humiliee,
Et de tous trois je me suis accointee,   665
Et de tous cas avec eulx appoinctee.

Alas, yes. For the source of my embarrassment
is the great love
of my husband, for whose honor
I don't mind declaring my shame.   630
    O my savior, who died on the cross for me,
this is not like abandoning a son,
or a child abusing a loving father,
or a sister grumbling and complaining.
    It is worse still, for the greater the love and understanding,   635
the more grievous the offense.
The greater God's intimacy,
the more reprehensible the infidelity.
    I was selected wife and partner,
loved as your very soul.   640
Shall I speak the truth? Yes.
I abandoned and forgot you, fled from you,
abandoned you to fulfill my own desires,
abandoned you for bad choices,
abandoned you, the source of all my happiness,   645
abandoned you by cutting the ties
of true love and promised loyalty.
Abandoned, but to go where?
There where there is nothing but wickedness.
I abandoned you, the true friend,   650
the friend above all friends admirable,
friend who loved before being loved.
I abandoned you, font of all goodness,
because of my weak will,
abandoned you, the good, the wise, the handsome,   655
the strong of arm and gentle of spirit.
I left you, and the better to remove myself
from your love, stand against you.
It is the enemy, the world, the flesh,
which cost you so dearly on the cross,   660
which you vanquished that I might be free,
I, who had been too long in their thrall,
a slave and so captivated,
I could not be further debased.
I mingled with all three   665
and shared in all their doings.

Et propre amour, qui est trop faulse et feincte,
A charité de vous en moy exteincte,
Tant que le nom de Jesus, mon espoux,
(Que paravant j'avoie trouvé si doulx)   670

Proverbe 2.   Avoie quasi en hayne et fascherie,
Et bien souvent en faisoie mocquerie.
Si on disoit, en oyant ung sermon:
Il a bien dit, je respondoie: ce a mon.
La parolle s'en voloit, comme plume,   675
A l'eglise n'alloie que par coustume.
Tous mes beaulx faictz n'estoient qu'hypocrisie,
Car j'avoie bien ailleurs ma phantasie.
Il m'ennuyoit d'ouyr de vous parler;
J'aymoie bien mieulx à mon plaisir aller.   680
        Pour faire court, tout ce que deffendez,
Je le faisoie; et ce que commandez,
Je le fuyoie et le trouvoie amair,
Tout par faulte, mon Dieu, de vous aymer.
        Mais, mon seigneur, pour vous avoir hay,   685
Habandonné, laissé, fouy, trahy,
Et vostre lieu à ung aultre donner,
Me regardant à luy habandonner,

Joel 2.   A'vous souffert que je fusse huee,
Monstree au doigt, ou battue, ou tuee?   690
M'avez vous mise en prison très obscure,
Ou bannie, sans avoir de moy cure?
M'a'vous osté voz dons et voz joyaux
Pour me punir de mes tours desloyaulx?
Ay je perdu mon douaire promys,   695
Pour les pechez qu'envers vous j'ay commis?
Feuz je par vous en justice accusee,
Comme femme meschante et abusee?
A tout le moins, a'vous point faict deffense
Que jamais plus devant vostre presence   700
N'eusse à venir, comme c'estoit raison,
Ne plus rentrer dedens vostre maison?
        O vray espoux, mari inestimable,
Parfaict amy, sur tous les bons amable,
Vous avez bien en moy faict aultrement,   705
Luc 15 et 18   Car cherchee m'avez diligemment,

And amour propre, which is false and deceiving,
extinguished charity in me.
So much so that the name of Jesus, my spouse
(which I once found so appealing),   670
I had come to treat as hateful and upsetting
and frequently even ridiculed.
If one said about a sermon
that he had spoken well, I promptly agreed.
My words floated like feathers   675
and I attended Mass through routine.
All my lovely gestures were mere sham,
for my thoughts lay elsewhere.
It annoyed me to hear you spoken of.
I preferred tending to my pleasures.   680
        In brief, everything you forbid,
I did. Whatever you command,
I found distasteful and fled,
my God, because I did not love you.
        But, Lord, having despised, abandoned,   685
deserted, forsaken, and betrayed you,
having replaced you
and given myself over to another,
did you allow me to be jeered at,
singled out, beaten, or killed?   690
Did you enclose me in a dark prison,
dispose of me carelessly?
Did you take from me your gifts and offerings
so as to punish me for my acts of disloyalty?
Have I lost my promised dowry?   695
Have I because of the sins I have committed against you
been brought to justice
as an unruly and abusive wife?
At the very least, have I,
as would have been altogether fitting,   700
been kept from you and prohibited
from entering your house?
        O true husband, inestimable partner,
perfect friend,²³ most admirable among the admirable,
you acted differently with me,   705
for you searched for me diligently,

Comme brebiz errante au plus profond
Du puitz d'enfer, où tous les maulx se font.
Moy qui estois de vous tant separee,
Et en mon cueur et mon sens esgaree.　　　　　710
Appellee m'avez à haulte voix,

Pseau. 44.　En me disant: Ma fille, oy et vois,
Et encline envers moy ton ouye;
Et ton peuple, où tu t'en es fouye,
Vueille oublier, et de ton premier pere　　　715
La grand maison, où as faict ton repaire;
Et le roy plein de toute loyaulté,
Couvoitera à l'heure ta beaulté.
　　　Mais quant ce doulx et gracieux prier
Ne me servoit, vous veniez crier:　　　　　720

Matth. 11.　Venez à moy vous tous qui par labeur
Estes lassez et chargez de douleur,
Je suis celluy, qui vous recepveray,
Et de mon pain refectionneray.
　　　Las! tous ces motz ne voulois escouter,　　　725
Mais, qui plus est, en les oyant, doubter
Si c'estoit vous, ou non; par adventure
Ce n'estoit riens qu'une simple escripture.
Car jusques là, j'estoie bien si folle
Que sans amour lisoie vostre parolle.　　　730
Je veoie bien que les comparaisons
De la vigne, qui vous donnoit poysons

Deuter. 32.　Et labrusques en lieu de fruict parfaict,
Esaie 5.　Estoit pour moy, qui ainsi avoie faict.
Assez pensoie que les vocations　　　　　735
De l'espouse et appellations,

Cantique 6.　Disant: tournez, retournez Sunamite,
Estoit affin que de tout le limite
De mon peché je voulsisse saillir,
Où en pitié me voyez defaillir.　　　　　740
De tout cela semblant ne faisoie mye;
Mais quant je vins à lire Hieremie,
Je confesse que j'euz en ce passage
Crainte en mon cueur et honte en mon visage.
Je le diray, voire la larme à l'oeil,　　　745
A vostre honneur, rabaissant mon orgueil.

like the lost sheep in the deepest
recesses of the pit of hell, where abides all evil,
I who was such a long way from you,
and so confused in both mind and body.   710
You called out to me in a loud voice,
saying: My daughter, listen and look,
turn your attention toward me.
Forget your people among whom you have taken refuge
and the grand house of your first father   715
which you have made your sojourn.
The king, moved by deep loyalty
will soon desire your beauty.
　　But when this so sweet and grace-inspired prayer
was of no avail, it was you who sought me out: 720
come to me all you who are weary
and heavy-laden with grief;
it is I who will comfort
and restore you with my bread.24
　　Alas, I did not heed these words;   725
worse still, hearing them, I questioned
whether they were yours.
Perhaps it was meaningless scripture,
for up to that point, I was so silly
that I read without feeling.   730
I came to understand that the vines
bearing poison
and wild grapes instead of good fruit
were intended for me who had acted in this fashion.
I rather believed that the wife's cries and pleadings,   735
saying: return, return, Sunamite,25
were so that, at the worst of my sinning,
I might seek to escape from that place
where you in your compassion saw me thrashing about.
In the midst of it all, I pretended indifference.   740
But when I fell upon the passage in Jeremiah,
I confess I had
fear in my heart, was shamefaced,
and indeed, let it be said,
even had tears in my eyes,   745
in your honor, lowering my pride.26

Vous avez dit par vostre sainct Prophete:

Si la femme au mary s'est forfaicte,
En le laissant et d'ung aultre abuser,
Jamais ne fut, ny l'on n'a veu user   750
Que le mary la vueille rappeller,
Ny plus la veoir, ny à elle parler.
N'est elle pas estimee polue,
Très meschante, et de nulle value?
La loy consent à justice la rendre,   755
Et la chasser, sans la vouloir reprendre.
    Mais toy, qui as faict separation
De mon doulx lict, par fornication
Avec aultruy meschantement commettre,
Et en mon lieu tes faulx amateurs mettre,   760
A moy tu peulx toutesfois revenir,
Car contre toy courroux ne vueil tenir.
Lieve tes yeulx et regard bien droit,
Et tu voirras en quel lieu et endroit,
A ceste heure ton peché t'a menee,   765
Et où tu gyz en terre prosternee.
    O paovre ame! regarde où tu tes mise,
Sur les voies du grand chemin assise,
Où tous passantz pour mal tu attendois.
A aultre fin certes tu ne tendois,   770
Comme ung larron caché en solitude,
A les tromper tu mettois ton estude.
Parquoy ayant ta malice accomplye,
Tout alentour de toy as remplye
Et couverte de ton infection   775
Toute la terre, par fornication.
Ton visage, ton oeil, ton front, ta face,
Avoit changé du tout sa bonne grace,
Car tel estoit que d'une meretrice,
Et si n'as eu vergongne de ton vice.   780
    Et le surplus que Hieremie dit,
Qui contraignoit mon cueur, sans contredict,
De congnoistre mon estat maleureux,
Et rejecter par souspir douloureux,
L'heure, le jour, le temps, le mois, l'annee,   785
Que vous laissay, me laissant condemnee,

Through your holy prophet you said:
If a wife forsakes her husband
and gives herself to another,
it is unheard of that the husband 750
should seek to take her back,
to look upon or ever speak with her again.
Is she not polluted,
evil, and of no worth?
The Law gives her up to justice 755
and permanently banishes her.
    But you who left
my sweet embrace and wickedly committed fornication with others,
and in my stead put false lovers,
you may nevertheless come back to me. 760
I do not wish to hold a grudge against you.
Lift your eyes and look with care
and you will see to what state
your sins have finally brought you,
and where at this moment 765
you lie prostrate.
    O unfortunate soul! Look where you have stationed yourself,
seated beside the great highway,
waiting to rob every passerby.
Certainly you have no other purpose. 770
Like a thief, hiding and alone,
you single-mindedly set upon trapping them.
Performing thus your malice,
you spread your poison every which way,
and with your fornicating, 775
cover the entire earth with your contagion.
Your look, your eyes, your forehead, your face
have relinquished all their beauty and grace,
you have the look of a prostitute,
and still you express no shame in your vice. 780
    Moreover, what Jeremiah said
clearly forced my heart to examine
my deplorable state and to regret
with a poignant sigh
the time, the hour, the day, the month, the year 785
that I forsook you, leaving me self-condemned,

Par moy mesme jugeant mon cueur infame
D'estre sans fin en l'eternelle flamme.

Prover. 15.   Ceste crainte (qui de moy ne procede,
Mais vient de vous qui tout plaisir excede)   790
M'avoit quasi par vive congnoissance
De mon peché mise en desesperance,
Si n'eust esté que ne m'avez laissee;
Car aussi tost qu'avez veu abbaissee
Ma volunté soubz vostre obeyssance,   795
Avez usé de vostre grand clemence,
Mettant en moy une si vive foy,
Que vous sachant mon seigneur, maistre, et roy,
(De qui debvoie par raison avoir crainte)
Par vray amour ma paour fut toute exteinte.   800
En vous croiant mary si gracieux,
Bon, doulx, piteux, misericordieux,
Moy (qui plustost me debvoye cacher)
N'ay eu crainte de vous aller chercher.
    A vous me suis vous cherchant retiree,   805
Mais paravant j'estoie de vous tiree.
Qu'avez vous faict? m'avez vous refusee?
Helas! mon Dieu, nenny, mais excusee.
A'vous de moy tourné vostre regard?
Non, mais vostre oeil m'a esté ung doulx dard,   810
Qui m'a navré le cueur jusques à la mort,
En me donnant de mes pechez remort.
Repoulsee ne m'avez de la main;
Luc 15.   Mais à deux braz, d'ung cueur doulx et humain,
M'estes venu, embrassant, approcher,   815
Sans mes faultes en riens me reprocher.
Point n'ay congneu à vostre contenance,
Qu'ayez jamais apperceu mon offense.
Vous avez faict de moy aussi grand feste,
Que si j'avoie esté bonne et honneste,   820
Couvrant à tous ma faulte et mon delict,
Me redonnant la part de vostre lict,
En me monstrant que mes pechez divers
Par la bonté de vous sont si couvertz,
Et si vaincuz par vostre grand victoire,   825
Que n'en voulez jamais avoir memoire,

judging that this burning heart
was to suffer eternal flames.
This fear (which proceeded not from me
but from you who surpass all joy),   790
through its intense self-awareness of my treachery,
might have left me in utter despair,
had it not been that you would not abandon me.
For as soon as you saw my will
bent under the yoke of obedience to you,   795
you used your overwhelming clemency
to instill in me a faith so strong
that knowing you to be my savior, master, and king
(whom by all reason I should have feared)
my trepidation was promptly vanquished by love.   800
Seeing in you a generous, kind,
loving, compassionate, and caring husband,
I (who ought to have hid myself)
did not fear to seek you out.
    Whereas once you drew me to you,   805
all the while searching for you, I pulled away.
What did you do? Did you reject me?
Ah, no, my Lord, you pardoned me.
Did you turn away from me?
No, your eye was rather like a gentle arrow   810
which pierced my heart to the quick,
causing me to regret my transgressions.
You did not push me away with your hand.
Rather, arms opened wide, with a kind and human heart,
you lovingly came toward me,   815
without ever a thought of blaming me for my errors.
I would never have believed from the look on your face
that you ever noticed my offense.
You made much of me
as though I had been good and honest.   820
You hid my flaws and dereliction from everyone,
invited me back into your bed,
proving that my countless sins
had been so completely exonerated
and vanquished by your great triumph,   825
that you did not wish to think about them.

Et que grace en moy avez enclose,
Qui vous garde de n'y veoir aultre chose,
Si non les dons donnez de vostre dextre,
Et les vertuz qu'il vous y a pleu mettre.   830
    O charité, bien voy que vostre ardeur
Icy brulle et deffaict ma laideur,
Et me refaict creature nouvelle,
Pleine de Dieu, qui me faict estre telle.
Ce qui est myen avez du tout destruict,   835
Sans y laisser renommee ne bruyt,
Et me daignant si parfaicte refaire,
Que tous les biens que mon espoux poeut faire
A une ame, vous l'avez fait à moy,
En me donnant de ses promesses foy.   840
    Or, ay je donc, par vostre bonne grace,
De l'espouse recouverte la place?
Bieneureux lieu, place tant desirable,
Gracieux lict, throne très honnorable,
Siege de paix, repoz de toute guerre,   845
Hauldays d'honneur, separé de la terre,
Recepvez vous ceste indigne personne,
Me redonnant le sceptre et la couronne
De vostre empire et royaume de gloire?
Qui ouyt onc parler de tel hystoire,   850
De moins que riens eslever si treshault,
Faire valoir qui de soy riens ne vault?
    Las! qu'est cecy? Jettant en hault ma veue,
Je voy en vous bonté si incongneue,
Grace et amour si incomprehensible,   855
Que la veue m'en demeure invisible,
Et par force faict mon regard cesser,
Qui me contrainct en bas mes yeulx baisser.
A l'heure, voy en ce regard terrestre,
Ce que je suis et ce qu'ay voulu estre.   860
Helas! je voy de mes maulx la laydeur,
L'obscurité, l'extreme profondeur,
Ma mort, mon riens, et ma nichilité,
Qui rend mon oeil clos par humilité,
Le bien de vous qui est tant admirable,   865
Le mal de moy trop inconsiderable,

You wrapped me in your grace,
which prevented you from seeing anything else
but the gifts awarded with your right hand
and the virtues it pleased you to place in me.   830
    O love, I see how your ardor burns
and destroys my ugliness,
and transforms me into a new creature,
fills me with the God who thus remakes me.
What was of my doing you totally undid,   835
leaving no signs of disgrace and rumor,
deigning to make me so perfect
that all the good things my husband could have brought
to my soul, you gave to me,
realizing his every promise.   840
    Have I then recovered, thanks to your grace,
my lost place as wife?
Blessed and much-desired status,
winsome bed, honorable throne,
seat of peace and refuge from struggle,   845
dais of honor, far removed from earth,
do you accept this unworthy person,
confiding in me the scepter and crown
of your glorious kingdom?
Who has ever heard tell of such a story,   850
to lift the lowliest to the summit,
to give value to the unworthy?
    And what do I see?
Raising my eyes on high,
I perceive in you unheard-of kindness,   855
grace and love so incomprehensible
that I am blinded, made to turn away,
to turn my sight downward.
And thus looking, I see what I am
and what I wanted to be.   860
I see the unsightliness of my misconduct,
darkness and a great abyss,
my death, my emptiness, my meaninglessness.
I shut my eyes in humility.
I see your inestimable kindness,   865
my own too-great mischief,

Vostre haulteur, vostre essence trespure,
Ma fragilité et mortelle nature,
Voz dons, vos biens, vostre beatitude,
Ma malice et grande ingratitude.   870
Quel vous m'estes et quelle je vous suis,
(L'ung à l'aultre comparer je ne puis)
Qui me faict bien sans fin esmerveiller,
Comme si fort vous a pleu travailler,
Pour vous unir à moy contre raison   875
Veu qu'il n'y a nulle comparaison.

Hebr. 5.   Vous estes Dieu, je suis vostre facture;
Mon createur, moy vostre creature;
Brief, ne povant ce que c'est diffinir,
C'est ce que moins à vous se poeut unir.   880
Amour, amour, vous avez faict l'accord,
Faisant unir à la vie la mort;
Mais l'union a mort vivifiee,
Vie mourant d'amour deifiee,
Vie sans fin a faict nostre mort vive.   885
Mort a donné à vie mort neïfve.
Par ceste mort, moy morte, reçoy vie;
Et au vivant, par la mort, je suis ravye.
En vous je vys; quant à moy, je suis morte.
Mort ne m'est plus que d'une prison porte.   890
Vie m'est mort, car par mort suis vivante.
Vie me rend triste, et mort me contente.
O quel mourir! qui faict mon ame vivre,
En la rendant par mort, de mort delivre.
Unie à vous par amour sy puissante,   895
Que sans mourir elle meurt languissante.
A elle tort l'ame, qui mort vouldroit,
Pour un tel bien? nenny. Elle ha bon droit,
Philip. 1.   Car pour avoir vie tant estimee,
Bien doibt nommer la mort sa bien aymee.   900
O doulce mort, gracieuse douleur,
Puissante clef, delivrant de malheur
Ceulx qui par mort estoient mortifiez,
Par foy s'estre en vostre mort fiez,
Vous les avez mys par ung doulx dormir   905
Hors de la mort qui les faisoit gemir.

your worth, your purity,
my fragile and mortal nature,
your qualities, riches, and beatitude,
my own wickedness and terrible ingratitude.   870
I marvel when I place side by side
what you are and what I am,
for there can be no comparison.
And seeing no comparison, I endlessly marvel
that you should have been so eager   875
to join yourself to me against all reason.
    You are God; I am of your making.
You are the creator, I the creature.
I am incapable of fathoming these matters,
how it is that I could possibly be united to you.   880
    Love, love, you have brought about this union,
joining death to life.
A union vivified by death,
deified life dying from love,
life eternal has brought life to death.   885
Death has given life to innocent death.
Through this death, I dead find life.
And while alive, through death, I am made to live.
I live in you while I am dead.
Death to me is no more than a prison door.   890
    Life is death to me since through death I am alive.
Life brings sadness while death provides happiness.
Such a death gives life to my soul.
Death delivers my soul from death.
United to you by such an overwhelming love,   895
without dying, my soul dies languishingly.[27]
    Is the soul in error in seeking death
in order to achieve such a gift? Not at all. It is right.
For to acquire such an inestimable life,
it must declare death its beloved.   900
    Oh, sweet death, delightful sorrow,
all-powerful means to deliver from misery
those who were mortified by death,
because they put faith in your death,
you have granted them a gentle sleep   905
which defies the death that made them grieve.

Las! bieneureux est de mort le sommeil
A qui trouve la vie à son reveil.
Par vostre mort, la mort n'est au chrestien
Que liberté de son mortel lyen.   910
La mort qui est au maulvais effrayable,
Elle est aux bons plaisante et aggreable.

Hebr. 2.   Or est donc mort par vostre mort destruicte.
Parquoy, mon Dieu, si j'estoie bien instruicte,
La mort diroye vie; et vie, mort,   915
Fin de labeur, et entrée de seur port;
Car de vie la grant fruition
M'empeschent trop de vostre vision.
O mort, venez; rompez moy cest obstacle.
O bien, amour, faictes en moy miracle.   920
Puisque par mort encores ne puis voir
Mon doulx espoux, par vostre grand povoir
Transformez moy en luy toute vivante,
Et en repos j'attendray mieulx l'attente.

Ionas 4.   Faictes moy donc, en luy vivant, mourir;   925
Aultre que vous ne me poeut secourir.

Rom. 11.   O mon saulveur, par foy je suis plantee,
Et par amour ne vous joincte et entee.
Quelle union! quelle bieneureté!
Puis que par foy j'ay de vous seureté,   930
Nommer vous puis par amour hardiemment:

Jean 1.   Filz, pere, espoux, et frere, entierement
Pere, frere, filz, mary. O quelz dons
De me donner le bien de tous ces noms!
O mon pere, quelle paternité!   935
O mon frere, quelle fraternité!
O mon enfant, quelle dilection!
O mon espoux, quelle conjunction!
Pere, envers moy plein de mansuetude;
Frere, ayant prins nostre similitude;   940
Filz, engendré par foy et charité;
Mary, aymant en toute extremité.
Mais qui est, ce que vous ayme? Helas!
Celle qu'avez retiree des laqs
Où elle estoit lyee par malice,   945
Luy redonnant le lieu, nom et office

And so blessed is the sleep of death
from which one awakens to life.
Because of your death, a Christian's death
is freedom from these mortal bonds.   910
Death which to the wicked is terrifying,
is to the pure of heart pleasant and agreeable.
  By your death is death destroyed.
Thus, Lord, if I have understood well your teachings,
death is life, and life is death,   915
the end of strife and access into a safe harbor.
For life's generous gifts
hinder me from seeing you.[28]
  O death, come and take from me this obstacle,
or love, perform for me a miracle.   920
Since death does not yet permit me
to see my loving spouse, by your great power
turn me living into him,
so that I may better resign myself to the delay.
Make me die by living in him.   925
Only you can help me.
  O savior, I am suffused with faith,
by love joined to and fixed in you.
Ah what a coming together, what bliss,
how I feel secure in your faith!   930
In love I can boldly call you
son, father, spouse, and brother.
Father, brother, son, and husband,
what a joy to be able to dedicate these titles to you.
As a father, such paternity;   935
As a brother, such fraternity;
As a child, such pleasure;
As a spouse, such a marriage;
A father overflowing with kindness toward me;
A brother taking on our human likeness;   940
A son engendered by love and faith;
A husband, loving in the extreme.
  But who is this person who loves you,
she whom you released from the snare
where wickedness had entrapped her,   945
and to whom you gave back the name, status, and place

De fille, soeur, mere, espouse. O saulveur,
Ceste doulceur est de grande saveur,
Très plaisante et très doulce à gouster.
Parlant à vous, ou bien, vous escouter.   950

Hiere. 3. Vous appellant pere (parlant à vous
Sans crainte avoir), enfant, frere et espoux,
Vous escoutant, je m'oy mere nommer,

Cant. 4, 5. Soeur, fille, femme. Las! c'est pour consummer,
Fondre, brusler, du tout aneantir   955
L'ame qui poeut ceste doulceur sentir.

    Est il amour auprès de ceste cy,
Qui trop pleine ne soit de maulvais si?
Est il plaisir dont l'on poeust tenir compte?
Est il honneur que l'on n'estime à honte?   960
Est il prouffit que l'on doye estimer?
Brief, est il rien que plus je sceusse aymer?
Helas! nenny, car tous ces mondains biens,

Philip. 3. Qui ayme Dieu, repute moins que fientz.
Plaisir, prouffit, et honneur sont corvee   965
A qui l'amour de son Dieu a trouvee.

    Amour de Dieu est si plaisant prouffit,

Psal. 106. Et tant d'honneur que seule au cueur suffit.
Elle rend content (je le puis dire)
Tant que riens plus ne veult ny ne desire;   970
Car qui ha Dieu, ainsi qu'il le commande,
Oultrageux est qui aultre bien demande.

    Or vous ay je par une foy latente,
Parquoy je suis satisfaicte et contente.
Or vous ay je, mon pere, pour deffense   975
Des folyes de ma trop longue enfance.
Or vous ay je, mon frere, pour secours
De mes ennuyz, que je ne trouve cours.
Or vous ay je, mon filz, pour ma vieillesse
Le seul baston, support de ma foiblesse.   980
Or vous ay je l'espoux sans fiction,
De tout mon cueur la satisfaction.
Puis que vous ay, je quicte le surplus.

Cantique 3. Puis que vous tiens, je ne vous laisray plus.
Puis que vous voy, riens ne veulx regarder,   985
Qui de vous veoir me puisse engarder.

of daughter, sister, mother, and spouse?
O savior, this benevolence is sweet,
and ever so satisfying to the taste,
this speaking to and hearing you,   950
calling you father, child, brother, and partner,
and conversing without fear.
Listening to you, I hear myself called
mother, sister, daughter, wife. It is enough to consume,
melt, burn, and completely destroy   955
the soul that can feel this sweetness.
     Is there a love, compared with this one,
which is not contemptible?
Is there a pleasure worthy of the name?
Is there an honor which should not be called a shame?   960
Is there any profit that one should esteem?
In short, is there anything in the world I could have loved more?
Indeed not. To the one who loves God,
all these mundane achievements are worth less than dung.
Pleasure, success, honor are like a heavy chore   965
to those who have found the love of God.
     God's love is so wondrous a bounty,
so great a mark of distinction that it is sufficient unto the heart.
It brings contentment (this I know)
beyond any desire or longing.   970
For whoever has God, as he commands it should be,
he is outrageous who demands anything else.
     Now you are mine because of an unpretentious faith
that makes me happy and pleased,
mine, my father, to protect me   975
from the foolishness of my persistent childish ways,
mine, my brother, to help me
against the deep sorrows which never go away,
mine, my son, the only buttress
against old age and deterioration,   980
mine, true husband,
the joy of my heart.
And since you belong to me, all the rest is like naught,
since I have you, I shall never let you go,
since I have my eyes upon you, I wish to see nothing   985
that would delay my seeing you,

Psal. 84. Puis que vous oy, aultre ne veulx ouyr,
Cant. 3, 8. Qui m'empesche de vostre voix ouyr.
Puis que propos à vous je puis tenir,
Aultre que vous ne veulx entretenir.   990
Puisqu'il vous plaist près de vous m'approcher,
Plustost vouldroye mourir qu'aultre toucher.
Puis que vous sers, je ne veulx aultre maistre.
Puis qu'à vous suis, à aultre je ne veulx estre.
Puis que mon cueur au vostre avez uny,   995
S'il s'en depart, qu'il soit sans fin puny;
Car plus dur est que la damnation
Sentir de vous la separation.
Dix mille enfers n'estime tant de peine,
Que de vous perdre ung seul jour la sepmaine.   1000
    Helas! mon Dieu, mon pere createur,
Ne souffrez pas l'ennemy inventeur
De tout peché avoir ceste puissance,
Psal. 37. Qu'il me face perdre vostre presence;
Car qui a faict de la substraction   1005
De vostre amour vraye probation,
Il dira bien qu'il vouldroit mieulx en fer
Estre lyé à jamais en enfer,
Que retomber encor ung seul moment
Au mal que faict de vous l'eslongnement.   1010
    O mon saulveur, plus ne le permettez,
Mais en tel lieu, s'il vous plaist, me mettez,
Que mon ame par peché ou folye,
De vostre amour jamais ne se deslye.
    En ce monde ne puis parfaictement   1015
Avoir ce bien, qui me faict ardemment
De tout mon cueur en desirer l'yssue,
Sans craindre mort, pic, paelle, ny massue.
Car quelle paour de mon Dieu puis je avoir,
Qui par amour a passé son debvoir,   1020
Et a prins mort dont il n'avoit que faire,
2. Tim 1. Pour nostre mort par la sienne deffaire?
    Mort est Jesus, en qui tous mortz nous sommes,
Et en sa mort faict vivre tous ses hommes.
Je diz les siens, qui de sa passion   1025
Ont par la foy participation.

since I hear you, I listen to nothing else
that might keep me from hearing you,
since I converse with you,
I have no interest in any other discourse, 990
since it pleases you to be near me,
I would die rather than approach another,
since it is you that I serve, I serve no other,
since I am yours, I do not wish to be another's,
and since my heart is joined to yours, 995
if it should separate, may it be forever punished.
Parting from you would be worse
than damnation.
Ten thousand hells are a lesser pain
than a mere day away from you. 1000
        My God, my father-creator,
let not the enemy, inventor
of all sins, exercise such power
that I should lose your presence.
Whoever has experienced that trial 1005
of the loss of your love
will tell you that it would be better
to be bound eternally in the chains of hell
than to endure a single moment
of the anguish of separation from you. 1010
        O savior mine, never again permit it
that I should be anywhere but here with you,
or that my soul through sin and folly
should ever be removed from your presence.
        Never without fear of mace, pickaxe, shovel, or death, 1015
could I enjoy in this world that perfection
which leads me to desire with all my heart
removal from it.
For what have I to fear from my God,
who far beyond duty's devotion, 1020
experienced an undeserved death
to save us from our own?
        Jesus died, in whose death we all participated,
and whose death gave life to all his followers.
I say his followers, those who through faith 1025
have shared in his passion.

Car où la mort avant le grand mystere
Ecclesiaste. 41.   De ceste croix estoit à tous austere,
En regardant sa face et sa rigueur,
Et n'y avoit cueur qui n'en eust frayeur,   1030
Veu l'union qui est de l'ame au corps,
L'ordonnance, l'amour, et les accordz,
Dont la douleur estoit du separer,
Extreme accès pour tout desesperer.
Depuis qu'il pleut au doulx agneau souffrir   1035
Esaie 53.   Dessus la croix et pour nous là s'offrir,
Sa grande amour a allumé ung feu
En nostre cueur si vehement, que jeu
Tout bon chrestien doibt la mort estimer,
Et l'ung l'autre à la mort animer.   1040
Et tout ainsi que mort nous retardoit,
Amour desir de mort donner nous doibt.
1. Jean 4.   Car, si amour est au cueur, sans mentir
Il ne sçauroit aultre chose sentir
Si grande elle est, qu'elle tient tout le lieu;   1045
Tout m'est dehors, riens n'y seuffre que Dieu
Où est amour, vray et vivant sans feinte,
Il ne souvient de paour, douleur, ne crainte.
    Si nostre orgueil, pour honneur acquerir,
Faict de la mort tant de moiens querir;   1050
Si pour avoir ung plaisir qui tant couste,
L'on oublye de la mort crainte et doubte;
Si pour avoir des richesses son saoul,
L'on met sa vie en danger pour ung soul;
Si l'envie de rober ou tuer,   1055
Battre, tromper, faict l'esperit muer,
Tant qu'il ne voit de la mort le danger,
Pour faire mal ou d'aultruy soy venger;
Si la force d'une grand maladie,
Ou la douleur d'une melancholie,   1060
Desirer faict la mort et souvent prendre
Par ce nayer, soubdain tuer, ou pendre;
(Car si grand est le mal ou le desir,
Qu'il faict la mort pour liberté choisir).
    Si ainsi est que ces grandz passions   1065
Pleines de mal et d'imperfections,

Before the great mystery of the cross,
death was for all a horror.
Seeing its pitiless countenance,
every heart shuddered with fear,   1030
in view of the union between body and soul,
the order, the love, the ties,
so that to separate them is painful
and causes great despair.
But since the gentle lamb of God chose to suffer upon the cross   1035
and to offer himself up as a sacrifice for us,
his great love placed so consuming a fire in our hearts
that every Christian must look upon death
as little more than a trifle
and inspire each other to seek it.   1040
And while death was once an obstacle,
love should make us wish for it.
For if love is truly embedded in our hearts,
its power is so great and takes up so much of the space there,
that we should feel nothing else.   1045
For with genuine and honest love,
I make room for naught but God,
and remember neither fear, nor pain, nor anxiety.
     If our pride in obtaining honor
leads us to seek out death,   1050
if the costly search for pleasure
causes us to forget our fear and dread of death,
if to have our fill of riches,
we endanger our lives for a farthing,
if in order to seek revenge, the desire to rob,   1055
kill, bruise, and deceive moves us
to the point of no longer seeing
the risk of death,
if some terrible illness
or great sadness   1060
causes us to seek out death
and to drown, hang, or kill ourselves
(for the suffering is so overpowering
that death seems like an escape),
     if such great emotions,   1065
full of imperfections and evil,

De la mort font peu craindre le hasart,
Mais maintesfois leur semble venir tard,
Que doibt faire amour juste et louable,
Obligee et plus que raisonable?   1070
Que doibt faire l'amour du createur?
Doibt elle point si fort brusler ung cueur,
Que transporté de telle affection,
Ne doibt sentir nulle aultre passion?

Psal. 115. Helas! si faict, car mort est chose eureuse   1075
A une ame de luy bien amoureuse;

Philip. 1. Gracieuse elle estime la porte
Par où il fault que de sa prison sorte.
Le dur chemin ne la sçauroit lasser
Par où elle va son espoux embrasser.   1080
O mon vray Dieu, que ceste mort est belle,
Par qui j'auray fin de toute querelle,
Par qui j'auray de vous fruition,
Et jouyray de vostre vision,
Par qui seray à vous si conformee,   1085
Que j'y seray divine transformee.
O Mort, par vous j'espere tant d'honneur,
Qu'à deux genoulx j'en cry, souspir, et pleur.

Psal. 119. Je vous requier, venez hastivement,
Et mettez fin à mon gemissement.   1090

Cantique. 5. O eureuses ames, filles très sainctes,
En la cité de Jerusalem joinctes,
Baissez voz yeulx par miseration,
Et regardez ma desolation.
Je vous supply que vous vueillez pour moy   1095
Dire à mon Dieu, mon seigneur, et mon roy,
Luy annonçant à quelqu'heure du jour,
Que je languyz pour luy de son amour.
O doulce Mort, par son amour venez,
Et par amour à mon Dieu me menez.   1100
O Mort, où est icy vostre poincture,
Vostre aiguillon, vostre rudesse dure?
Helas! elle est de mes yeulx divertie,
Car en doulceur, rigueur m'est convertie.
Puis que par vous mon amy est passé,   1105
Et sur la croix pour moy mort trespassé.

cause us not to fear death,
but rather frequently to long for it,
then what could a just, laudable,
engaging, and reasonable love accomplish? 1070
What could the love of the creator achieve?
Should it not so burn our hearts
that moved by such intensity,
we feel nothing else?
Indeed, yes, for death is a happy occurrence 1075
for a soul so much smitten by it.
Filled with grace, it values the door
through which it must flee its prison.
The difficult journey toward its husband's embrace
should not weary it. 1080
     Truest God, how beautiful is this death,
which frees me from all struggles,
which brings me the rewards of your riches,
and I will have the joy of beholding you
by which I will be so shaped by you 1085
that I will be transformed into your divine image.
     O Death, through you I hope for such honor,
that on bended knee I weep, sigh, and cry out for it.
I call for you to come in haste
and put an end to my torment. 1090
     Happy souls, saintly daughters,
in union at Jerusalem,
lower your eyes in compassion
and look upon my desolation.
I beg you to intercede with my God, 1095
my savior, and my king,
and report to him that, at all hours of the day,
I languish for the love of him.
     O sweet Death, in the name of his love,
come to me and lead me to my God. 1100
O Death, where is your sting,
your hurt, your harsh cruelty?[29]
They are without significance,
for severity has been changed to kindness,
since by your means my lover has passed on 1105
and died on the cross for me.

Sa mort si fort à mourir mon cueur poulse,
Que vous m'estes pour le suyvir bien doulce.

1. Cor. 13. O Mort, o Mort, venez, quoy que je dye
Mettre ensemble avec l'amy l'amye.   1110

Puis que la mort m'est vie si plaisante,
Que plus me plaist qu'elle ne m'espouvente,
Craindre ne doib si non le jugement
(Qui vient après) de Dieu qui point ne ment.
Tous mes pechez par sa juste balance   1115
Seront poisez et mys en congnoissance.
Ce que j'ay faict, mon penser, ma parolle

Luc 12 et Sera congnu, mieulx escript qu'en ung rolle.
Matth. 10. Et ne fault pas penser que charité
Vueille offenser justice et verité,   1120
Car qui aura vescu comme infidele,
Puny sera d'infinité cruelle.

Psal. 7. Dieu est juste; son jugement est droict;
Tout ce qu'il faict est juste en tout endroit.
Là, où je suis, regarde sa droicture,   1125

Job. 15. Moy miserable et paovre creature.
Veu que je sçay que toutes les justices

Micheas. 7. Des plus justes sont si pleines de vices,
Que devant DIEU sont hordes, salles, villes

Esaie 64. Plus infames qu'immundices des villes,   1130
Psal. 129 et 37 Que sera ce des pechez que j'ay faictz,
Dont trop je sens importable le faix?
Dire ne puis aultre conclusion,
Sinon que j'ay gaigné damnation.
Est ce la fin? sera desesperance   1135
Le reconfort de ma grande ignorance?

Matth. 19. Las! mon Dieu, non; car ma foy invisible
Me faict croire que tout mon impossible
Est facile à vous, tant que mon rien

Rom. 5. Convertissez en quelque peu de bien.   1140
Rom. 8. Donc, mon seigneur, qui me condemnera?
Et quel juge jamais me damnera,
Quand cestuy là qui m'est donné pour juge

Psal. 8, 9. Est mon espoux, mon pere, et mon refuge?
Pere, mais quel? qui jamais son enfant   1145
Ne condemne mais l'excuse et deffend.

His death draws me so inexorably toward dying
that to pursue it is like bliss.
Death, Death, whatever my words,
come and join lover to lover.   1110
    Since death is to me like a life of joy,
more pleasing than frightening,
I have nothing to fear save the final judgment
of God who never lies.
All my sins will be placed in the balance,   1115
fairly weighed and examined.
Everything I have done, thought, or spoken
will be known, better recorded than in any record book.
Nor must I think that kindness will conflict
with justice and truth,   1120
for whoever has lived as an infidel,
will be punished with everlasting cruelty.
God is just, his judgment fair.
He is entirely fair-minded in everything that he does.
In the place where I am I behold his justice,   1125
miserable, sad creature that I am.
    Knowing as I do that even the just acts
of the most just are tainted with dishonesty,
that in the eyes of the Almighty they are sullied, corrupt, and vile,
more depraved than the filth of cities,   1130
what are we to say of the sins I have committed,
whose burden I find unbearable?
I can come to no other conclusion
than that I deserve damnation.
    Is that all? Will despair be the only recompense   1135
for my colossal negligence?
Let it not be so, my God. My simple faith
leads me to believe that what is impossible
for me is easy for you. You are able
to convert my nothingness into a hint of some decency.   1140
Thus, my Lord, who will condemn me?
What judge dares censure me
since the judge I am given
is my spouse, my father, and my refuge?
    And what sort of father? The kind that never rebukes his child, 1145
but rather forgives and defends.

Et puis, je voy n'avoir accusateur
Que Jesuchrist, qui est mon redempteur,
Qui par sa mort nous a restitué
L'heritage, et s'est constitué   1150

1. Jean 2 et   Nostre advocat, devant Dieu presentant
1. Tim. 1.   Ses merites, qui sont et vallent tant
Que ma debte en est si surmontee
Qu'en jugement el' n'est pour rien comptee.
    Mon redempteur, voicy ung bien grant cas: 1155
Il se treuve peu de telz advocatz.

Esaie 53.   Doulx Jesuchrist, c'est à vous que je doy;
Hebr. 7.   Et vous payez et playdoiez pour moy.
Roma. 8.   Et qui plus est, quant paovre me voiez,
De vostre bien, ma grand debte payez.   1160
O de bonté, mer, abisme, et deluge,
Vous mon pere, daignez estre mon juge
Ezech. 18. Qui ne voulez veoir la mort du pecheur.
Matth. 4.   O Jesuchrist, des ames vray pescheur
Et seul sauveur, amy sur tous amys,   1165
Mon advocat icy vous estes mys,
Parlant pour moy, me daignant excuser,
Où me povez justement accuser.
    Plus je ne crains de nul estre deffaicte,
Car justice est du tout satisfaicte.   1170
Mon doulx espoux en a faict le payement
Si suffisant et tant abondamment,
Que justice de moy ne poeut vouloir
Riens que de luy elle ne puisse avoir;
1. Pet. 2. Car il a prins tous mes pechez sur soy,   1175
Et m'a donné ses biens, comme je croy.
    Quant voz vertuz, mon seigneur, presentez,
Certes, assez justice contentez.
Quant mes vices el' me veult reprocher,
Vous luy monstrez qu'en vostre propre chair   1180
Vous les avez portez de bon courage
Par l'union de nostre mariage;
Et sur la croix par vostre passion
En avez faict la satisfaction.
Et, qui plus est, par vostre charité   1185
M'avez donné ce qu'avez merité.

And what is more, I see that none other than
Jesus Christ is my plaintiff, who is my redeemer,
and who, by his death, has returned to us
our birthright. He has made himself   1150
our advocate before God,
offering up virtues of such worth
that my debt is more than paid
and thus entirely expunged at the time of my judgment.
    My redeemer, this is worthy of note.   1155
Such advocates are rare.
Sweet Jesus, I am beholden to you
and yet you plead my case and pay my debt.
Moreover, seeing me destitute,
from your boundless resources you redeem me.   1160
Oh, generosity, as boundless as sea, abyss, and flood.
You, my father, unwilling to see the death of any sinner,
deign to be my judge.
Jesus, true fisher of souls,
unique savior, friend above all friends,   1165
my advocate, you have been placed here
to speak on my behalf and to forgive
where you could easily have accused.
    I no longer fear the danger of anything,
for wrong has been put right.   1170
My dearest husband has paid the debt
so amply and so abundantly
that justice can ask nothing of me
that has not been forfeited by him,
for he has taken upon himself all my transgressions   1175
and, as I earnestly believe, given me of his bounty.
    When, my Lord, you offer your inestimable worth,
justice is paid in full.
When justice seeks to reproach me my failings,
you prove that with your very flesh   1180
and through the union of our marriage,
you have taken them upon yourself with courage.
By your passion on the cross
you have fully redeemed me.
By love you have given me   1185
the merit that was rightly yours.

Parquoy voyant vostre merite mien,
Psal. 84. Justice plus ne me demande rien;
Mais sa soeur, Paix (comme toute appaisee
Vous regardant) est doulcement baisee.   1190
  Du jugement n'auray donc plus de crainte,
Mais par desir trop plus que par contraincte
L'heure j'attentz que mon juge verray,
Et jugement juste de luy auray.
Si je sçay bien que vostre jugement   1195
Est si juste, qu'il ne fault nullement,
Et congnois bien mon infidelité,
Digne d'enfer et sa crudelité.
Si seulement mon merite regarde,
Rien je ne voy qui de ce feu me garde,   1200
Il est tout vray qu'il n'est que pour le diable,
Et n'est point faict pour l'homme raisonnable;
Mais toutesfois, s'il a mys son estude
De l'ennemy prendre similitude,
C'est bien raison que (comme luy) il soit   1205
Retribué du loyer qu'il reçoit.
  Car si l'homme, par contemplation,
Amour, vertu, bonté, perfection,
Tient de l'ange et à la fin herite
Au ciel, le lieu de semblable merite,   1210
Le vicieux en enfer est puny
Sapien. 18. Avec celluy à qui il s'est uny.
Puis qu'à Satan du tout s'est comparé,
Matth. 25. Il tient le lieu qui luy est preparé.
Cecy bien peu mon esperit conforte,   1215
Pensant des deux la differente sorte
Nier ne puis qu'au maulvais ne ressemble
Trop plus qu'au bon: parquoy je crains et tremble;
Car de l'ange la vie est si celeste
Que rien n'en tiens: cela je le proteste;   1220
Mais de l'aultre, j'en ay tant de semblance,
Tant de malice, et tant d'accoustumance,
Que de son mal, sa peine, et son tourment,
Participer doib par vray jugement.
  Grand et trop grand est le cruel peché   1225
Qui en enfer a mon cueur attaché.

Thus seeing me joined to your preeminence,
justice asks no more of me.
But her sister, Peace (appeased
in your presence), is gently embraced.   1190
    I no longer fear judgment,
but more by choice than by force,
await the hour when I will see my true judge
and receive his just verdict.
I know your rulings to be just   1195
and in all ways equitable,
and I also acknowledge my own infidelities,
worthy of the torments of hell.
If I look only upon my merit,
I see nothing that would save me from damnation.   1200
Hell surely was intended for the devil
and not any reasonable person.
And yet, if one has devoted oneself
to imitating the enemy,
it is only reasonable that (like him)   1205
he should get his just deserts.
    For if man is by meditation,
love, virtue, goodness, and perfection
similar to angels and in the end inherits
in heaven a place of similar merit,   1210
then the reprobate ought to be punished in hell
in the company of the one with whom he has joined forces.
Since he has modeled himself on Satan,
he should go where he belongs.
This nowise gives me comfort.   1215
Viewing the two different categories,
I cannot deny that I resemble far more the sinner
than the saint, and so am anxious and tremble.
I must firmly maintain that I have no likeness
to the celestial life of the saint.   1220
And as for the other, I am so similar,
so equal in evil and so much a disciple,
that because of his malevolence,
I ought to share in his sentence of pain and torment.
    And just so powerful is the terrible sin   1225
which has drawn my heart into darkness.

Enfer est fort, ne laissant rien saillir,
Ny ne craingnant qu'on le vienne assaillir.

Luc 11.   Le fort est fort; mais quant le plus fort vient,
Le fort ne sçait que sa force devient.   1230
Peché est fort, qui en enfer nous meine;
Et ne voy nul qui, par merite ou peine,
Ayt jamais sceu vaincre et tuer ce fort,
Fors celluy seul qui a faict tel effort

Philip. 2   Par charité, que mort humilié,   1235
Ephese. 4.   Son ennemy a vaincu et lyé,
Enfer rompu, et brisé son povoir,
Dont maintenant ne poeut puissance avoir
De plus tenir captive et en tutelle
La paovre ame qui est à Dieu fidele.   1240
        Par quoy croiant de luy la grand vertu,
Enfer, peché, je n'estime ung festu.
Dequoy me nuyst peché, sinon de mieulx
Monstrer mon Dieu misericordieux,
Fort et puissant, entierement vainqueur   1245
De tout le mal qui est dedens mon cueur.
Si mon peché pardonné est, la gloire
De mon saulveur, pareillement puis croire,
Et la mienne en est donc augmentee,
Puis qu'en luy suis inseree et entee,   1250
Son honneur seul honore tous les siens,
Sa richesse remplit chascun de biens.
        Enfer est donc par luy du tout destruyt,
Peché vaincu, qui tant a eu de bruit.
Puant enfer, où est vostre deffence?   1255
Villain peché, où est vostre puissance?

1. Cor. 15. O Mort, où est icy vostre victoire,
Vostre aiguillion, dont tant est de memoire?
En nous cuidant donner mort, donnez vie;
Le contraire faictes de vostre envie.   1260
        Et vous Peché qui à damnation
Voulez tirer tous, sans remission,
Vous nous servez d'esperon et d'eschelle
Pour atteindre Jerusalem tresbelle,
Cuidant faire par maligne nature   1265
Au createur perdre sa creature.

Hell is relentless, allowing no one to escape
and fearing no counterattack.
The powerful one is powerful, but when the still more powerful arrives,
his strength is as nothing.[30]   1230
The sin that leads us into hell is mighty
and I cannot envision anyone who by wit or will
has ever been able to overcome and kill this great force
save the one who made such an effort
for the sake of love that having died humiliated,   1235
he conquered and shackled his enemy,
and destroyed his netherworld. His authority crushed,
the devil can no longer have the power
to hold captive and under his tutelage
the poor soul who remains true to God.   1240
    Thus believing in God's inestimable virtue,
I care not a wit for sin and hell.
Sin can do no harm; it merely draws attention
to a compassionate, strong, and authoritative God,
who has completely undone the evil   1245
that was buried in my heart.
If my transgressions are pardoned,
I can believe in the glory of my savior,
and my own glory is thereby increased.
Since I am entirely in and of him,   1250
his honor, singularly bestowing honor on his own,
enriches each and every one.
    He has completely vanquished hell
and conquered sin, which had enjoyed so much favor.
Foul-smelling underworld, where now is your defense,   1255
and villainous sin where now your power?
Death, where is your victory,
your long-remembered sting?
Thinking you have given us death, you have given life.
You have managed the very contrary of your wishes.   1260
    And you, Sin, who wish to condemn us all
without remission,
you act as our spur and ladder
to reach beautiful Jerusalem,
thinking you will by cunning   1265
cause the creator to lose his creation.

Par sa grace advancez son retour,
Et à son Dieu la faictes, par amour,
Plusque jamais revenir humblement,
Roma. 5   Et le servir et aymer doublement.   1270
Sa grand bonté vous faict perdre la peine
Que vous prenez le long de la sepmaine.
Parquoy enfer n'a pas eu tout le nombre
Qu'il pretendoit par vous, pource que l'umbre
Et la vertu de ceste passion   1275
Est à l'ame telle protection,
Qu'elle ne doibt avoir ne peur ne doubte
De mort, peché, ne d'enfer une goutte.
     Y a il riens qui me puisse plus nuyre,
Si Dieu me veult par foy à luy conduire?   1280
Ephes. 2.   J'entens la foy toute telle qu'il fault,
Digne d'avoir le nom du don d'enhault:
Foy, qui unist par charité ardente
Au createur sa treshumble servante.
Unie à luy je ne puis avoir peur,   1285
Peine, travail, ny ennuy, ne douleur;
Car avec luy croix, mort, et passion
Ne poevent estre que consolation.
Trop foyble suis en moy, ny assez forte,
Philip. 4.   Et si puis tout en luy qui me conforte.   1290
Son amour est si ferme et permanable
Que pour nul cas elle n'est variable.
     Qui sera ce donc qui me tirera
De sa grace et m'en separera?
Certes, du ciel la tresgrande haulteur,   1295
Ny de l'enfer l'abisme et profundeur,
Ny la largeur de toute ceste terre,
Mort, ne peché, qui tant me font de guerre,
Ne me pourront separer ung seul jour
De la grande charité et amour   1300
Que mon pere, par Jesuchrist, me porte;
Car son amour est de si bonne sorte,
Roma. 5.   Que sans l'aymer il m'ayme, et est l'aymant
1. Cor. 14.   Par son amour (sans l'aymer) doublement.
Mon amour n'est pour l'aymer, mais la sienne   1305
En moy ame, que je sens comme mienne.

Thanks to his grace, you encourage her return
and because of love lead her back to her God,
more humble than ever
and doubly ready to serve and love.   1270
His infinite kindness nullifies the efforts
you exert all week long.
And so hell has not been able to gather in
as many as desired, since the virtuous presence
of our Lord's passion   1275
has been such an effective shield to the soul
that it need neither fear nor be anywise alarmed
about death, sin, or hell.
    Is there anything which can harm me
while faith in God draws me to him?   1280
I understand faith just as it is necessary to understand it,
as worthy of having the name of a gift from on high:
a faith which through burning love
unites a humble servant to his creator.[31]
In league with him, I need not suffer   1285
terror, pain, travail, hurt or sorrow.
Because of him, the cross, death, and the passion
can only mean comfort.
I myself am too weak, lack the necessary fortitude,
and thus it is his strength that gives me solace.   1290
His love is so firm and enduring
that nothing can unseat it.
    What then can possibly remove
his grace from me?
For certain neither the heavens above   1295
nor the deep abyss of hell below,
nor this enormous planet,
nor Death, nor sin which wages war against me
can ever separate me
from the bounteous love and devotion   1300
that through Christ, my father bestows upon me.
For his is of that kind of love
that loves without being loved,
loves doubly without being loved.
My love does not love him, but his love   1305
in me loves him, which I feel as my own.

Il s'ayme donc en moy et par m'aymer,
Il faict mon cueur par amour enflammer.
Par ceste amour il se faict aymer tant,
Que son effect (non moy) le rend content.   1310
Se contentant, tousjours il multiplie
Trop plus d'amour, qu'amour ne luy supplie.
        O vray aymant, de charité la source,
Et du tresor divin la seule bourse,
Doib je penser, ny oseroie je dire   1315
Que c'est de vous? le puis je bien escripre?
Vostre bonté, vostre amour se poeut elle
Bien comprendre de personne mortelle?
Et s'il vous plaist ung petit l'imprimer
Dedans ung cueur, le poeut il exprimer?   1320
Certes, nenny! car la capacité
N'est pour tenir la grande immensité
Qui est en vous, veu que vive raison
Nous monstre bien n'avoir comparaison
Psal. 14.   De l'infiny à la chose finie;   1325
Mais quant à luy par amour est unie,
Si remply est son riens d'ung peu de tout,
Qu'à declairer ne poeut trouver le bout.
Plus ha de bien qu'il n'en poeut soustenir,
Parquoy il croit tout le monde tenir.   1330
        Quant le soleil d'une seule estincelle
Aveugle l'oeil, sa grand lumiere celle;
Mais demandez à l'oeil qu'il a senty;
Il dira tout; mais il aura menty;
Car aveuglé de petite lumiere,   1335
Il ne poeut veoir la grand clarté entiere;
Et demeure toutesvoies si content,
Qu'il luy semble s'il en avoit autant,
N'estre puissant pour endurer
Ceste clarté qu'il ne poeut mesurer.   1340
        Aussi le cueur qui par façon subtile
Sent de l'amour de Dieu une scintille,
Treuve ce feu si grand et si terrible,
Si doulx, si bon, qu'il ne luy est possible
Dire que c'est d'amour; car ung petit   1345
Qu'il a senty, rend tout son appetit

He loves himself in me and by loving me,
he fills my heart with love.
In such loving he makes himself to be so loved
that its consequence (not mine) brings him joy.   1310
Making himself happy, he endlessly multiplies
greater love than love can give.
    True lover, source of all devotion,
the unique font of heavenly riches,
may I believe, dare I say   1315
that it comes from you? Am I able to write it?
Your munificence and love,
can a human heart understand them?
And whatever small amount you implant
in a heart, can the heart express it?   1320
Surely not. For it is not large enough
to contain your vastness.
Our human reason proves
that there can be no comparison
between an infinite and a finite thing.   1325
But when by love one is brought into union,
the small amount of the infinite so fills the finite
that one is not able to perceive its limits.
One so overflows with its content
that one thinks to contain the entire universe.   1330
    When a single ray of the sun blinds the eye,
it does not reveal its fullest power.
But ask the eye what it has felt
and it will say everything; but it lies.
For blinded by a little light,   1335
it cannot see the whole thing.
And yet it is so satisfied
that it seems, were it to have still more,
it would not be able to endure
that light whose limits it cannot measure.   1340
    In like manner the heart,
which experiences a hint of God's love,
finds its intensity so overwhelming,
so delicious, and so wonderful,
that it is not able to identify it as love.   1345
For the small amount that it feels,

Ecclesiast. 24 Si satisfaict et non moins desirant,
Que plus que semble, et vit en souspirant.
Le cueur sent bien que trop il a receu;
Mais tel desir en ce trop a conceu,   1350
Qu'il desire tousjours à recepvoir
Ce qu'il ne poeut, ny n'est digne d'avoir.
Indicible congnoist estre son bien,
Et veult le plus, où il ne congnoist rien.
Sentir ne poeut quel est son bien vrayement,   1355
Et si ne poeut penser son sentement.
        Le dire donc n'est pas en sa puissance,
Puis que du feu il n'ha la congnoissance.
Amour sçait bien, au vray, diffinir
Qui la cuide tant en son cueur tenir;   1360
Bieneureux est qui en ha tel excès
Qu'il poeut dire: Mon Dieu, j'en ay assez.
Qui l'a en soy, il n'en sçauroit parler:
(Craignant, partant, de la laisser aller)
Si non faisant l'edification   1365
De son prochain, à sa salvation.
        L'impossible me fera donques taire;
Car il n'est si parfaict ou bien austere
S'il veult parler de l'amour du treshault,
De sa bonté, doulceur, de ce qu'il vault,   1370
De sa grace, et de ce qu'à luy touche,
Qu'il ne ferme (baissant les yeulx) sa bouche.
        Moy doncques, ver de terre, moins que riens,
Chienne morte, pourriture de fientz,
Cesser doy bien parler de celsitude   1375
De ceste amour; mais trop d'ingratitude
Seroit en moy, si je n'en eusse escript,
Satisfaisant à trop meilleur esprit.
Car de celer les biens d'ung si bon maistre,
C'est ung crime, qui assez ne poeut estre   1380
A droict puny, sans l'eternel lycol.
Parquoy venez, o bieneureux saint Paul,
Actes 9 *et*
2. *Cor.* 12. Qui tant avez gousté de ce doulx miel,
Trois jours sans veoir, ravy jusques au ciel,
Satisfaictes mon ignorance et faulte.   1385
Qu'avez vous sceu de vision si haulte?

so completely satiates its needs,
that it fully believes itself to be living in ecstasy.
The heart realizes that it has gathered in too much,
but has developed such a powerful desire, 1350
that it wishes for more
than it can either absorb or that it merits.
Appreciating its ineffable pleasure,
it longs for more of what it does not understand.
It cannot comprehend its true happiness 1355
and thus cannot express its feelings.
    It is incapable of putting it into words,
inasmuch as it has no understanding of this ardor.
He knows well enough how to define love
who knows how to hold so much of it in his heart. 1360
Happy he who has so much
that he can say: God, I have enough.
Whoever possesses this love dares not speak of it,
(fearing to lose it)
save for the edification 1365
and salvation of his neighbor.
    Thus the impossible will keep me silent.
For there is no one so perfect or so severe,
who if he wishes to talk about the love of the most high,
of his goodness, sweetness, whatever he wishes, 1370
his grace, whatever touches him,
does not (lowering his eyes) become silent.
    I then, worm, less than nothing,
dead dog, rotting dung,
should cease talking about 1375
the immensity of this love.
But it would be ungrateful of me not to write about it
so as to give some pleasure to a better soul.[32]
To hide the bounty of so exceptional a master
would be a crime so great that only the eternal noose 1380
would be punishment enough.
Therefore, come, O blessed Saint Paul,
who has tasted so plentifully of this sweet honey,
blind for three days and in celestial ecstasy,
come and correct my ignorance and weakness.[33] 1385
What did you see during your heavenly vision?

Rom. 11.   Oyez qu'il dit: O immense haultesse,
          Du grand thresor de divine richesse
          De la source de toute sapience
          Et fonteine de divine science,   1390
          Voz jugementz sont incomprehensibles,
          Et voz voies, selon tous noz possibles,
          A tous noz sens investigables sont.
          O bon sainct Paul, voz parolles nous font
          Bien esbahir, que vous si tressçavant   1395
          D'ung tel secret ne parlez plus avant.
          Mais encores dictes: de ceste amour
          Qu'esperons nous en avoir quelque jour?
              Escoutez le, et voilà qu'il nous dit:
          Onques nul oeil d'homme mortel ne vit,   1400
          Ny aureille ne sceut jamais entendre,
          Ne dans le cueur, tant soit il bon, descendre
          Ce que Dieu a preparé et promiz
          A la parfin à tous ses bons amyz.
              N'en direz vous plus oultre? Certes non.   1405
          Ce qu'il en dit, encores n'est, sinon
          Pour nous faire estimer et aymer,
          Ce qu'il ne poeut declarer ne nommer,
          Tirant noz cueurs, nostre amour, et espoir
          A desirer ce qui ne se poeut veoir.   1410
          Que diz je veoir? mais penser, ny sentir:
          Qui rend content de mourir ung martyr.
              O tresgrand Don de foy, dont tel bien vient,
          Que posseder faict ce que l'on ne tient!
          Foy donne espoir par seure verité   1415
          Qui engendre perfecte charité.
1. Jean 4.   Et charité est Dieu, comme sçavons.
          Si en nous est, Dieu ainsi nous avons.
          Il est en nous, et trestous en luy sommes.
          Tous sont en luy, et luy en tous les hommes.   1420
          Si nous l'avons par foy, tel est l'avoir,
          Que le dire n'est en nostre povoir.
              Donques, puis qu'ung si tresgrand apostre
          Comme sainct Paul n'a voulu parler oultre,
          A l'exemple de sa tressage escolle,   1425
          Je tairay, mais suyvant sa parolle

Listen to his response: "O most heavenly expanse,
divine wealth from the great treasury,
source of all wisdom,
fountain of sacred science,   1390
your mind and your ways are,
according to our methods and means,
well beyond our understanding."
O most wonderful Saint Paul, you who are so wise,
you astonish us that your words go no further   1395
in interpreting the divine mysteries.
Tell us: What can we hope for
one day from this love?
     Listen to what he had to say:
"However worthy,   1400
no human eye has ever seen,
nor human ear ever heard
what God has prepared for
and promised to us for the end of time."
     Have you nothing further to add? "Nothing."   1405
What he has told us of the ineffable
serves to inspire our love and admiration,
that which he can neither declare nor name,
drawing our hearts, affections, and aspirations
toward what we cannot ourselves see,   1410
indeed, imagine, or feel:
the will to die as martyrs.
     O mighty gift of faith, from which such good comes,
that we possess what we do not have.
Faith gives hope of certain truth,   1415
which in turn engenders perfect love.
And, as we know, God is love.
And if that love abides in us, then so too does God.
He lives in us, and we in him;
we are all in him and he is in us.   1420
And if we possess him through faith,
such possession is not within our power to define.
     Since so great an apostle
as Saint Paul says no more,
following his example,   1425
I am silent.[34] But according to his promise

(Bien que pouldre je me confesse et fanges)
Ne puis faillir à rendre la louenge
De tant de biens qu'avoir je ne merite,
Qui luy plaist faire de moy sa Marguerite.   1430

1. Tim. 1. Au roy du ciel, immortel, invisible,
Seul Dieu puissant, et incomprehensible,
Soit tout honneur, gloire, louenge, amour
Par les siecles des siecles sans sesjour.
AMEN

(though I be but dust and dirt),
I cannot fail to give thanks
for the many undeserved blessings
he deigns to bestow on his Marguerite.   1430
To the heavenly, eternal, and invisible God,
all-powerful and beyond understanding,
be honor, glory, praise, and love,
world without end.
AMEN.[35]

III
LA COCHE / THE COACH

Marguerite de Navarre spent the spring of 1541 in Cauterets, a spa in the Pyrenees where she went to relax, take care of her rheumatism, and recover from the court intrigue that so tired her. This was a particularly difficult year for Marguerite; her brother had arranged the marriage of her daughter, Jeanne, to the duke of Clèves, and neither Marguerite, Henri d'Albret, nor Jeanne herself had much enthusiasm for this political arrangement designed to build up the king's alliances against the Holy Roman Emperor. The months between July 1540, when the marriage contract was signed, and the spring of 1541 were filled with secret negotiations between the king of Navarre and Charles V over a possible marriage of Jeanne with Charles's son, Philippe. Marguerite was caught between her husband and her brother during this time, arguing for each case to the opposing party and having to succumb, in the end, to carrying out the king's wishes against those of both her husband and her daughter. The marriage took place in June of 1541. Sometime during that year, Marguerite composed for presentation to the duchess of Étampes, the king's mistress, a 1,401-line poem about friendship among women.

Marguerite is the narrator of the poem, and the fatigue and alienation she must have felt during this trying time are represented in the attitude of her character at the beginning of the poem. She finds herself walking away from the court to find solace in nature. She ends up meeting with three friends who are also seeking solace away from the court. While Marguerite never talks about her own suffering as narrator, her three friends reveal to her the pains they have suffered in love as well as the bonds of friendship that sustain them.

Marguerite sets out to discover which of the three suffers the most, agreeing with their request that she write down their arguments. Each woman explains her situation and contends that she bears the greatest pain. The first lady feels as though her lover has abandoned her even though he insists he still loves her. She is tormented by her doubt. The second lady has truly been abandoned by her lover; he has declared his love to the first lady. Finally, the third lady has decided to abandon her perfect lover so that she can suffer in solidarity with her two friends. The women agree to give their debate over to the duchess for judgment.

The poem is structured in the tradition of the debate poem, a medieval form that was abundantly popular in fourteenth- and fifteenth-century France. The popularity of the form was waning at the time that Marguerite wrote her poem, and she was surely inspired by her predecessors of the past two centuries. Her most immediate influence is mentioned in the poem itself, Alain Chartier. His *Belle dame sans merci* (Beautiful Lady Without Mercy) was written in debate form as well as his *Livre des quatre dames* (Book of Four Ladies, 1415) which poses the same question as *The Coach*: which of the women telling her story has suffered the most because of her beloved? The frame of these debate poems is similar and descends from Guillaume de Machaut's *Jugement du Roy de Behaingne* (Judgment of the King of Bohemia, 1340). The setting is pastoral; the poet is walking alone when he comes upon a group of strangers debating a question on love. When the debate remains unresolved at its end, the poet offers to deliver it to a person of distinction who will sit in judgment.

Marguerite distinguishes herself from Alain Chartier in two important ways in her frame. First, while Chartier depicts himself as a melancholic lover seeking distraction from his sorrow, Marguerite realistically portrays herself as an older woman who has lost all interest in matters of the heart. She even visits briefly with a local peasant, inquiring about his family and work, a gesture in keeping with her role as queen. And while Chartier is consoled by the beauty of the scenery around him, Marguerite is untouched by the same beauty; her sorrow is too deep to be so easily unseated.

It is perhaps Christine de Pizan who was the inspiration for the most original detail in *The Coach*. In her *Dit de Poissy* (Story from Poissy), she relates, as poet, the debate of two traveling companions, friends whom she knows well. Marguerite also meets up with friends rather than strangers and emphasizes the intimacy of their relationship. This intimacy allows Marguerite to write about the reflection of suffering between herself and her companions without revealing her own story hinted at in the beginning of the poem. Her fifteenth-century predecessors, especially Christine de Pizan, must also have been inspiration for the suffering female voice, unusual in the tradition of courtly love. Women were more typically objects of veneration in this tradition, often indifferent or hostile toward their suitors, not usually talking subjects who are just as devoted to love as men.

While Marguerite's poem is original in a number of ways, then, the most striking element here is the exposition of an *amitié d'alliance* among the three women. Marguerite proposes such an alliance as the remedy against the alienation and powerlessness women feel in literary and social milieus. In Marguerite's poem this oath of friendship translates into the creation of a female community whose purpose is to act as readers of other women's stories and to mediate the introduction of these stories into court culture. Marguerite builds her argument on a transformation of the concept of *couverture*. Traditionally women are expected to "cover" themselves in silence; the literary domain does not belong to them. Marguerite argues that women should, on the contrary, "cover" themselves with their writing. This redefinition of *couverture* involves two levels of "covering." The first is the power to represent oneself and one's experience through writing. The writing of one's own story gives the author the power to recreate herself and her life through the text, and thus to "cover" herself with her own interpretation of that life. The second *couverture* is that of the female community which provides a safe place in which a woman can tell her story without fear of losing her honor. Healing takes place through this series of *couvertures* in which each of the storytellers in *La coche*—three women as well as the narrator—creates a protective distance from her narrative through the female community. For example, rather than telling her own story of loss to which she refers at the beginning of the poem, Marguerite tells the stories of the other women. These women tell their stories orally to another woman but wish to have them written down by her to be read at court. The community of women supports the telling of tales as well as the act of writing. The strong identification among the women is established in *La coche* through a gendered rewriting of the literary tradition of *amitié d'alliance*. In emphasizing friendship among women, Marguerite uses the tradition of *amitié d'alliance* to question the social structures that alienate women not only from court society and courtly literature but also from each other.[1]

1.   A version of a portion of this introduction appears as "Reading a Woman's Story in Marguerite de Navarre's *La coche*," *Explorations in Renaissance Cultures* 31, no. 2 (Winter 2005): 279–303, and is reprinted with permission (copyright 2006 South-Central Renaissance Conference).

LA COCHE

Soit noté qu'en ce livre sont contenues unze hystoires jouxte le subject d'iceluy, lesquelles
hystoires sont devisées chascune en son endroict. Et icy est la premiere où est ung pré dedans
lequel est une compagnie d'hommes et femmes se esbatans. Au bout duquel pré est une femme
acoustrée comme la Royne de Navarre, cheminant par une petite sente loing des autres. Et
contre une haye qui est le long dudict pré est ung bon homme de village vestu de grix auquel
parle ladicte dame.

Ayant perdu de l'aveuglé vaincueur
Non seullement le sentement du cueur,
Mais de son nom, dictz et faictz la memoire,
Ayant perdu le pouvoir et la gloire,
Et le plaisir de la doulce escripture,   5
Où tant je fuz incline de nature,
Me trouvant seulle en ung lieu si plaisant
Que le hault ciel se rendoit complaisant
Par sa doulceur et par sa temperance
A la verdure du pré plein d'esperance   10
Environné de ses courtines vertes,
Où mille fleurs à faces descouvertes
Leurs grandz beaultez descouvroient au soleil,
Qui, se couchant à l'heure, estoit vermeil
Et laissoit l'air sans chault ny froid, si doulx   15
Que je ne sçay cueur si plein de courroux
De ire et d'ennuy, qui n'eust eu guarison
En ung tel lieu, fors moy, qui sans raison
Fuyant les gens me retiray à part,
Pour n'avoir plus à leur passetemps part,   20

THE COACH

Let it be noted that this book contains eleven stories that make up The Coach, *each of which is told in its proper order. Here is the first, which takes place in a meadow where a company of men and women are enjoying themselves. At one end of the meadow there is a woman, dressed like the queen of Navarre, who is walking on a little path far from the others. Standing by a hedge bordering the meadow, there is a man from the village dressed in gray to whom the woman speaks.[2]*

Having lost not only the ability to love
but also the memory of the name,
the words, and the deeds of that blind conqueror,
having lost the power, the glory,
and the sweet pleasure of writing,   5
to which I am naturally inclined,
I found myself that day in a place so pleasant
that the heavens would be calmed
by its sweetness and warmth.[3]
The greenery of the meadow, full of hope,   10
was surrounded by curtains
on which thousands of blossoming flowers
uncovered their beauty to the sun,
which, a beautiful red as it set,
left the air neither hot nor cold, just sweet.[4]   15
I know of no heart so full of anger,
rage, and sorrow that it would not find solace
in such a place. Except mine;
I fled the company of others for no reason,
withdrawing from taking part in their pastimes,   20

Car cueur qui n'a de plaisir une goutte,
D'en veoir ailleurs il a peine sans doubte.

Par une sente où l'herbe estoit plus basse
Me desrobay, comme femme non lasse,
Hastivement, pour n'estre point suyvie,   25
Car de parler à nul n'avoye envie
En mon chemin je trouvay ung bon homme;
La m'arrestay en luy demandant comme
L'année estoit et qu'il en esperoit,
Qu'il avoit faict, qu'il faisoit, qu'il feroit   30
De sa maison, femme, enfans et mesnage,
De son repos et de son labourage,
Prenant trop plus de plaisir à l'ouyr
Qu'en ce que plus me soulloit resjouyr.

Cy endroict est la seconde hystoire laquelle contient le mesme pré beau et verd, au bout
duquel est ung hault boys separé d'un ruysseau, duquel boys sortent troys dames, toutes
vestues de noir, ayans leurs cornettes basses, leurs touretz de naiz et leurs colletz haultz,
toutes troys d'une grandeur et d'une sorte, les testes baissées vers la terre; à l'autre bout
dudict pré est encore la Royne de Navarre parlant au bon homme et soy retournant devers
lesdictes dames comme si elle s'advanceoit pour aller devers elles.

Ainsi parlant, pensant toute seulle estre,   35
Je veis de loing troys dames apparestre,
Saillans d'un boys hault, foeillu et espais,
Dont ung ruysseau trescler, pour mettre paix,
Entre le boys et le pré se mectoit.
Portant le noir et l'une et l'autre estoit   40
D'une grandeur; colletz, touretz, cornettes
Couvroient leurs colz, leurs visaiges et testes.
Leurs yeulx je vey vers la terre baissez,
Et de leurs cueurs par trop d'ennuy pressez
Sailloient souspirs dont tout l'air raisonnoit,   45
Mais ung seul mot leur bouche ne sonnoit.
Leur marcher lent monstroit bien que tristesse
Rendoit leurs piedz agravez de foiblesse.

Lors quant je vey ung si piteux object,
Pensé en moy que c'estoit ung subject   50

probably because a heart that contains no pleasure
is pained to see it in others.[5]

I stole away on a path where the grass was worn,
quickly, like a woman who is not wearied,
so as not to be followed,   25
because I did not wish to speak with anyone.
On the path, I met a man from the village
and I stopped to ask him how the year was going
and what his hopes were for it.
I asked how his house, his wife, his children, and household   30
were doing and what plans they had for the future;
I asked about his work and his leisure.
I took more pleasure from this conversation
than from those I am more used to enjoying.[6]

*Here is the second story that takes place in the same beautiful, green meadow at one end of
which there is a large wooded area separated from the meadow by a stream. Three ladies
dressed in black come out of the woods, wearing shadows, mufflers, and high collars.[7] All
three are of the same stature and attitude, their heads down. At the other end of the meadow,
the queen of Navarre is still talking to the man from the village as she turns in the direction
of the three ladies as though she is going to proceed toward them.*

As I was speaking to the man,   35
thinking that I was the only other one in the meadow,
I saw three ladies appear from afar.
They emerged from a large, leafy, thick woods,
peacefully separated from the meadow by a clear stream.
They were wearing black, and all were of the same stature.   40
Their collars, mufflers, and shadows
covered their necks, faces, and heads.
I saw that their eyes were turned toward the ground,
and the air resonated with the sighs that their hearts,
burdened by too much sorrow, projected.   45
Not a word sounded from their mouths.
Their gait was weakened by a sadness
reflected in the slow pace.

When I saw such a pitiful object,
I thought to myself that this was a subject   50

Digne d'avoir ung Alain Charretier
Pour les servir comme elles ont mestier.
Car moy qui ay trop grande experience
Povoys tresbien juger soubz patience
Leur passion tresextreme estre close: 55
J'ay maintes foys soustenu telle chose!
Qui me feist lors desirer de sçavoir
Si pis que moy elles povoient avoir.

En ce desir vers moy les vey venir,
Tousjours leurs yeulx contre terre tenir,   60
Que j'apperceu, quand furent près de moy,
Jecter ruysseaulx dont ne puys ny ne doy
La verité trop estrange celer,
Car je les vey comme ung fleuve couller.
Je feis du bruyt, dont elles m'adviserent   65
Et l'une à l'autre ung petit deviserent;
En essuyant leurs yeulx secretement
Vindrent vers moy, me disans doulcement:

Cy endroict est la tierce hystoire contenant les mesmes pré et boys et les troys dames
parlantes à la Royne de Navarre, leurs touretz de naiz baissez au dessoubz du menton, la
Royne faisant contenance de les voulloir mener et pourmener dans ledict pré.

« Il vous seroit, Madame, mieulx duisant
Parler à nous qu'à ce fascheux paisant. »   70
Mais quant je vey descouvers leurs visages,
Ausquelz Nature avoit faict telz ouvrages
Qu'à leurs beaultez nulle aultre n'approchoit,
Il me sembla que Nature pechoit
D'avoir laissé amortir leur couleur,   75
Car je ignoroys encores leur douleur.
Je congneu lors que c'estoient les troys dames
Que plus j'aymois, de qui Dieu corps et ames
Avoit rempliz de vertuz, de sçavoir,
D'amour, d'honneur, autant qu'en peult avoir   80
Nul corps mortel, de bonté et de grace.
Mais de beaulté l'une l'autre ne passe,
Ny de façon, parolle et contenance.
Leur trinité, sans nulle difference,

worthy of an Alain Chartier
to serve them as they need.[8]
For I, who have much experience in such matters,
could judge well that an extreme emotion
was hidden under their calm facades.   55
Many times I've endured such a thing,
and I wanted to know then
if they could be in a worse state than I.[9]

As I stood watching and wanting to know more,
I saw them come toward me with their eyes still down.   60
I noticed when they got closer to me
that from their eyes flowed streams of tears,
a strange truth I neither can nor should hide,
for I saw them flow like a river.
I made a noise and they noticed me.   65
After briefly consulting each other
and secretly wiping their eyes,
they came over to me, speaking softly:

*Here is the third story that takes place in the same meadow and woods. The three ladies
speak to the queen of Navarre, their mufflers down under the chin. The queen gives the
impression of wanting to lead them to the meadow to walk.*

"It would be more pleasant for you, Madame,
to talk to us rather than this tedious peasant."   70
When I saw their faces uncovered,
formed by Nature so that
no other came close to their beauty,
it seemed to me that Nature had sinned
in letting the color deaden,   75
for I did not yet know their suffering.
I recognized then that they were the three ladies
whom I loved above all, whose bodies and souls
God has filled with as much virtue, knowledge,
love, honor, goodness, and grace   80
as any human body could possess.[10]
Yet, not one exceeds the others
in beauty, form, word, or countenance.
Through the harmony[11] of their bodies, not one

Demonstroit bien par l'union des corps   85
Qu'Amour leurs cueurs unist par doulx accords.
Croyez pour vray que pitié et desir
De soulaiger leur couvert desplaisir
Me contraignit leur dire en soupirant:
« Ung mal caché va tousjours empirant,   90
Et, s'il est tel qu'il ne puisse estre pire,
Il s'amoindrist quelque foys à le dire.

Moy donc jugeant par trop apparens signes
Que vous portez le mal dont n'estes dignes,
Je vous requier par l'Amour qui commande   95
Sur tous bons coeurs, octroyez ma demande
Et dictes moy la douleur et la peine
Que vous souffrez, dont chacune est si pleine
Que sans mourir ne la povez porter.
Si je ne puis au moins vous conforter,   100
Je souffriray par grant compassion
Avecques vous la tribulation.
Vous estes troys, il vault mieulx estre quatre
Et nous aller dedens ce pré esbatre.
Et ne craignez privéement parler,   105
Car comme vous je promectz le celer. »

« Las! ce n'est pas par doubte de secret
Que nous craignons compter nostre regret,
Lequel vouldrions estre par vous escript.
Mais nous voyons maintenant vostre esprit   110
Si paresseux, si fasché ou lassé
Que ce n'est plus celuy du temps passé;
Qui nous faict peur que la peine d'entendre
Nostre malheur reffuseriez de prendre. »

« Dames, pour Dieu, n'attribuez à vice   115
Si j'ay laissé long temps a cest office,
Pensant pour vray qu'Amour n'avoit obmis
Ung seul des tours qu'il faict en ses amys
Qu'en mes escriptz passez ne soit trouvé
Et de mon temps veu, ouÿ ou prouvé. »   120
Et si leur dis: « je reprendray la plume

different from the others, these women formed a trinity   85
that showed that Love had joined their hearts with sweet accords.[12]
Please believe that it was true compassion
and the desire to sooth their hidden pain
that moved me to say to them with a sigh:
"A hidden pain will always worsen,   90
and if it is as bad as it can be,
it sometimes lessens with the telling.

Judging by appearance,
you endure pain you do not deserve;
I ask, through Love which rules over all good hearts,   95
that you grant my request
and tell me about the pain and grief that you suffer
and which fill each of you so much
that only death could bring respite.
If I cannot comfort you,   100
at the very least I offer you compassion
in suffering the pain with you.
There are three of you; it is better to be four
and take pleasure in going to the meadow together.
And do not be afraid to speak openly,   105
for I promise to keep your suffering hidden, as do you."[13]

"Alas! It is not because we doubt you will keep our secret
that we fear telling our story.
In fact, we would like you to write it down.
But we see that your spirit is now so low,   110
so vexed or wearied
that it is no longer the same as it was in the past.
We are afraid that you would refuse
to take up the burden of hearing our misfortune."

"Ladies, in the name of God, do not blame me   115
if long ago I left behind the pleasure of writing.
I truly think that Love has not kept back
a single one of the tricks that he plays on his friends,
and these all can be found in my past writings
and seen, heard, or proven during my lifetime."[14]   120
And then I said to them: "I will take the pen up again

Et feray mieulx que je n'ay de coustume
Si le subject me voullez descouvrir. »

Ainsi disant vei leurs doulx yeulx couvrir
D'une nuée de larmes dont la presse   125
Les feist sortir par pluye trop espesse.
Me regardans me prindrent pour aller
Dedans le pré, où long temps sans parler
Allasmes loing. Et lors leur prins à dire:
« Si ne parlez, je n'ay garde d'escrire!   130
Pour Dieu tournez le pleur qui vous affolle
A descharger vostre ennuy par parolle. »
L'une me creut, non la moins vertueuse
Ny ennuyée, et dist à voix piteuse:

Icy est la quarte hystoire où sont la Royne de Navarre et lesdictes troys dames qui se
pourmenent ensemble par le pré; l'une desquelles dames parle à la Royne luy monstrant une
de ses compagnes. Et toutes troys ont leurs mouchouers chascune en sa main. Et les deux qui
ne parlent font contenance de fort plourer.

          « O vous Amans, si pitié jamais eut   135
Sur vous pouvoir de convertir en larmes
Voz tristes yeulx, si jamais douleur peut
          Brusler voz coeurs par ses cruelz alarmes,
Et si jamais Amour voz langues feist
Fondre, disant piteux et tristes termes,   140
          Oyez le plainct du cueur non desconfit,
Mais en mourant tousjours prest de porter
Ce que luy donne Amour, qui luy suffist.
          Nous sommes troys dont le reconforter
Impossible est, car sans nostre amytié,   145
Sans mort tel mal ne sçaurions supporter
          L'une de l'autre a egale pitié,
Egale amour, egale fantaisie,
Tant que l'une est de l'autre la moyctié.
          Entre nous troys n'y eut onc jalouzie   150
Oncques courroux, oncques diversité:
Si l'une a mal, l'aultre en est tost saysie.
          Du bien, aussi de la foelicité
L'une n'en a que l'autre n'y ait part,

and will do even a better job then usual
if you want me to make the subject of your story known."

As I was saying this I saw their eyes fill
with a heavy cloud of tears   125
that fell like a torrent.
Looking at me they took my arm to go into the meadow
where we walked a long while without talking.
And then I said to them:
"If you don't speak, I won't have to worry about writing!   130
For the love of God, use words to turn the lament
that is your undoing into a release of your grief."
One of them, not the least virtuous or distressed,
believed me, and said in a gentle, afflicted voice:

*Here is the fourth story where the queen of Navarre and the three ladies are walking
together in the meadow. One of the three ladies speaks to the queen, pointing out one of her
companions. All three have handkerchiefs in their hands, and the two who are not speaking
are crying profusely.*

　　"O you lovers, if ever compassion had power over you   135
to transform your cheerless eyes into tears,
if ever suffering was able to burn your hearts
　　　　with its cruel alarms,
and if ever Love melted your tongue
with pitiful and sad words,   140
　　　　then hear my heart's complaint.
It will not be defeated even in death and will always be ready to bear
that which Love gives to it, which satisfies it.[15]
　　　　We are three women who cannot be comforted,
for without either our friendship or death   145
we would not know how to bear such pain.
　　　　Each one of us feels the same torment,
the same love, the same desire;
each one of us completes the others.
　　　　There has never been jealousy among the three of us,   150
never anger, never division;
if one of us is in pain, the others are also completely taken by it.
　　　　Goodness and happiness
we share and share alike,

Pareillement part en l'adversité.   155
　　　Mort pourra bien des corps faire depart,
Mais nul malheur n'aura jamais puissance
De mectre ung cueur des deux autres à part.

　　　Or eusmes nous toutes troys joÿssance
Du plus grant bien qui peult d'amour venir   160
Sans faire en riens à nostre honneur offence.
　　　Helas que dur m'en est le souvenir,
En me voyant advenir le contraire
Du bien tresseur que je pensoys tenir!
　　　O fainct Amour, pour noz troys coeurs attraire,   165
Tu leur donnas la fin de leur desir
Que tu leur viens hors de saison substraire!
　　　Troys serviteurs telz que l'on doit choysir
Eusmes par Toy, dont la perfection
D'ung paradis nous estoit le plaisir.   170
　　　Beaulté, bonté, tresforte affection,
Tresferme amour, bon sens, bonne parolle,
C'estoit le pis de leur condition.
　　　Leur amytié n'estoit legiere ou folle;
Leur grace estoit saige, doulce, asseurée;   175
Et de vertu povoyent tenir escole.

　　　Par leur amour, grande et desmesurée
Noz coeurs aux leurs rendirent si unis
Que la douleur nous en est demourée;
　　　Car d'un tel heur furent si bien garnis   180
Qu'ilz n'eussent sceu jamais souhaitter mieulx;
Las, ilz en sont maintenant bien punis!
　　　Sur tous le mien, malheureux, ennuyeux,
Qui sent tresbien le coeur de son amy
Tout different du parler et des yeulx.   185
　　　O trop cruel et mortel ennemy
Qui veois mon cueur languir de telle sorte,
Que ne mectz tu ton espée parmy,
　　　En m'asseurant qu'à une autre amour porte
Et que de moy plus il ne te souvient?   190
Bien tost seroye ou consolée ou morte!
　　　Mais je ne sçay quel malheur te retient

just as we do adversity.   155
    Death could very well separate our bodies,
but no misfortune will ever have the power
to separate one of our hearts from the others.[16]

    Now, all three of us have had the pleasure
of the greatest good that can come from love,   160
without having done anything to offend our honor.
    Alas, the memory of this is so difficult for me;
just when I felt sure to possess the treasure of love,
I saw its opposite befall me!
    O cunning Love, in order to seduce our three hearts,   165
you gave them what they desired
only to come and take it away too soon.
    We received from you three servants,
exactly of the sort we should choose;[17]
their perfection was for us heavenly pleasure.   170
    Beauty, goodness, strong affection,
enduring love,[18] good sense, and elegant speech
were the worst they had to offer.
    Their friendship was neither easy nor foolish;
their grace was wise, sweet, and assured;   175
and they could have taught a lesson on virtue.

    Through their great and extraordinary love,
they so united our hearts to theirs
that the pain of the separation is still with us.[19]
    Our hearts were so well supplied with such happiness   180
that they would never have known to wish for better.
Alas, they[20] are well punished for that now!
    Especially mine; unhappy and vexed,
it knows so well that its lover's heart,
is different from his words and eyes.   185
    Oh, you cruel and mortal enemy
watching my heart languish like this!
Why don't you pierce it with a sword;
    why won't you tell me that you love another
and that your heart has forgotten me?   190
I would then soon be consoled or dead!
    But I don't know what pain is holding you back,

De m'en celer ainsi la verité,
Ou si à toy ou si à moy il tient.

A moy? Las non! Amour et Charité   195
Ont bien gardé mon coeur de t'offenser,
Comme toy moy, sans l'avoir merité.
    Je ne sceu onc nulle chose penser,
Que pour ton bien et honneur se peust faire,
Où l'on ne m'ait soubdain veue advancer.   200
    J'ay bien voullu mon ferme cours parfaire
Et te monstrer qu'amour leale et bonne
Tu ne sçaurois par ta faulte deffaire.
    De ton costé, o trop faincte personne!
Je ne sçay riens dont te puisse argüer,   205
Fors que ton coeur au mien plus mot ne sonne.
    De ton parler je ne voy rien müer:
Tu dis m'aymer ainsi qu'as de coustume,
Mais par mentir, je croy, me veulx tüer.
    Car en t'aymant ma vie je consume   210
Et en sentant que tu ne m'aymes point
Mon coeur se faict de patience enclume.
    Il est au tien, ainsi comme il fut, joinct
Et le tien non, bien qu'en mentant tu dis
Qu'il est tout mien et Dieu le te pardoint!   215
    Qu'est devenu le regard de jadis,
Qui messager estoit de ton fainct coeur,
A qui du mien jamais ne contredis?
    Et le parler qui par doulce liqueur
Le rendoit mol et foible à se deffendre,   220
Dont toy, Amy, demouroys le vaincueur?
    Tu dis m'aymer? Mais qui le peult entendre,
Quant tous les tours et les signes d'amour
En toy voy mors et convertiz en cendre?
    O malheureux pour moy ce premier jour   225
Où je cuidoys mon heur prendre naissance
Et pour jamais faire en moy son sejour!
    Or ne voy plus en toy forme ne essence
De ceste amour que je cuidoys si ferme;
Je n'en ay plus tant soit peu congnoissance.   230
    J'ay bien doubté souvent, je le t'afferme,

hiding the truth from me,
or if it's your fault or mine.[21]

    Mine? Alas, no! Love and Charity   195
have kept my heart from offending you,
as you have me; I do not deserve it.
    In the past I would only have to think of something
that could be done for your good and honor
and immediately I would set about advancing your cause.   200
    I truly wanted to complete my steady course
and prove to you that you could not purposefully
undo a loyal and good love.
    As for you, you impostor!
I have no proof with which to accuse you,   205
except that your heart no longer speaks a word to mine.
    I have not seen anything change in your speech;
you tell me that you love me just as you used to,
but it seems to me that you would kill me with your lies.
    My whole life is consumed in my loving you,   210
and enduring the constant blows of unrequited love,
my heart has become an anvil.
    My heart is yours, joined to you just as it was;
yours is not, however, even though, lying,
you say that it is all mine. May God forgive you this lie.   215
    What has become of that gaze you used to send my way,
a messenger from your false heart?
I always responded in kind.
    And of the speech that softened my heart with sweet nectar
and rendered it too weak to defend itself?   220
You, beloved, were always its conqueror.
    You say you love me? But who can believe it
when I see that all the gestures and signs of love
are dead and transformed into ashes?
    Oh, how sad it is now for me, that day   225
when I first thought my happiness had come into being
and would make its home with me forever.
    I no longer see in you either the form or the essence
of the love that I thought would endure;
I can no longer recognize it.   230
    I assure you that I have often wondered

Qu'en autre lieu eusses ton amour mise,
Qui t'eust mis hors de cest honneste terme.

    La vérité diligentement quise
J'ay sans cesser et trouvé pour certain   235
Que tu ne l'as encor en nulle assise.
    Qu'esse de toy? Sera ton amour vain?
Ou bien est il de toy du tout sailly?
Dictz le moy franc et me baille la main
    En me quictant, sans que j'aye failly   240
La foy promise et de moy bien gardée
Et non de toy, vaincu non assailly.
    Assez tu m'as hantée et regardée,
Mais en nul cas qui sceust ou peust desplaire
A ung amy, ne m'as veue hazardée.   245
    Or ne sçay je, malheureuse, que faire,
Puis que de toy ung mot ne puis tirer
De verité, qui me peult satisfaire.
    Je te voy triste et souvent souppirer;
Crainte me dit que ce n'est pas pour moy   250
Que ainsi te voy par douleur martyrer.
    Amour me dit que si et que sa loy
Permect telz cas pour mieulx faire la preuve
De ma tresferme et trop leale foy.
    Crainte veult bien que ung autre amy je treuve   255
Pour ne mourir en ce cruel tourment.
Amour deffend que je face amour neufve.
    Helas mon cueur, quel est ton sentement?
Es tu de luy aymé? Ou si aymer
Ung autre doibz? Diz le moy franchement: 260
    « Aymé ne suis, qui m'est cas trop amer,
Car je le sens, malgré son apparence;
O fainct Amy que tu es à blasmer!
    Aymer ne puis: je n'ay pas la puissance,
Car long temps a qu'en luy mis mon voulloir   265
Et en perdy du tout la joÿssance. »
    Las, coeur qui n'as d'un autre aymer pouvoir
Et d'estre aymé as perdu le plaisir,
Tu n'as pas tort de te plaindre et douloir!
    Regarde, Amy, si tu as le loysir,   270

whether you had placed your love elsewhere,
outside of our honest love.

    I've diligently and tirelessly sought out the truth
and I've found for certain   235
that you have yet to tell anyone.
    What has become of you? Will your love be indifferent?
Or has it completely left you?
Tell me frankly and give me your hand as you leave me.
    I have not failed you in the faith that I promised;   240
you have failed,
who were conquered but not assaulted.
    You have followed and watched me enough,
but you have never seen me try anything
that would displease a lover.   245
    But now I am miserable; I don't know what to do
since I can't get one word of truth from you
that would satisfy me.
    I see you sad, often sighing.
Fear tells me that it's not for me   250
that sorrow makes a martyr out of you.
    Love tells me 'yes,' it is so,
and that his law permits such cases
in order to better prove my solid and ever loyal faith.
    Fear wants me to find another lover   255
to prevent my death from such cruel torment.
Love forbids me to find new love.
    Alas, my heart, how do you feel?
Are you loved by him?
Or should you love another? Tell me frankly: 260
    'I am not loved, a bitter pill for me,
for I feel it despite appearances.
O false lover, you are to blame!
    I cannot love; I no longer have the strength;
for it has been such a long time that I've placed my desire in him   265
and I've lost all joy from it.
    Alas, heart that does not have the strength to love another
and has lost all the pleasure of being loved,
you are right to complain and to suffer!
    Look, my love, if you have the time,   270

S'il est tourment qui soit au mien semblable,
N'ayant nul bien, ny de nul bien desir?
  Je n'ay nul bien, te congnoissant muable,
Ny je n'en veulx, craignant de rencontrer
Amy de toy moins parfaict, variable.   275
  D'aussi parfaict l'on ne m'en peult monstrer,
Quant à beaulté, vertu et bonne grace,
Sur qui n'y ait nul vice à remonstrer.
  Et qu'un qui fust moindre que toy j'aymasse,
Plus tost mourroys que de m'y consentir: 280
Point ne mectray mon amytié si basse.
  Je ne me puis et me veulx repentir
De ceste amour: fermeté la tient forte,
Mais la douleur la veult aneantir.
  Fut il jamais malheur de telle sorte?   285
J'ayme ung amy qui dit m'aymer, mais quoy?
Je voy et sçay qu'amour est en luy morte.
  Laisser le doy, car clerement je voy
Qu'il est menteur; mais mon amour honneste
Ne me permect faire ce que je doy.   290
  Et tant que d'oeil, bouche, pied, main ou teste
Signe d'amour verray, rompre ne veulx
Ceste amytié prise à sa grant requeste.
  Si fermes sont les lyens et les noeudz
Que, si rompuz ilz sont de son cousté,   295
Ilz sont du mien encor entiers et neufz.

  Dames, croyez qu'il m'a bien cher cousté,
Ce faulx amy, et couste et coustera
Tant qu'à la mort coeur et corps soit boutté.
  La seulle mort de mon coeur oustera   300
L'amour de luy, qui sans luy me demeure,
Car autre amour mon coeur ne goustera.
  Et, qui pis est, ung autre ennuy sur l'heure
M'est survenu, qui le premier augmente,
Dont je ne suis pas seulle qui en pleure.   305
  Le serviteur de ceste vraye amante,
Qui tant long temps l'a aymée et servie
Qu'el'en estoit tresheuruese et contente,
  Enfin a eu de la laisser envie;

to see if there exist other torments like mine,
possessing neither riches nor the desire for riches.
    I possess no riches since I know you are inconstant,
nor do I want any for fear of meeting a lover
who is less perfect than you and fickle.   275
    No one could show me another man as perfect
in beauty, virtue, and grace
and in whom there is no vice to expose.
    I would rather die than consent
to loving someone inferior to you;   280
I will not lower my friendship to that level.
    I cannot nor do I want to repent of this love.
Steadfastness holds it tight,
but sorrow wants to destroy it.
    Has there ever been misery of this kind?   285
I love a lover who says he loves me,
but I see and know that love is dead in him.
    I need to leave him for I see clearly
that he is a liar; but my honest love
doesn't allow me to do what I must.   290
    As long as I will see a sign of love from eye, mouth,
foot, hand, or head, I don't want to break
this friendship that we entered into at his request.
    The bonds and knots are so solid
that even if they are broken from his side,   295
from mine they appear whole and new.[22]

    Ladies, believe me that this false lover has cost me greatly.
He still does and will continue to do so
until death separates heart and body.
    Only death will remove his love from my heart,   300
which stays with me even without him,
for my heart will not taste another love.
    And to make matters worse, another problem
has come up for me recently that makes the first problem greater;
and I am not alone to suffer from it.   305
    The beloved of this true lady,
who had loved and served her for a long time
making her very happy and satisfied,
    finally decided to leave her.

Dont de l'ennuy qu'el'en prend et a pris   310
J'ay bien grant peur qu'el'abrege sa vie.
    Il luy a dit, estant d'elle repris
Et bien inquis de sa mutation,
Qu'il est ainsi de mon amour espris.

    Moy qui sçavoys sa grande affection   315
Et devant qui faillir à sa maistresse
Eust crainct de peur de ma correction,
    Seroys je bien si meschante et traitresse
Le recevoir, voyant qu'il faict mourir
Par son peché ma compaigne en tristesse?   320
    J'aymeroye mieulx par mort me veoir perir
Qu'en la voyant porter si grant tourment
Je feisse riens pour ceste amour nourrir.
    En sa faveur je laisse entierement
Veoir et parler où se puisse atacher   325
L'oeil et le cueur d'un si meschant amant.
    Je l'aimoye tant et le tenoye si cher
Quant il l'aymoit, comme s'il m'eust aymée,
Mais maintenant ne le veulx approcher.
    S'amye estoit digne d'estre estimée,   330
Il devoit bien pour jamais s'i tenir,
Et elle aussi d'aymer n'estoit blasmée.

    Dames, celuy qui veult mien devenir
Je n'en veulx point et son amour me fache;
L'autre, que j'ayme, je ne puis retenir.   335
    L'un est meschant, trop variable et lasche,
Lequel me suyt et toujours je le fuys;
S'amye et moy avons trop ferme atache!
    Celuy me fuyt que j'ayme et que je suys,
Je l'ay perdu et si ne le puis croyre.   340
Helas jugez en quel travail je suis!
    Je n'ay plus rien sinon que la memoire
Du bien passé qui entretient mon dueil:
Je croy que nul n'a veu pareille hystoire.

    Or faictes donc, Madame, le recueil   345
De mes douleurs que n'ay voullu celer.

She is so taken by the pain of this   310
that I am afraid that she might end her life.
    When, in admonishing him, she asked him
why he had changed his mind,
he told her simply that he is taken with love for me.[23]

    I've always known of his great affection for her.   315
Thus, he was afraid of failing his mistress
for fear of my reprimand.
    Would I be such a traitor to take him in,
seeing that with his transgression
he is killing my friend with whom I suffer?   320
    I would rather see myself perish
than to see her suffer so greatly.
I do nothing to nurture this love.
    For her I let it be seen and said
where the eye and heart of such a wretched lover   325
can attach themselves.
    I loved him very much, and he was very dear to me
when he loved her, as if he had loved me,
but now I don't want to be near him.
    If his lady was worthy of being esteemed,   330
he should have stayed with her forever.
And she should not be blamed for having loved.

    Ladies, I want nothing to do with the one
who wants to become mine; his love annoys me.
The other one, whom I love, I can't hold on to.   335
    The first is worthless, too changeable and cowardly;
he pursues me and I flee him constantly.
His lady and I are too tightly bound.
    The one that I love and that I pursue flees me.
I've lost him and I cannot believe it.   340
Alas, judge the distress that I find myself in!
    I have nothing left but the memory
of past riches to sustain my mourning;
I doubt that anyone has ever heard such a story.

    Now, then, Madame, write the collection   345
of these sorrows I do not wish to hide.

Taire me fault ayant la lerme à l'oeil,
Car les souppirs empeschent le parler. »

Icy est la quinte hystoire où est une des troys dames levant les yeulx en hault comme pasmée
et couchée par terre, et une de ses compagnes la soustient par derrière en son gyron, et la
Royne de Navarre luy couppe son lacet. L'autre des dames prent la Royne par la main et
de l'autre main faict signe qu'elle veult parler à elle, et apparest le ciel et le soleil en couleur
telle qu'il est une heure avant son coucher.

Les yeulx levez au ciel, crevez de pleurs,   350
Jectans torrens dont arrousoit les fleurs,
Donna silence à sa bouche vermeille,
Car la douleur qui semblait nompareille
Faisoit sa voix par souppirs estoupper
Tant qu'il fallut destacher et coupper
Ses vestemens pour soulaiger son cueur,   355
Ou elle fust crevée de douleur.
Au bout d'un temps que nous l'eusmes tenue
Dessus le pré, elle fut revenue
Et si me dist: « Telle est ma maladie
Que qui a pis souffert que moy le dye. »   360
Lors se coucha près de moy morte et blesme,
Les autres deux feirent aussi de mesme,
Car ung chacun de leurs doulx cueurs sentoit
L'ennuy trop grant que la tierce portoit.
Moy qui d'un mal en veoye troys pleurer,   365
Dys: « Vous pourriez jusques au soir demeurer
En ce plourer que ne povez finer,
Et ne sçauriez me faire deviner
Qui de vous troys seuffre plus de martyre,
Si ne voullez le me dire ou escripre. »   370

Voyant du lict le soleil approcher,
Vint la seconde ma main prendre et toucher
Et me prier ne m'ennuyer d'attendre
Qu'elle me peust au long son compte rendre.
       « Je sens, dist elle,   375
Cent et cent foys douleur aspre et mortelle
Plus que ne faict, point ne fault que le cele,
       Nulle des deux,

I have to stop now; tears are coming to my eyes,
and my sighs prevent me from speaking."

*Here is the fifth story in which the lady who has just spoken falls back on the ground as
if she is fainting, her eyes reflecting the pain she feels. One of her companions supports her
around her waist from behind, and the queen of Navarre loosens her laces. The other lady
takes the queen's hand and indicates with her other hand that she wants to speak. The
position of the sun in the sky and its color indicate that it is one hour before sunset.*

Eyes raised to the heavens, the lady poured out a stream of tears,
watering the meadow flowers around her.   350
The tears silenced her crimson mouth,
for the pain that seemed unparalleled to her
broke up her voice with sighs,
so much so that the others had to loosen her clothing
to ease her breathing   355
or she might have died of pain.
After a moment of us holding her in the meadow,
she came to and said to me,
"Such is my suffering;
may she who has suffered worse than I speak."   360
She then lay down next to me, pale and exhausted.
The two others did the same,
for each one of their two hearts felt the heavy anguish
that the third carried within it.
And I, who saw all three cry of the one sorrow, said,   365
"You could continue to cry like this
without end into the night,
but you would never reveal to me
which of the three of you suffers the most
if you do not tell me or write it down for me."   370

Seeing that the sun was close to setting,
the second lady came to reach out and take my hand
and begged me to be patient
so that she could tell her story from beginning to end.
    "I feel," she said,   375
"a bitter and mortal pain;²⁴ I must not hide
that it is a hundred times worse than that
    of either of these two ladies.

Car le cruel, lequel nommer ne veulx
Amy, qui ha d'amour rompu les voeux,   380
    Certes n'est digne
Qu'à luy je parle ou que luy face signe,
Ny de plaisir, ny de colere mine.
    D'en dire mal,
De l'appeller traistre, faulx, desloyal   385
Et plus cruel que nul autre animal,
    Ce seroit peu
Pour amoindrir de mon courroux le feu.
J'ayme bien mieulx laisser jouer ce jeu
    A la premiere,   390
Qui de luy dire injure est coustumiere.
Elle luy est ainsi qu'une lumiere
    Devant ses yeulx.
Son cueur changeant, trop fainct et vicieux,
Elle congnoist et si luy siet bien mieulx   395
    De le blasmer
Que non à moy, car de desestimer
Celuy que tant l'on a voullu aymer
    N'est pas bien faict.
S'il est meschant, variable, imparfaict,   400
D'elle le voy si tresmal satisfaict,
    Si desdaigné,
Si reffuzé, desprisé, esloigné,
Qu'il a tresmal en ce cas besoigné
    D'aller à elle.   405
Pas ne pensoit la trouver si cruelle:
Elle le hait bien fort et ne luy cele
    Ses fascheux tours.
Elle le fuyt en tous lieux et tousjours.
Or a il bien maintenant le rebours   410
    De son attente.
Mais de son mal je suis si mal contente
Et en soubstiens douleur si vehemente
    Que plus n'en puis.
Je suis quasi dessus le bord de l'huys   415
De desespoir et ne crains profond puitz
    Ny haulte tour
Où voluntiers, sans espoir de retour,
Ne me jectasse pour deffaire l'amour,

For this cruel man, whom I do not want to call
my beloved, has broken the vows of love.   380
     It is certainly not dignified
that I speak of him or that I acknowledge him
with looks of either pleasure or anger.
     To speak badly of him,
to call him a traitor, false, disloyal,   385
the cruelest of creatures,
     would hardly be enough
to lessen the fire of my anger.
I prefer to leave this game
     to the first lady;   390
it is natural that she insult him.
To him, she is like a light
     before his eyes.
She knows his changing heart, weak and immoral,
and so it is more fitting for her   395
     to blame him
than it would be for me. For to scorn
the one that you truly wanted to love
     is not an honorable thing to do.
If he is mean, changeable, and imperfect,   400
I see that she gives him no satisfaction;
     he is so disdained,
so refused, despised, distanced,
that he acted very foolishly
     in going to her.   405
He did not think that he would find her so cruel.
She hates him greatly and does not hide from him
     her exasperation.
She flees him wherever and whenever she sees him.
Now he has the opposite   410
     of what he hoped.
But I am so unhappy about his sorrow;
I too bear a pain so intense
     that I can no longer endure.
I am near the threshold of despair   415
and I fear neither deep wells
     nor high towers
where I could throw myself with no hope of return
in order to undo this love.

La paction,   420
Le souvenir, memoire, affection
Qui de mon mal sont generation
      Si importable
Et, qui pis est, si irremediable
Qu'à ma doulleur n'en est nulle sembable.   425
      Je l'ay aymé
De si bon cueur, tant creu, tant estimé
Que cueur et corps estoit tout abismé
      En l'amytié
Que luy portoys; encor ay je pitié   430
D'ainsi le veoir puny et chastyé
      De son peché.

Helas, mon Dieu, comment s'est il fasché
De mon amour et ainsi detaché?
      Oncques offence   435
Je ne luy feis, fors que la resistence
Pour quelque temps, où il feist telle instance
      Et si honneste,
Qu'avec honneur je pouvoys sa requeste
Bien accorder. Et puis, par longue queste,   440
      Par long service,
Par forte amour qui faisoit son office,
Gaigna mon cueur, voyant le sien sans vice.
      O la victoire
Dont le vaincu recevoit telle gloire   445
Que le vaincueur! Helas, qui eust peu croire
      Qu'elle eust duré
Si peu de temps, ny que j'eusse enduré
Si longuement mal si desmesuré
      Sans souffrir mort?   450

Helas, jugez, mesdames, si son tort
N'est pas égal à l'amour qui trop fort
      Mon cueur tormente,
Et si autant ne suis leale amante
Comme il est faulx, dont, si je me lamente,   455
      J'ay bien raison.
En me cuidant tromper par trahyson,

The pact we made,   420
the memory of our past love,
the passion we shared,
    all magnify unbearably my sorrow.
And to make it worse, mine is so beyond repair
that it is not possible that anyone has ever felt such pain.   425
    I loved him so sincerely;
I put my faith in him and cherished and admired him so
that I was completely taken in, body and soul,
    by the friendship
that I carried for him. I still feel pity   430
to see him punished and chastised
    for his sin.

Alas, my God, how did it happen
that he tired of my love and became detached?
    I caused him no offense,   435
except to resist him for some time
during which he insisted
    so respectably
that I could easily and honorably
grant his wish. And then, through long pursuit   440
    and long service,
through a strong love that defined his duties,
he won my heart; I saw that his was without vice.
    O what victory
that gives to the conquered the same glory   445
as the conqueror! Alas, who would have thought
    that it would last
such a short time or that I would have to endure
this undue sorrow for so long
    without suffering death?   450

Alas! Ladies, judge whether his wrong
is not equal to the love, too great,
    that torments my heart.
And judge whether I am not as loyal a lover
as he is false; if I lament,   455
    I am right to do so.
He knowingly treated me treacherously;

Luy mesme a beu ceste amere poyson
    Qui tant le blesse.
Il est puny par beaulté et rudesse, 460
Mais son ennuy n'amoindrist ma tristesse,
    Car son cueur lasche
M'ennuye fort et me desplaist qu'il fasche
A celle là qui ne peult avoir tache
    D'avoir permis 465
Qu'il la servist: ailleurs son cueur a mis
Lequel ne peult endurer deux amys,
    J'en suis bien seure.
Son desplaisir avec le mien je pleure,
En la cherchant il la fasche à toute heure, 470
    Mais plus à moy
En me laissant, dont suis en tel esmoy,
En tel ennuy, où nulle fin ne voy,
    Qu'à bien grant peine
Se peult penser la douleur qui me meine: 475
Je me contrainctz, et rys, et foys la saine,
    Et je me meurs!
Ces dames cy qui congnoissent mes moeurs
Sçaivent quelz maulx, foiblesses et douleurs
    Je dissimule! 480
Dont au dedans le double en accumulle
Par desespoir qui sans fin me stimule
    De me donner
Du tout à luy. Mais peur d'abandonner
Ces deux me vient si treffort estonner 485
    Que mieulx veulx vivre
En ce tourment, sans en estre delivre,
Que leurs deux cueurs à tel ennuy je livre.
    Pour elles vis,
Et vivre veulx du tout à leur devis, 490
Et pour moy non; parquoy il m'est advis
    Que pis que morte
Chascun me peult tenir en ceste sorte,
Puis que la mort, qui seulle me conforte,
    Je veulx fouyr. 495
C'est tout mon bien, mais je n'en veulx joÿr

now he too has drunk the same bitter poison
    that hurts so.
He is punished by beauty and harshness.   460
Yet his troubles do not lessen my sadness,
    for his cowardly heart
troubles me greatly and it is displeasing to me
that he displeases my friend here
    who could never allow him   465
to serve her. She has placed her heart elsewhere,
and her heart cannot bear two lovers,
    of that I am sure.
I lament over her displeasure with him;
by seeking her out he constantly angers her.   470
    But he upsets me even more
by leaving me. There is no end in sight;
I am so troubled and distressed by this
    that only with great pains
is it possible to imagine the suffering that grips me.   475
I force myself to laugh and pretend to be in good health,
    and yet I am dying!
These women here who know my ways
know the sorrows, weaknesses, and sufferings
    that I hide!   480
It builds inside me, doubling
through the despair that constantly urges me
    to give myself to it
completely. But the fear of abandoning
these two women overwhelms me so strongly   485
    that I would rather live
in this torment without ever being freed from it,
than give their two hearts over to such pain.
    I live for them
and I want to live completely according to their will   490
and not for myself. This is why I am convinced that,
    as everyone can see,
I am in a state worse then death
since I want to flee the only thing that brings me comfort,
    death.   495
Death is the only help left me,

Que leurs deux corps je ne voye enfouyr
Avecques moy en noyre sepulture.
Noz troys malheurs me feront resjouyr
D'estre assemblez soubz une couverture. »   500

Cy endroit est la sixiesme hystoire pareille à la quinte, fors que la premiere des troys dames
estant couchée et pasmée a sa teste appuyée ou gyron de la Royne de Navarre, la seconde
des dames est tombée d'autre costé comme esvanoye et la tierce est levée à genoulx faisant
signe de la main comme parlante d'audace et est tournée vers la Royne.

    Soit noté que aux hystoires precedentes et ceste cy est ung arbre au coing dudict pré
soubz lequel arbre sont couchées esvanouyes lesdictes troys dames.

Lors ung despit et courroux nompareil
Feirent soubdain son visaige vermeil
Et la doulleur sa parolle couppa
Tant qu'à peu près elle ne sincopa,
Car par troys foys je la vey deffaillir   505
Sans que des yeulx il peust larmes saillir.
Le cueur serré jecta si piteux crys
Que à les monstrer deffaillent mes escrips.
Mais en voyant la tierce que la place
Luy demouroit, me dist de bonne grace: 510

    « Madame, autant que douleur les tormente,
Souffrans l'ennuy de leurs ingratz amys,
L'amour parfaict qui dans mon cueur s'est mis
Faict qu'i n'ont mal qu'ainsi qu'elles ne sente.
    Car mon voulloir au leur est si uny   515
Que, si leurs cueurs ont peine pour aymer
Ceulx que l'on peult creulz amys nommer,
Le mien en est comme les leur puny.
    Comm'elles j'ay creu leurs amys loyaux,
Lesquelz j'aimoys comme le propre mien,   520
Participant en leur plaisir et bien
Comme je veulx avoir part en leurs maulx.
    Si j'ay eu part en leur felicité,
Où si bien fut nostre union gardée,
Seroit donc bien maintenant retardée   525
Ceste union pour leur necessité?

but I would only want to savor this pleasure
if their two bodies were buried with me in our communal tomb.
I will rejoice that our three misfortunes
brought us together under one cover." 500

*Here is the sixth story similar to the fifth, except that the first of the three ladies, lying down
and pale, is resting her head on the queen of Navarre's lap; the second lady has fallen to the
other side as if she has fainted; and the third is on her knees making a sign with her hand as
if she is speaking with courage and resolve. She is turned toward the queen.*

*Let it be noted that in the preceding stories as well as in this one there is a tree in the
corner of the said meadow under which the three ashen ladies are lying.*

Then an unequaled anger and spite
suddenly colored her face red
and pain cut her voice
so much that she almost fainted.
I saw her falter three times 505
without being able to let the tears flow from her eyes.
Her heart was so constricted that she let out such pitiful cries;
my writing fails to render them.
But then I saw the third lady
who still had to speak; she said gracefully: 510

"Madame, as much as they are tormented by sorrow
and suffer the pain of having ungrateful lovers,
the perfect love that has placed itself in my heart
makes it so that they have no pain that I don't feel as they do.[25]
    For my will is so tied to theirs 515
that if their hearts suffer for having loved
those that can be called cruel lovers,
mine is punished like theirs.
    I, like them, believed that their lovers were loyal;
I loved them as I do my own 520
and took part in their pleasure and goodness
just as I want to take part in their pain.
    If I partook in their happiness,
where our union was well preserved,
should this union now be precluded 525
because of their needs?

Non! Mais courir veulx aussi vyste qu'elles
A leur malheur, sans jamais departir,
Jusques à ce que l'ame pour partir
Aura repris ses aelles immortelles.   530
    Peine, torment, voire dix mille mortz,
Ne me feront peur de m'en tenir près.
Si mort les prend, pourroys je vivre après,
Sentant mourir les deux partz de mon corps?
    Si j'avoye mal et les deux eussent bien,   535
Il suffiroit pour me reconforter,
Car leur amour pourroit mon mal oster:
Contre une, deux ont grant force et moyen!
    Si mon ennuy perdoye pour leur plaisir,
Pour leur ennuy perdre je doy aussi   540
Tout mon plaisir, sans point avoir mercy
De cueur, de corps, d'amour ny de desir.
    Or je le veulx et ainsi le concluz
Puys que je voy leur mal intollerable,
Je veulx le mien faire irremediable   545
Et que de moy tout plaisir soit forcluz.
    Pleines d'ennuys sont, que porter leur fault,
Non pas pour moy, mais contre leur voulloir:
Moy de plaisir, auquel, pour mon devoir,
Hors de mon cueur je foys faire le sault.   550

    Madame, helas, pensez l'extremité
Là où je suis! Ayez pitié de moy!
Voyez mon mal, mon trouble, mon esmoy,
Voyez amour par amour lymité!
    L'amour des deux me dict: « O meschant cueur,   555
Vous vouldriez vous tant à plaisir donner
Et ces dames ainsi abandonner
En leur malheur pour ung seul serviteur?
    Las, rirez vous quant elles ploureront?
Et à plaisir tiendrez les yeulx ouvers   560
Quant de douleur verrez les leur couvers
En regretant leur amour qui se rompt?
    Jouÿrez vous du veoir et du parler
De vostre amy par grant esjoÿssance

No! On the contrary, I want to run as fast as they
to their sorrow, without ever separating myself from them
until my soul will have spread
its immortal wings to leave.[26]   530
    Pain, torment, even ten thousand deaths
would not scare me away from being with them.
If death would take them, could I live
after feeling two parts of my own body die?
    If I were suffering and my two friends were happy,   535
that would be enough to comfort me,
for their love could take away my pain;
against one person, two have great power and means.
    If I would abandon my pain because of their pleasure,
I must also abandon all my pleasure   540
for their pain, without mercy
for my heart, my body, my love, or my desire.
    So this is what I want and I've come to the conclusion
that since I see that their pain is unbearable
I want to make my own irremediable   545
and to exclude pleasure from my own life.[27]
    They are so full of tribulation that they must carry
not for me, but against their will.
I am forcing pleasure out of my heart,
just as I should.   550

    Madame, alas, think of the position
I find myself in! Have pity on me!
See my pain, my trouble, and my emotion,
see love limited by love!
    My love for these two ladies says to me,   555
'O selfish heart, would you so like to give yourself over
to pleasure and thus abandon these ladies
to their sorrow for the sake of a single man?[28]
    Alas, will you laugh when you see them cry?
And will you open your eyes to pleasure   560
when you see theirs covered with sorrow,
regretting their broken promises?
    Will you take pleasure in the sight
and the words of your lover with great joy

Quant elles n'ont d'un tel bien joÿssance?   565
Les laisrez vous? Ne le vueillez celer. »

    D'aultre costé l'amour du plus loyal,
Du plus parfaict qui soit dessus la terre,
Me vient mener une cruelle guerre
En me disant: « Pensez au plus grant mal.   570
      Vous sçavez bien qu'en laissant vostre amy,
Duquel si bien avez esté servie,
Vous luy ostez soubdainement la vie,
Car son cueur est du vostre le demy.
      Que fera il se voyant separé   575
De sa moytié? Croyez qu'il ne peult vivre.
Sera chacun des cueurs d'elles delivre
De leur ennuy, le voyant esgaré?
      Si vostre mort leur apportoit secours
Droict à la mort il vous fauldroit courir,   580
Mais ung amy loyal faire mourir
Sans leur servir? C'est estrange discours.
      Las, quel amy est ce que vous laissez?
Vous n'en sçavez au monde ung plus parfaict!
Et nul bien n'ont les deux en ce beau faict,   585
Fors que leur mal par le vostre oppressez. »

    Voyla comment les deux amours ensemble
Me combattent en grant confusion,
Si m'y fault il mectre conclusion;
Je la diray bien que le cueur m'en tremble: 590
      Puis que leur mal est ma mort et leurs vies
Ma vie aussi, si j'ay receu plaisir
De leurs plaisirs, je n'ay moindre desir
Qu'en leurs malheurs de moy soyent suyvies.
      Or ont perdu, sans sçavoir bien pourquoy,   595
Leurs deux amys, soit par faulte ou malheur,
Mais moy je perdz, sans raison ny couleur,
Celuy qui n'a jamais faulcé sa foy.
      Sa loyaulté est vrayement nompareille;
Il n'a rien faict qui jamais me despleust;   600
Sa grand amour que chacun chercher deust
Je laisse et fuys: n'est ce pas grant merveille?

when they don't possess such joy?   565
Will you leave them? Please be honest.'

    On the other hand, love for the most loyal,
the most perfect of lovers who ever lived on the earth
makes cruel war on me,
saying, 'Think of the greatest pain.   570
    You know well that in leaving your lover
who has served you so well,
you will take away his life,
for half of his heart is yours.
    What will he do when he sees that he has been separated   575
from his other half? Know that he will not be able to live.
Will each one of these ladies' hearts be delivered
from their pain upon seeing him cast aside?
    If your death would be of help to them,
then you should run straight into death,   580
but to make a loyal lover die
without serving these ladies? This is a strange argument.
    Alas, what kind of lover are you leaving?
You know of no other more perfect than he!
And these two ladies receive no good from this beautiful deed   585
except that you burden their pain with your own.'[29]

    This is how the two loves battle
within me with great clamor[30]
such that I must put an end to it.
I will say it although my heart will tremble from it: 590
    since their pain is my death and their lives
my life also, as I have received pleasure
from their pleasures, I have no other desire
than to imitate their sorrows.
    So without knowing why, either by fault or misfortune,   595
they have lost their two lovers.
However, I lose, without reason or pretext,
one who has never gone back on his word.
    His loyalty is unequaled;
he has never done anything displeasing to me.   600
I leave and flee his great love, the kind that everyone must be seeking.
Is it not a great wonder?

Je le tiens tel, si parfaict et si bon,
Que je vouldroys le mectre en troys parties
Et si serions toutes troys bien parties   605
Quand des deux pars je leur feroys le don.
    L'honneste amour de parler et de veoir,
Là où l'honneur trouve contentement,
Se peult partir quant voluntairement
Le bien on laisse où l'on a tout pouvoir.   610
    J'ay le povoir de bien les contenter:
De chasque jour les deux pars je leur donne
Et mon plaisir toutesfoys n'abandonne,
Car par le leur il pourra augmenter.
    Car en sentant de chacune d'eulx l'ayse,   615
J'en auray plus que je n'ay de la mienne
Et mon amy aussi aura la sienne,
Ne faisant riens qui bien fort ne me plaise.
    Mon amy seul, qui en vault plus de troys,
Sera des troys amy. O quel lien   620
Qui quatre cueurs unira sans moyen
En ung voulloir! Helas, je le vouldroys!
    Mais j'ay grant peur que pour ces deux follastres,
Qui sont payez trop d'une larme d'oeil,
Vueillent plus tost ainsi mourir de dueil   625
Que d'avoir mieulx. Tant sont opiniastres!
    Puis qu'elles n'ont cure d'un tel party,
Mon cueur au leur est uny si tresfort
Que, sans avoir regard à peine ou mort,
De mon amy il sera departy.   630
    Las, qu'il est dur ce mot à pronuncer!
Laisser ainsi mon bien, mon heur, ma vie!
Helas, Amy, à la mort te convie
Lors qu'on t'ira cest adieu annuncer.
    Que diras tu, Amy, de ton amye?   635
Ou que l'amour luy a trop cher cousté?
Ou tu pourras juger d'autre costé
Qu'elle te hayt, la nommant ennemye?
    Amour me mect en ung merveilleux trouble,
Qui d'un costé loue ma fermeté   640
Et d'autre part deffaict de seureté
Le vray lyen qui rendoit ung ung couble.

He is so perfect and so good; I hold him so dear
that I would like to divide him in three parts,
and all three of us would have an equal share 605
when I would give to them the two other parts.
 Honest expressions of love like speaking and seeing,
those things in which honor finds contentment,
can be shared when one gives freely
of those things in her possession. 610
 I have the power to make them happy
by giving them two parts of each day.
But I don't have to abandon my own pleasure,
for it will grow greater through theirs.
 When I feel that each one of them is comforted, 615
I will have more pleasure than I have from my own joy.
My lover will also have his joy
through pleasing me.
 My one lover, who is worth three,
will be the lover of three. Oh, what a bond 620
between four hearts united directly in one will!
Alas, how I would like it to be!
 But I fear greatly that these two foolish women
who have already paid too much with their tears
would rather die in mourning than have better. 625
They are so stubborn!
 Since they have no desire to share my love,
my heart is so tied to theirs
that it will be separated from my lover
without regard to pain or death. 630
 Alas, it is so difficult to pronounce this word!
To be separated from my treasure, my happiness, my life!
Alas, beloved, I summon you to your death
when this farewell will be announced to you.
 What will you say about your lady, beloved? 635
That love cost her too much?
On the other hand, could it be that you decide
that she hates you? Will you call her your enemy?
 Love has put me in an unbelievable turmoil:
on the one hand, it praises my steadfastness; 640
on the other, it undoes the real bond
that has firmly made one from two.

O que la mort viendroit bien à propos!
Car luy ne moy en ce departement
N'aurons jamais qu'à son advenement   645
Contentement, bien, plaisir ne repos.
    Or venez donc et par compassion
Mectez noz corps uniz en terre obscure
Avant souffrir qu'au departir j'endure
Si tresextreme et dure passion. »   650

Cy endroit est la septiesme hystoire semblable aux deux precedentes sinon que l'une des troys
dames est couchée ou pré, acoultée sur le coulte, l'autre qui estoit à genoulx près de l'arbre
est en son seant appuyée contre ledict arbre, toute pale et transie, et la Royne de Navarre
luy frotte une main entre les siennes pour la faire revenir, et l'autre dame qui estoit couchée
ou gyron de la Royne est comme assise oudict gyron parlant et faisant signe de la main
comme si elle parloit à celle qui est appuyée contre ledict arbre.

Ainsi parlant, s'appuyant contre ung arbre,
En la façon d'une femme de marbre
Qui n'a chaleur, vie ne mouvement,
Les yeulx fermez, les dens pareillement,
A ses souppirs deffailloit son alaine.   655
Moy qui la veis en si cruelle peine,
Je pris ses mains à frotter et tenir,
Tant qu'un petit je la feis revenir,
Et, en tournant son oeil triste vers nous,
Nous dist: « Helas, que vostre ennuy est doulx   660
Au pris du mien, qui ne peult plus durer! »
Ce que ne peut la premiere endurer:

    « Vous n'avez mal, dist elle, qu'un tout seul
C'est de laisser pour nous vostre plaisir.
Mais j'en ay deux qui agravent mon doeul: 665
    Las, je n'ay pas seullement le loysir
De regreter de mon amy la perte,
Que le second ne me vienne saysir.
    Amye, helas, si ma douleur couverte
Sentiez, qui est fondée en ignorance,   670
Dont ne m'est point la verité aperte,
    Vous jugeriez n'avoir pas la puissance
De la porter, car el'est par trop griefve.
Or Dieu vous gard de telle congnoissance!

Oh, would that death come soon!
For neither he nor I will feel either happiness,
goodness, or the pleasure of peace   645
before its coming.
    So come, death,
and put our three united bodies in the dark earth
before I must bear the suffering,
so extreme, of this separation."   650

Here is the seventh story, similar to the two preceding stories, except that one of the three
ladies is lying down in the meadow supported on her side; the other who had been on her
knees next to the tree is now seated and leaning against the tree, pale and paralyzed; the
queen of Navarre is rubbing one of her hands between her own to make her come to; and the
other lady who was lying in the queen's lap is now seated, speaking, and raising her hand
as if she were speaking to the one who is leaning against the tree.

She spoke thus, leaning against a tree
like a marble statue
that has neither heat, life, nor movement.
Her eyes were closed as was her mouth.
Her breath weakened with her sighs.   655
When I saw her in such pain
I took her hands to rub and hold,
such that I did bring her to a little.
Turning her sad eye towards us,
she said to us, "Alas, yours is such sweet sorrow   660
compared to my own that must not last!"
The first lady could not endure this:

    "You have but a single sorrow," she said,
"that of having left your pleasure behind for us.
But I have two sorrows that worsen my pain.   665
    Alas, I barely had time
to regret the loss of my lover
when the second one came around to seize me.
    My friend, alas, if only you could feel my hidden pain;
its truth is not revealed even to me,   670
for it is kept in the dark.
    It is so painful that you would see
that you do not have the strength to bear it.
May God keep you from such knowledge!

Puis que l'honneur mect en vostre amour trefve,   675
Plaisir avez, gardant la longue foy
Que nous devez, de la rendre ainsi briefve.

Si vous sçaviez aussi bien comme moy
Que c'est de vivre en doubte et en suspens,
Peu vostre mal estimeriez, je croy.   680

S'il me disoit: « D'aymer je me repens, »
J'en osteroys mon cueur qui de douleur
Perpetuel en payeroit les despens,

J'estimeroys à grant heur ce malheur,
Bien que ce n'est peu de despit ou honte   685
D'estre laissée ainsi d'un serviteur.

Le desplaisir en est tel et tant monte
Que d'en laisser cent de sa volunté
Ce n'est ennuy dont l'on deust tenir compte.

Votre cueur est de desespoir tenté   690
Par vostre amy: c'est chose raisonnable,
Aussi est il d'honneur bien contenté.

Rendant l'amour de l'union louable
D'entre nous troys, la gloire en recevez,
Qui vostre ennuy doibt rendre tolerable.   695

Certes le mien, si bien l'appercevez,
Voirrez plus grant que le vostre troys foys,
Si par faveur vous ne vous decevez.

Le moindre ennuy, de quoy compte ne foys,
C'est de fuyr le plaisir d'estre aymée   700
D'un treshonneste et parfaict toutesfoys.

L'autre ennuy est que je voy abismée
En desespoir celle que j'ayme tant
Par celuy seul dont je suis estimée.

Le tiers ennuy trop cruel qui pretend   705
Me mectre à mort, c'est la doubte craintifve,
Aymant tresfort, de n'estre aymée autant.

Que dis je autant? Mais que l'amour naïfve
Soit morte en luy ainsi que je la sens
Dedens mon cueur plus parfaicte et plus vifve.   710

Ces troys ennuyz me mectent hors du sens
Et si ne voy moyen de m'en deffaire
Sinon mourir, à quoy je me consens.

Since honor has put an end to your love,   675
you have the pleasure of preserving the long faith
you owe us, thus making the pain seem brief.[31]
    If you knew as well as I
what it means to live in doubt and suspense,
you would consider your own pain negligible, I believe.   680
    If he would say to me 'I repent of having loved,'
I would remove his love from my heart,
although it would pay the price in perpetual sorrow.
    I would consider this sorrow to be a great happiness,
even though there is great spite and shame   685
in being left in such a way by a lover.
    Compared with my grief that worsens every day,
to leave one hundred lovers voluntarily
is hardly suffering to take into account.
    It is right that your heart is afflicted   690
with despair for your lover.
This is why honor comforts it well.
    The glory that you receive
from the love of our worthy union
should make your pain tolerable.[32]   695
    If you look well and don't deceive yourself
through bias, certainly you will see
that mine is three times greater than yours.

    The least sorrow, really of no account,
is to flee the pleasure of being loved.   700
even by an honest and perfect lover.
    The second sorrow is that I see the lady
whom I love so much drowned in despair
by the only man who holds me in esteem.
    The third most cruel sorrow,   705
the one that threatens to destroy me,
is the fearful doubt of not being loved as much as I love.
    Why am I saying 'as much'? Rather, that true love
is dead in him even as I feel it
more perfect and more alive in my own heart.   710
    These three sorrows are driving me mad
and I see no means of freeing myself of them
except death; this I accept.

Il n'est ennuy, qui tant de mal sceust faire,
S'il est congneu, qu'on ne treuve moyen   715
Pour quelque peu au moins y satisfaire.
    Mais mon mal est incapable de bien,
Car je le sens et n'ay nulle asseurance
Si mon amy tient ou rompt ce lyen.
    Si juger veulx par tresseure apparence,   720
Je dis qu'il est rompu, mais son jurer
Me vient donner du contraire esperance.

    Las, mon ennuy est pour long temps durer,
Car le suspens de la conclusion
Qu'il faict d'aymer me contrainct d'endurer.   725
    Son doulx parler m'est une illusion
Qui m'aveuglist sens et entendement
Et de l'aymer me donne occasion.
    Helas, ses faictz parlent bien autrement:
Par eulx je voy que de luy suis laissée.   730
Il dit que non; verité dit qu'il ment.
    Par ses effectz ma joye est rabaissée,
Par son parler elle se ressuscite;
Ainsi des deux sans cesser suis pressée.
    Si grand douleur grande pitié incite,   735
Plus que de vous ayez compassion
De mon malheur, qui à la mort me cite.
    Celle qui n'a riens qu'une passion
Dont la cause est congneue et bien certaine,
O qu'el'est près de consolation!   740
    De si et non j'ay la teste si pleine,
Que, si le pis des deux povoye sçavoir,
Je le tiendroys à grace souveraine.
Mais le suspens surmonte mon pouvoir. »

    «Comment? Comment?   745
Soustenez vous estre plus grant torment
Doubter l'ouy ou non de vostre amant »
    Dist la seconde,
«Que de sçavoir par espreuve et par sonde
Que changement au plus parfond abonde   750
    De son faulx cueur?

There exists no sorrow, no matter how painful,
that, as long as it is understood,   715
can't be relieved at least a little.
    But it is impossible to relieve my pain,
for I feel it and yet I have no assurance
whether my lover is still true or has broken our bond.
    If I judge by appearance,   720
I say that he has broken all ties,
but his words of assurance give me hope that he has not.

    Alas, my sorrow will endure a long time,
for his postponement of the end
of his love for me forces me to hang on.   725
    His sweet words are an illusion
that blinds my senses and reason
and gives me occasion to love him.
    Alas, his actions speak otherwise:
through them, I see that he has abandoned me.   730
He says that he hasn't; truth tells me that he's lying.
    My joy is diminished by his actions;
it is brought back to life by his words.
I am continually harassed by both.
    Such great sorrow brings about great compassion.   735
Have pity on my pain more than yours,
for it summons me to death.
    She who suffers
from only one certain cause
is already practically consoled!   740
    My head is so full of 'yes' and 'no'
that if I could know for certain
the worst of the two I would cherish it.
But the suspense overwhelms my strength."

    "What!" said the second lady,   745
"Do you contend that you are in greater torment
not knowing whether your lover
    loves you or not
than knowing by proof and by probing
that change has entered abundantly   750
    into his heart?

Estimez vous souppeçon, doubte et peur
Comme ung sçavoir certain sans nul erreur?
    C'est cas estrange!
Mais moy qui sçay de mon amy le change,   755
Que je tenoye aussi parfaict qu'un ange,
    Que puis je faire?
Il le m'a dit sans point se contrefaire
Qu'il se voulloit de mon amour deffaire
    Pour la remectre   760
Du tout en vous, ce que jamais permectre
N'avez voullu, mais bien vous entremectre
    Par la pityé
Qu'aviez de moy, rabiller l'amytié
Dont je retiens moy seulle la moyctié.   765
    Si vous avez
Peine à fuyr ce qu'aimer ne devez,
Que doy je avoir sinon les yeulx crevez
    De lamenter
Celuy qui tant me soulloit contenter,   770
Qui ne me veult plus aymer ny hanter.
    Las, je le perdz
Qui fut tout mien et à beaulx yeulx ouvers
Le voy fouyr, non pas par les desers
    Ny lieu sauvage,   775
Mais droict à vous; et devant mon visage
Il a tourné son sainct pelerinage.
    Il auroit bien
Changé en mieulx, s'il ne sçavoit combien
Nous nous aymons et que ce qui est mien   780
    Est vostre aussi.
Il fuyt de moy, cherchant de vous mercy;
Pour vostre non, il pert de moy le sy.

    O cruaulté!
En mon endroit par sa desloyaulté,   785
Et dans son cueur par vostre grant beaulté!
    Car ung seul compte
Vous n'en tenez. O mon Dieu! quelle honte
Il doit avoir et peur que je racompte
    A vous, amye,   790

Do you really think that suspicion, doubt, and fear
are the same as knowing for certain with no mistake?
    This is strange!
And what about me; I know that my lover,   755
who I thought was as perfect as an angel, has changed,
    and what can I do?
He told me without question
that he wanted to get out of our love
    in order to give all of his to you.   760
You have never wanted this
but rather you have put him off.
    Through the pity
that you have for me you have reconciled our friendship
and I hold my half of the friendship dear.   765
    If you have difficulty
fleeing from someone who does not deserve your love,
imagine how I must have cried
    my eyes out
for the man who always comforted me   770
and who now wants neither to love nor to be with me.
    Alas, I am losing the man
who was all mine, and with my eyes wide open
I see him flee not to the desert
    or to some wilderness   775
but straight to you! Right in front of my face
he has changed direction on his holy pilgrimage.
    He might well have
changed for the better, if only he knew
how we love one another and that that which is mine   780
    is also yours.
He flees from me, looking to you for mercy:
to hear your 'no' he has lost my 'yes.'

    O cruelty!
It has entered in my life through his unfaithfulness   785
and in his own heart through your great beauty!
    For you don't take that at all into account.
O God! What shame he must feel!
He must fear that I will tell
    you, friend,   790

Et vous à moy le discours de sa vie.
Car entre nous sa trop faulce alquemye
    Est descouverte,
Dont à moy seulle en demeure la perte.
Vous ne sçavez si elle est meure ou verte   795
    Ceste douleur.
Plus il vous dit sa peine et son malheur,
Plus vous mocquez de son mal et couleur
    Point n'en changez.
Et puis de luy si fort vous estrangez   800
Que je voy bien que mon tort vous vengez
    Tout en riant.
Et je m'en voys à part pleurant, criant,
Et Dieu et sainctz requerant et priant
    Pour mon aÿde.   805
Car je n'y voy sans miracle remyde.
Je l'ay perdu et n'y a croix ne guyde
    Qui radresser
Le sceust vers moy. Je ne le veulx presser
Et si ne puis son amour delaisser,   810
    Qui est plantée
Dedans mon cueur et si tresfort entée
Que, bien qu'il m'ait du tout mal contentée,
    Je n'ay vigueur,
Force ou povoir de l'oster de mon cueur,   815
Qui est nourry et plein de sa liqueur
    Et transmüé
En cest amour tant que, s'il n'est tüé,
Il n'en sera separé ne müé.

    Or donc pensez   820
Quel vostre ennuy est que vous advancez
Plus que le mien: en quoy vous m'offencez.
    Le pis de vous
C'est le doubter. Las, qu'il me seroit doulx!
Je jugeroys mon amy tous les coups   825
    Avoir le droict.
Ce souppeçon pour ung temps me vauldroit
Et contre non, ouy me soustiendroit.
    Mais de ce non

and that you will tell me the story of his life.
Between us, his false alchemy
   has been discovered.
And I alone suffer the loss.
You don't know whether this pain has matured 795
   or is still green.
The more he tells you of his pain and his sorrow,
the more you make fun of his pain
   and you show no emotion from this.
And then you distance yourself from him so much 800
that I see that you have well revenged the wrong against me,
   laughing all the while.
I, in the meantime, watch from afar, crying,
praying, and asking God and the saints
   for help. 805
For without a miracle, I see no remedy for myself.
I have lost him and there is no cross nor guide
   that can direct him back to me.
I don't want to harass him
and yet I don't want to let go of his love. 810
   It is planted
in my heart and so grafted on that,
even though he has displeased me in every way,
   I don't have the vigor,
strength, or power to pull it from my heart. 815
My heart has been so nourished and filled by his elixir;
   it is transformed into this love,
so much so that unless it is killed,
it will never be separated from it or changed.

   So think about what the pain is 820
that you pretend is greater than mine;
I am offended by this.
   The worst thing for you is doubt.
Alas, doubt would be so sweet to me!
I would think that my lover 825
   was always right.
Suspicion would be worth something to me for a time
and 'yes' would sustain me against 'no.'
   But I am certain

Certaine suis, non point par faulx renom.   830
Car toutes troys pour meschant le tenon,
   Pour variable,
Traistre et menteur et moy pour immuable
En fermeté honorable et louable.
   Qui me contrainct   835
Qu'autant de temps qu'en amour juste et sainct
Je l'ay porté dedans mon cueur empraint
   Par amour forte,
Autant de temps pour meschant je le porte.
Impossible est que jamais il en sorte.   840
   Sa lascheté
Donnera foeille à ma grant fermeté.
O que l'honneur sera cher acheté
   De ne partir
Hors de l'amour dont le voy departir!   845
Où est l'esprit comme le mien martyre?
   Il n'en est point.
Loyaulté l'a si fort en moy conjoinct
Que mon cueur sien n'est plus mien; c'est le poinct.
   Et si mourir   850
Me fault sans cueur, à la mort puis courir,
Car, arrachant celuy qui peult nourrir
   En luy la vie,
De luy bien tost elle seroit ravie.
Las, j'auroys bien de ceste mort envie!   855
   Mais luy en moy
Vivre me faict en tel dueil et esmoy
Qu'il me faisoit vivre d'amour et foy
   En grant plaisir,
Durant le temps que par heureux loysir   860
Me racontoit son honneste desir.
   Or est passé
Tout ce beau temps où je n'ay amassé
Riens que regret et espoir que son tort
M'apportera, bien congneu par ma mort,   865
De tous amans: Requiescat in pace. »

La tierce, oyant leur gracieux debat,
Plus par ennuy que par plaisant esbat,

of this 'no,' and not from false rumor.   830
All three of us think of him as mean
        and changeable;
he's a traitor and a liar while I am steadfast,
honorable, and praiseworthy.
        What restrains me   835
is that I have carried him imprinted on my heart
with great love
        for as much time in a just and holy love
as I carry him now as mean and changeable.
It is not possible that he will ever be removed from it.   840
        His cowardice
highlights my great steadfastness.
Oh, the honor of staying true
        to the love from which I see him turn away
will be dearly bought!   845
Where is there a martyred spirit like my own?
        There does not exist another.
Loyalty has joined him to me so well
that my heart is no longer mine but his; this is enough.
        And if I must die   850
without a heart, I can run to death,
for having torn out the one that can nourish
        life in it,
its life will soon be taken.
How I would welcome this death!   855
        But from within me
he makes me live in mourning and anguish
just as he sustained me with love and faith
        in great pleasure
during the days of happy leisure   860
when he would speak to me of his honest desire.
        Well, this beautiful time is past;
I collected nothing but regret and hope
that his wrong, made known because of my death,
will bring me this prayer from all lovers: 865
may she rest in peace."

The third lady, listening to their amiable debate, said,
more from affliction than pleasure,

Dist: «Je vous pri' et requiers toutes deux
N'estimer tant, l'une sa peur et doubte,   870
L'autre son dueil, qu'ung peu l'on ne m'escoute,
Puis que pour vous de bon cueur souffrir veulx.
　　Vos maulx sont grands, nulle doubte n'en foys,
Vivre en suspens, sans resolution,
Par l'amy plein de toute fiction.   875
Mais le mien n'est pas moindre toutesfoys,
　　Car mon amy, loyal et veritable,
Où j'ay trouvé tout ce que je desire,
Me fault laisser pour me faire, en martyre
Et en malheur, à vous autres semblable.   880
　　Las, si en luy sçavoye riens d'imparfaict
Ou qu'envers moy en quelque cas eust tort,
Nostre lyen, qui en seroit moins fort,
Sans grant douleur plus tost seroit deffaict.
　　Mais il n'y a occasion aucune   885
Entre nous deux, qui double mon torment,
D'ainsy laisser ung si parfaict amant
Pour recevoir part en vostre infortune.
　　S'il ne m'aymoit, il me seroit aisé
De le laisser, ou bien si en doubtance   890
J'estoys de luy par sa grand inconstance,
Mon dueil seroit doulcement appaisé.

　　Helas, il n'a riens d'imperfection,
Car son corps est parfaict, son cueur sans vice,
En tout honneur m'a faict loyal service,   895
Las, dure en est la separation!
　　Laisser celuy de qui ne suis aymée,
Qui ne le vault, qui est fainct et meschant
Ou qui de nous la honte va cherchant,
Je n'en pourroye estre mal estimée.   900
　　Mais d'ung parfaict qui m'ayme tant, helas,
Le departir m'en est trop importable,
Car son amour demourra pardurable
Dedans mon cueur qui de l'aymer n'est las.
　　Je pers de luy la parolle et la veue   905
Et tout le bien dont je soulloys jouyr,
Et ne retiens riens pour me resjouyr
Que son amour, dont je suis bien pourveue

"I beg of you please, both of you,
do not consider your fear and doubt   870
and your mourning so much that you don't listen to me,
for I sincerely want to suffer for you.
    I do not doubt that your pain is great,
to live in suspense without any resolution
from a lover who is full of fiction.   875
However, mine is not less.
    For I have to leave my loyal and true lover
who has given me everything I desire
in order to make myself like you two,
in martyrdom and sorrow.   880
    Alas, if I knew of anything imperfect in him
or if he had ever done anything wrong toward me,
our bond, which would be weaker from these things,
would soon be undone without much pain.
    But there has never been such a reason between us   885
to abandon in this way such a perfect lover
in order to take part in your misfortune.
This just doubles my torment.
    If he didn't love me
it would be easy to leave him,   890
or if I doubted his faithfulness
my mourning would be gently soothed.

    Alas, he has no imperfection
because his body is perfect, his heart without vice.
He has honorably paid loyal service to me.   895
Alas, our separation is so hard!
    To leave someone who does not love me,
who does not deserve my love, who is false and mean,
or who seeks out our shame
would bring no dishonor to me.   900
    But the separation from a perfect lover who loves me so much
is unbearable for me.
His love will rest eternally in my heart,
for it has not tired of loving him.
    I lose the sight of him and his words   905
and all the good that I used to enjoy.
I have nothing left to enjoy
except his love; of that I am well supplied.

C'est bien raison qu'après le congié pris,
Que dis je pris? Mais donné sans sa faulte,   910
Sa grand amour, tant vertueuse et haulte,
Se mecte ailleurs, ja n'en sera repris.
    Mais ceste là que j'ay par luy conceue
Me demourra pour doulce nourriture,
Dedans mon cueur, de tant ferme nature,   915
Nulle autre amour ne sera plus receue.

    Vous deux perdez l'amour de voz amys,
Mais d'eulx avez la parolle et la veue,
Moy j'ai l'amour trescertaine et congneue,
Mais tout plaisir pour vous j'ay dehors mis.   920
    Car le parler et la veue je quitte.
C'est tout mon bien que pour vous j'abandonne,
O quel thresor, amyes, je vous donne!
Fault il qu'Amour ainsi vers vous m'acquitte?
    L'on tient qu'il n'est nul plus cruel martyre   925
Que pour son Dieu, d'ung propos voluntaire,
Fuyr plaisir et, en lieu solitaire,
Soy separer du bien que l'on desire.
    Car le martyre, souffrant cruel torment
Par main d'autruy, mect toute sa science   930
De soustenir son mal par patience,
Qui de tous maulx est le soulagement.
    Vous endurez, par le tort et le vice
De voz amys, en despit de voz cueurs,
Pis que la mort. O petites douleurs   935
Mises auprès de mon grand sacrifice!
    Pour vous aymer, celuy où je me fie
Trop plus qu'à moy, que j'ayme, que j'estime,
Mon bien, mon heur, j'en foys une victime
Et voluntiers pour vous le sacrifie.   940
    Non pas que mort le vueille presenter,
Mais tout vivant, qui m'est plus grand regret,
Sans retenir ung seul bien en secret,
Ny d'ung seul mal me voulloir exempter.
    Avecques luy tout plaisir je renunce   945
De veoir, d'ouyr, de penser, de parler,
Parquoy d'ennuy, point ne le fault celer,
J'en ay le marcq si vous en avez l'unce.

It is only right after the leave that I have taken—
what am I saying, "taken"? 910
It has been given by me rather without any fault of his own.
That his great love, so virtuous and exalted,
 be placed elsewhere, he will never be blamed for this.
But the love that I knew through him
will stay with me and be my sweet sustenance. 915
No other love will ever be received in my steadfast heart.

 The two of you have lost your lovers' love
but you can still see them and hear their words;
I still have a certain and known love,
but for you I've dismissed all pleasure. 920
 I leave behind the sight of him and his words;
I've abandoned all my treasure for you.
What a treasure I give to you, friends!
Must Love repay my debt to you?
 They say that there is no crueler martyrdom 925
than to flee from one's pleasure
voluntarily for God and, all alone, to be separated
from the treasure that one desires.
 For the martyr, suffering cruel torment
at someone else's hand, puts all his mind 930
and will to bearing the pain through patience,
which is solace from all pain.
 Despite your hearts, you endure worse than death
because of the wrong and the vice of your lovers.
What small sorrow this is 935
compared with my great sacrifice![33]
 Because I love you I have made a victim
of the man whom I trust more than myself,
whom I love and esteem, my treasure, my happiness;
willingly I sacrifice him for you.[34] 940
 Not dead do I give him to you,
but fully alive, which is an even greater sorrow for me.
I have not withheld even one secret treasure,
nor do I wish to exempt myself from even one sorrow.
 I renounce all pleasure of seeing him, 945
hearing him, thinking of and speaking with him,
and so, it must be said,
your pain is only a fraction of mine.

Sa grant bonté et sa perfection
Entretiendront en moy ceste amour forte   950
Qui n'aura fin tant que je soye morte,
En ce poinct seul j'ay consolation.
    Car d'esperer jamais plus le ravoir,
L'ayant laissé, ce seroit grant follie:
Ou il mourra par grand melancolie,   955
Ou il fera d'aymer ailleurs devoir.

    Las, s'il en meurt, je pers mon esperance,
S'il ayme ailleurs, plus à moy ne viendra
Car où l'amour le lyera se tiendra;
Je congnoys bien sa grand perseverance.   960
    Mort ou aymant je le pers sans espoir
De le ravoir; ma perte est toute entiere.
Mais vous avez, dames, d'espoir matiere,
Ce que je veulx bien cler vous faire veoir.
    Si l'une voit les effectz accorder   965
De son amy avecques sa parolle,
Je ne la tiens si sotte ne si folle
Qu'elle voullust ses faultes recorder.
    A l'autre aussi l'amy qui s'en viendroit
Luy demander en grande repentence   970
Pardon, en lieu de dure penitence
Plus de ses maulx il ne luy souviendroit.
    Or tous ces biens vous peuvent advenir,
Car vous n'avez pas esleu vostre peine.
Mais moy je suis de ma perte certaine   975
Sans nul espoir qu'il puisse revenir.
    Que perdez vous? Ung maulvais et ung fainct,
Et moy ung bon, sans vice ny sans faincte,
Lequel perdant d'aymer je suis contraincte,
Laissant le bien que perdre j'ay tant crainct.   980
    Fortune ou Dieu ce bien icy ne m'ouste,
C'est moy sans plus qui de mon cueur l'arrache
Affin que mieulx unie je m'attache
A voz malheurs. O que cher il me couste!
    Brief, voz espoirs et ma desesperance,   985
Les meschans tours de voz cruelz amys,
Et les vertuz que Dieu au mien a mis
Font de voz maulx au mien la difference. »

His great goodness and his perfection
maintain in me this strong love   950
that will end only when I die.
In this end lies my only consolation.
    For having abandoned him,
it would be a great folly to hope to ever see him again.
Either he will die of great melancholy   955
or he will make it his duty to love elsewhere.

    Alas, if he dies from this, I will lose all hope.
If he loves elsewhere he will never again come to me,
for he will stay where love has tied him;
I know well his perseverance.   960
    Dead or in love I lose him with no hope
of seeing him again; my loss is complete.
But you, ladies, have the treasure of hope;
I will show this to you clearly.
    If you see the actions of your lover   965
correspond to his words,
I do not think you so stupid or so crazy
that you would want to recall his faults.
    And if your lover came back
repenting and asking forgiveness of you,   970
instead of imposing a harsh punishment,
you would no longer remember his crimes.
    So all these good things can happen to you
for you did not choose your sorrow.
I, on the other hand, am absolutely sure of my loss;   975
there is no hope that he could return.
    What do you lose? An unfaithful lover and a false lover;
I lose a good lover who has no vice and is without falsehood.
All the while I am still in love with him;
I leave behind the treasure that I so feared losing.   980
    Neither Fortune nor God has taken away this treasure from me;
it is I alone who tears him from my heart
so that I can better tie myself
to your sorrow. Oh, it costs me dearly!
    In short, your hopes and my despair,   985
the mean tricks of your cruel lovers
and the virtues that God has placed in mine
make all the difference between your pain and mine."

Icy est la huytiesme hystoire qui est pareil lieu que les precedentes, mais la Royne de
Navarre et les troys dames sont leveés sur piedz près ledict arbre et la Royne leur monstre
le soleil se couchant et la nuyt prochaine et toutes les troys dames font signes de leurs mains
comme estans en grande querelle.

Plus tost le jour nous eust peu deffaillir
Que ces dames de leurs propos saillir,   990
Qui me sembloit estre à recommencer.
Mais, regardant la nuict trop s'avancer,
Contraincte fuz d'empescher le discours
De leurs propos, que je trouvoys trop cours,
Car je n'ouÿ oncques femmes mieulx dire,   995
Pour sentir tant qu'elles d'ennuy et d'ire.
Et si le lieu où failloit retourner
Eust esté près, voluntiers sejourner
L'on nous eust veu jusques au lendemain,
Passant la nuict à ce doulx air serain.   1000
Celles en qui serain, travail, sommeil
N'estoit senty, et du trescler soleil
L'absence estoit de leurs yeulx incongnue
Et de la nuyct la soubdaine venue,
Congnurent bien, escouttans ma raison,   1005
Que du partir estoit heure et saison,
Qui leur despleut, car chacune n'avoit
De son ennuy dict ce qu'elle sçavoit.
Parquoy en pleurs voulurent reveler
Ce que le temps les contraignoit celer,   1010
Et de lermes et souspirs feirent langues
Pour achever sans parler leurs harangues.

Las, ce plourer me monstra le torment
Dont ne sçavoys que le commencement:
Par leur parler les lermes confirmerent   1015
Quel fut l'ennuy de celles qui aymerent.
Je ne croy pas que perdre pere et mere
Sceust engendrer passion plus amere
Que je leur vey porter et soustenir.
Mais sur le poinct de nous en revenir   1020
Prindrent leurs criz et pleurs à redoubler,
Tant que soubdain feirent le ciel troubler

Here is the eighth story which takes place in the same place as the preceding ones, but the queen of Navarre and the three ladies are standing near the tree and the queen is pointing out to them the setting sun and approaching night. All three ladies are gesturing as though they are seriously quarreling.

The sun was setting more quickly
than the ladies were resolving their argument,   990
which, it seemed to me, was starting up again.
But, as I watched the night come upon us,
I was unfortunately forced to interrupt
their discourse, which I found too short,
for I had never heard women speak more eloquently   995
despite the pain and anger that they felt.
If the place where we had to return had been closer,
I would have gladly stayed and spent the night
in this sweet, clear air,
hidden from the world until the next day.   1000
The ladies, who felt no calm,
fatigue, or sleep, hadn't noticed
that the sun was setting
and that night had come.
They listened to reason   1005
and understood that it was time to leave,
although they were not happy about it;
each one had not said all she could about her pain.
And so through tears they sought to reveal
that which time forced them to hide.   1010
They made a language out of their tears and sighs
to finish their arguments without speaking.

Alas, this crying made me realize
that I was only beginning to understand their torment.
Their tears spoke and confirmed   1015
how great is the pain of women who have loved.
I believe that even the loss of father and mother
could not cause emotion more bitter
than that which I have seen them bear.
But just as we were about to go back,   1020
their cries and tears worsened,
so much so that they made the sky darken.

Qui d'elles print telle compassion
Que sa doulceur par grant mutation
Se convertit en tonnoirre et tempeste,   1025
En pluye et vent tant qu'aulx champs n'y eut beste
Qui ne cerchast caverne ou couverture
Pour se cacher, voyant telle adventure.

En essuyant leurs yeulx et leurs visages
Toutes les troys, tant honnestes et sages,   1030
D'abandonner ce pré furent contrainctes,
Laissans au ciel achever leurs complainctes.
La pluye en creut, lors chacune descoche
Et nous meismes toutes quatre en la coche
Qui attendoit nostre departement;   1035
Après les autres courusmes vystement.

Icy est la neufiesme hystoire où est une grande pluye et obscurité, et les troys dames
plorantes saillent hors dudict pré dans ung chemin ouquel est une coche tyrée à quatre
jumentz noyres attelées deux à deux, en laquelle coche est desja entrée la Royne de
Navarre; l'une des dames est en l'eschelle pour y monter, l'autre passe la haye du pré et
la tierce est encores dedans ledict pré, toutes troys plourantes, leurs mouchouers es mains.
Et apparoissent en ceste hystoire plusieurs bestes cachées à demy à raison de la pluye
violente.

Mais en allant, pour oster le discord
De leur propos et les mectre d'accord,
Je leur requis voulloir ung juge prendre
Qui leurs debatz voullust et peust entendre.   1040
Car aussi tost que l'une j'escouttoys
De son costé soubdain je me mectoys;
Et puis, quant l'autre avoit compté son cas,
A qui ne fault bailler nulz advocatz,
Je me rendoys à son opinion.   1045

Pour les tenir doncques en union
Ung bon esprit leur estoit necessaire,
Et quant à moy, je m'obligeoye de faire
Tout mon povoir, que je sens trop petit,
Pour reciter, non à mon appetit,   1050
Tous leurs propos, mais au moins ma puissance

It felt for them such compassion
that it transformed its sweetness
into thunder and storms, wind and rain,   1025
so much so that there was not a beast in the field
that did not look for cave or cover
to hide upon seeing such a tempest.

Wiping their eyes and faces,
the three wise and honest ladies   1030
were forced to abandon the meadow,
leaving the sky to finish their complaints.
The rain got heavier as we ran
all four of us to the coach
that awaited our departure;   1035
we ran quickly after the others.

Here is the ninth story in which there is a great storm darkening the sky. The three ladies,
crying, leave the said meadow by a path where there is a coach pulled by four black
mares harnessed two by two.[35] *The queen of Navarre has already entered the coach; one*
of the ladies is on the step to climb into it; another is going through a hedge that encloses
the meadow; and the third is still in the meadow. All three of them are crying, their
handkerchiefs in their hands. Several beasts, partly hidden because of the violence of the
rain, appear in this story.

As we were leaving, in order to rid them of their discord
and to get them to agree,[36]
I asked them to please choose a judge
who could willingly listen to their debate.   1040
For as soon as I would hear one of the ladies,
I would immediately take her side.
And then when another,
who needed no lawyer to plead for her,
would have argued her case, I would side with her.   1045

Thus they needed a reasoned mind
to keep them together.
As for me, I committed myself to using all my ability,
though it seems meager to me,
to tell their whole story,   1050
not as I would have liked,

N'espargneray à donner congnoissance
De leurs ennuyz comme leur ay promis,
Sans qu'un seul mot de leurs dictz soit obmis.

« Nostre debat, ce me dist la premiere,   1055
Mect nostre esprit en tell'obscurité
Qu'il ne nous fault pas petite lumiere.
    Je n'en sçay qu'un qui, à la verité,
Puisse juger qui plus a de doleur
Et plus d'honneur par souffrir merité.   1060
    C'est celuy seul duquel la grant valeur
N'a son pareil et à tous est exemple
Des grans vertuz par qui s'acquiert honneur.
    C'est luy qui peult triumpher en son temple,
Ayant passé par celuy de Vertu.   1065
C'est luy que ciel, et terre, et mer contemple.
    La terre a joye, le voyant revestu
D'une beaulté qui n'a point de semblable,
Au prix duquel tous beaulx sont ung festu.
    La mer, devant son povoir redoutable,   1070
Doulce se rend, congnoissant sa bonté,
Et est pour luy contre tous favorable.
    Le ciel s'abaisse et, par amour dompté,
Vient admirer et veoir le personnage
Dont on luy a tant de vertuz compté.   1075
    C'est luy lequel tout le divin lignage
Des Dieux treshaulx ont jugé qu'il doit estre
Monarche ou plus si se peult davantage.
    C'est luy qui a grace et parler de maistre
Digne d'avoir sur tous gloire et puissance,   1080
Qui sans nommer assez se peult congnoistre.
    C'est luy qui a de tout la congnoissance
Et ung sçavoir qui n'a point de pareil,
Et n'y a riens dont il ait ignorance.

    De sa beaulté il est blanc et vermeil,   1085
Les cheveulx bruns, de grande et belle taille;
En terre il est comme au ciel le soleil;
    Hardy, vaillant, saige et preux en bataille,
Fort et puissant, qui ne peult avoir peur
Que prince nul, tant soit il grant, l'assaille.   1090

but at least I will spare none of my power
to make known their suffering as I had promised,
without omitting a single word.

    The first one said to me, "Our debate   1055
has plunged us so into darkness
that we need more than a small light.
    I only know of one person, truthfully,
who could judge which of us suffers more
and which has earned the most honor through suffering.   1060
    He is the one whose great valor
has no equal, who is an example to all
of the great virtues through which one acquires honor.
    He is the one who can triumph in his own temple
because he has passed through Virtue's temple.[37]   1065
He is the one that the sky, the earth, and the sea contemplate.
    Earth is joyous seeing him adorned
with unrivaled beauty;
all other beauties are nothing in comparison.
    The sea is calmed before his formidable power;   1070
she knows his goodness
and is favorable toward him against all others.
    The sky, overcome with love, comes down
to admire and see the one
about whom so much virtue has been told.   1075
    He is the one designated by the divine lineage
of the gods most high to be monarch,
or more if it were possible.
    He is the one who has the grace and the speech of a master
worthy of having glory and power over all.   1080
He is known without being named.
    He is the one who possesses all knowledge
and learning that has no equal;
there is nothing of which he is ignorant.

    He has a beautiful cream and rose complexion,   1085
brown hair and a grand, striking stature.
On earth he is like the sun in the sky.
    Hardy, valiant, wise, and courageous in battle,
strong and powerful, he could never fear
that another prince, no matter how great, would attack him.   1090

Il est begnin, doulx, humble en sa grandeur,
Fort et constant et plein de patience,
Soit en prison, en tristesse ou malheur.
  Il a de Dieu la parfaicte science
Que doit avoir ung roy tout plein de foy,   1095
Bon jugement et bonne conscience.
  De son Dieu garde et l'honneur et la loy,
A ses subjectz doulx support et justice.
Brief luy seul est bien digne d'estre roy.
  Si pour l'enfant estainct par trop grant vice,   1100
A Salomon demanderent les femmes
Le jugement, par son royal office,
  Nous ne povons encourir aucuns blasmes
Quand à ce roy, plus grant que Salomon,
Presenterons la douleur de noz ames   1105
  Et, s'il luy plaist lire ce long sermon,
Il jugera qui soustient la plus grande,
Aussi l'amour dont point ne nous blasmon.
  Dames, le roy pour juge je demande,
Qui jugera à nostre affection   1110
L'honneur, aussi à nostre fiction
Punition par honorable amende. »

Quant je la vey choysir sy haultement,
Crainte me print en luy disant: « Vrayement,
Si devant l'oeil d'un si parfaict esprit   1115
Falloit monstrer mon trop mal faict escript,
Vous pourriez bien prendre ailleurs secretaire.
J'aymeroys mieulx me desdire et me taire,
Car d'empescher sa veue et son bon sens
Sur mes beaulx faictz, jamais ne m'y consens.   1120
Les plus parfaictz où n'y a que remordre
Lyment leurs faictz et les mectent en ordre
Premier que ozer, sans bien les acoustrer,
Devant tel roy si sçavant les monstrer,
En craignant plus de luy le jugement   1125
Que du surplus de tout le firmament.

Moy donc qui suis des escrivans la moindre
Et moins que rien, ne doy je pas bien craindre

He is benevolent, gentle, humble in his grandeur,
strong and constant and full of patience,
whether it be in prison, in sadness, or in misfortune.
    He has the perfect knowledge of God
that a king who is full of faith should have,   1095
as well as good judgment and a good conscience.
    He upholds the honor and the law of his God;
he gives gentle support and justice to his subjects.
In short, he is the only one worthy of being king.
    If, by virtue of his royal office,   1100
the women asked Solomon for a judgment
for the child who was viciously suffocated,
    we should not be blamed for asking this king,
who is greater than Solomon.[38]
We will present the suffering of our souls,   1105
    and if it pleases him to read this long speech
he will judge which one of us bears the greatest pain
as well as the greatest love, for which we are not ashamed.
    Ladies, I request the king as judge;
he will judge which of our loves has the honor of being the greatest, 1110
and for our mistakes he will assign us punishment
to make honorable amends.

When I realized that she was choosing someone of such stature,
I was taken with fear. I said to her,
"Truly, if I must present my scribbling   1115
before the eyes of such a perfect mind
you would do well to find another secretary;
I would prefer to withdraw and be silent,
for I would never consent to burdening his eye
and his good sense with my work.   1120
The most perfect writers, of whom no critique can be made,
polish their works, putting them in order,
and only after first beautifying them
do they dare to present them to such a learned king.
They fear his judgment more   1125
than that of the heavens.

And so I, who am among the least of those who write
and less than nothing, should I not fear

Voz bons propos bien dignes d'estre veuz
Rendre par moy indignes d'estres leuz   1130
Devant le roy, où ne fault presenter
Rien qui son sens ne puisse contenter?
Plus le louez, plus de crainte me prent.
Car c'est celuy de qui chacun apprent,
Qui sçait louer le bien en verité   1135
Et rendre au mal ce qu'il a merité.
Or choysissez ung juge tel que moy,
Car, s'il failloit monstrer devant le roy
Ung si tresbas et mal tyssu ouvrage,
Je n'auroye pas d'escrire le courage. »   1140

      « Le roy vrayement,
Dist l'autre après, j'eusse esleu justement,
Car qui est plus que luy parfaict amant?
      Ne qui entend
Mieulx qu'il ne faict où vraye amour pretend?   1145
Il a aymé si fort, si bien et tant
      Qu'il peult entendre
Ce qui en est et la raison en rendre
Par son bon sens, qui à tous peult apprendre.
      L'amour loyal,   1150
Ferme et parfaict dedans son cueur royal
A faict son throsne et son hault tribunal
      Pour juger tous
Les vrays amans, saiges, hardiz et doulx,
Et se mocquer des glorieux et foulz   1155
      Qui font les braves,
Oultrecuydez, pensans faire les graves,
Puis reffusez, bien sotz, font les esclaves.
      Car c'est le rolle
Qu'il fault jouer où deffault la parolle   1160
Et le bon sens. Et quelque povre folle
      Ou les craindra
En bravegeant, ou pour morts les tiendra,
Ne parlant plus, ce que point n'adviendra
      A une sage   1165
Qui prend plaisir d'ouyr ung bon langage
Dit d'un bon cueur vertueux, d'un visage

presenting to the king your good speech, so worthy to be seen,
rendered by me unworthy to be read?   1130
Nothing should be presented to him
that cannot satisfy his mind.
The more you praise him, the more I am taken by fear,
for he is the source of knowledge for all.
He rightly praises the truly good   1135
and gives to the bad that which it deserves.
So choose a judge more like me,
for if I had to present to the king
such an inferior and poorly woven work,
I would not have the courage to write."   1140

    The second lady then said,
"In truth I would have also chosen the king,
for who is a more perfect lover than he?
    Nor is there anyone
who understands better than he what true love is.   1145
He has loved so strongly, so well, and so much
    that he can understand
what love is and make sense out of it
with his reason so that we can all learn.
    A faithful, enduring, and perfect love   1150
has built its throne and its tribunal
in his royal heart
    in order to judge
all true lovers who are wise, strong, and gentle,
and to scorn the proud and vain,   1155
    who pretentiously boast,
thinking they come off as serious.
When they are rejected these idiots play the part of slaves,
    for it is the only role left
to those who lack both elegant speech   1160
and good sense.
    And some poor foolish woman
will either fear them for their bravado
or think them dead if they no longer speak.
    This would never happen to a wise woman   1165
who finds pleasure in elegant language
spoken from a virtuous heart,

Plein d'une audace,
D'une doulceur et d'une bonne grace
Qui plaist tousjours à chacun quoy qu'il face.   1170
    Celuy aura
Du roy l'honneur: bien choysir le sçaura.
Par luy chacun bien recevoir pourra
    Juste sentence.
Luy seul congnoist l'estre et la subsistance   1175
D'Amour, le bien, aussi la penitence
    Qu'il peult donner.
Combien qu'il soit roy et puisse ordonner,
Son cueur humain n'a craint d'habandonner
    L'auctorité   1180
De commander contre la charité:
Il ayme mieulx souffrir l'austerité,
    La passion
Que donne à tous le dieu d'affection,
Et, comme estant d'autre condition,   1185
    Veult s'asservir
Par ferme amour, par seur et long servir,
Et par vertuz, des dames desservir
    Bon traictement,
En desprisant force et commandement.   1190
S'il luy plaisoit, il feroit autrement.
    Mais son hault cueur
A joinct l'amour, la vertu et l'honneur,
Qui l'a rendu de cruaulté vainqueur.
    Parquoy la palme,   1195
Louenge et gloire, et renommée et fame
Luy doit d'amour tout homme et toute femme.
    Puis que luy seul
Vous n'acceptez pour juge, dont j'ay dueil,
Vous qui avez faict ce piteux recueil   1200
    De nostre hystoire,
Vous en avez mieulx qu'un autre memoire
Et n'estes pas sans quelque experience
Que c'est d'amour, je vous en veulx bien croyre
Or jugez nous en bonne conscience. »   1205

« Je ne veulx point de mon sens abuser,
Mesdames, dis je, ains tresbien m'excuser

from a face full of courage,
sweetness, and grace
that is pleasing to all no matter what he may do.   1170
    This is the one who will receive honor
from the king. He will know to choose him.
Each one will receive
    a just sentence from him.
He alone knows the essence and substance   1175
of Love, the joy as well as the sorrow
    it can give.
Even though he is king with power to command,
his human heart is not afraid to abandon
    this authority   1180
to command against charity;
he prefers to suffer austerity
    and the passion
that the god of love gives to everyone.
And, as if he were of another status,   1185
    he wants to subjugate himself
through enduring love, long and steady service,
and virtue, scorning force and command,
    deserving to be treated well
by women.   1190
If he wanted to, he could act otherwise.
    But love, virtue, and honor
come together in his superior heart,
and this has made him triumph over cruelty.
    This is why every man and woman   1195
owes him acclaim, praise, and glory
for his renown and fame in love.
    Since you,
who have made this pitiful account of our story,
refuse to accept him as our only judge,   1200
    to my chagrin,
you have a better memory than another of what love is,
and you are not without experience in this matter.
I put my faith in you,
in good conscience be our judge. "   1205

"Ladies," I said, "I do not want to seem unreasonable,
but I do want to excuse myself

Que je ne suis pour juger suffisante
Et aussi peu à escrire duysante
Vostre debat, mais desir de sçavoir   1210
Tous voz ennuyz, ignorant mon povoir,
Me feist soubdain, sans y penser, promectre
De les escrire et dans ung livre mectre.
Ma foy promise, aussi vostre priere
Meirent ma peur et ma raison derriere.   1215
Ceste premiere et trop folle entreprise
Veulx mectre à fin, mais, si vous plaist, reprise
Je ne seray de la seconde erreur,
Qui doy avoir de la premiere horreur.

Mes cinquante ans, ma vertu affoyblie,   1220
Le temps passé commandent que j'oublye,
Pour mieulx penser à la prochaine mort,
Sans avoir plus memoire ny remort
Si en amour a douleur ou plaisir.
Doncques veuillez autre juge choysir   1225
Qui justement vous puisse satisfaire.
Je ne le puis ny ne le sçauroys faire. »

    La tierce dist: «Dames, voicy pitié,
Quant celuy seul nous ne povons avoir
Qui est l'abisme et source de sçavoir   1230
Et qui congnoist la parfaicte amytié.
    Seure je suis que, plus tost presenté
N'eust à ses yeulx ce livre pour le lire,
Que tout soudain ne nous eust bien sceu dire
Qui a le cueur de douleur plus tenté.   1235
    Son oeil deffaict toute faintise et ruze,
Son sens entend la fin de tous propous,
Et son cueur sent mieulx qu'en touchant le poulx
Qui ayme au non. Brief, nully ne l'abuse.
    Si nous perdons de luy le jugement   1240
Et de sa seur, qui de luy doit tenir
Et ses propos vertueux retenir,
Ung autre j'ay en mon entendement.

    C'est ceste là qui n'a gloire petite
De nostre temps, mais la plus estimée   1245

for not being an adequate judge,
or a barely suitable writer, of your debate.
The desire to know your troubles,   1210
forgetting about my skill,
made me suddenly promise without thinking
to write them down and put them in a book.
The promise that I made along with your pleading
shifted my fear and my reason to the background.   1215
I want to finish
this first foolish undertaking,
but, please, I will not be taken up in a second error;
I can only feel trepidation for the first.

My fifty years of life, my failing strength,   1220
demand that I forget the past
in order to better think of my approaching death,
without memory of or remorse over
whether I had pain or joy in love.
Therefore please choose another judge   1225
who could do you justice.
I have neither the strength nor the knowledge to do it.

    The third lady said, "Ladies, it is a shame
that we cannot have the one person
who is the first and endless source of knowledge   1230
and who knows what perfect friendship is.
    I am sure that as soon as this book
was presented to him to read,
we would know immediately
who among us has the heart most inclined toward sorrow.   1235
    His eyes discern all falsehood and deception,
his mind understands the purpose of every argument,
and his heart senses who loves or not more accurately
than the beat of the pulse. In brief, no one can deceive him.
    If we must lose his judgment   1240
as well as that of his sister who is much attached to him
and holds him dear to her heart,
I have another in mind.

    I speak of the woman
who has more than a little glory in our times;   1245

Est et la plus parfaictement aymée,
Ce que tresbien par ses vertuz merite.
　　Si par beaulté se congnoissent les femmes,
Allez où sont dames ou damoyselles,
Comme ung soleil au mylieu des estoilles　　　　　　　1250
Vous la verrez parmy toutes les dames.
　　Si par vertu son nom se doit congnoistre,
Voyez ses faictz, qui ne sont point cachez,
Tous pleins d'honneur, de nul vice tachez
Vous la verrez dessus toutes paroistre.　　　　　　　1255
　　Des ses bienfaictz chacun luy rend louenge,
Ils sont congneuz de tous les gens de bien;
Pour ses amys elle n'espargne rien
Et des meschans ennemys ne se venge.
　　Si on congnoist le nom par la fortune　　　　　　1260
De biens, d'honneur, de richesse et faveur,
Voyez qui ha de son maistre et seigneur
Ce qui luy plaist sans luy estre importune.
　　Mais tous les biens qu'elle en peult recevoir
Ne luy sont riens, car seullement heureuse　　　　　1265
Se tient de veoir par amour vertueuse
Tenir les cueurs uniz comme on peult veoir
　　Les cueurs du plus parfaict et plus parfaicte
Que l'on peult veoir, en qui Dieu et Nature
N'ont riens obmis de ce que creature,　　　　　　　1270
Pour acquerir perfection, souhaitte.
　　Acceptez donc madame la duchesse
Qui en vertuz et honneur passera
La plus parfaicte qui soit ne qui sera,
Ne qui fut onc. A elle je m'adresse.　　　　　　　1275
　　Elle congnoist que c'est de bien aymer:
Le vray amant la tient à son escolle,
On le peult bien congnoistre à sa parolle
Qui tant se doit priser et estimer.
　　Quand elle aura veu nostre doulx combat,　　　1280
Seure je suis que, sans favoriser
L'une partie et l'autre despriser,
Fera la paix de nostre long debat. »

Toutes, voyans sa bonne election,
A la duchesse où gist perfection　　　　　　　　　1285

she is the most esteemed and the most perfectly loved woman,
and this is as it should be; she has earned it through her virtues.
    If women are known by their beauty,
go to where there are women and young ladies;
you will see her among all these ladies   1250
like a sun among the stars.
    If her name is known by her virtue,
consider also her works which are full of honor
and there for all to see, not marred by any vice.
You will see her appear above all others.   1255
    Everyone praises her kindness
which is known to all gentlemen and gentlewomen.
She would do anything for her friends,
but does not seek revenge against her worst enemies.
    If fortune brings fame,   1260
see how she has received from her lord and master
possessions, honor, riches, and favor
without imposing herself on him.
    But all the possessions she receives
from him are nothing to her,   1265
for her only happiness lies in the virtuous love
that unites their hearts, as all can see:
    the hearts of the most perfect man and the most perfect woman
ever seen, in whom God and Nature
have omitted nothing that a being desires   1270
in order to achieve perfection.[39]
    Thus accept the duchess
who surpasses in honor and virtue
the most perfect woman who is, who will be,
and who has ever been. I ask her for help.   1275
    She knows what it is to love well:
she is at the school of her truly beloved.
This is easy to see in her speech
which should be highly prized and esteemed.
    I am sure that when she will have seen our gentle fight,   1280
she will bring peace to our long debate
without favoring one party
or underestimating the other."

When they saw this good choice,
all of the ladies willingly agreed to hand the judgment over   1285

Le jugement ont remis de leur faict.
Et moy, voyant que juge plus parfaict
L'on ne pourroit en ce monde trouver,
Leur bon advis voullu bien approuver,

En leur disant: « Possible n'est de mieulx,　　　　　　1290
Dames, choysir pour moy dessoubz le cieulx.
Par son bon sens de justice usera
Et sa doulceur ma faulte excusera.
Et s'il advient, et que bon il luy semble
Que le propos et l'escripture ensemble　　　　　　1295
Devant le roy puisse estre descouvert,
Seure je suis qu'ayant le livre ouvert
Regardera les poinctz où le lecteur
Se doit monstrer advocat de l'acteur
Et, en louant voz entreprinses haultes,　　　　　　1300
Excusera mes ignorantes faultes
Et servira de doulce couverture
Sa grant bonté à ma povre escripture.
Et si povez croire que sa sentence
Telle sera comme le roy la pense.　　　　　　1305

Ainsi pourrez par ce tresseur refuge
Avoir le roy, que desirez, pour juge,
Qui, sans reffuz, d'un cueur doulx et humain,
Regardera, venant de telle main,
Tout ce discours qui est digne de luy　　　　　　1310
Et l'escripture aura pour son appuy
Celle qui peult la deffendre de blasme
Et l'excuser comme une oeuvre de femme.
Ainsi pourra couvrir sa charité,
Devant les yeulx de la severité　　　　　　1315
Du roy, qui faict à tous jugement droit,
Ce que j'ay trop failly en chasque endroit. »

Cy endroict est la dixiesme hystoire où est une court en laquelle est arrivée la coche et toutes
les dames descendues d'icelle; la Royne de Navarre disant adieu aux troys dames et les
troys dames à elle. Et est ung page habillé de noir portant deux torches, mesme sont quelques
gentilz hommes attendans pour conduire la Royne à son logeis estant à l'opposite de celuy
desdictes troys dames.

to the duchess in whom all perfection lies.
And when I saw that we could never
in the world find a more perfect judge,
I wanted to approve their choice.

I said to them, "For me, ladies,   1290
there could not be a better judge under the skies.
She will use her good sense of justice,
and her sweetness will excuse my faults.
And if it happens that she thinks
the arguments and the writing together   1295
should be uncovered before the king,
I am sure that having opened the book,
she will look at those places where the reader
should be the advocate of the author.
Praising your great undertakings,   1300
she will excuse my ignorant faults,
and her great kindness will serve
as a gentle cover to my poor writing.
And so you can believe
that the king will share her verdict.   1305

Thus, through this safe refuge,
you will be able to have the king as your judge, just as you wanted.
Without refusing, he will look at all these arguments
worthy of him with a sweet and human heart,
especially as it will be given by the hand of the duchess.   1310
And the writing will have the support
of a woman who can defend it
and excuse it as the work of a woman.
In this way her charity will be able to conceal
the many mistakes I have made   1315
before the severity of the king
who judges all soundly."

*Here is the tenth story, where there is a courtyard in which the coach has arrived and all
the ladies have come out of it. The queen of Navarre is saying goodbye to the three ladies
and they to her. There is a page dressed in black who is carrying two torches and several
gentlemen waiting to drive the queen to her lodging which is across from theirs.*

Lors d'un accord sur le poinct nous trouvasmes
Que dans la coche au logeis arrivasmes.
La nuict me feist aux troys donner l'adieu,   1320
Non pour dormir, mais pour trouver ung lieu
Où, sans avoir de nul empeschement,
Peusse acquitter ma promesse et serment.
Mais, en voyant du propos la grandeur,
De mon langage et termes la laydeur,   1325
Honte me faict finer ma mauvaise oeuvre.
Mais verité veult que je la descoeuvre
A celle là que je prens pour aÿde,
Pour mon secours et souverain remyde

Cy endroit est la unziesme et derniere hystoire qui contient comment la Royne de Navarre
baille son livre à madame la duchesse d'Estampes toutes deux estans en une chambre fort
bien tapissée et parée; ladicte dame d'Estampes ayant une robbe de drap d'or frisé, fourrée
d'hermines mouchetées, une cotte de toylle d'or incarnat esgorgetée et dorée avec force
pierreries. La Royne de Navarre, tant en ceste hystoire que les autres, est habillée à sa façon
acoustumée, ayant ung manteau de veloux noir couppé ung peu soubz le braz, sa cotte
noyre assez à hault collet fourrée de martres, attachée d'esplingues par devant, sa cornette
assez basse sur la teste, et apparest ung peu sa chemise froncée au collet.

C'est donc à Vous, ma cousine et maistresse,   1330
Que mon labeur et mon honneur j'adresse,
Vous requerant comme amye parfaicte,
Que vous teniez ceste oeuvre par moy faicte
Ainsi que vostre et ainsi en usez
Et la monstrez, celez ou excusez.   1335
Faictes au roy entendre la substance
Pour à ces troys donner juste sentence.
Vostre parler luy fera mieulx sçavoir
Tout le discours que de luy faire veoir
Ce livre auquel mon escripture efface   1340
Tout le plus beau et la meilleure grace
De leurs propos, desquelz j'ay bien suyvie
La verité, mais la grace et la vie
Qui est dedans, je l'ay toute souillée
De fascheux motz, empeschée et brouillée   1345
Tant que je doy, en lieu d'augmenter, craindre
La grant valeur du propos faire moindre.

When we had reached an agreement on this point
we found that we had arrived at our lodgings.
Because night was upon us,   1320
I said goodbye to the three ladies,
not in order to sleep but to find a place
where I could fulfill my promise and oath without delay.
But upon seeing the greatness of the subject matter
and the ugliness of my language and words,   1325
shame drives me to put an end to my awful work.
Yet truth demands that I make it known
to the woman whose help I seek
for encouragement and sovereign remedy.

*Here is the eleventh and last story, which tells how the queen of Navarre gives her book
to the duchess of Étampes. Both women are in a room richly decorated and hung with
tapestries. The duchess is wearing a robe made of cloth of gold frisé, trimmed with flecked
ermine, over a dress of crimson gold, cut low at the neck and gilded with precious stones.
The queen of Navarre, in this story as in the others, is dressed in her usual fashion, wearing
a black velvet cloak slightly cut under the arms, a black dress with a high collar trimmed
with sable and fastened in the front with pins. She wears her shadow low on her head, and
her chemise, gathered at the neck, peeks out.*

To you, my cousin and my mistress,[40]   1330
I give my labor and my honor,
asking that you, as an example of perfect friendship,
accept this work that I have done,
as your own. Use it, share it,
hide it, or excuse it as you want.   1335
Make the king understand the substance of the work
so that a just judgment will be given to these three ladies.
Your speech will make him understand better
all the arguments than if he were to simply look at[41] this book.
My writing effaces the most beautiful   1340
and the most graceful of their arguments;
I have followed closely the truth of their speech
but have spoiled the grace and the life
contained within with awkward words;
I've hindered and clouded its understanding,   1345
so much so that instead of increasing the value of their arguments
I fear that I have reduced it.

Quant est de Vous, honteuse je ne suis
De vous monstrer le mieulx que faire puis.
S'il y a riens digne de mocquerie,   1350
Mocquez vous en, point n'en seray marrye,
Car seure suis qu'à ung second ne tiers
Ne monstrerez ma faulte voluntiers
Fors à celuy qui sur tous a povoir,
Envers lequel vous ferez tout devoir   1355
De m'excuser, j'en suis bien asseurée.
Car ceste amour, en noz cueurs emmurée,
Soit de monstrer ce livre ou le cacher
Fera si bien qu'on ne pourra toucher
A mon honneur qu'entre voz mains je mectz,   1360
Comme à la Dame en qui, je vous promectz,
J'ay mis cueur, corps, amour, entendement
Où ne verrez jamais nul changement.

Parlant de moy, oublier je ne doy,
Celles de qui la douleur, je le croy,   1365
Merite bien que vous vueillez entendre
Leurs passions, car elles veullent tendre
A qui aura de bien aymer l'honneur
Et d'avoir plus dans le cueur de douleur.
Ou ceste là qui en suspens demeure   1370
Pour ung amy, chassant l'autre à toute heure;
Ou ceste là de l'amy delaissée
Qui de regret importable est pressée;
Ou l'autre qui laisse ung amy parfaict
Pour ressembler, et en dit et en faict   1375
Aux autres deux et l'union tenir
Où ferme amour leurs troys cueurs faict unir.
Et ceste là se teindra bien heureuse
Que vous direz des troys plus douloureuse,
Et son malheur à tresgrant bien tiendra,   1380
Quand sur les deux vostre arrest obtiendra
De plus avoir qu'elles d'aspre douleur,
Ennuy, tourment, desespoir et malheur.
Les deux aussi, quant jugées seront
De vostre main, bien s'en contenteront.   1385
Et je seray trop plus qu'elles contente

But with you, I am not embarrassed
to show you the best that I can do.
If there is anything worthy of mockery,   1350
go ahead and make fun. I will not be angered
for I am sure that you will not readily show my faults
to a second or third person,
except to the one who has power over all.
With him you will do all that you should   1355
to excuse me, I am sure.
Whether you share this book or hide it,
the love that is encased in our hearts
will make it so that no one
will be able to question my honor;   1360
I put it in your hands now
just as I have placed my heart, my body, my love, my mind with you.
I promise that this will never change.

In speaking of myself, I must not forget
those whose pain deserves to be heard,   1365
I believe that you should hear about their passions.
They want to know which one will have the honor
of having loved well
and having felt pain most acutely in her heart.
Is it the one who hangs in suspense for a lover   1370
while constantly chasing off another?
Or is it the one who has been abandoned by her lover
and is burdened with unbearable sorrow?
Or is it the other who has left a perfect lover
in order to come together, in word and in deed,   1375
with the other two and to unite with them
in an enduring love that holds their hearts together?[42]
The one that you name the most sorrowful of the three
will be joyful, and she will embrace her pain
like a cherished treasure   1380
when the judgment is handed down
that she possesses more cruel pain,
anguish, torment, despair, and sorrow than the two others.
The two others will also be satisfied
when they are judged by your hand.   1385
And I will be the most content of all

Si mon labeur, lequel je vous presente,
Vous donne autant, en lysant, de plaisir
Qu'en l'escrivant j'en ay eu de desir.

Or le prenez et pensez qu'il procede   1390
De qui le lieu à nulle autre ne cede
De vous aymer et, actendant le bien
Que Dieu ung jour me donne le moyen
De vous monstrer par effect ma pensée,
Je luy requiers qu'ainsi que commencée   1395
Il a en vous fortune si tresbonne,
Que maintenant et pour jamais vous donne
Autant de bien, d'honneur et de santé
Comme il en fault, pour estre contenté,
A vostre cueur plein d'amour et de foy,   1400
Et tout autant que j'en desire au roy.

PLUS VOUS QUE MOY

if my labor that I present to you
gives you as much pleasure in reading
as I had desire in writing.

So take it and remember that it comes   1390
from someone who loves you above all others.
As I wait for the day
when God will give me the means
to show you in deed my thoughts for you,
I ask him that, just as he has already   1395
placed in you such great fortune,
for now and forever he give to you
as much treasure, honor, and health
as your faithful heart, full of love,
requires to be content;   1400
And I desire no less of the same for the king.

YOU MORE THAN I

IV

LA FABLE DU FAUX CUYDER / THE
FABLE OF FALSE PRIDE

EDITOR'S INTRODUCTION

It was the marriage of her namesake niece, Marguerite de France, to Emmanuel-Philibert, duke of Savoy, in 1541 that prompted the queen of Navarre to honor the occasion with this cautionary tale. The mythological *La fable du faux cuyder*, composed in decasyllabic couplets, enjoyed several printings in its author's own lifetime, in 1543, 1545, and 1547, and again was included in the second volume of her 1547 anthology, though under the changed title *L'histoire des Satyres et nymphes de Diane* (The Story of the Satyrs and Diana's Nymphs).

While the work readily lends itself to an evangelistic interpretation, the need to avoid false pride,[1] Marguerite sees the problem in terms of male/ female relations. She aims to warn her niece against the wiles and ruses of prowling males, depicted here in the guise of Satyrs, the modern synonym for lecher.[2] Was Marguerite thinking of her own experience with attempted rape, described in novellas 4 and 10 of the *Heptameron*?[3] The text would seem also to say something of the author's views on maternal love.[4] Diana's anger

---

1. Jourda, *Marguerite d'Angoulême*, 2: 417.

2. The Satyrs were mythological creatures, half human, half goat or horse, often depicted "ithyphallically," that is, with erected penises, symbol of their lecherous appetites. The god Pan was probably a Satyr of a milder and more subdued variety. They, along with their female counterparts, the Maenads, were part of the lively, drunken entourage of the god Dionysus. The creature of myth gave its name to a style of writing. In attic drama, authors created "Satyric" plays, and the Roman poets Horace and Juvenal both became famous for their biting verse satires.

3. See the analysis of these two stories and their autobiographical significance in Patricia Cholakian, *Rape and Writing in the Heptameron*, chaps. 2 and 7; and also in Cholakian and Cholakian, *Marguerite de Navarre*, chap. 2.

4. There has always been a considerable debate about just how "maternal" Marguerite was. Certainly, as a woman of royal standing, she inevitably hired tutors and a governess for her

against her five disobedient nymphs is mitigated by devotion, and like the irate animal mother, she is "prepared to fight to the end" to protect her children from the ravenous wolf. Like any fable, this one too has an explicit moral, placed, however, at the beginning of the tale rather than at the end. But Marguerite by no means is satisfied with a simple statement in the manner of Aesop or La Fontaine. She plunges into a lengthy philosophical commentary.

only surviving child, Jeanne d'Albret, and her complicated court life did not permit her to spend endless time with her. On the other hand, in any crisis situation, she was involved, when, for example, Jeanne as a young girl fell ill, and in later years when Jeanne was forced to marry a man she did not love. On that occasion, her distraught mother worked diligently to see that the marriage was properly annulled.

LA FABLE DU FAUX CUYDER

Le mal qui est l'absence de tout bien,
Et qui se peult hors de tout nommer rien,
Qui n'est creé ne fait: car le facteur
De tout n'est point de mal et vice autheur;
Ce rien, lequel hors de tout fault vuyder,   5
N'est plus qu'un vain menteur, et Faux Cuyder,
Lequel produit un depravé desir
Dessoubs l'espoir d'un incongnu plaisir.
Et n'ont Cuyder, Desir, ny esperance,
Nul fondement, qu'aveuglée Ignorance.   10
Ce mal icy, receu au cœur des hommes,
Au plus profond ha engendré grands sommes
D'inventions, moyens, subtilitez,
Deceptions, feintes, habilitez,
Pour parvenir au poinct jà pretendu,   15
Du bien, non bien, si bien feust entendu.
Dont le desir, par espoir, sans propos
Oste la paix de l'homme, et le repos.
Et si travail ha du commencement,
Ne pensez pas moindre en fin le tourment: 20
Car arrivé à la fin, où il pense
De tous ses maux avoir la recompense,
Son espoir vain, sans congé l'abandonne;
Son fol desir tant de travail luy donne,
Qu'en lieu d'avoir grand joye de sa prise,   25
Maudit le jour, l'espoir, et l'entreprise,
Comme verrez en la presente histoire:

THE FABLE OF FALSE PRIDE

Evil, which is the absence of all good[5]
and which above all things can be called nothingness,
is neither created nor made: for the inventor
of all creation is not the creator of vice and evil.
This nothingness, which we should do away with,   5
is false pride.
In the disguise of hope, it gives birth
to a depraved desire for some unknown pleasure.
Pride, desire, and hope have no other origin
than blind ignorance.   10
This evil, buried in the human heart,
is at the root of countless dissimulations,
schemes, deceptions, shams,
deceitful maneuvers, and plots
to achieve premeditated   15
and so-called good ends.
Such desires, driven by vain hope,
deprive one of peace and tranquility.
And if the effort is great in the beginning,
do not expect the torment at the end to be any less.   20
For once at the end, when one expects
a reward for all the exertion,
vain hope with no further ado disappears.
Foolish ambition causes so much distress
that instead of the joys of a prosperous issue,   25
one curses the expectation, the undertaking, and its results.
As you shall see, ladies-in-waiting,[6]

Où je pretens paindre en vostre memoire
(Dames d'honneur) des hommes la malice,
Et leurs regrets, quand par vertu, leur vice   30
Est surmonté: joint aussi qu'ignorance
Du mal, couvert soubz honneste apparence,
Souvent deçoit celles qui n'ont apris,
Que prendre peult celuy, que l'on ha pris,
Et que vertu d'ignorance guydée,   35
En fin, des Dieux est bien souvent aydée.

Un jour trescler, que le soleil luysoit,
Et sa clarté un chacun induysoit
Chercher les boys, haults, fueilluz, et espais,
Pour reposer à la frescheur, en paix.   40
Faunes des boys, Satyres, Demydieux,
Sceurent pour eux tresbien choisir les lieux
Si bien couverts que le chault en rien nuire
Ne leur pouvoit, tant sceult le Soleil luyre,
Sur le lict mol, d'herbette, espesse et verte,   45
Se sont couchez, ayans pour leur couverte
Une espesseur de branchettes, yssues,
Des arbres verds, jointes comme tyssues,
Et auprès d'eux (pour leur soif estancher)
Sailloit dehors d'un cristallin rocher   50
Douce et claire eau, tresagreable à voir,
Qui d'arroser le lieu faisoit devoir,
Mais en voulant courir par les præries,
Gros Dyamans et riches pierreries
Luy faisoyent tort, et à son cours injure,   55
Dont il sailloit d'entre eux si doux murmure,
Que les lassez du chault, par terre mis,
Furent soudain d'un tel somme endormis,
Que long repos, soubs Cedres et Cyprès,
Leur amena un tel resveil après,   60
Que riz et jeux, dont ils feirent assez,
Monstrerent bien qu'ilz estoyent delassez.
A ce resveil leur faim point ne tenterent,
Ne de l'eau pure ilz ne se contenterent,
Mais de fort vin du far de Silenus,   65
Lors se sont paints ces Satyres cornus,

in this present tale, where I wish to impart to you
the malevolence of men and their regrets
when virtue overcomes vice.   30
With this I shall also show that ignorance
of a wickedness that is hidden behind an honest appearance
can often deceive those who have not learned
that the conqueror can become the conquered,
and that the gods⁷ can often in the end   35
come to the rescue of virtuous innocence.

One clear day, when the sun was shining,
its brilliance inspired people
looking for quiet rest in the fresh air
to head for thick, leafy woods in high places.   40
Wood fauns, Satyrs, and demigods
knew how to choose the most sheltered spots,
where the heat, however strong,
could do them no harm.
They lay down on soft, thick,   45
green grasses, using as covering
blankets woven together
from tree branches.
Nearby, to quench their thirst,
a sweet, clear stream, lovely to look at,   50
and a water source for the surrounding area,
came pouring forth from out of the crystalline rocks.
But in its attempt to wend its way through the fields,
diamonds and precious stones
encumbered its path,   55
making such a gentle noise
that all the sun-weary
suddenly fell into a deep sleep.⁸
Their lengthy sleep under the cedars and cypresses
brought about a lively awakening.   60
The laughing and frolicking
showed how thoroughly rested they were.
Wide awake, they now desired
neither food nor pure water, but the strong wine
taken from the towers of Silenus.⁹   65
Then these horned Satyrs painted themselves,

Dont la chaleur, qui brusloit leurs entrailles,
Entrepreneurs les feit de grands batailles:
Non contre Mars, pas n'ont la hardiesse,
Mais ouy bien contre la grand'Deesse   70
Dyane chaste, et contre ses pucelles.
Parquoy l'un dit qu'estre separé d'elles
En ces beaux lieux, en ce temps gracieux,
Pleins de plaisirs et biens delicieux,
Leur estoit mort et tourment importable.   75
Mais que nous est (disoyent ilz) profitable
D'estre sains, forts, abondans en tous biens,
Quand celuy seul sans lequel ne sont riens
Les autres tous nous default maintenant?
A ce mot là, chacun incontinent   80
Cria: Il fault sans plus de temps attendre,
Ou par amour ou bien par force, en prendre.
Mais un vieillard tout gris, bien entendu,
Les ha fait taire, et leur ha respondu:
Enfans, amys, pensez à cest affaire,   85
Et ne cuydez chose legere à faire
De force user sur celle qui commande:
Car vous sçavez que Dyane la grande
Ha tel povoir que, si vous approchez
De son tropeau et la moindre touchez,   90
Son coup divin vous fera tost sentir,
Tant que trop tard viendra le repentir.
De les penser par voz vives raisons,
Par long servir, prieres, oraisons,
En fin gaigner jusqu'à mettre en oubly   95
L'honneur duquel leur cœur est anobly,
Vous perdez temps, car si bien sont apprises
Que par parole elles ne seront prises.
Mais il y ha une seule science
Pour decevoir, c'est d'avoir patience,   100
Dissimulant du tout l'affection
Que vous portez, et par grand' fiction,
Fuir les boys ausquelz elles se tiennent,
Prez et ruisseaux où elles vont et viennent,
Sans plus les voir ne plus les pourchasser,   105
Et les laissant sans crainte prou chasser.

and the heat, which burned their insides,
made them hanker for a confrontation,
not with Mars—they were not so daring—
but with the great goddess,   70
the chaste Diana and her virgins.
And so one of them said that to be separated from them,
in this beautiful setting full of many delights,
and during this lovely weather,
was unbearable torment and even death.   75
"But what does it profit us," they all said,
"to be healthy, strong, and rich in goods,
if we lack the one thing without which
all the rest means nothing?"
At these words, they all cried aloud: 80
"With no further delay we must either by force
or seduction take what we desire."
A gray-haired, respected old man
silenced them and said:
"Friends and children, think carefully about this matter   85
and do not act in haste to use force
against the one who commands.
As you must know, the mighty Diana
has such power that if you approach
her charges and in the least way harm them,   90
she will so quickly cause you to feel her divine wrath
that it will be too late to repent.
You are wasting your time if you think
that with your clever tactics, long service, prayers, and supplications
you will persuade them to forsake   95
the noble principles engraved on their hearts.
They are so well tutored
that no words are going to win them over.
There is but one strategy that will work
and that is to bide your time,   100
conceal your emotions,
pretend to flee from the woods
where they are gamboling about
through fields and along riverbanks,
and, avoiding them altogether,   105
allow them to hunt at will.

De vos costez, prenez voz passetemps
A mille jeux, ainsi que gens contens;
Et si de loing vous viennent regarder,
Reculez vous, laissez les hazarder   110
De s'approcher du lieu où, soubs le jeu,
Pourront trouver (sans y penser) le feu
Qui peu à peu, par un desir d'ouyr,
Vous pourra bien d'elles faire jouyr.
Plus tost ne fut ce conseil recité,   115
Que chacun dit: Il ha dit verité.
Alors ont fait leur conjuration,
Mettans à fin leur conspiration,
Qu'un chacun d'eux feroit tout son devoir,
Par trahison, de vaincre et decevoir   120
Celles par qui leur force est impuissance
Et leur raison trop congue ignorance.
Or ont leurs cœurs (ce semble) contentez
D'estre remplis de faulses voluntez.
Le desespoir de jamais n'estre aymez   125
Les ha ainsi de fureur enflammez.
Il ne leur chault de faillir à leurs esmes,
Ayans du tout satisfait à eux mesmes;
Et vont disant: qui ne peult faire amye
Jouyesse donc de l'aymée ennemye.   130
Courans s'en vont, en remplissant les boys
De leurs chansons et tresplaisantes voix,
Que l'on oyoit jusques dela la prée
Où la Deesse estoit sur la vesprée
Venue au bort, et soubs les verds Sapins,   135
Soubs cabinets de flouris Aubepins,
Pour reposer son corps laz, s'estoit mise,
Et au mylieu de ses vierges assise,
En leur faisant de la chasse records,
Et du grand Cerf portant dixhuit cors,   140
Qu'elle avoit pris, leur disant qu'exercice
Estoit la mort de tout peché et vice;
Les exhortant de si bien se garder,
Que le Soleil peussent bien regarder:
Car, sans rougir ny honte recevoir,   145
L'œil chaste et pur ne craint point de le voir,

Meanwhile, take your pleasure in the pastimes
and thousands of games of the happy.
And if perchance they come to spy on you,
draw back and let them take the initiative   110
to come closer until, innocently and slowly
fired up by your sport and wanting to hear,
they make it possible for you
to get the better of them."
This good advice was hardly given   115
when each shouted: "He has spoken the truth."
And thus they all agreed
and perfected their plans,
that each would perform his traitorous task
in order to deceive and conquer   120
those for whom their strength is weakness
and their too-well-known reason, ignorance.
And so the Satyrs seemed eager
to surrender to their cunning desires.
Fear of never finding love   125
had filled them with longing.
Overly sure of themselves, they were not the least concerned
that they might fail in their endeavors.
They shouted out: "Who lacks a lover,
let him take his pleasure with his beloved enemy."   130
And so they went rushing through the woods,
filling them with their songs and pleasant voices,
audible as far as the edge of the field,
where at evening tide, under the green pines
and flowering hawthorns,   135
the goddess had come
to rest her weary body.
Seated among her virgins,
she told them of her hunt
and the eighteen-point stag she had caught.   140
She told them that exercise
was death to sin and vice
and exhorted them to be on their guard
so that they could stand in the light of the sun
without turning red with shame.   145
A chaste and pure countenance does not fear

Ny d'estre veu ny de luy ny du monde;
Mais l'œil meschant dont le cœur est immunde,
Quand il se fault au cler Soleil monstrer,
Ne se peult tant couvrir ny acoustrer   150
Que verité ne luy paingne en la face
Le meschant cas qui son honneur efface.
En ce disant la main soubs son chef mit,
Et en dormant les Vierges endormit.
Le grand travail leur causa un sommeil   155
Auquel nul bruit n'apporte le resveil;
Car si profond estoit et si pesant
Que bruit ou son, feust il triste ou plaisant,
Ne l'empeschoit; dont la plus travaillée
Estoit plus forte à estre resveillée.   160
Celles qui moins de labeur avoyent pris
Furent plus prompts au resveil les esprits;
Parquoy de cinq sur l'herbette estendues
Furent les voix plaisantes entendues
Des Dieux cornus, qui, rompans leur dormir,   165
Feirent leurs cœurs soudainement fremir,
Tant de la peur d'estre par eux surprises
Que du plaisir. Lors (comme mal apprises),
Le lieu heureux pour reposer laisserent,
Et au travail malheureux s'avanserent.   170
Du bout des boys les doux chants escoutans,
Veirent près d'eux les Satyres chantans,
D'elles si près que de peur d'arresterent.
Eux, les voyant, à fuyr s'appresterent,
Disans tout hault: Fuyons, Dyane est là.   175
Elles, ryans en entendant cela,
Creurent pour vray qu'auprès de leur maistresse
N'eussent osé leur faire ennuy ou presse,
Qui feit leurs pas en silence mouvoir,
Pour les cuyder tromper et decevoir.   180
Ce cuyder là fut d'eux mieux apperceu
Que ne fut pas d'elles le cœur deceu,
Dont en cuydant decevoir, les deceües
Dedens le pré bien avant sont yssues.
Eux, les voyans peu à peu approcher,   185
Se vont asseoir et les cordes toucher

its gaze or that of the world.
But the evil one with mischievous intent,
when she appears before the sun's light,
however much she cowers or hides,   150
shows upon her face the truth of the wickedness
of deeds which have obliterated honor.
Saying this, she placed her hand under her head
and put herself and her virgins to sleep.
Hard work caused a sleep   155
that no sound could disturb.
So deep and heavy was their slumber
that no noise, pleasant or sad,
could awaken them. The most exhausted
were the hardest to arouse,   160
and those who had done the least
were the easiest to stir into motion.
Thus five of those spread out on the grass
heard the agreeable sounds
coming from the horned creatures,   165
and they arose, their hearts suddenly aflutter,
as much from the abruptness of the disturbance
as from pleasure. And so, alas,
they left their pleasant retreat
and headed toward their unhappy end.   170
Attracted by the sweet sounds from the forest's edge,
they saw singing Satyrs approaching so close,
that, afraid, they came to a complete standstill.
The Satyrs, upon seeing the virgins, made ready to flee,
saying out loud: "Let us run away, Diana is near."   175
The virgins, laughing at this remark,
actually believed that, with their mistress close by,
the Satyrs would not dare bother or come after them.
This gave them the courage to move closer,
stealthily, in order to trick and deceive them.   180
That blind trust was better perceived by the Satyrs
than the virgins in their unsuspecting hearts.
Believing they had deceived them,
the foolish virgins moved further out into the meadow.
Watching as they approached,   185
they returned to their places to pluck the strings

Des instrumens et les Fleustes sonner.
Doubles Flageolz faisoyent lors raisonner
Avec les voix, et, sans faire semblant
Des derobeurs, ilz vont les cœurs emblant.   190
Les cœurs, saisiz de si plaisans accords,
Sans y penser approcherent les corps
De celles qui paravant eussent craint
De regarder un de ces Cornus paint.
Mais le plaisir, usant de sa puissance,   195
De leur danger leur osta congnoissance.
L'une disoit à l'autre: Retournez.
Où fuyez vous? Ilz ont le doz tournez;
Regardez les, nul d'eux ne nous regarde.
Approchons nous, d'avoir mal n'avons garde: 200
A leurs doux chants ilz sont trop amusez,
Et ne sont pas si folz, ny abusez
De nous toucher, car croyez qu'ilz ont crainte
De courroucer notre Dyane sainte.
Ilz sont meilleurs que nous ne les pensons.   205
Or escoutons leurs plaisantes chansons,
Oyez leurs voix, leurs diminutions;
Oyez des gens les fortes passions,
Oyez leurs voix, leurs accords, leur mesure.
Un jour icy un moment ne nous dure.   210
Pour mieux ouyr, chacune s'est assise
Dessus le pré, estimant à sottise
D'avoir tant craint et si long temps eu peur
D'un tel plaisir, qui ressuscite un cœur
Et faisoit bien là chacune son compte   215
De ne laisser jamais plaisir pour honte.
Après avoir les chansons bien ditées
Sur le verd pré longuement escoutées,
Ces Dieux chantans, pensans leur gaing certain,
Dirent un son plus plaisant et hautain,   220
Et si treshault ilz ont sonné un bransle
Qu'une chacune en s'eslevant s'esbransle,
Et à danser toutes mettre se vont,
Monstrans que point d'effroy ne crainte n'ont.
Sautans, dansans par excessive joye,   225
Nulle n'y ha qui son ennemy voye.

of their instruments and to sound their flutes.
They blended their voices with the double flageolets,
and giving no appearance of being debauchers,
harbored villainous thoughts in their hearts.   190
Inspired by such seductive sounds,
those who had previously shied away
from the painted horns,[10]
moved their bodies closer.
Desire, exercising its power,   195
blinded them to their danger,
and they whispered amongst themselves: "Turn around.
Why should we flee? Their backs are turned toward us.
Look, not a one of them is even looking at us.
Let us move closer. We have nothing to fear.   200
They are enjoying themselves too much with their music.
Moreover, they are not so foolish as to dare
to touch us, for, rest assured, they would be too afraid
to irritate the divine Diana.
They are not as bad as we think.   205
So let us listen to their entertaining songs
and how they modulate their voices.
Let us soak in the deep feelings of these people,
their harmonious and measured singing,
for a day is but a moment here."   210
Imprudently, believing that they had too much
and for too long dreaded such heart-warming delights,
in order to hear better, they all sat down
on the grassy field,
each in her way convincing herself   215
that there was no shame in enjoyment.
Having performed with skill,
and on these verdant fields given sound to their songs,
these singing gods, thinking their conquest assured,
began playing a more lively and catchy tune.   220
They struck up so animated an air
that each virgin rose to rock to the rhythm.
They all began to dance in order to prove
that they had neither fear nor hesitation.
Hopping and jumping with such delight,   225
none gave a thought to her enemy.

Eux qui n'ont rien perdu, pour leurs doux chants,
Des faux desirs de leurs cœurs tant meschants,
En les voyant plus près d'eux approcher,
Moins font semblant de les voir ny chercher.   230
O la douceur, ô la sagesse feinte!
O l'abstinence et bonté de contrainte!
O faux semblant, destruction des ames,
Qui sçavez bien seduire simples femmes!
Simplicité, d'ignorance conduite,   235
Souvent avez (sans y penser) seduite.
Où allez vous (povres vierges), helas!
Voyez vous point que vous tombez ès laz
De ceux qui n'ont autre soing dens leurs cœurs
Qu'estre de vous et voz honneurs vainqueurs?   240
Helas! où est Dyane vostre dame?
Où est la peur d'acquerir d'elle blasme?
Levez en hault ceste veüe abaissée;
Voyez le lieu où vous l'avez laissée
Des ennemys bien près et d'elle loing,   245
Tard vous pourra secourir au besoing.
Considerez comme à ce plaisant jeu
Plaisir vous ha tirées peu à peu.
Où est la peur des Satyres cornus?
Osez vous bien regarder leurs corps nuds?   250
Osez vous bien approcher leur repaire,
Ce que jadis vous n'eussiez osé faire?
Est mort en vous le chaste enseignement
De vous garder soliciteusement
De ces trompeurs, tant seulement d'ouyr   255
Leurs plaisans sons, ne vous en resjouyr,
Que si souvent Dyane la divine
Vous exhortoit, et que d'œil ny de mine,
Ne vous advinst de leur donner attrait?
Car dangereux en estoit le retrait.   260
Tant bien vous ha d'Amour dit les merveilles,
Et que plus tost ha gaigné les oreilles
Par un plaisir couvert d'honnesteté,
Que l'œil n'estoit à l'oreille arresté,
Et qu'en ayant l'œil et l'oreille ensemble,   265
Il n'y ha cœur si chaste qui ne tremble.

Thanks to their captivating music,
the Satyrs had lost none of the wicked thoughts
of their evil minds. Watching them come ever closer,
they made less pretense of indifference.   230
O sweet seduction, O bogus prudence,
O pretend kindness and abstinence,
O sham, destroyer of souls,
you know how to seduce naïve women,
you have often unthinkingly taken in   235
the simple and the innocent.
Miserable virgins, where are you headed?
Do you not see that you are falling into the trap
set by those who have no other thought in mind
than to conquer you and your honor?   240
Alas, where is your Lady Diana
and where your fear of her displeasure?
Raise your eyes.
Look where you have set your sights,
near enemies, and far from the one who in your need   245
is probably too late to come to your aid.
See how desire has slowly drawn you
toward this pleasant distraction.
Where is your apprehension of these horned Satyrs?
Do you dare look upon their nakedness,   250
approach the lair which earlier
you would never have dared come close to?
Have you forgotten the lessons in prudence
that the divine Diana taught you,
to eschew at all costs such debauchers,   255
never to listen to or take pleasure
in their bewitching songs,
or by eye or gesture
give them encouragement?
Theirs is a dangerous haunt.   260
She has also told you of the wonders of love,
that love has no sooner won over your ears
with beguiling words of pleasure
than the eye is joined to the ear;
and when ear is joined to eye,   265
there is no pure heart that will not tremble.

Que pensez vous? irez vous plus avant?
Avez vous mis ainsi l'honneur au vent?
Las! retournez et plus cy n'attendez,
Et ceste voix de Dyane entendez,   270
De qui l'Esprit (en songeant) bien fort crie:
Las! retournez, mes filles, je vous prie.
Mais, tout ainsi qu'un corps yvré de vin
Ne peult juger rien qui soit de divin,
Ayant perdu voix, ouye et parole,   275
Ainsi advint à ceste bende folle,
Qui, sans ouyr ne penser rien de bien,
Ont approché de leur mortel lien.
Ces Dieux, voyans desja l'heure venue
Que chacun pense avoir s'amye nue,   280
Cessans leur voix, ont tous jetté par terre
Leurs instrumens pour commencer la guerre.
Elle saultans n'ouyrent plus nul son,
Mais aux Cornus veirent changer façon,
Car leur douceur en rigueur fut tournée.   285
O la cruelle et piteuse journée!
Pour evader leurs mains pensent fuyr,
Eux en courant pensent d'elles jouyr.
Courir les fait le mal qui se doit craindre,
Suyvre les fait l'amour qui peult contraindre.   290
Crainte et amour font chacune leur course.
Helas! venez, Dyane, à leur recourse.
Vous estes loing, leurs ennemys sont près;
Despechez vous, venez y tout exprès.
Tous courent bien pour le commencement,   295
Mais la force est de durer longuement.
L'herbe trop haulte et la longue distance
Ayans perdu faveur et assistance
De vous, en qui ont mis tout leur espoir,
Leur ha osté toute force et povoir.   300
Ainsi s'en vont courantes et criantes,
Celles qui sont de Dyane priantes,
Et congnoissans leur corps n'estre assez fort.
Chacune crie au secours de la mort.
Droit au torrent grand et inevitable,   305
Où finissoit ce pré tant delectable,

What are you thinking? Will you venture farther?
Have you thrown caution to the wind?
Turn back, give no further heed,
and listen to Diana's voice,   270
who in her thoughts cries out this message to you:
"Come back, my girls, I beg you."
But like a body drunk with wine
and having lost speech and hearing,
and unable to attune to the divine,   275
so it was with this foolish band,
which, without speech or reasonable thought,
marched headlong towards its demise.
These gods, seeing the moment ripe,
each to seize his naked victim,   280
ceased to sing and dropped all instruments
in order to begin the attack.
Leaping about, the virgins no longer heard music,
but noticed a great change in the horned creatures' manner.
Their gentleness abruptly disappeared.   285
Oh, what a cruel and pitiful day was this!
While the virgins looked to avoid grasping hands,
the Satyrs rushed in to have their fill.
While frightening malevolence caused these to flee,
ardent passion caused those to pursue.   290
Passion and fear each ran its course.
It is time, Diana, to come to the rescue.
You are far and the enemy near.
Make haste and come at once.
Your virgins managed well enough in the beginning   295
but have not the stamina to endure.
The grasses are high and the distance great.
Having lost your aid and goodwill,
in which lies all their hope,
they are without force and energy.   300
And so shouting and pleading
to Diana, they proceed.
Knowing themselves too weak,
they ask for death,
and head straight for the wide and unavoidable torrent   305
at the end of the delectable field.

S'en vont courant pour abreger leurs vies
Et n'estre point des ennemys ravies.
Venans au bord, gueres ne sejournerent,
Que bras et yeux vers le Soleil tournerent,   310
Luy presentant en lamentation
Et treshaults cris leur desolation;
Car leur courir, leur travail et leur peine
N'empeschoit point, ny leur faute d'alaine,
De dire au long à Dyane en plourant,   315
Ainsi que font femmes qui vont mourant:
Si nous eussions (ô Deesse sans vice)
Failly vers toy par certaine malice;
Si dens noz cœurs fut le consentement
De n'obeïr à ton commandement;   320
Si ceste amour de toy tant defendue;
Y fust par nous contre toy descendue,
Si nous avons ce grand crime commis,
De nous renger devant tes ennemys;
Si nostre cœur n'estoit de chasteté   325
Plein, net et pur, ainsi qu'il ha esté,
Les yeux vers toy nous craindrions de lever,
Sans te prier de nous vouloir sauver.
Mais, congnoissans que ta chaste rigueur
De ta douceur n'empesche la vigueur,   330
Nous t'appellons à ceste heure à nostre ayde,
Ne voyans plus en terre nul remede.
Si nous t'avons par folie offensée,
Qui fut plus tost mise en fin que pensée,
En eslongnant la place trop heureuse   335
D'auprès de toy (ô Dame vertueuse),
Nous confessons ce peché estre tel
Que meritons de toy tourment mortel;
Duquel tourment ne te demandons grace:
Nous le voulons recevoir sur la place,   340
Ce que de toy voulons avant mourir.
Las! ce n'est pas de noz corps secourir
De l'aspre Mort où les sacrifions;
Mais c'est que toy, en qui nous nous fions,
Par ton honneur vueilles sauver le nostre,   345
Ne permettant que nostre mal plus oultre

They run to end their lives
and escape their ravenous pursuers.
Reaching the river's edge,
they promptly raised eyes and arms toward the sun,   310
expressing their desolation
in cries and lamentation,
despite their fatigue
and pain from running,
they supplicated Diana at great length,   315
like condemned women:
"O most untainted goddess,
if we had failed you through willful malice,
if in our hearts we had plotted
to disobey your commandments,   320
if we had set out to attack
that love which you have nourished in us,
if we had committed the crime
of allying ourselves with your enemies,
if our hearts were not, as always,   325
pure, wholesome, and full of kindness,
we would have hesitated to turn to you
and beg that you wish for our deliverance.
But knowing that your demanding love
does not restrict your vow of kindness,   330
and seeing ourselves without assistance,
we beseech you now for your help.
If we have foolishly offended you—
more through circumstances than premeditation—
by abandoning, O most virtuous lady,   335
that happy place next to you,
we confess that this transgression
deserves from you mortal torment,
for which we do not ask your grace.
We seek urgent forgiveness   340
before our demise.
We do not ask that you give us protection from cruel death,
to which we sacrifice our bodies,
but that you, in whom we have put our trust,
through your honor, save ours,   345
and not allow this iniquity to continue,

Face son cours, mais arrester les pas
De ces meschans, qu'ilz ne nous prennent pas:
Dix mille mortz nous sont plus agreables
Que de tomber en leurs mains redoutables.   350
A ta bonté (dont sans cesse tu uses)
Nous supplions faire à toy noz excuses,
Et regarder que sommes ignorantes,
Icy, sans toy, comme brebis errantes.
En abaissant l'œil de ta grand'haultesse,   355
Voy qu'il n'y a en nous nulle finesse,
Et que le mal que n'avions esprouvé,
Avons plustout que bien pensé trouvé.
Las! comment peult un chaste cœur douter
Que soubz un chant plaisant à escouter   360
Soit tant de mal et de vice caché?
Qui penseroit que le cœur fust taché
D'aspre rigueur, ne voyant apparence
Que de douceur? Qui n'auroit esperance
De se garder et l'honneur et la vie   365
Devant ceux là où l'on ne void envie,
Ne signe aucun d'amour et de poursuite,
Plustot monstrans grand' nonchalance et fuite?
Qui eust cuydé l'amour au cœur de ceux
Qui de hanter Dames sont paresseux?   370
Qui eust douté avoir en leur cœur part,
Quand nous voyans s'enfuyoient autre part?
On dit que l'œil est du cœur messager,
Et qu'au parler est le plus grand danger.
Ceste leçon avons bien retenue,   375
Et n'est jamais leur parole venue
Jusques à nous; et de nous regarder
Se sont tresbien les traytres sceu garder.
Doit on fuyr n'estant point assailly?
Doit on juger un homme estre sailly   380
Hors de raison, sans avoir apparence?
Que peult juger innocente ignorance,
Quand le rebours de leur cruelle fin
Monstré nous ont? Et nostre cœur peu fin,
Pensant trouver auprès d'eux seureté,   385
Acquis n'ha rien que malheureuseté.

but put a halt to the plot of these evildoers
who wish to ravish us.
We would rather die ten thousand deaths
than fall into these terrifying hands.   350
We offer up our apologies to your bounteous generosity
and ask that you take into account our ignorance
and acknowledge that without you
we are like so many lost sheep.
As you look down upon us from on high,   355
observe that there is no deceit in us,
and that whatever evil we have experienced
came rather from our having mistaken it for virtue.
Alas, how can a chaste heart suspect
deception and trickery to be hidden   360
behind such pleasant-sounding melodies?
Who could have guessed
that under the guise of amiability
lay a heart of malevolent dishonesty?
Who would not have expected to keep   365
honor and life intact where there were no signs
of avidity, lust, or aggression,
but rather indifference and timidity?
Who would have imagined passion in the hearts of those
who seemed reluctant to frequent the opposite sex?   370
How could we have imagined arousing interest
in those who were fleeing?
They say that the eye is the messenger of the soul
and speech a great danger.
We have learned that lesson well.   375
But nothing they said ever reached our ears,
and they gave no indication
of wanting to look at us.
Should one run away when not pursued?
Is it reasonable to consider oneself attacked   380
without any evidence?
What, in our total innocence, could we have concluded,
when everything they did
concealed their evil motives?
Our naiveté, anticipating safety,   385
was rewarded with nothing but mischief.

Cecy disant, ne nous voulons fier
Que noz raisons puissent justifier
Nostre piteux et malheureux affaire:
Car envers toy ne pretendons que faire   390
Humilier le regard de ton œil,
Et regarder par pitié nostre dueil,
Qui est si grand, si extreme et si fort
Que plus ne peult. O divin reconfort,
Nous sçavons bien qu'ignorance n'est digne   395
De nous couvrir; mais ta bonté divine,
Par charité qui toutes autres cœuvre,
Effacera le mal de ton chef d'œuvre.
Nous ne voulons compter pour tous merites,
Sinon qu'à toy (encores trespetites   400
Et du tout riens) avons esté vouées.
Tu nous retins, dont nous fusmes louées:
Souvienne toy qu'à ce commencement
Tu nous nourris du laict tant doucement;
Et puis, ainsi que la force croissoit,   405
Ta douce main chacune repaissoit
D'herbe, de pain et chair viande forte,
En nous donnant tous habitz à ta sorte.
Si à noz corps tu as pourveu si bien,
Donnant travail et repos sans moyen,   410
Sans nous laisser par grand repos tomber,
Ny au travail extreme succomber,
A noz espritz as donné nourriture,
Bien congoissant de chacun la nature:
Car des vertus que l'on doit adorer   415
Par toy n'avons nulle peu ignorer.
Toutes vertus sont peintes dens ton Temple;
En toy se peult de tout ce prendre exemple.
Bref nous avons de toy tout bien apris,
En qui tous biens sont encloz et compris.   420
Apris? Las! non; mais, ainsi qu'un festu
Retire à soy l'Ambre, ta grand'vertu,
Nous unissant à toy, nous rendoit telles
Que nous estions par ta grand' beauté belles,
Promptes à bien par ta grand' diligence,   425
Prudence ayant aussi par ta prudence;

This said, we do not think
that our excuses justify
our pitiful and unhappy state.
We merely hope to soften   390
the harshness of your judgment
and to make you look with kindness upon our grief,
which could not be more powerfully strong or violent.
O divine comfort, we know
that our ignorance does not excuse us,   395
but your blessed benevolence,
which so generously pardons so many others,
will wipe out the errors in your best work.
Although we are of small significance and value,
we ask your indulgence   400
because of our devotion to you.
You took us in, which earned us honors.
Remember how in the beginning
you so lovingly nourished us with your milk.
And then as we grew,   405
how your kind hand fed us
cereals, bread, and tasty meats,
and dressed us all in your manner.
If you tended to the needs of our bodies,
giving us equal doses of work and play—   410
neither overindulgence of amusement nor
excess of labor—
you also cultivated our minds,
recognizing each of our particularities.
As for your admirable virtues,   415
we have in no way disrespected any of them.
All these are inscribed in your temple,
with you as their principal model.
In short, we have learned well all that you,
who incorporate every good,   420
have taught us. Taught? No! But just as amber
attracts straw, your inestimable worth,
joining us to you, has so transformed us
that by your great beauty we have become beautiful,
through your diligence become quick to do good,   425
through your prudence become prudent,

Fortes en cœur, par le tien invincible,
Et tout pouvant par ton puissant Possible.
Ceste union de ta sainte presence,
Où tout honneur et richesse et plaisance   430
Trouvé avons, nous satisfaisoit tant,
Que de chacune estoit l'esprit contant.
O le malheur qui nous a separées
De la vertu dont tant fusmes parées,
Nous separans de ceste grand clarté,   435
Avons ainsi, comme un cœur escarté
Par un desert tenebreux et sans voye,
Et te perdant, perdu repos et joye.
Las! les vertus que de toy recevions,
Et que de nous, comme de nous n'avions,   440
Nous feirent voir la separation,
Que rien, sinon participation
De ta bonté et grace tant requise,
Ne nous donnoit cette vertu exquise;
Et tout ainsi que lampe sans lumiere   445
On voit tourner en sa laideur premiere,
Ainsi de toy l'eslongnement nous feit
Voir que de toy venoit nostre proufit.
Avecques toy fusmes tresacomplies,
Hors d'avec toy sommes toute remplies   450
Et de malheurs et d'imperfections;
Rien plus n'avons que les affections
De conserver le chaste et le pur nom
Dont nous, par toy, avons eu le renom.
Vueille nos piedz et noz corps secourir,   455
En nous donnant la force de courir
Jusques au lieu auquel chacune tasche,
Par dure mort, sauver son blanc de tache.
Nostre peché soit par toy pardonné,
Et prompt secours aux povres corps donné   460
Qui vont mourir pour observer ta Loy,
Car en toy gist nostre esperance et Foy.
Envoye (las!) ton bon et prompt secours,
En retardant leur impetueux cours!
Les voicy près, leurs haleines sentons;   465
Quasi leurs mains nous tiennent, que doutons,

through your stalwart heart, stalwart,
and through your matchless capability become capable.
This union with your blessed presence,
where we found all manner of honor, riches, and joy,   430
was so rewarding
that each of us in her soul felt contented.
Oh, the misfortune of having been separated
from that virtue which once adorned us!
Removed from this extraordinary light,   435
we, like souls lost
in a dark and murky desert,
surrendered all joy and tranquility.
Alas, all the good qualities we once received
from you and could never obtain through our own efforts   440
made us appreciate our loss, and realize
that only by participation in your goodness
and much desired grace
could we regain this wondrous gift.
And like the lamp without light,   445
which returns to its primitive ugliness,
so our separation from you has taught us
that all our value emanates from you.
With you we have everything
and without you we are flooded   450
by misfortune and imperfection.
Our only desire
is to conserve in us the fame
of your chaste and pure name.
We beg you to come to the aid of our feet and bodies   455
and to give us the strength to run
to that place where by harsh death
we can wash away our blemishes.
May you forgive our transgressions
and offer immediate assistance to our unfortunate bodies,   460
ready to die so as to obey your law,
for in you lies our faith and hope.
Quickly send us your valuable help.
Slow down their impetuous pace.
They are near. We can hear their panting.   465
It is as if we feel their terrifying hands upon us,

Leurs boutz de pieds touchent à noz talons;
Ilz vont cent fois plus fort que nous n'allons.
Voyci le point, las! Dyane, venez,
Et en voz mains noz chastes corps prenez.   470
Tel fut leur cry, et si forte leur plainte
Que jusqu'au cœur de Dyane la sainte
Frappa le traict de miseration
Que luy tira leur desolation.
Parquoy son œil retourna promptement   475
Pour regarder leur peine et leur tourment.
Et, tout ainsi que la mere offensée
A chastier l'enfant s'est avancée
Et par fureur frappe sur luy grands coups,
Quand son enfant se vient mettre à genoux,   480
En confessant sa faulte sans excuse,
De grand' douceur après grand' rigueur use,
Tout ainsi feit Dyane: car soudain
De la fureur que Cerf, Sanglier, ou Dain
Souloit chasser jusqu'au bout de leurs vies,   485
Voyant du Loup les cinq brebis ravies,
Ne peult souffrir aux ennemis la gloire
D'avoir sur rien du sien eu la victoire.
Premierement sa colere s'esmeut
Dessus les cinq, que chastié elle eust   490
Bien asprement, si leur necessité
N'eust surmonté leur grande cecité:
Car en voyant leur orgueilleuse audace,
Qui leur avoit fait eslongner la place
Où commandé leur estoit le sejour,   495
Pour le travail pris le long de ce jour,
Ainsi parla: O Cuyder, tu affoles
Par ton orgueil le cœur des povres folles.
Las! en pensant sans moy quelque chose estre,
Pensent leur cœur de toute vertu maistre;   500
Cuydans sans moy avoir telle puissance,
Et de tout bien et mal la congnoissance;
Cuydans avoir de resister pouvoir,
Cuydans avoir la prudence et sçavoir
Pour se garder et seules cheminer;   505
Cuydans les maux advenir deviner;

their toes against our heels.
They move a hundred times more swiftly than we,
and it is none too soon, Diana, for you to come
and take our virgin bodies into you hands."   470
Such was their lamentation
and such their pained grievance
that it struck deep into the saintly Diana's heart.
Their cry of misery saddened her.
And so she immediately turned   475
to look upon their suffering and torment.
In the same way that an irate mother
might press forward to strike
its child with angry blows,
but change violence to sweetness   480
when the child confesses
its inexcusable bad behavior,
so too did Diana respond, for suddenly
she was taken with the same fury
with which she hunted stag, boar, or deer to their death,   485
seeing the wolf attacking the five sheep.
She was unable to endure the triumph of her foe
over anything of hers.
At first her anger burst upon the five,
and she would have cruelly punished   490
her virgins if their need had not been greater
than their blindness.
Seeing the presumptuous audacity
that had drawn them away from where
they had been ordered to remain   495
for that day's work, she said:
"O vanity, you have with your arrogance
tricked these poor young women.
Believing themselves to be of value without me,
to have power without me,   500
and without me, knowledge
of all good and evil,
believing themselves strong enough to resist,
to have the wisdom and discretion
to manage on their own,   505
to recognize the approach of evil

Les devinant, cuydans y mettre l'ordre
Se bien que nul n'y peust trouver que mordre;
Cuydans sans moy estres bonnes et sages
Et se garder de tous mauvais passages,   510
En ignorant qu'elles sont moins que rien,
Et que leur sens, leur grace et leur maintien
N'estoit sinon qu'une chacune unie
Estoit à moy, et que ma compaignie
Je remplissois des biens qui sont en moy;   515
En elles non, fors quand amour et foy
Avecques moy les rendoit toutes unes,
Participans en toutes mes fortunes,
En tous mes biens, en toutes mes vertus,
Tant que jamais ne furent abbatuz   520
De mon fort arc Cerf, Ours ne Leopart,
Que comme moy elles n'y eussent part:
Car tout mon bien, mes vertus, ma puissance,
Tant qu'ell' ont eu à moy obeissance,
Sans rien sentir d'elles, vivre voulu,   525
Sans rien avoir refusé ny tollu,
Leur ay donné et rendu sy commun
Qu'elles et moy par amour n'estions qu'un.
Par ce Cuyder, par qui se sont senties
Telles que moy, hors de moy sont sorties.   530
Il n'a tenu à leur dire souvent
Que ce Cuyder estoit moins que le vent;
Il n'a tenu à faulte de doctrine,
De bon propos, d'exemples et discipline,
Qu'avecques moy demeurées ne sont;   535
Mais mon parler retenu elles n'ont.
Ce Cuyder là semble un mal sy petit
Que ce n'est riens; mais petit à petit
Se fait sy grand que l'on congoit à l'œil
Que c'est le chef de tout peché qu'Orgueil.   540
Par ce Cuyder estre vierges parfaictes,
En s'eslongnant de moy se sont defaictes,
Non entendans que leur perfection
Ne venoit pas de leur condition.
Helas! pensez quelle melancolie   545
Je pensois lors, regardant leur folie,

and to stave it off
so well that nothing can harm them,
believing themselves to be good and wise without me,
able to avoid all dangers,   510
they did not realize that they are less than nothing.
They did not realize that their
understanding, grace, and survival
came about through their connection to me
and that it was I who furnished them with worth.   515
Save for their union with me
in love and faith, they were as nothing.
Because they partook of all my fortunes,
all my riches, and all my virtues,
never was a stag, bear, or leopard   520
brought down by my mighty weapon
that they didn't share the credit with me.
So long as they remained obedient
and without resentment,
I unstintingly wished for them to flourish.   525
I wished neither to refuse nor deprive them of anything.
And since they and I were united in love,
I shared with them all my goods, wealth, and power.
Because of this pride that led them
to want to be my equal, they grew apart from me.   530
In vain I told them how pride
was often less than the wind.
In spite of doctrines, preaching,
good examples, and discipline,
they did not stay faithful to me.   535
They did not heed my advice.
This presumptuousness seems harmless enough,
but little by little it grows
and turns into pride,
the worst of all sins.[11]   540
Because of it, these perfect virgin beings,
not understanding that their perfection
was not of their doing,
destroyed themselves by straying away from me.
Think of my despair when   545
seeing their foolishness,

De loing les voir Cuyder les pourmener
Parmy ce pré et peu à peu mener
Dedans les laz jà tenduz pour les prendre,
Soubs un plaisir d'escouter et apprendre   550
Les plaisans chants et les mots gracieux
Dont le desir meschant et vicieux
Des ennemys estoit si bien caché
Qu'on estimoit à vertu le peché.
Quel tremblement soudainement m'esprit,   555
Quelle fureur dedens mon cœur se prist,
Voyant faillir ainsi ma nourriture,
Voyant perir ainsi ma creature!
Mon cœur esmeu par elle et par amour
Me cuyda lors forcer de faire un tour,   560
C'est de tirer de mes flesches contre elles,
Rendant mes mains maternelles cruelles,
Les preservant par un soudain trespas
Du prochain mal couvert de doux appas.
Mais mon amour tant vertueuse et haulte,   565
Qui ne se rend subjette à nulle faulte,
Me retiroit la main qui jà la flesche
En l'arc tenoit pour faire en leur cœur bresche,
Considerans qu'il n'estoit pas mestier
De promptement ainsi les chastier   570
Et que trop mieux valoit dissimuler,
En les laissant à leur vouloir aller,
A celle fin que par experience
Peussent venir à la vraye science
De voir que peult un Cuyder vain et faux,   575
Par aucun temps de malheur et de maux,
Deliberant priver ces malheureuses
De leur malheur, les laissant langoureuses,
Leur deniant toute faveur de moy.
Ce que n'ay fait; mais, voyant leur esmoy,   580
Leur dueil, leur plaint, leurs soupirs et leurs larmes,
Leur grand douleur, leurs crys, leurs piteux termes,
Leur seul espoir en ma grande puissance,
Et de leurs maux la vraye congnoissance,
J'oy que chacune en m'invoquant m'adjure,   585
Par ma bonté. Je ferois donc injure

and having to watch from a distance
how pride led them astray into that field,
and how they, under the influence
of hearing sweet sounds and ingratiating words,   550
were slowly caught in the trap that had been laid for them.
The destructive wickedness of the enemy
was so well conceived
that one mistook bad for good.
What a terrible trembling took hold of me,   555
what a great furor seized me,
when seeing the failure of all my work,
the destruction of my creation!
My aching heart, moved by this sight and by my love,
made me want to take revenge,   560
to direct my arrows against them,
to give my maternal hands over to cruelty
and to protect them by a quick demise
from an evil masquerading as pleasure.
But my too virtuous and high-minded love,   565
opposed to wrongdoing,
held back my hand, which had already placed the arrow
in the bow in order to pierce their hearts.
I concluded that it was not necessary
to punish so hastily,   570
and that it was better to dissimulate
and let them do as they liked,
in order for them to learn
the truth by experience,
and to see what vain and false pride could bring about.   575
No matter what evil befell them,
I thought I would not prevent them,
and allow them to languish,
while I denied them my favor.
But I did not. I saw their distress, sorrow,   580
lamentations, supplications and tears,
their overwhelming anguish, their weeping and pitiful outcry,
their utter dependence on my strength
and genuine recognition of their failings.
I heard how each called upon me,   585
pleading for my compassion.

A la bonté qui se fait appeller,
Si au secours je l'empeschois d'aller.
Ceste bonté par moy d'elles congnue,
Voire par moy dens leurs cœurs retenue,   590
Leur fait sentir qu'en moy est leur recours.
Ceste bonté m'esmeult à leur secours,
Recongnoissant en elles mon ouvrage
Que j'ay tousiours de parfaire courage:
Car mon honneur est mon don couronner   595
En quelque lieu qu'il m'ayt pleu m'adonner.
Donné leur ay ce que garder je veux.
Si elles ont osé faillir leurs vœux,
Faillir ne veux à ma grande bonté,
Par qui tout mal par le bien est dompté.   600
Je voy leurs piedz de courir agravez,
D'elles si près les meschants despravez,
Que les cheveux d'elles souvent ils touchent,
Las! peu à peu qu'à terre ne se couchent.
Leur cœur leur fault, leur alaine se pert,   605
Le poulx leur bat, la sueur leur appert
Comme ruisseaux tout le long de leur corps.
Rien plus ne font, fors qu'en piteux records,
Crier à moy, qui ne puis plus porter
Ceste douleur sans les reconforter.   610
Si je permets qu'elles meurent en l'eau,
Tant est le corps d'une chacune beau
Que j'aurois peur qu'après mort abusassent
De leur beauté, et que d'elles usassent
Mes ennemys, dont la fureur est telle   615
Que par la Mort ne peult estre mortelle.
Je ne veux point que corps à moy vouez
Soient prestez aux meschans, ni louez.
Si chastes sont vivantes preservées,
Chastes seront après mort conservées.   620
Souffrir ne veux pour nulle passion
Ce qui est mien souffrir corruption.
Par quoy je veux, et arreste, et ordonne,
Que pour jamais cette grace leur donne
Que leur esprit avec le mien uny   625
Soit à toujours sans en estre banny.

I would have done an injustice to their cry for sympathy,
if I did not respond to their appeal.
That well-known kindness which indeed
I had instilled in their hearts   590
is what made them come to me for help
and what moved me to act in response.
I recognized in them the handiwork
which I needed to perfect
and my responsibility to refine those gifts,   595
wherever I had chosen to bestow them.
I wished to protect what I had given them.
If they had failed in their vows,
I did not wish to fail in that generosity
by which good conquers all evil.[12]   600
I saw their wounded feet
and the proximity of their depraved pursuers
who reached out to touch their hair.
They came close to collapsing.
Their hearts were beating rapidly, they were running out of breath.   605
Their pulse was hammering, perspiration flowed down
like streams from their bodies.
They could do little more than cry out
to me repeatedly; I could no longer
bear this sorrow without coming to their aid.   610
If I were to allow them to expire in the water,
so lovely are their bodies,
I fear that after death my enemies would take advantage
of their loveliness and abuse them.
Their fury was such that Death   615
would not slow them down.
I could not permit that bodies dedicated to me
should be admired by or surrendered to these evil creatures.[13]
Preserved pure in life,
pure they had to remain in death.   620
I could not tolerate that what belonged to me
should be corrupted by lust.
And so I wish, proclaim, and ordain
that this grace shall forever
and without separation   625
unite their souls to mine.

Ce qui est un ne se peult diviser,
Quoy que l'œil sot ayt cuydé adviser.
Ce qui estoit en elles immortel
Aussi en moy à jamais sera tel.   630
Mais pour donner au corps punition,
Sauvant l'honneur pour leur contrition,
Soudain les veux en saules transformer,
Sans porter fruit qui soit doux ou amer,
Auprès des eaux et au bout des præries   635
Où elles ont eu tant de fascheries.
Si leur beauté a fait les sotz pecher,
Ilz la verront devant leurs yeux cacher.
Si leur desir les a fait inconstantes,
Je les feray pour jamais demeurantes   640
En un seul lieu, regardant les rivieres,
Comme pleurans leurs façons trop legeres.
Ainsi sera leur peché satisfait,
Et le Cuyder des ennemys deffait.
Ainsi sera pour toutes ceste exemple.   645
Ainsi feray punition tresample
Des ennemys, qui point ne jouyront
De leur desir et ne s'esjouyront
D'avoir de moy ne des miennes rien eu,
Fors le Cuyder dont chascun est deceu.   650
Arbres tresdurs pour dames trouveront,
Voire et du fruit jamais ne gousteront:
Car vierges sont sans porter fruit d'enfans.
De porter fruit à jamais leur defens,
A celle fin que leur virginité   655
Soit en memoire: elles l'ont merité.
Et cest honneur, qu'en nul temps ne mourra,
En moy tousjours par elles demourra.
Sy tost n'eut dit la Divine Puissance
Le dernier mot de sa juste sentence,   660
Que trouvé ont les cinq Nymphes le bort
Du grand torrent pour recevoir la Mort;
Ayans les bras levez pour s'y jetter,
Desirans biens et plaisirs rejetter
Pour eviter par Mort toute infamie.   665
Des Dieux ardans chacun d'eux tient s'amye,

What is one cannot be divided,
however it may appear to flawed vision.
That which was immortal in them
will in me remain immortal.   630
But to punish the body and,
because of their contrition, to save honor,
I wish to transform them immediately into weeping willows
that produce no fruit, either sweet or bitter,
and to place them along riverbanks and at the borders of the fields   635
where they suffered so much.
If beauty caused the fools to sin,
it will be hidden before their eyes.
If their desires caused them to be impure,
I shall make them immovable,   640
stuck in one place, where they can watch the river
and weep because of their imprudence.
Thus will their sins be absolved
and the arrogance of their enemies reproved.
Thus will they be an example.   645
And thus will I adequately chastise their foes,
who will no longer satisfy their yearnings
nor gloat over having abused
me and my followers.
They will have earned nothing but the sham of their pride.   650
In lieu of women they will find
hardened trees and inedible fruit,
for virgins bear no children.
I forbid that they should ever produce fruit,
to the end that their virginity   655
will be remembered. They deserve no less.
And honor will never die,
but live through them forever."
No sooner had the Divine Authority
pronounced the last word of her sentence   660
that the five nymphs found themselves prepared
to accept death at the agitated river's edge.
Eager to flee pleasure and comfort,
they lifted their arms in readiness to dive into the torrent
and thereby through death to avoid all infamy.   665
The gods, burning with the desire to have each his favorite,

Bien les cuydans de la Mort engarder,
Et avec eux les tenir et garder,
Pour en jouyr comme de preis acquis
Par grand labeur, tant aymé, tant requis,   670
Tant desiré, et par si longue espace
Qu'à bien peu près chacun d'eux n'en trespasse.
Entre leurs bras cuydent ferme tenir
Le plus grand bien qui leur peust advenir.
Elles contre eux se mettent en defence;   675
Eux, ne craignans faire à leurs corps offense,
Prendre les vont, et si fort embrasser
Que d'embrasser ne se pouvoient lasser.
Ilz sont transis et quasi morts de joye,
Il ne leur chault qui les oye ou les voye: 680
Or ont ilz bien la fin de leur desir,
La voix leur pert par excessif plaisir.
Mais, tout soudain bruslans par grand chaleur,
A la blancheur virent changer couleur;
Et la douceur de la chair en rudesse   685
Tournée fut, dont soudaine tristesse
Leurs cœurs saisit, voyant la blanche chair
Perdre couleur, s'endurcir et seicher.
Si que, cuydans les mener hors de là,
Feirent effort les tirer; mais cela   690
Rien ne servit, car leurs piedz arrestez
A cheminer ne furent apprestez:
Les convertir en racine sentirent,
Les bras aussi en branches tourner virent.
Lors de serrer et redoubler leurs forces;   695
Mais dens leurs bras ne tindrent rien qu'escorces.
Dont vers le hault, pour le cœur appaiser,
Cerchent leur face et les cuydent baiser.
Ce fut le pis: car pour la bouche douce
Et les yeux verds ilz ne trouvent que mousse,   700
Dont il saillit une voix foible et lente,
Telle que peult de personne dolente,
Disant: Meschans importuns amoureux,
Or demeurez à jamais malheureux,
Nous en allons à Dyane contentes,   705
De noz vainqueurs en la fin triomphantes.

hoped to save the nymphs from the arms of death
and have them and hold them.
After so much effort, so much passion,
and so much lust to have the fulfillment   670
finally of their hard-earned prize,
they were near the point of collapsing.
They longed to hold firmly in their arms
the greatest reward ever to have come their way.
While the nymphs fought against their advances,   675
the Satyrs, not fearing any offense,
seized and embraced them with such force
that they could in no way escape.
They were transfixed and nearly lifeless from the extreme pleasure of it.
Nor did they care a whit as to who heard or who saw,   680
for at last they had their fullest satisfaction.
So great was the joy that they became speechless.
But suddenly, all afire,
they saw the whiteness change colors
and the sweet flesh turn stiff.   685
They despaired as they watched
the loss of color and the hardening
and drying up of this fair flesh.
They were so anguished
that they did all they could to pull them away.   690
But it was to no avail, for their feet
had lost the ability to move
and were converted into roots,
and their arms were transformed into branches.
They redoubled their efforts,   695
but held only bark in their arms.
To find some redress, they looked up,
hoping to discover a face on which to plant a kiss.
Here's the worst of it: in place of a sweet mouth
and green eyes, they found only moss.   700
And with the weak and feeble voices
of pained victims,
the nymphs said: "O miserable importunate lovers,
may you forever suffer so, as we, in the end,
triumphant over our pursuers,   705
happily return to Diana."

Et, crians hault, luy dirent grans mercis.
La voix cessa. Eux, demeurans transis
Et demy morts, ont changé leur esbas
En pleurs et cris, regardans hault et bas   710
S'il se peult rien en elles voir d'humain.
Las! trouvé n'ont teste, corps, pied ne main,
Qui encontre eux ne se soit endurcy.
O leur Cuyder, secourez les icy,
Qui, sur le poinct de recevoir loyer   715
De leur travail, ne les povez payer
Que du rebours de toute leur entente,
Après si longue et si pensible attente.
Où est, Cuyder, vostre ferme promesse
Qui leur causa ce trop de hardiesse?   720
Où est, Cuyder, l'amye que pensoit,
Avoir chacun si tost? Quoy que ce soit,
De toy ne peult sinon Cuyder saillir,
Qui fait les folz en qui tu es faillir.
Cuyder avoir leur donne grand repos,   725
Cuyder n'avoir leur fait changer propos.
Cuyder tenir les faisoit hault chanter,
Cuyder laisser les fait mal contenter.
Cuyder en fin acquerir leur amye
Leur fait sonner Flageolz et Chalemye,   730
Cuyder avoir leurs amyes perdues
Fait que ruisseaux de larmes espandues
Jettent leurs yeux, et leurs crys font tel vent
Que renverser font leur arbre souvent.
O fol Cuyder, on voit bien vostre effect,   735
Que de rien rien est engendré et fait!
Que ferez vous, Satyres importuns,
Qui desprisez les sages oportuns,
Qui par amour gaignent l'amour des cœurs,
Dont par amour ilz en sont les vaincqueurs?   740
Las! apprenez que, si leur cœur n'est pris,
Et par amour mis en un les espritz,
Il perd le temps qui le corps pense avoir.
Ce Cuyder là ne fait que decevoir,
Et là ou plus pense trouver le fol   745
Le corps aisé et le cœur faible et mol
C'est là où plus le cœur et le corps pur

Thus with their last breath
they cried out their thanks to her.
The Satyrs, immobile, and as if half-dead,
went from astonishment to weeping and wailing.   710
They looked up and down in the hopes of finding some human remnant,
but everything they had held was now turned to wood;
there was neither head nor body, neither foot nor hand.
Where was pride when they were about to enjoy
the rewards of their labors?   715
After so long and painful a wait,
it gave them only the reverse
of what they had hoped for.
Where, Pride, was your determined promise
which so much contributed to their boldness,   720
and where the prize each thought to have
so easily? In any case,
from you comes naught but the arrogance
that makes fools of those whom you corrupt.
Pride gives a strong feeling of self-assurance.   725
Lack of pride makes them talk differently.
Pride produces singing aloud.
Without pride they did not get what they desire.
Finally Pride turns to the flageolet
and the chalumeau in order to seduce,   730
but Pride causes the loss of love
and torrents of tears.
And often this shedding of tears and sobbing create
so strong a breeze that it makes the trees fall.
O foolish Pride, one sees what you can accomplish,   735
for nothing comes from nothing.
And what will become of you, importunate Satyrs,
you who disdain the prudent sages
who by love win the love of hearts
of which through love they are the conquerors?[14]   740
Take note that if the heart remains uncommitted
and not given over to affection,
one seeks in vain to win the body.
Such pride can only deceive.
And the more one believes one has found   745
a willing body and feeble and vulnerable heart,
the more one is in fact likely to find a chaste heart and body

Par chasteté s'endurcit comme un mur.
C'est le vray poinct où l'amour de la gloire
Fait aquerir à la vertu victoire: 750
Car chasteté n'est jamais approuvée,
Si elle n'est du contraire esprouvée.
Cerchez l'amour vertueux et honneste,
Et vous ferez honorable conqueste,
Ou autement tousjours vous adviendra,   755
Comme il ha fait, quand Cuyder vous prendra.
Pourquoy icy, Satyres, sejournez?
Pourquoy ainsi honteux ne retournez?
Je sçay que c'est, vous craignez les moqueurs,
Qui vous diront: Où vont les gens sans cœurs?   760
Où est la peau du Lyon? où la teste
De ce grand Cerf dont on fait si grand feste?
Où est de l'Ours la redoutée patte?
Du Léopart, du Chat sauvage ou Chatte,
Qui vous faisoit courir si promptement,   765
Pour n'apporter un seul enseignement?
Si celle là que chacun loue et prise
Chassée avez, monstrez nous vostre prise.
Et si le corps n'en rapportez tout nud,
Monstrez au moins comme à vous n'ha tenu.   770
Apportez nous la guymple ou la seinture,
Que nous puissions juger par conjecture
Qu'il n'ha tenu à faire bon devoir
Que n'ayez eu ce que vouliez avoir.
Mais vous n'avez riens de quoy vous vanter,   775
Dont conseiller veux, pour vous contenter,
Voz corps jetter en ce ruysseau courant,
Pour effacer voz hontes en mourant.
Las! de noz ditz ilz ont fait peu de compte.
Cuyder par mort ne veult couvrir sa honte,   780
Elle promet qu'en fin auront honneur.
Le prometteur n'est icy le donneur.
Lors par orgueil dirent: A qui tient-il?
Avons nous eu faute de cœur gentil?
Si nous avons failly quand à les prendre,   785
Failly n'avons au moins à l'entreprendre,
Failly n'avons à force et diligence:
Car, sans avoir aucune intelligence

which will stiffen into a wall.
It is at that very point that love of glory
makes virtue triumphant.   750
Chastity cannot be admired
until it is put to the test.
Seek an honest and virtuous love
and you will make an honorable conquest.
Otherwise you will experience   755
what happens when pride takes over.
And why, Satyrs, do you linger on?
Why do you not shamefacedly withdraw?
I think I know why. You are afraid of what people will say:
"Where are these heartless ones headed?   760
Where is the lion's pelt? Where is the head
of that great stag they boasted about?
Where is the bear's fearsome paw,
and where all the leopards and wildcats
that lured them into the chase?   765
Where are the results?
If you in fact hunted down this much-admired
and prized prey, show us evidence of your victory.
If you cannot present the naked cadaver,
at least give some proof that it was not your fault.   770
Show us a belt or headpiece
so we can at least guess
why you were not able to accomplish
what you set out to do.
But you have nothing to boast about.   775
And so I suggest, if you would listen to me,
that you bury your shame in death,
by throwing yourselves into this flowing stream."
Alas, they paid little heed to what we had to say.
Pride does not choose to hide its shame in death,   780
but instead it promises ultimate vindication.
But there is many a slip from cup to lip.
They superciliously responded: "And what concern is it of yours?
Have we not behaved properly?
If we did not have our fill of these women,   785
it was not from not trying.
We lacked neither effort nor diligence.
Having no further dealings with them now,

A elles cinq, ne pouvons faire plus.
Or sommes nous de nostre espoir forcluz,   790
Chacun n'a pas eu le bien qu'il cuydoit,
Puisque fureur sans amour nous guidoit.
Bien facile est de prendre reconfort,
Femmes assez nous trouverons au fort;
Mais, si l'amour noz cœurs eust contentez,   795
Plustost à mort se fussent presentez
Que vivre après perte si desplaisante.
Mort ou amour à l'avant est duysante.
Nous qui n'avions riens que nostre plaisir,
N'avons tourment, fors que nostre desir   800
N'est mis à fin, dont la fureur portons
Dedens noz cœurs, que si fort nous sentons
Que du despit qui tant les vient grever
Bien peu s'en fault qu'on ne les voit crever.
Mais nonobstant semblant nous n'en ferons,   805
Et leurs rameaux par force arracherons
Pour emporter chapeaux à noz amys,
Qui, les voyant dessus noz testes mis,
Nous cuyderont dignes de quelque gloire,
Et qu'ayons eu honorable victoire.   810
Par ce Cuyder, nous cuydons satisfait
Le tresgrand tort que Cuyder nous ha fait.
Et si diront tout hault et en tous lieux:
Mieux eussions fait, n'eussent esté les Dieux.
Mais si par eux l'un de nous est contraint   815
De dire vray, et n'estre fin ne feint,
Dire povons: Cuyder nous feit pretendre
Chasse honnorable, et sur le point de prendre
Corps, corne, pied, dents, ongle, chair et peau,
Rien n'avons eu que ce povre chapeau.   820
C'est tout le bien qu'avons pu acquerir
Du fol Cuyder qui nous ha fait querir
L'amour du cœur par tourmenter le corps;
Mais cest amour qui ne gist qu'au dehors
Avons si mal requise et pourchassée,   825
Veu qu'elle estoit par Dyane enchassée,
En corps mortelz si pleins d'honnesteté,
Que nous n'avons d'elles rien conquesté
Fors temps perdu et rigoureux reffuz,

we can do no more;
we have no further prospects.   790
We did not have the satisfaction we hoped for
because it was loveless lust that led us on.
We can easily console ourselves,
for there are lots of other women to be had.
If love had prompted us,   795
we would have chosen death
rather than survive after such a painful defeat.
It is customary for either death or love to reign.
We who seek nothing but our pleasure,
suffer only when our desires are not met.   800
The disappointment that we agonizingly bear
in our hearts
is so deeply engraved there
that we nearly fall dead.
Nevertheless we will pretend, put on a good face,   805
pull up their roots
and wear them in our hats,
so that our friends, seeing them on our heads,
will assume us to be worthy of respect
for having won some great victory.   810
Through such self-assurance, we believe we are receiving satisfaction
for the great wrong pride has done to us.
And so we everywhere will shout:
We would have done better had they not been gods.
But if they force us to speak freely   815
and without deception
we can say: Pride made us pretend
an honorable pursuit and at the very moment when we might have gained
body, horns, feet, teeth, nails, flesh and skin,
we have only this poor hat to show for our efforts.   820
It is all that is left us
because foolish pride made us seek
the heart's love by tormenting the body.
We chased and pursued this superficial love
for creatures protected   825
by Diana's cloak of honesty,
but so ineffectively
that we got nothing out of it
except lost time and unequivocal rejection.

Parquoy portons, ainsi que gens confuz,   830
Ces chapeaux verds, dont à jamais prendront
Nostre façon les amans qui perdront
Soit par courroux, par mariage ou mort,
Leur belle amye ou à droit ou à tort.
Et la couleur, qui en est grise et verte,   835
Demonstrera le travail de leur perte,
Et le despit qui fait travail durer.
Or nous faut il ceste honte endurer,
De noz labeurs n'emportans seulement
Fors le loyer d'un importun amant.   840
Lors (comme gens qui desesperez sont)
S'en vont cerchant l'obscur et le profond
De la forest, et leur dueil lamentable
Parachever en lieu inhabitable,
Entre rochers, cavernes, baricaves,   845
Ceux qui jadis feirent si fort les braves,
Cuydans cacher leur cuyder et leur honte,
Tant qu'oncques puis d'eux n'ouys un seul compte;
Mais tout ainsi comme je l'entendis,
De mot à mot, ma Dame, le vous dis,   850
Et vous sçavez que lors vous pleut me dire
Et me prier de la vouloir escrire:
Ce prier là, qui m'est commandement.
Ha fait la fin et le commencement.
Puis que je sens d'obeïr satisfait   855
Le mien desir, je dy que j'ay bien fait.
Si faulte y ha, qui payera l'amende,
Ou celle là qui telle œuvre commande,
Ou celle qui obeït sans excuse?
Vous donc, ma Dame, envers laquelle j'use   860
Tant seulement de vraye obeissance,
Et qui sçavez quelle est mon impuissance,
Devez portez le mal que je merite,

Et Marguerite excuse Marguerite.
Il me suffit et seray bien contente,   865
Mais que croyez vostre treshumble tante
N'estre jamais de vous obeïr lasse,
Et la tenir en vostre bonne grace.

And thus, like embarrassed fools,   830
we must don these green hats, to be worn by all those
who have rightfully or wrongfully
lost their women,
either through anger, marriage, or death.
The color, gray and green, stands for futile efforts   835
and the continued scorn
which adds to our distress.
Aggressive lovers, we must endure this shame.
We have nothing to show
for our efforts but this humiliation."[15]   840
And so, hoping to hide their shame and pride,
these once brave souls,
ran despairingly
into the darkest and deepest recesses
of the forest to bewail their lamentable grief   845
among inhospitable rocks,
caverns, and caves,
such that nothing more was ever heard of them again.
So my lady, I recounted this tale to you,
word for word, just as I myself had heard it,   850
and it was you who asked
that I should write it down.[16]
That request, which was my command,
has produced both beginning and end.
And inasmuch as to obey accords   855
with my own desires, I think I have done well.
But if there are any flaws, who should be held responsible,
she who gave the order,
or she who obediently executed it?
You, my lady, to whom I have been   860
an obedient servant
and who recognize my shortcomings,
must absolve my guilt.

Marguerite must excuse Marguerite.
It is payment enough for me that you should see me   865
as your unstintingly dutiful
and most humble aunt,
and that you hold me in your esteem.

V

CHANSONS SPIRITUELLES / SPIRITUAL SONGS

EDITOR'S INTRODUCTION

Marguerite's major biographer, Pierre Jourda, ranks the *Chansons spiritu-elles*, short pieces which the queen of Navarre created over a long pe-riod of time, as among the most lyrical and sensitive of her poetic works.[1] Moving and thought-provoking, they also often show a remarkable pro-sodic dexterity. These truly lyrical pieces differ from the other verse in this collection, in which content generally outweighs form.

"Si quelque injure" is composed of five seven-line stanzas in octosyl-labic meter, with the rhyme scheme ABABCDD, in which the rhyme at the C line is repeated throughout the five stanzas. In this poem Marguerite pre-dates Rudyard Kipling's famous poetic meditation "If" by several centuries, expressing something of the same stoic sentiment but, unlike the British author, revealing her strong evangelistic leanings.

"Si la douleur," written in her carriage as she set off to visit her dying brother, the king, consists of seventeen eight-line stanzas in octosyllabic meter, in a mirroring rhyme sequence of ABABBABA. Distressed at the thought that she may not be there when her brother most needs her, Mar-guerite's words here seem to pour out of her agonized soul, as if in spite of her paralyzing anguish.

The second sequence was written when, exhausted by her race with time, she stopped at the convent of Tusson and belatedly learned of her brother's death.[2] The terrible ache of loss and the smarting wound of not

---

1. Marguerite herself opted to include many of these pieces in her 1547 anthology.

2. The story goes that Marguerite overheard one of the nuns weeping and thus learned that the cause for her sorrow was the death of the king. The queen of Navarre's deep mourning was such that she stayed on with the nuns for at least another month, meditating, praying, and pouring out her emotions in writings which include these songs and large portions of two other works inspired by her grief, her long poem *La navire* and the play *Comédie sur le trépas du roi*.

having arrived in time give these verses a driving pathos and poignancy. Repeating the meter and rhyme of the first sequence, Marguerite, however, has reduced her affecting royal dirge to twelve stanzas of only six lines each.

We do not know whether Marguerite was herself musical, but she unquestionably demonstrated great interest in music. Did she, for example, encourage her poet friend Clément Marot to do translations of the psalms for musical reasons? Many of that poet's vernacular translations are to this day sung in French Protestant churches. And as for her plays, they are full of instances of singing and dancing. Marguerite introduces a chorus at the close of *L'Inquisiteur*, a dance routine in the last scene of her *Comédie des quatre femmes*, and a Latin religious chant to end her *Comédie sur le trépas du rois*. In the *Comédie de Mont-de-Marsan*, translated in this anthology, the playwright invents a charming shepherdess who much prefers singing to talking.

Throughout her life, Marguerite composed individual songs, some secular and some not, some comical and satirical, some profoundly moving, like those represented here and composed at the time of the illness and death of her beloved brother. We remember that *spirituel* in French has the double meaning of religious and witty. In a few cases she creates words for already-known tunes, a practice that had been in fashion since the late Middle Ages and called by musicologists *contrafata*, or parodies. The poem that begins "Si la douleur," for example, she tells her readers is to be sung on the chant "Ce qui m'est deu et ordonné."

CHANSONS SPIRITUELLES

CHANSON

Las, tant malheureuse je suis
Que mon malheur dire ne puys,
Sinon qu'il est sans espérance:
Désespoir est desjà à l'huys,
Pour me jetter au fond du puits   5
Où n'a d'en saillir apparence.
    Tant de larmes jettent mes yeux
Qu'ilz ne voyent terre ne cieux:
Telle est de leur pleur l'abondance.
Ma bouche se plaint en tous lieux,   10
De mon cœur ne peult saillir mieux
Que souspirs, sans nulle allégeance.
    Tristesse, par ses grans efforts,
A rendu si foible mon corps
Qu'il n'ha ny vertu ny puissance: 15
Il est semblable à l'un des morts,
Tant que, le voyant par dehors,
L'on perd de luy la congnoissance.
    Je n'ay plus que la triste voix,
De laquelle crier m'en vois   20
En lamentant la dure absence.
Las, de celuy pour qui je vivois,
Que de si bon cœur je voyois,
J'ay perdu l'heureuse présence.
    Seure je suis que son esprit   25
Règne avec son chef Jésus Christ,
Contemplant la divine essence.

SPIRITUAL SONGS

SONG

    Alas, I am so miserable[3]
That I cannot speak of my pain,
Except to say that it is beyond repair:
Despair is already at my door
Ready to jettison me to the bottom of the well   5
From which there is no easy escape.
    My eyes pour out so many tears
That they no longer see land or sky:
Such is the extent of their weeping.
My mouth voices its sorrow everywhere,   10
From my heart comes nothing
But never-ending sighs.
    Sadness through its great efforts
Has so weakened my body
That there is neither will nor strength left: 15
It so resembles a cadaver
That, looking at it,
One has no sense of its existence.
    I am left with only a sad voice
With which I go sounding   20
A lament over the painful loss.
Alas, of that one for whom I lived,
Whom I looked upon with a gladdened heart,
I have lost the joyous presence.
    I am sure that his soul   25
Abides with his Lord Jesus Christ,
Contemplating his divine essence.

Combien que son corps soit prescript,
Les promesses du saint Escrit
Le font vivre au ciel, sans doutance.   30.
    Tandis qu'il estoit sain et fort,
La foy estoit son réconfort
Son Dieu possédoit par créance.
En ceste Foy vive il est mort,
Qui l'a conduit au très-seur port   35
Où il ha de Dieu jouyssance.
    Mais, hélas, mon corps est banny
Du sien, auquel il feut uny
Depuis le temps de nostre enfance.
Mon esprit aussi est puny   40
Quand il se trouve desgarny
Du sien plein de toute science.
    Esprit et corps de dueil sont pleins,
Tant qu'ilz sont convertiz en plainctz:
Seul pleurer est ma contenance.   45
Je crie par bois et par plains,
Au ciel et terre me complains;
A rien fors à mon dueil ne pense.
    Mort, qui m'as fait sy mauvais tour
D'abattre ma force et ma tour,   50
Tout mon refuge et ma défense,
N'as sceu ruyner mon amour
Que je sens croistre nuict et jour,
Qui ma douleur croist et avance.
    Mon mal ne se peut révéler,   55
Et m'est si dur à l'avaller
Que j'en perds toute patience.
Il ne m'en fault donc plus parler,
Mais penser de bientost aller
Où Dieu l'a mis par sa clémence.   60
    O mort, qui le Frère as domté
Vien donc par ta grande bonté
Transpercer la Sœur de ta lance.
Mon dueil par toy soit surmonté;
Car quand j'ay bien le tout compté   65
Combattre te veux à outrance.
    Vien donques, ne retarde pas;

Though his body is no more,
The promises of Holy Scripture
No doubt sustain him above.   30
     While he was safe and sound,
Faith was his comfort,
Because of his belief, he had his God.
In that living faith he died,
Which bore him to safety,   35
Where he enjoys the divine presence.
     But, alas, my body is banished
From his, to which it was united
Since the time of our childhood.
My soul too is punished   40
When it is deprived
Of his, full of all knowledge.
     Body and soul are heavy with grief,
So much so that they are turned into suffering;
Tears alone bring me comfort.   45
I moan through woods and plains,
To heaven and earth I cry out;
I think of naught but my sorrow.
     Death who has dealt so unfairly with me
By taking from me my force and my will,   50
My very refuge and my defense,
Has not destroyed my love,
Which I feel growing night and day,
increasing and advancing my grief.
     I cannot talk of my pain   55
And it is so difficult to keep in
That I lose patience.
I must not speak of it any longer
But prepare to go soon
Where God in his mercy has taken him.   60
     O death who has undone the brother,
In your great kindness come
Pierce the sister with your lance.
Let my sorrow be brought to an end by you;
For as I look upon all that has transpired,   65
I am prepared to do battle with you to the bitter end.
     Come then, do not tarry,

Non: cours la poste à bien grands pas,
Je t'envoye ma deffiance.
Puisque mon Frère est en tes laz,   70
Prens moy, afin qu'un seul soulas
Donne à tous deux esjouyssance.

CHANSON

    Si quelque injure l'on vous dit,
Endurez le joyeusement;
Et si chacun de vous mesdit,
N'y mettez vostre pensement.
    Ce n'est chose nouvelle   5
D'ouyr ainsi parler souvent:
Autant en emporte le vent.
    Si quelcun parle de la Foy
En la mettant quasi à riens
Au prix des œuvres de la Loy,   10
Les estimant les plus grans biens,
    Sa doctrine est nouvelle;
Laissez le là, passez avant:
Autant en emporte le vent.
    Et si pour vostre Foy gaster,   15
Vous vient louer de voz beaux faits.
En vous disant (pour vous flatter)
Qu'il vous tient du reng des parfaitz,
    Fuyez parole telle,
Qui ameine orgueil décevant: 20
Autant en emporte le vent.
    Si le monde vous vient tenter
De richesse, honeur, et plaisir,
Et le vous vient tous présenter,
N'y mettez ni cœur ni desir: 25
    Car chose temporelle
Retourne où estoit paravant:
Autant en emporte le vent.
    Si l'on vous dit qu'en autre lieu
L'on puisse trouver réconfort   30
Et vray salut, qu'en un seul Dieu,
C'est pour mettre vostre âme à mort;

No: approach as quickly as you can,
I throw down my gauntlet.
Since my brother is caught in your net,   70
Take me too, so that one single consolation
Brings eternal joy to us both.

SONG

    If someone offends you,
Endure it cheerfully;
And if someone speaks ill of you,
Do not give it a second thought.
    There is nothing new   5
In hearing this kind of talk everywhere.
It is gone with the wind.
    If someone speaks of faith,
Counting it as naught
When compared with the works of the law,   10
Considered far superior,
    That's a new one,
Just ignore it, move on:
It is gone with the wind.
    And if to spoil your faith,   15
They come praising your fine deeds,
Telling you flatteringly
That you are to be ranked among the perfect,
    Avoid such talk,
Which leads to deceitful pride: 20
It is gone with the wind.
    If they come tempting you
With wealth, honor and pleasures,
Offering these all to you,
Give neither heed nor heart to it,   25
    For temporal things
Return whence they came:
It is gone with the wind
    If they tell you that in some other place,
One can find solace   30
And true salvation, other than in one God,
They mean to destroy your soul;

Monstrez vous lors rebelle,
Et desmentez le plus sçavant:
Autant en emporte le vent.   35

CHANSON

Si la douleur de mon esprit
Je povois monstrer par parole
Ou la déclarer par escrit,
Onques ne feut sy triste rolle;
Car le mal qui plus fort m'affole   5
Je le cache et couvre plus fort;
Parquoy n'ay rien qui me console,
Fors l'espoir de la douce mort.
      Je sçay que je ne dois celer
Mon ennuy, plus que raisonnable;   10
Mais si ne sçauroit mon parler
Atteindre à mon dueil importable:
A l'escriture véritable
Defaudroit la force à ma main;
Le taire me seroit louable,   15
S'il ne m'estoit tant inhumain.
      Mes larmes, mes souspirs,mes criz,
Dont tant bien je sçay la pratique,
Sont mon parler et mes escritz,
Car je n'ay autre rhétorique;   20
Mais leurs effectz à Dieu j'applique
Devant son throne de pitié,
Monstrant par raison et réplique
Mon cœur souffrant plein d'amitié.
      O Dieu, qui les vostres aymez,   25
J'adresse à vous seul ma complainte;
Vous qui les amys estimez,
Voyez l'amour que j'ay sans feinte,
Où par vostre loy suis contrainte,
Et par nature, et par raison;   30
J'appelle chacun Saint et Sainte
Pour se joindre mon oraison.
      Las, celuy que vous aymez tant
Est détenu par maladie,

Take a firm stand,
And show yourself the wiser:
It is gone with the wind.   35

SONG

If my soul's sorrow
I could reveal in speech
Or demonstrate by the written word,
No sadder task could there ever be.
For the pain that drives me to greater madness   5
I keep hidden and completely concealed;
And so find no consolation,
Save in the hope of sweet death.
I know that I should not mask
My grief more than it is reasonable to do,   10
But if my speech
Cannot do justice to my great sorrow
And if at meaningful writing
The force of my hand fails me,
It would be better that I keep silent   15
If it were humanly possible.
My tears, my sighs, my cries,
To which I am far too accustomed,
Are my words, spoken and written;
For I have no other language;   20
And thus these signs I offer God
Before his throne of mercy,
To give proof by reason and argument of
My lovesick and wounded heart.
Dear God who so loves his own,   25
To you alone I bring my plaintive cry;
You who love the loving,
Look upon my unfeigned tenderness,
Born of your commandment,
By nature and by reason;   30
I call upon all the saints
To join in my prayer.
Alas, he whom you so love
Is in the grips of illness,

Qui rend son peuple mal content,   35
Et moy envers vous sy hardie
Que j'obtiendray, quoy que l'on die,
Pour luy très parfaite santé:
De vous seul ce bien je mendie
Pour rendre chacun contenté.   40
    C'est celuy que vous avez oinct
A Roy sur nous par vostre grâce,
C'est celuy qui ha son coeur joint
A vous, quoy qu'il die ou qu'il face,
Qui vostre Foy en toute place   45
Soustient, laquelle le rend seur
De voir à jamais vostre face;
Oyez donc les criz de sa sœur.

    Helas! C'est vostre vray David,
Qui en vous seul ha sa fiance;   50
Vous vivez en luy tant qu'il vit,
Car de vous ha vraye science;
Vous régnez en sa conscience,
Vous estes son Roy et son Dieu;
En autre nul n'ha confiance,   55
Ny n'ha son cœur en autre lieu.
    Pour maladie et pour prison,
Pour peine, douleur ou souffrance,
Pour envie ou pour trahison,
N'ha eu en vous moindre espérance.   60
Par luy estes congnu en France
Mieux que n'estiez le temps passé;
Il est ennemy d'Ignorance,
Son sçavoir tout autre a passé.
    De toutes ses grâces et dons   65
A vous seul a rendu la gloire:
Parquoy les mains à vous tendons,
Afin qu'ayez de luy memoire.
Puis qu'il vous plaist luy faire boire
Vostre calice de douleur,   70
Donnez à nature victoire
Sur son mal et nostre malheur.
    O grand Medecin tout puissant,
Redonnez luy santé parfaite,

Which causes his unhappy people 35
And myself to turn boldly to you,
That, despite what some say, I might obtain
His perfect health:
To you only do I make this wish
So that all may find happiness. 40
     It is he whom you have anointed
By your grace to be our king;
He who has joined his heart
To yours, whatever he says or does;
Who everywhere your faith 45
Upholds, which assures him
Of seeing your face eternally:
Hear then the supplications of his sister.

     Alas, it is your true David
Who in you alone puts his trust; 50
So long as he lives you live in him;
For he knows you well,
You reign in his conscience,
You are his king and his God.
In no other does he confide. 55
Nor to any other place surrender his heart.
     In sickness or prison,
In pain, sadness, or suffering,
In spite of jealousy and treason,
He has never lost his hope in you. 60
It is because of him that you are known in France,
Better than ever before:
He is the enemy of ignorance,
His knowledge has surpassed all others.
     For all his blessings and gifts 65
To you alone he has given thanks.
And so we raise up our hands toward you,
That you may remember him.
Since it is your will that he should drink
From the cup of sorrow, 70
Let nature triumph
Over his infirmity and over our misery.
     O most powerful doctor,
Give him health,

Et des ans vivre jusqu'à cent,   75
Et à son coeur ce qu'il souhaite,
Lors sera la joye refaite,
Que douleur brise dans noz cœurs,
Dont louange vous sera faite
De femme, enfans et serviteurs.   80
      Par Jésus Christ nostre Sauveur
En ce temps de sa mort cruelle,
Seigneur, j'attens vostre faveur
Pour en ouyr bonne nouvelle.
J'en suis loing, dont j'ay douleur telle   85
Que nul, ne la peult estimer.
O que la lettre sera belle
Qui le pourra sain affermer!
      Le desir du bien que j'attens
Me donne de travail matière,   90
Un heure me dure cent ans,
Et me semble que ma Litière
Ne bouge, ou retourne en arrière,
Tant j'ay de m'avancer désir.
O qu'elle est longue, la carriere   95
Où à la fin gist mon plaisir!
      Je regarde de tous costez
Pour voir s'il arrive personne,
Priant sans cesser, n'en doutez,
Dieu, que santé à mon Roy donne.   100
Quand nul ne voy, l'œil j'abandonne
A pleurer, puis sur le papier
Un peu de ma douleur j'ordonne:
Voila mon douloureux mestier
      O qu'il sera le bien venu   105
Celuy qui, frappant à ma porte,
Dira: Le roy est revenu
En sa santé tres bonne et forte.
Alors sa sœur plus mal que morte
Courra baiser le Messager   110
Qui telles nouvelles apporte,
Que son frere est hors de danger.
      Avancez vous, homme et chevaux,
Asseurez moy, je vous supplie,

And a hundred years more life, 75
And everything that his heart desires;
Then will the joy return
That grief has removed from our hearts;
For this thanks will be given you
By women, children, and servants. 80
     Through Jesus Christ our Savior
At this season of his cruel death,
Lord, I await your favor
That I might hear good news.
I am far away, which grieves me more 85
Than anyone can imagine.
Oh, how wonderful will be that letter
Which will confirm his health.
     The desired news I await
Gives me cause to suffer; 90
An hour is like a hundred years,
And it seems to me that my coach
Does not advance, but turns back,
So great is my need to move forward.
How interminable the path 95
At the end of which is my delight.
     I look in every direction
Hoping to see someone,
Praying continuously, doubt me not,
To God, that he give health to my king. 100
When I see no one, I give my eyes over
To crying; then on paper
I give some expression to my distress.
This is my sad preoccupation.
     Oh, how welcome, 105
He who, knocking on my door,
Announces: The king has been restored to
Good and sound health!
Then his sister, more dead than alive,
Will run to embrace the messenger 110
Who brings news to the effect
That her brother is out of danger.
     Oh, press ahead you men and horses,
Assure me, I beg you,

Que nostre Roy pour ses grands maux   115
A receu santé acomplie;
Lors seray de joye remplie.
Las, Seigneur Dieu, esveillez vous,
Et vostre œil sa douceur desplie,
Sauvant vostre Christ et nous tous.   120
    Sauvez, Seigneur, Royaume et Roy,
Et ceux qui vivent en sa vie;
Voyez son espoir et sa Foy,
Qui à le sauver vous convie.
Son coeur, son désir, son envie,   125
A tousjours offert à voz yeux:
Rendez nostre joye assouvie,
Le nous donnant sain et joyeux.
    Vous le voulez, et le povez;
Aussi, mon Dieu, à vous m'adresse;   130
Car le moyen vous seul sçavez
De m'oster hors de la destresse,
De peur de pis, qui tant me presse
Que je ne sçay là où j'en suis.
Changez en joye ma tristesse;   135
Las, hastez vous, car plus n'en puis.

That our king has from his great pain   115
Been fully delivered to health.
Then shall I be filled with joy.
Alas, my Lord, arise,
And look with kindness,
Saving your Christ and us all.   120
    Save, Lord, kingdom and king,
And those who take their sustenance from him!
Look upon his hope and his faith,
Which inspire you to cure him.
His heart, his desires, his wishes   125
He has always given over to your judgment.
Make possible our joy
By returning him to us healthy and happy.
    You wish it and you can do it:
And so, my God, I look to you: 130
For you only know how
To remove from me this distress
Of fearing the worst, that oppresses me,
Such that I know not where I am.
Transform my sadness into joy.   135
Make haste for I can bear no more.

VI

LA COMÉDIE DE MONT-DE-MARSAN / THE
COMEDY OF MONT-DE-MARSAN

EDITOR'S INTRODUCTION

In the winter of 1548, Marguerite de Navarre retired for a time to Mont-de-Marsan, a small port city on the edge of the Landes forest in the Aquitaine region, to spend the Easter season. Just as she had been seven years before, Marguerite was occupied with negotiations for her daughter's marriage. Francis I had passed away the year before, and his son, Henry II, had plans to marry Jeanne to Antoine de Bourbon. Henry of Navarre was still trying to negotiate a marriage between Jeanne and the prince of Spain. Marguerite, again trying to maneuver between the two powers, felt her influence and her strength waning. So it was that she wrote a *comédie* to be performed at Mont-de-Marsan on Mardi Gras.

As she entered into what would be her last year of life, Marguerite's mind had wandered far from political concerns toward things spiritual. Having continued to surround herself with evangelical humanists, she was still very much connected to reformist thinking in France in the 1540s. While much of the language that she uses in the *Comedy of Mont-de-Marsan* was inspired by her earlier mentor, Guillaume Briçonnet,[1] the group that has been most closely tied to the ideas contained in the play is the *libertins spirituels*. The leaders of this group, Quintin de Hainaut and Anthony Pocquet, both held positions at Marguerite's court in Nérac. The spiritual libertines believed in three ages of man, the reign of the Father (Old Testament), the reign of the Son (New Testament), and the reign of the Spirit, toward which each individual could strive. Those believers who let themselves be

---

1. See V. L. Saulnier's introduction to the critical edition of *Théâtre profane*, 242. Saulnier refers specifically to turns of phrase Marguerite uses to refer to God, as well as the themes of justification by faith and the spiritual movement the different steps of which are embodied in the four characters of the play: sensuality, superstition, reason, and union with God.

absorbed by the Spirit did not need to concern themselves with religious practice or knowledge. They believed that the Spirit worked through them, that they were regenerated through possession by the Spirit, and that therefore they were like Christ. This possession prevented sin from entering into their lives, and since every act is caused primarily by God's will, they believed it was wrong to try to correct sinful behavior in others. The spiritual libertines also advocated a "prudent conformism," however, that kept them, for a time, out of danger.

The theology of the spiritual libertines was refuted vigorously by John Calvin, who wrote an invective against them in 1545, *Contre le secte phantastique et furieuse des Libertins que se nomment Spirituelz* (Against the Eccentric and Excessive Sect of the Libertines Who Call Themselves Spiritual). Calvin had spent time at Nérac himself in 1533 but left France a year later after the *affaire des placards*, when the situation became much more dangerous for reformers in France. If Calvin's *Institutes of the Christian Religion* is a warning against ritual practices in the church that he considered abuses, his essay against the spiritual libertines is a warning against an excessive dismissal of ritual practices.[2] Calvin used this document as an opportunity to criticize not only these reformist thinkers at Nérac but also the French court as a whole, which he characterizes as "full of vanity, of excessive pomp, of pride, of licentiousness and insolence, of blasphemy, and of ambition."[3] Understandably, Marguerite felt personally assailed by these attacks. She never directly responded to Calvin;[4] nevertheless, a response can be found in her later writings, most notably the *Comedy of Mont-de-Marsan*.[5]

The *Comedy* is a morality play with four characters: the Worldly Woman, the Superstitious Woman, the Wise Woman, and the Woman Enraptured by the Love of God(the Shepherdess). As each woman enters, she introduces herself with a monologue before engaging in dialogue with the woman or women who preceded her. The characters have been interpreted in slightly

2. *Théâtre profane*, ed. Saulnier, 249–50.

3. Quoted in Carol Thysell, *The Pleasure of Discernment: Marguerite de Navarre as Theologian* (Oxford: Oxford University Press, 2000), 34.

4. Although they had at times corresponded in the past, Calvin's critique in his invective put an end to that.

5. Thysell's book, *The Pleasure of Discernment*, is a convincing demonstration of how the *Heptameron* is in many ways a response to Calvin's critique, especially in its frame where the group of *devisants* represents a community of lay people engaged in theological discussions under the guidance of the spirit. The spiritual libertines believed that an individual could become one with the "single spirit" and be free from sin in this life. Thysell argues that Marguerite was influenced by this view of divine inspiration and the libertines' use of allegorical interpretation of Scripture. Marguerite would never, however, advocate the view that humans could be without sin. On this topic she agreed closely with Calvin (see esp. 24–38).

different ways by various scholars, but the general outline of the voices seems clear: the first represents materialism, the second represents religious bigotry and pietism,[6] and the third the spirit of reform or evangelism. The first two are converted by the third before the appearance of the fourth character, who is slightly more difficult to discern. Abel Lefranc has labeled her a spokeswoman for the spiritual libertines; Pierre Jourda sees in her an embodiment of mystical love;[7] and V. L. Saulnier calls her simply "la foi du charbonnier."[8] In any case there is surely a great divide between this character and the three others who prove themselves incapable of understanding her relationship with her beloved. She embodies the theme of the play: salvation through pure and simple faith.[9]

Marguerite's response to Calvin is especially embodied in the Shepherdess who is characterized as "folle" and who speaks in such a way that the others cannot understand her. One of Calvin's principal criticisms of the spiritual libertines was their use of obscure language that Calvin qualified as fraudulent. Marguerite pokes fun at Calvin by using refrains of popular songs to mark the "ramage d'oiseau" (warbling) of the Shepherdess, the same term Calvin used when writing of the spiritual libertines. The Shepherdess's speech takes up certain ideas dear to Marguerite's heart: justification by faith alone, love as the only path to salvation, the rapture of man (Rien) absorbed in God (Tout), and the inability of language to translate this experience.[10]

While there is much in the Shepherdess that reveals the spiritual thought of Marguerite, many scholars identify her with the Wise Woman. The reading of the Bible, the dignity of the human body, the value of ritual and good works in the spiritual life are all privileged in the speech of the Wise Woman. Perhaps especially, she represents open exchange of ideas. Marguerite never developed a fixed "doctrine" of reform that she followed throughout her life. Instead, she followed her own spiritual itinerary that always involved open dialogue with new ideas.[11] *The Comedy of Mont-de-Marsan* is such a dialogue. The four characters represent different opinions that

6. Traits that would most likely be associated with, more specifically, a narrow-minded Catholicism. See Abel Lefranc, *Les idées religieuses de Marguerite de Navarre d'après son oeuvre poétique* (1898; Geneva: Slatkine, 1969), 111; and Jourda, *Marguerite d'Angoulême*, 1: 602.

7. Jourda, *Marguerite d'Angoulême*, 1: 603.

8. Blind and simple faith, literally the "faith of a coalman." *Théâtre profane*, ed. Saulnier, 259.

9. Ibid., x and 263.

10. Ibid., 263–64.

11. Thysell argues that Marguerite's project in the *Heptameron* is to bring voices, which seem antagonistic, together in a "communal discernment of theological truths in both sacred and secular literature" guided by "the belief that such discernment is itself part of the process of sanctification or regeneration because it is guided by the Spirit" (*Pleasure of Discernment*, 99).

Marguerite wished to juxtapose, even if the different voices cannot always hear each other. If the Shepherdess and the Wise Woman represent two different tendencies in the queen's spiritual life, it is telling that it is the Wise Woman who has the least patience with the Shepherdess. Reading the two characters together, one can imagine the questions that occupied the author in the twilight of her life.

COMÉDIE JOUÉE AU MONT DE MARSAN,
LE JOUR DE CARESME-PRENANT MIL
CINQ CENS QUARENTE SEPT

A quattre personnages, c'est assavoir
La Mondainne, la Supersticieuse, la Sage et la Ravie de l'amour de Dieu,
bergère

SCENE I

La Mondainne commance:
J'ayme mon corps, demandez moy pourquoy:
Pource que beau et plaisant je le voy;
Quant à mon âme qui est dedans cachée,
Je ne la puis toucher d'œil ny de doy.
(N'en avoir point, ou qu'invisible soit,)   5
Ce m'est tout ung, poinct n'y suis empeschée.
Ame soit âme à qui l'a bien cherchée,
Mon corps est corps, je le sens vivement.
S'il a du mal, j'en suis toutte fâchée,
S'il a du bien, j'en ay contantement.   10
          Je le pare et dore,
          Acoustre et decore
          De tous ornemens.
          Je le painctz et farde,
          Remire et regarde   15
          Voire à tous momens;
              De le tenir sain,
          C'est tout mon desain,
          Car je veulx qu'il vive.
          De melencolie   20

THE COMEDY OF MONT-DE-MARSAN, PRESENTED AT MONT DE MARSAN, DURING SHROVETIDE,[12] 1547

With four characters, that is to say:
The Worldly Woman, the Superstitious Woman, the Wise Woman, and the Woman Enraptured by the Love of God.

SCENE I

The Worldly Woman begins:
I love my body; ask me why.[13]
Because I see that it is beautiful and pleasing.
As for my soul that is hidden within,
I cannot touch it with either my eye or my finger.
Not to have one or that it be invisible,   5
It is all the same to me, I am not at all hindered by it.
May the soul be the soul for the one who looks hard for it;
My body is of flesh, I feel it intensely.
If it is in pain, I am greatly vexed;
If it feels good, I am content.   10
                    I adorn it with gold,
            Dress it up and decorate it
            With all sorts of ornaments.
            I make it up with paint and rouge,
            I contemplate it   15
            continually.
                    My entire purpose
            Is to keep it healthy,
            For I want it to live.
            For it, I am fearful   20

Et de maladie
Pour luy suis craintive.
    Je luy cherche joye
Et ne veulx qu'il voie
Rien qui luy desplaise.   25
Honneurs pour luy chasse
Et biens luy pourchasse
Pour le tenir aise.
    Et tout le plasir
Que l'œil peult choisir,   30
Au ceur je le donne,
Tant qu'il en peult prandre:
A ce veulx entendre
Sans aymer personne.
    Bref, tout mon penser   35
C'est de l'advencer
En plaisir parfaict;
Par peine non grande,
De ce qu'il demande
Le rendz satisfaict.   40

SCENE II

La Supersticieuse chante:
    Je m'en vois faire ung voiage,
De bon ceur et bon couraige:
C'est ung sainct pelerinage
De Marie et son enfant,
Qui de mal et toute rage   45
Le vray pellerin deffend.
Puis elle dict:
Le chemin long m'a aux piedz agravée,
Dont ma personne est sy tresfort grevée
Que j'en sens bien des douleurs non petites;
Mais quant j'ay bien mes pennes esprouvées,   50
Doulces en moy doibvent estre trouvées,
Veu que j'aquiers par elles gros mérites.
Tant aise suis quant j'ay mes heures dictes
Et mon saultier de cent cinquante Avez.
Cestuy mien est du Mont des Hermittes,   55
Dont plusieurs sont en le disant sauvez.

Of melancholy
and sickness.
    I seek out joy for it
And do not want it to see
Anything that is displeasing to it.   25
I hunt down honors for it and
Pursue things
to make it comfortable.
    And every pleasure
That the eye can discern   30
I give to its heart,
As much as it can take.
I want to strive for this
Without loving anyone.
    In a word, all my thoughts   35
Go to achieving for it
Perfect pleasure.
I will satisfy
Its every demand
Without much difficulty.[14]   40

SCENE II

The Superstitious Woman sings:
    I am leaving on a trip
    Happily and bravely:
    It is a holy pilgrimage
    To Mary and her child
    Who protects the true pilgrim   45
    From evil and violence.
Then she says:
The long road has made my feet heavy;
I am so beleaguered by this
That I feel pain none too small.
But when I have suffered my agony,   50
In me it should become a sweetness,
Seeing that I earn great merit through it.
I am so comforted when I have said my hours
And the one hundred and fifty Aves of my rosary.[15]
Mine is from the Hermit's Mount;[16]   55
Many people who recited it were saved.

Des oraison m'aÿde
De la saincte Bregide,
Qui révélation
Eut de tout le torment,   60
Que souffrit justement
Christ en sa passion.
        De tous sainctz, oraisons
J'ay pour toutes saisons,
Pour garder et guérir   65
De tous dangiers et maulx,
D'ennuis et de travaulx,
Où je puis encourir.
        Puis voici ma neufvaine,
Qui n'est pas chose vainne.   70
Voiez ces neuf chandelles:
S'elles sont allumées
Et que droict les fumées
Voy monter au ciel d'elles,
        Je sçay que ma prière   75
N'est pas mise en arrière,
Mais est receue aux cieulx.
De ces trois qui sont blanches,
Je les garde au dimanche
Dont j'espère bien mieulx.   80
        Bref, pour sauver mon âme,
Par eau, par feu et flame,
Espargner je ne veulx.
Le corps d'une âme saincte,
Quant la vie est estainte,   85
On luy porte des veulx.

La Mondainne chante:

    Il est jour dict l'alouette:
    Surbout, alon jouer sur l'herbette.

Puis elle dict:

    Or sus; puis que je suis coiffée,
    Je croy que ma journée est faicte.   90
    En est il de mieulx estoffée,
    Ny en beauté aussy parfaicte?
    Puis que je me sens satisfaicte
    De moy, en parle qui vouldra.

I seek help from the prayers
Of Saint Bridget,[17]
Who had a revelation
Of all the torment   60
That Christ suffered
In his passion.
  I have prayers of every saint
For every season,
To protect me from and heal me of   65
all dangers and evils,
Troubles and tribulations
That I could fall into.
  And then here is my novena,
A very useful thing.   70
See these nine candles:
If they are lit
And I see the smoke from them
Rise directly to the sky,
  I know that my prayer   75
Is not sent back,
But is received in the heavens.
I keep these three that are white
For Sunday
When I hope for even better.   80
  In short, in order to save my soul,
Through water, through fire and flame,
I wish to spare nothing.
When life is extinguished,
To the body of a blessed soul   85
Divine honors are paid.[18]

The Worldly Woman sings:

 It is day, says the lark:
 Get up, let us go to the meadow to play.[19]

Then she says:

 So, get up; since I have done my hair,
 I think that I am ready to start my day.   90
 Is there anyone better dressed
 Or of a more perfect beauty than I?
 As I am satisfied with myself,
 Let others talk about me if they want.

Leur bouche en demourra infecte,   95
Et qui pis est ne m'en chauldra.

La Supersticieuse

Glorieuse Vierge Marie,
Et que le ceur au corps me bat!
Celle qui deust estre marrie,
Et contre elle prendre combat,   100
Prent son plaisir et son ebat,
Comme le porceau dans la fange,
A faire en péché son sabat
Par sa paresse; ô cas estrange!

La Mondainne

Mais où va ceste pelerine,   105
Qui me semble si foible et lasse?

La Supersticieuse

Au chemin par où je chemine,
La mondanité point n'y passe.

La Mondainne

Vous tenez bien la teste basse:
Je croy que vous jurez sans faulte.   110

La Supersticieuse

Mais à vous, mocqueresse agasse,
Set mal de la tenir sy haulte.

La Mondainne

Je lève ma teste,
Et mon corps honneste
A chascun je monstre;   115
Il est beau et doux,
Et tenu de tous
Pour bonne rencontre.

La Supersticieuse

Vostre corps de chair
Estimez trop cher: 120
Ce n'est que charongne.
Il le fault mourir:
(Au poinct fault venir,)
Qui qu'en parle groigne.

La Mondainne

Ha! Mes beaulx yeux vers   125
Nourriture à vers
Ne deviendront poinct.

Their mouths will be infected by it.   95
And the worst of it is of no importance to me.
The Superstitious Woman
  Glorious Virgin Mary,
  How my heart beats in my chest!
  This woman who should be doleful
  And fight against herself   100
  Finds her pleasure and amusement
  In transforming the Sabbath into sin
  With her laziness.
  Like a pig in the mud. How strange!
The Worldly Woman
  Where is this pilgrim going,   105
  Who seems so weak and tired?
The Superstitious Woman
  Worldliness never travels
  On the path that I am taking.
The Worldly Woman
  You hold your head very low;
  It seems to me that you find yourself without fault.   110
The Superstitious Woman
  But it is not seemly to hold yours so high,
  Contemptuous magpie.
The Worldly Woman
    I raise my head
    And to everyone
    I show my worthy body.   115
    It is beautiful and soft
    And is thought by all
    To be good company.
The Superstitious Woman
    You place too high a value
    On your fleshly body: 120
    It is nothing more than carrion.
    It has to die;
    (We must come to the point)
    Where it is only spoken of in disdain.
The Worldly Woman
    Ha! My beautiful green eyes   125
    Will never become
    Food for worms.

La Supersticieuse

>   Vous ferez ce sault;
>   Mourir il vous fault,
>   C'est le plus seur poinct.   130

La Mondainne

>   Ceste mort rebelle
>   Sy june et sy belle
>   Ne m'oseroit prendre.

La Supersticieuse

>   Nul de sa main forte,
>   Quelque arme qu'il porte,   135
>   Ne se peult deffendre.

La Mondainne

>   Poinct n'y veulx penser,
>   Mais mon temps passer
>   Sans ce dur remort,
>   Durant ma junesse;   140
>   Puis apres, viellesse
>   Finira par mort

La Supersticieuse

>   La mort n'a nulle heure
>   Ny ne faict demeure
>   Pour force ou junesse;   145
>   Soudain vous prendra.
>   Donc ne vous fauldra
>   Fier en viellesse.

La Mondainne

Puis que ainsy est que demain je mourray,
A belle bride abatue je courray   150
A tout plaisir, dourmir, manger et boire;
Et passeray mon temps sy plaisamment,
Que j'auray eu parfaict contentement
Avant le jour de la dame tant noire.

La Supersticieuse

Non, non, ma seur, mieulx vault faire cecy: 155
Pour vray plaisir prenez peine et soucy,
En obliant pour l'âme vostre corps.
Quant est du mien, tous les jors je le tue.
Car pour gaigner paradis m'esvertue,
A tout le moings je y faictz tous mes efortz.   160

The Superstitious Woman

> You will make that leap;
> There is nothing more sure than
> That you must die.   130

The Worldly Woman

> This rebellious death
> Would never dare take me
> So young and so beautiful.

The Superstitious Woman

> No one can defend himself
> From death's strong hand   135
> No matter what weapon he carries.

The Worldly Woman

> I don't want to think about it.
> I want to pass the time of my youth
> Without thinking of this
> Cruel heartbreak.   140
> And then, later, old age
> Will end in death.

The Superstitious Woman

> Death has no hour
> And does not delay
> For strength or youth.   145
> She will take you
> Without notice;
> Thus you must not count on old age.

The Worldly Woman

Since it is such that tomorrow I will die,
I will rush toward every pleasure.   150
I will sleep, eat, and drink
And spend my time so pleasantly
That I will have achieved perfect contentment
Before the day of that so black lady.

The Superstitious Woman

No, no, my sister! It is better to do this: 155
Take up pain and doubt as true pleasure,
Forgetting your body in favor of your soul.
As for my own body, I kill it every day;
For I struggle hard to gain paradise.
Whatever happens I direct all my efforts there.   160

SCENE III

La Sage commance:
Dieu a bien faict ung tresbeau don à l'homme
De luy donner raison, savez-vous comme?
Comme à ung ange. Est-ce pas don honneste?
Par la raison il assemble et assomme,
Ayme et congnoist les vertus et les nomme: 165
Par la raison il differe à la beste;
Dieu luy a mis en hault regard et teste
Pour contempler ce qui est par sur luy:
La beste en bas à la terre s'areste,
Et l'homme en hault, dont vient tout son appuy.   170
   L'homme raisonnable
   Est faict agréable
   A Dieu et au monde;
   Dieu croid, ayme, adore,
   Loue, prie et honore: 175
   Là son esprit fonde.
   Quant à son prochain,
   Le bon ceur la main
   Mect à le servir.
   Ce qu'il doibt il paie,   180
   Et a tousjour joye
   A vertus suivir.
La Supersticieuse
  Ma mie, voilà ung propos
  Qui est au vostre differant.
  Elle vit en ung grand repos: 185
  Oions qu'elle va referant.
La Mondainne
  Mais allons à elle en courant,
  Et luy declairons toutte chose.
  A la veoir il est apparent
  Qu'elle entend la rime et la proze.   190
La Sage
  Voilà deux dames bien contraires
  A leurs avis, venans ycy;
  Entendre fault de leur affaire.

SCENE III

The Wise Woman begins.
God has given a beautiful gift to man
In giving him reason. Do you know what it's like?
It is just like a gift to an angel. Is that not a worthy gift?
With reason, man gathers together and calculates,
He loves and knows the virtues and names them. 165
Through reason he is set apart from the beast.
God has put his vision and his head up high
In order to contemplate what is above him.[20]
The beast looks no further than the earth below,
While man looks up to where he gets all his support. 170
       Reasoning man
       Is pleasing
       Before God and the world.
       He believes in, loves, adores,
       Praises, prays, and honors God; 175
       That is where his spirit rests.
       As for his neighbor,
       He gives his heart and hand
       To serve him.[21]
       What he owes, he pays, 180
       And he is always glad
       To follow the virtues.
The Superstitious Woman
    That, my friend, is an argument
    That is quite different from yours.
    She seems at peace with herself; 185
    Let us listen to what she is saying.
The Worldly Woman
    Yes, let us go straight to her
    And tell her everything.
    By the looks of her it is clear
    That she understands rhyme and reason. 190
The Wise Woman
    Here come two ladies
    Of very different opinions;
    I must hear their concern.

La Supersticieuse
   Madame, la Bonté sans si
   Vous doint bon jour.   195
La Sage
       Hé, grand mercy,
   A vous deux j'en désire aultant.
La Mondainne
   Pour nous hoster hors de soucy,
   A vous nous en venons baptant.
La Supersticieuse
   Ça, Madame, à vous veoir de loing,   200
   Seullement à vostre apparence,
   Nous semble qu'à nostre besoing
   Nous debvez donner allegence.
La Sage
   Or, parlez, car j'ay esperance,
   En me monstrant comme advocas   205
   Ce dont estes en difference
   Que je donray ordre à voz cas.
La Mondainne
   Madame, je suis corporelle,
   Aymant mon corps, tant naturelle
   Qu'à riens fort à vivre ne pense: 210
   J'entens vivre joieusement
   En biens et honneurs longuement,
   En tous plaisirs, jeux, ris et dances.
   J'ayme mon corps, voylà la fin:
   C'est mon amy, c'est mon afin;   215
   C'est mon tout, mon Dieu, mon idolle.
La Sage
   Voilà trop bestialle amour;
   Si vous y faictes long sejour,
   Par cest amour deviandrez folle.
La Supersticieuse
   Pas ne suis comme elle, Madame,   220
   Car je n'ayme riens que mon âme
   Et ne veulx, sinon la saulver.
   Et pour la rendre necte et pure,
   Mal et peine en mon corps j'endure,
   Pour ma vertu mieulx esprouver.   225

The Superstitious Woman

> Madame, may the goodness of God[22]
> Bring you a good day.   195

The Wise Woman

> Thank you very much;
> I wish the same to you.

The Worldly Woman

> We've come to you promptly
> So that you can take away our doubt.

The Superstitious Woman

> Having seen you from afar, Madame,   200
> Judging from your appearance,
> It seems to us that
> You could relieve our burden.

The Wise Woman

> Speak, then, for I have hope that,
> In interceding in that   205
> Which divides you,
> I will find a solution to your dispute.

The Worldly Woman

> Madame, I am a physical being.
> I love my body so that it is natural
> That I think only of living.   210
> I intend on living joyously
> And for a long time in worldly treasures and honor,
> In all pleasure, games, laughter, and dance.
> I love my body, that's all there is to it.
> It is my friend, it is my ally.   215
> It is everything to me; my god, my idol.

The Wise Woman

> Well, there's a beastly love.
> If you stay with it for too long,
> This love will make you crazy.

The Superstitious Woman

> I am not like her, Madame,[23]   220
> For I love only my soul
> And desire nothing except its salvation.
> And to make it clean and pure,
> I endure suffering and pain in my body
> In order to better test my virtue.   225

La Sage

    Vostre âme sauver! las, m'amye,
    Elle n'a plus grande ennemye
    De vostre gloire par trop grande.

La Supersticieuse

    Quoy? est-ce mal faict de deffaire
    Son corps, pour son âme parfaire,   230
    Madame, je le vous demande?

La Sage

    Premier voulez le corps destruire
    Que vostre âme en vertu instruire:
    C'est ruiner tout l'édifice.

La Supersticieuse

    Qu'est ce cy? n'est-ce pas bien faict   235
    De deffaire ung corps imparfaict,
    En jeunant, disant mon office,
    Portant la hère tous les jours
    Et la discipline tousjours;
    Pleurer, demourer sollitaire,   240
    Estre à beaulx genoulz nus au temple,
    Donner par jeunes bon exemple,
    Priant Dieu sans jamais se taire?

La Sage

    Dieu a vostre corps mis sur terre,
    Auquel ne debvez faire guerre,   245
    Sinon qu'il est contraire à Dieu.
    Souvent, cuidant bien faire, on erre,
    Faisant cas de casser ung verre
    Ou de jouer à quelque jeu.

La Mondainne

    Madame, aussy ne faictz-je pas,   250
    Car j'ayme mieulx ung bon repas
    Que tous les jûnes d'un caresme.
    Garde je n'ay de mon corps baptre,
    Mais en tous lieux le faiz esbattre.
    Bref, je n'ayme rien que moy mesme.   255

La Sage

    Vous mesmes n'aimez vous pas bien:
    Par vous, comme vous, n'estes rien,
    Si du corps parlez seulement.

The Wise Woman

> To save your soul! Alas, my friend,
> Your soul has no worse enemy
> Than your enormous pride.

The Superstitious Woman

> What! I ask you, Madame,
> Is it wrong to undo one's body   230
> For the sake of perfecting one's soul?

The Wise Woman

> You will destroy your body
> Before your soul is taught virtue.
> You're undermining the whole structure.

The Superstitious Woman

> What is this? Is it not good   235
> To defeat an imperfect body
> By fasting, saying my prayers,
> Wearing a hair shirt every day,
> Enduring flagellations,
> Crying, seeking solitude,   240
> Worshiping on my bare knees in church,
> Being a good example through fasting,
> Praying to God incessantly?

The Wise Woman

> God put your body on this earth.
> To attack it in this way   245
> Is contrary to God's will.
> Often, thinking we do good, we go astray,
> Atoning for breaking a glass,
> Or playing some game.[24]

The Worldly Woman

> Madame, I don't act like that,   250
> For I prefer a good meal
> To all the fasts of Lent.
> I do not worry about beating up my body;
> On the contrary, I let it enjoy itself always and everywhere.
> In short, I love only myself.   255

The Wise Woman

> You don't love yourself well.
> Through yourself, as yourself, you are nothing,
> If you speak only of your body.

La Mondainne

> Que mon corps n'est rien? Je le touche.
> N'ay-je pas deux yeulx, une bouche?   260
> Vous parlez bien estrangement.

La Sage

> Bien ung corps avez, je l'aloue,
> Qui est faict de fange et de boue:
> Mais pas n'est l'homme ce corps là.

La Mondainne

> N'est pas l'homme ce que je voy,   265
> Que je puis bien toucher au doy:
> Je ne puis entendre cela.

La Sage

> Le corps sans âme n'est que masse
> De terre et dure peu d'espace.
> (Sans elle ne mange ny boit)   270
> Un tas de chose dure ou molle,
> Il n'a veue, oye, ny parolle.
> Est-il pas vray? Respondez-moy.

La Mondainne

> Mon corps sans mon ame n'ay veu,
> Ny que tousjours mangé et beu   275
> Il n'ait, parlé, veu ny ouy.
> Je le sans oÿr, veoir, parler,
> Odorer, toucher, puis aller
> Ung jour triste et l'autre esjouy.

La Sage

> Ce n'est pas luy qui parle et voy,   280
> Mais la chair ainsy vous deçoit,
> Qui vous faict cuider que c'est elle.
> Elle est la flûte du chantant,
> Mais la voix qui en sort portant
> Ne vient pas de chair mortelle.   285

La Mondainne

> Qui est ce qui par mes yeulx void,
> Qui par ma bouche parle et boit,
> Sinon, moy, le corps que voicy?

La Sage

> Du corps pour son masque se sert
> Vostre ame, et très bien il appert,   290
> Si vous voullez oyr cecy:

The Worldly Woman

    My body is nothing? I touch it;

    Do I not have two eyes, one mouth?   260

    What strange things you say.

The Wise Woman

    You certainly do have a body, I admit that.

    But it is made of mud and dirt.

    Man is not the body of which you speak.

The Worldly Woman

    Man is not what I see,   265

    What I can touch with my finger?

    I don't understand that.

The Wise Woman

    The body without a soul is nothing more than a mass

    Of earth that lasts only a short time.

    Without the soul we can neither eat nor drink.   270

    A pile of hard or soft matter

    Does not see, hear, or speak.

    Isn't that true? Answer me.

The Worldly Woman

    I have never seen my body without my soul,

    Nor that it does not still eat,   275

    Drink, speak, see, or hear.

    I feel it hear, see,

    Speak, smell, touch

    And then be sad one day and happy the next.

The Wise Woman

    It is not the body that speaks and sees;   280

    The flesh has thus deceived you

    That makes you believe that it is the one.

    The body is the flute of the performer,

    But the voice that comes from it

    Does not come from mortal flesh.   285

The Worldly Woman

    Who is it then who sees with my eyes,

    Who speaks and drinks with my mouth

    If it is not me, the body that is right here?

The Wise Woman

    Your soul uses the body as a mask,

    And this will be very apparent   290

    If you are willing to listen to this:

Quant votre corps dort et sommeille,
Vostre ame, qui sans dormir veille,
Travaille vostre corps par songes.
Dans vostre corps l'ame immortelle   295
Est mise, et doibt prandre en tutelle
Le corps, vray masque ou bien mensonge.
Elle est de luy le mouvement,
Il n'est d'elle que l'instrument
Exerçant ses affections.   300
Quant mort a l'instrument cassé,
Que l'on dict l'homme est trepassé,
L'ame cesse ses actions.
Le corps convient ung jour pourrir,
L'ame ne peult jamais mourir.   305
Oblie donc ton corps pour elle:
Car, quelque grand beauté qu'il ayt,
Il deviendra puant et laid,
Et l'ame bonne tousjours belle.

La Mondainne

Madame, l'ame separée   310
Du corps, dont elle est tant parée,
Se doibt-elle l'homme estimer?

La Sage

Non, car l'ame tant seullement
N'est l'homme; mais l'assemblement
Des deux, hommes lon doibt nommer.   315
Corps sans ames sont cadavers,
Charongnes pour nourrir les vers,
Qui de l'homme n'ont nul effect;
L'ame sans corps ne peult veoir
Et des euvres pert le pouvoir,   320
Dont elle n'est l'homme parfaict:
Mais l'ame au corps joincte et unie,
C'est l'homme: en cest compaignie
De parfaicte confaction
Ceste union apporte vie: 325
Mais si l'ame est du corps ravie,
C'est mort leur separation.

La Mondainne

Ce que vous dictes bon me semble,
Que l'homme soit les deux ensemble.

When your body sleeps and slumbers,
Your soul, which stays awake and keeps watch,
Works on your body through dreams.
Your immortal soul is put into your body   295
And it must take the body,
A real mask or even a lie, under its wing.
The soul is the body's movement
And the body is simply the soul's instrument,
Doing its bidding.   300
When death breaks down the instrument,
When they say that one has passed away,
The soul ceases its work.
While the body must rot away one day,
The soul can never die.   305
Accordingly forget your body in favor of your soul,
For whatever great beauty it possesses,
It will become putrid and ugly.
Your soul will always be beautiful.

The Worldly Woman

Madame, should one then consider   310
The soul, separated from the body
That adorns it, man?

The Wise Woman

No, because the soul by itself is not man.
It is the joining of the two
That should be called man.[25]   315
Bodies without souls are cadavers,
Corpses to feed worms,
Which have none of the effect of man.
The soul without the body cannot see
And loses the power of action,   320
So it alone does not complete man.
It is the joining of the body and the soul
United that is man.
In the company of this perfect concoction,
This union brings life.   325
But if the soul is taken from the body,
Their separation is death.

The Worldly Woman

What you are saying seems good to me,
That man is the two together.

Parquoy je veux plus que jamais   330
Garder l'ame du corps saillir,
Et de le nourir ne faillir
En tout plaisir: je le prometz.

La Sage

Plus ne te fault estre amoureuse
Du corps, mais estre desireuse   335
De l'entretenir sobrement.
Mais tu doibz estre socieuse
De veoir ton ame vertueuse,
Ce doibt estre ton pensement;
Car l'ame plaine de malice   340
Au corps exercera son vice,
En se damnant avecque luy.
Mais l'ame de vertu remplie
Fera au corps euvre accomplie,
Car il n'est d'elle que l'estuy.   345
Bien ou mal qu'ensemble feroit,
Bien, mal, ensemble sentiroit,
Pour tout jamais en bas ou hault.

La Mondainne

Je crainctz ceste pugnition;
Pensant telle damnation,   350
A tout jamais le cueur me fault.
Helas! je suis si très mondaine,
Si tressubtile et si très vaine
Qu'a peu que ne me desespere.

La Sage

Desesperer, c'est bien le pire.   355
Il fault que vostre cueur desire
La grace de son Dieu et pere.

La Mondainne

Moy qui n'ay aymé que ma chair
N'oserois de luy approcher,
Car en moy ne sens que peché.   360

La Sage

C'est l'heure que au grand vaincueur
Fault declarer le mal du cueur
Qui par peché est tout taché;
Sur peché aura la victoire,

This is why I want more than ever 330
To keep the soul from leaving the body
And to not fail to nourish it
With every pleasure. I promise this.

The Wise Woman

You should no longer be in love
With your body, but rather 335
Desire to maintain it soberly.
You should be more worried
About seeing that you have a virtuous soul;
This should be your first concern,
For a soul that is full of malice 340
Will work its vice on the body,
Condemning the body along with the soul.
But a soul full of virtue
Will make of the body an accomplished work,
For the body is only the casing of the soul. 345
Good or bad, they will do it together,
Good, bad, they will feel it together,
Forever either down below or up above.

The Worldly Woman

I fear this punishment.²⁶
My heart falters when I think 350
Of such an eternal condemnation.
Alas! I am so worldly,
So very clever, and so very vain
That I despair greatly.

The Wise Woman

To despair is the worst of things; 355
Your heart must desire
The grace of its God and father.

The Worldly Woman

And I, who have only ever loved my flesh,
Would never dare approach him;
I feel only sin in myself. 360

The Wise Woman

Now is the time that you must declare
To the great victor the evil in your heart,
All blemished with sin.
He will be victorious over sin,

Et n'en demande que la gloire,   365
Vous en donnant tout le profit.

La Mondainne

Las! puis je croyre, moy villaine,
Que ceste bonté souveraine
Si grant honneur et bien me feist?

La Sage

Croire il te fault fermement,   370
Puis suyvre son commandement,
Et le servant de cueur et d'euvre.

La Mondainne

Je ne sçay pas où commencer:
Je craindz seullement de penser
Au mal qu'il fault que je desceuvre.   375

La Sage

Pour vous metre toute à delivre,
Je vous faictz present de ce livre:
C'est la loy et vielle et nouvelle.
En luy verrez ce qu'il fault faire
Et qui pour vous peult satisfaire,   380
Pour vous metre en vie eternelle.

La Mondainne

Puis qu'il vous plaist de le me dire,
Incessament je le veux lire,
Pour y chercher mon sauvement.

La Sage

Ignorance, des folz marrastre,   385
A sapience pour emplastre,
Bon sens, raison, entendement.

La Supersticieuse

Dieu soit loué de veoir reduicte
Ceste pouvre folle seduicte.
Vous avez faict ung grand meritte: 390
Elle alloit à bridde avallée
Jusques au fondz de la vallée
De perdition très mauldite.

La Sage

Vous qui jugez sa vie infecte,
Cuydez vous estre plus parfaicte   395
Qu'elle et mener meilleure vie?

And he asks only the glory,   365
  Giving you all the rewards.

The Worldly Woman

  Alas! Can I, so despicable, believe
  That this sovereign goodness will do me
  Such a great honor and give me such gain?

The Wise Woman

  You must believe firmly,   370
  Then follow his commandment,
  Serving him with heart and deed.

The Worldly Woman

  I don't know where to begin.
  It scares me to think simply
  Of the evil that I have to reveal.   375

The Wise Woman

  To put you at ease
  I give you the gift of this book:
  It is the law, old and new.[27]
  You will find in it what you must do
  And who can give you satisfaction   380
  To assure your eternal life.

The Worldly Woman

  Since it pleases you to tell me about it,
  I will read it continually
  Seeking my salvation in it.

The Wise Woman

  Ignorance, cruel mother of the feeble-minded,   385
  Has a remedy in wisdom,
  Good sense, reason, and understanding.

The Superstitious Woman

  Praise God to see
  This poor deceived fool won over.
  You have done a great service.   390
  She was heading at full speed
  Into the depths of the horrid
  Valley of perdition.

The Wise Woman

  You, who judge her life to be impure,
  Do you believe that you are more perfect than she   395
  And that you lead a better life?

La Supersticieuse

    Meilleure: je ne le dis pas,
    Mais j'aurois bien perduz mes pas,
    Si sur son euvre avois envye.
    Je ne joue ny je ne dance,   400
    Ny ne despens en habondance,
    Comme elle faict et jour et nuit.

La Sage

    N'y a il peché que dancer?
    Examinez vostre penser
    Qui trop plus que le dancer nuict.   405

La Supersticieuse

    Ma pensée est de faire bien
    En faict, en dict et en maintien,
    Profitant à moy et au monde.
    Je dictz les sept heures du jour
    Et de travailler n'ay sejour;   410
    Pour me sauver là je me fonde.

La Sage

    Mais vous la jugez toutesfois.

La Supersticieuse

    Sans faulte, Madame, non fais:
    Je parle par compassion.

La Sage

    Si vous voyiez vostre peché,   415
    Vostre œil en seroit empeché
    De juger sa condiction.

La Supersticieuse

    Vous me faictes bien enrager:
    Tenue suis de corriger
    Mon prochain, voiant son default.   420
    Mais si son mal faict ne regarde,
    De le corriger je n'ay garde.
    Qu'est ce donc que faire me fault?

La Sage

    Aux magistratz est bien l'office
    De juger et faire justice;   425
    Par eulx Dieu gouverne la terre.
    Mais si sans peché vous sentez,
    Contre elle vostre main metez
    Et jectez la premiere pierre.

The Superstitious Woman

    "Better" I would not say,

    But I would really have lost my way

    If I desired her life.

    I don't play or dance   400

    Or spend abundantly

    As she does day and night.

The Wise Woman

    Is dancing the only sin?

    Examine your thoughts,

    Which are much more harmful than dancing.   405

The Superstitious Woman

    My thought is to do well

    In deed, in word, and in conduct,

    Benefiting both myself and the world.

    I pray the seven hours of the day[28]

    And I never cease working.   410

    I anchor myself in that in order to save my soul.

The Wise Woman

    Yet nonetheless you judge her.

The Superstitious Woman

    Truly, Madame, I do not.

    I speak with compassion.

The Wise Woman

    If you could see your own sin,   415

    Your eye would be unable

    To judge her condition.

The Superstitious Woman

    You are making me quite angry.

    It is my duty to correct

    My neighbor when I see her fault.   420

    If I do not take notice of her bad behavior,

    Then I do not have to be concerned with correcting her.[29]

    What is it, then, that I should do?

The Wise Woman

    It is the role of judges

    To judge and render justice.   425

    God governs the earth through them.

    But if you feel that you are without sin,

    Raise your hand against her

    And throw the first stone.[30]

La Supersticieuse

    Sans peché ne me sens je pas;   430
    Si ay je retiré mes pas,
    Tant que j'ay peu, de toute ordure;
    J'ai delaissé accoustremens,
    Festins, amours et instrumens,
    Prenant une vie aspre er dure.   435

La Sage

    Puis que peché encores faictes,
    Pas juge competant vous n'estes.
    Or vous jugez dont la premiere.

La Supersticieuse

    Je me juge bien pecheresse
    Et que je failly, mais si est ce   440
    Que ne suis paillard' ny meurtriere;
    J'en loue le Dieu de bonté,
    Pour lequel mon corps j'ay doubté
    Tant qu'il ne se peult soubstenir.
    Je le bas, je le fais jeusner   445
    Et en voiage cheminer,
    Et de tous plaisirs abstenir.

La Sage

    N'esperez pour ce rien gaigner,
    Pour vostre corps en sang baigner,
    Ou faire sur le feug rostir;   450
    Car, si vostre cueur n'est joieulx
    Et charitable et amoureux,
    A Dieu ne faictes que mentir.
    Dieu regarde du cueur le fons.
    Vos peines, voiaiges et dons   455
    Faictz sans charité il desprise.
    Car luy qui est d'amour vray dieu
    Veult le cueur brusler de son feug,
    Ainsi qu'umilité le brise;
    Car, s'il n'est bien humilié   460
    Et par amour à luy lié,
    Rien ne sert vostre barboutter:
    Et si en Dieu vous ne trouvez
    Et sa presence n'esprouvez,
    Vous avez beau partout trotter.   465

The Superstitious Woman

    I do not feel that I am without sin;   430

    Because of this I have retreated

    As much as I can from all filth.

    I have abandoned all trappings,

    Parties, loves, and music,

    Taking up a bitter, difficult life.   435

The Wise Woman

    Since you continue to sin,

    You are not a competent judge.

    Yet you are the first to judge.

The Superstitious Woman

    I judge myself to be a sinner;

    I do fall short.   440

    But if I am not a loose woman or a murderer,

    I praise the God of goodness for it.

    It is for him that I have feared my body

    So much that I can hardly bear it.

    I beat it, I force it to fast,   445

    Go on pilgrimages,

    And abstain from all pleasures.

The Wise Woman

    Do not hope to gain anything[31]

    By bathing your body in blood

    Or by roasting it over a fire;   450

    For if your heart is not joyous,

    Charitable, and loving,

    Then you do nothing but lie to God.

    God looks at the depth of the heart.

    He despises your suffering, travels, and gifts   455

    That are done without charity.

    For he who is the true God of love

    Wants your heart to burn with his fire,

    Just as humility breaks it.

    If your heart is not humbled   460

    And linked through love with God,

    Your mumblings are useless.

    And unless you find yourself one with God

    And feel his presence within yourself,

    Then all your journeys are to no avail.   465

Et voiez vous ceste mondaine
Qui à bien faire n'a prins peine?
Je dy que sous peché infame,
Duquel elle a la congnoissance,
A par humilité puissance   470
Estre de Dieu amye et femme.
Voiant Celluy qui luy pardonne,
Elle l'ayme d'une amour bonne
Et d'une charité ardante.
Elle est plus près de Dieu toucher   475
Que vous qui cuydez le chercher
Par une fidélité lante.

La Supersticieuse

La loy de Dieu est icy nulle:
Celluy va tost qui se reculle,
Et qui faict bien il a mal faict.   480
Il fault donc à la chair complaire
Et plus nulle bonne œuvre faire,
Et suivre le plus imparfaict.

La Sage

C'est orgueil qui vous faict parler.
Je vous dis qu'il vous fault aller   485
Le chemin des commandemens,
Et faire bien sans vous lasser,
Et de prier ne vous passer,
Rememorant ses Testamens.
Mais si vostre cueur n'est bien net   490
D'orguel, et une tache en ayt,
Je dis que peu vault vostre ouvraige.
Le cueur doux, humble et charitable,
A seulement Dieu agreable;
Aymer le fault de bon couraige.   495
Mais vous qui jugez le peché,
Dont vostre cueur est entaché,
Je dis que vous avez besoing
De premier avoir la science
De juger vostre conscience,   500
Ou de Dieu vous estes bien loing.

La Supersticieuse

Plustost ma langue en ung feu arde,
Que je me confesse paillarde,

Do you see this worldly woman
Who has never bothered to do good?
I say that she,
Who is very familiar with vile sin,
Has the power through humility   470
To be the beloved and wife of God.
Upon seeing the One who forgives her,
She loves him with a good love
And with fervent charity.
She is closer to touching God   475
Than you who think you are reaching him
Through your tenacious fidelity.

The Superstitious Woman

Then the law of God doesn't apply here:
The one who steps back goes first,
And the one who does good is wrong.   480
One must please the flesh then,
Stop doing all good deeds
And follow the most imperfect.

The Wise Woman

Pride is speaking in you.
I say to you that you must take   485
The path of the commandments
And do good without tiring yourself
Or forgetting to say your prayers,
Remembering his Testaments.
But if your heart is not clean of pride   490
And is blemished with it,
I say that your work is worth little.
Only a sweet, humble, charitable heart
Is pleasing to God.[32]
You must love him with a good heart.   495
But you who judge in others
The sin that spots your heart,
I say that you need first
To develop the knowledge
To judge your own conscience   500
Or you will be very far from God.

The Superstitious Woman

I would rather burn my tongue in a fire
Than confess to being a loose woman,

    Moy qui suis chaste devant tous,

    Et qu'omicide je me nomme,   505

    Qui n'ay frappé ne tué homme,

    Mais plustost j'ay souffers des coups.

La Sage

    M'amye, je ne vous puis taire

    Qu'il n'est nulle pire adultaire

    Que celle qui l'espoux delaisse   510

    Et ayme son contraire et suict,

    Et sa faincte doctrine ensuict

    Et soubz luy s'incline et abaisse.

La Supersticieuse

    Mon mary je ne laissés oncques,

    Dont veufve je demeure adoncques,   515

    Ny n'ay suyvy autre que luy.

La Sage

    Le vray mary, le dieu puissant,

    Ne l'allez vous pas delaissant,

    Mectant en autre vostre appuy?

    En autre que luy vous fiez,   520

    En esperant edifier

    Vostre salut, plaisir, honneur;

    Et luy, qui est le Dieu jaloux,

    Ne veult, autre amy et espoux

    Ayez, où mectez vostre cueur,   525

    Car tout vostre cueur veult avoir,

    Vostre vouloir, vostre pouvoir,

    Et le veult luy seul posseder,

    Et ne vous permect le cueur metre

    En mary, enfans, pere ou maistre;   530

    Le cueur à nul ne veult ceder.

La Supersticieuse

    Dieu ne nous a il pas permis

    D'aymer noz enfans et amys?

    Autrement serions pis que bestes.

La Sage

    Si vous aymez, comme il commende,   535

    Le bon dieu, à vostre demande

    Trouverez les responces prestes.

    Car en l'aymant parfaictement,

I who am chaste before all,
And to call myself a murderer, 505
I who have never hit nor killed anyone,
But rather have suffered many blows.

The Wise Woman

My friend, I must tell you
That there is no worse adultery
Than that of the woman who leaves her spouse 510
To follow and love his enemy,
Becoming a devotee of his false doctrine,
Bowing down and humbling herself before him.

The Superstitious Woman

I never abandoned my husband;
I am his widow 515
And I followed no other than him.[33]

The Wise Woman

Have you not gone about abandoning
The true husband, God Almighty,
Finding your support in another?
You put your trust in another, 520
Hoping to increase your chances
Of salvation, pleasure, and honor.
And he who is a jealous God
Does not want you to have another beloved and spouse
In whom you place your heart. 525
For he wants to possess your entire heart,
He wants to be the only keeper
Of your will, your potential;
He does not allow you to place your heart
In a husband, in children, a father, or a master. 530
He does not want to surrender your heart to anyone.[34]

The Superstitious Woman

Hasn't God allowed us to
Love our children and our friends?
Otherwise we would be worse than animals.

The Wise Woman

If you love God as he demands, 535
You will find the answers
Ready at your request.[35]
For by loving him perfectly,

Vostre prochain parellement
Aymerez, voiant en lui Dieu: 540
Ainsi aymerez dieu haultain
Et aymerez vostre prochain,
Voiant dieu en luy en tout lieu.

La Supersticieuse

Ceste doctrine m'est bien dure.

La Sage

Or, me lisez ceste escripture   545
Où verité se faict entendre.

La Supersticieuse

Madame, je suys bien trop sotte
Pour chanter de si haulte notte:
Certe, je n'y puis rien comprandre.

La Sage

M'amye, lisez hardiment   550
Le viel et nouveau Testament
Que vous a laissé vostre pere.

La Supersticieuse

C'est à la personne savante:
Mais moy qui suis tant ignorante,
Cela me seroit impropere.   555

La Sage

Si vous fuyez la medecine,
Qui vous peult guerir la racine
De vostre mal, vous estes morte.

La Supersticieuse

Bien que malade ne me sens,
Toutsefoye, à vous me consens.   560

La Sage

Laissez là donc de bonne sorte
Pour guerir vostre maladie.
Lors, ne soyez plus si hardie
De dire que vous estes saine,
Mais quant vostre mal à planté   565
Sentirez, alors la santé
Vous y trouverez toute plaine.

La Supersticieuse

J'y veulx lire pour vous complaire.

You will love your neighbor in the same way,
Seeing God in him.   540
In this way you will love God most high
And you will love you neighbor,
Seeing God in him everywhere.

The Superstitious Woman

This is a most cruel doctrine for me.

The Wise Woman

Then read for me this scripture   545
Where truth can be found.

The Superstitious Woman

Madame, I am really too foolish
To sing so high a note:
I will surely understand nothing in it.

The Wise Woman

My friend, read now   550
The Old and the New Testament
That your father has left you.

The Superstitious Woman

This is for the learned.
It would be improper for me;
I am too ignorant.[36]   555

The Wise Woman

If you flee the medicine
That can cure your illness at its root,
Then you will die.[37]

The Superstitious Woman

Even though I do not feel sick,
I give myself over to you anyway.   560

The Wise Woman

Leave it at that, then, as you should,
To cure your illness.
Don't be so bold now
As to say that you are healthy;
On the contrary, it is when   565
You will feel your sickness fully
That you will find yourself full of health.

The Superstitious Woman

I want to read it to please you.

La Sage
>   C'est le mirouer qui esclaire
>   Vos cueurs, et puis qui les descouvre.   570
>   Grande joye j'ay de vous deux
>   Veoir lire en ces livres si neufz,
>   Que neufves serez en ceste euvre.

SCENE IV

La Ravie de Dieu, Bergère, chante:
>   Helas! Je languys d'amours . . .
>   Helas! je meurs tous les jours.   575

Puis dict elle:
Qui vit d'amour a bien le cueur joieulx,
Qui tient amour ne peult desirer mieulx,
Qui scet amour n'ignore nul sçavoir,
Qui void amour a tousjours rians yeulx,
Qui baise amour il passe dans les cieulx,   580
Qui vainc amour il a parfaict pouvoir,
Qui ayme amour acomplyt son debvoir,
Qui est porté d'amour n'a nulle peine,
Qui peult amour embrasser prandre et veoir,
Il est remply de grace souveraine.   585

La Mondainne
Oyez quel chant!

La Supersticieuse
>   Mais oyez sa parolle.

La Sage
Ha! Ce n'est pas langage d'une folle?

La Bergère chante:
>   La, la, la, la, la, la, la, la
>   Quelle bonne chere elle a   590
>   Quant son amy près d'elle est là,
>   Berger pour la bergere!

La Sage
>   A sa voix et à sa maniere,
>   Elle ayme, poinct n'en fault doubter.

La Mondainne
>   Arrestons nous pour l'escouter.   595

The Wise Woman
> This is the mirror that lights up
> Your hearts and then reveals them. 570
> I feel such joy in seeing you two
> Read these newfound books;
> In them you will be renewed.

SCENE IV

The Woman Enraptured by the Love of God, shepherdess, sings:[38]
> > Alas! I languish from love. . .
> > Alas! I die every day. 575

Then she says:
She who lives on love has a joyous heart,
She who possesses love cannot want better,
She who knows love is ignorant of nothing,
She who sees love always has laughing eyes,
She who kisses love passes into the heavens, 580
She who conquers love has perfect power,
She who loves love accomplishes his duty,
She who is uplifted by love suffers not,
She who can embrace, grasp, and see love
Is filled with supreme grace. 585

The Worldly Woman
Listen to that song!

The Superstitious Woman
> But listen to her words.

The Wise Woman
Ha! Is this not the language of a fool?

The Shepherdess sings:
> > La, la, la, la, la, la, la, la
> > How joyful she looks 590
> > When her beloved is close to her,
> > > A Shepherd for the Shepherdess.

The Wise Woman
> There's no doubt about it; as you can see
> In her voice and in her manner, she is in love.

The Worldly Woman
> Let us stop and listen to her. 595

La Bergère chante:
Amours m'ont faict du desplaisir mainte heure,
Mais le parfaict, qui dans mon cueur demeure,
M'a satisfaict et garde que ne meure
　　Dont pour luy chante et pleure.
La Sage
C'est pure amour qui si fort la tourmente.　　　　　　　600
La Supersticieuse
Aussi d'amour seullement elle chante.
La Mondainne
Saluons la pour la faire parler.
La Sage
Il ne fault pas soubdain à elle aller:
Approchons nous nostre beau petit pas.
La Bergère chante:
Jamais d'aymer mon cueur ne sera las,　　　　　　　605
Car dieu l'a faict d'une telle nature
Que vray amour luy sert de noriture:
Amour luy est pour tout plaisir soulas.
La Mondainne
Saluons là.
La Sage
　　C'est bien dit.　　　　　　　610
La Supersticieuse
　　　　Dieu vous gard.
La Bergère
Et vous aussi.
La Supersticieuse
　　Nous venons ceste part
Vous visiter, sçavoir qu'icy vous faictes.
La Bergère chante:
　　　　Je garde mes brebiettes.　　　　　　615
La Mondainne
　　Quoy? n'avez vous autre exercice?
La Sage
　　Oysiveté engendre vice.
La Bergère chante:
　　Je fille quant dieu me donne dequoy
　　Je fille ma quenoille, ouoy.

The Shepherdess sings:
Loves have often brought me much displeasure,[39]
But the perfect love that lives in my heart
Satisfies me and protects me from death;
    It is for him that I sing and cry.
The Wise Woman
It is pure love that greatly torments her.   600
The Superstitious Woman
And she sings only of love.
The Worldly Woman
Let us greet her to get her to talk.
The Wise Woman
We must not startle her;
Let us approach slowly.
The Shepherdess sings:
My heart will never be tired of loving,   605
For God has made it of such a nature
That true love is its nourishment.
Love is my heart's complete and never-ending pleasure.
The Worldly Woman
Let us greet her.
The Wise Woman
    Well said.   610
The Superstitious Woman
      May God protect you.
The Shepherdess
And you also.
The Superstitious Woman
    We've come by to visit with you
And to find out what you do here.
The Shepherdess sings
    I am guarding my flock.   615
The Worldly Woman
    What? Have you no other occupation?
The Wise Woman
    Idleness engenders vice.
The Shepherdess sings:
    I spin when God provides,
    I spin my distaff, indeed I do.

La Supersticieuse

    Mais d'amour est tout vostre chant.   620

La Mondainne

    Helas! c'est ung dieu trop meschant.

La Sage

    Certes, il faict d'estranges tours.

La Bergère chante:

        O bergere, m'amie,

        Je ne vy que d'amours.

La Supersticieuse

    Amour est dangereux pour vray.   625

La Bergère chante:

        Je vy d'amourette et vivray.

La Sage

    Lon vous en doibt moins estimer.

La Bergère chante:

Ces facheux sotz qui mesdisent d'aymer,

Et n'en eurent en leur vie congnoissance,

Je vous jure dieu et ma conscience   630

Qu'ilz ont grant tort d'un tel plaisir blasmer.

La Mondainne

    Amour est ung fin ennemy.

La Bergère chante:

        J'ayme bien mon amy

        De bonne amour certaine,

        Car je sçay bien qu'il m'ayme   635

        Et aussi fay je luy.

La Sage

    La femme, s'elle est raisonnable,

    Doibt panser amour dommageable.

La Bergère chante:

        Amour, nulle saison,

        N'est amy de raison.   640

La Supersticieuse

    Puis qu'amour mect raison dehors,

    De son salut n'a nul remors.

La Sage

    Son estat va de mal en pire.

La Bergère chante:

        Laissez parler, laissez dire,

The Superstitious Woman
> But your entire song is about love.   620
The Worldly Woman
> Alas! Yours is a cruel god.[40]
The Wise Woman
> It is true, he does strange things.
The Shepherdess sings:
>> O Shepherdess, my beloved,
>> I live only on love.
The Superstitious Woman
> Love is truly dangerous.   625
The Shepherdess sings:
> I live and will always live on love.
The Wise Woman
> You should be respected less for it.
The Shepherdess sings:
Those annoying fools who speak ill of love
And who have never in their lives known it,
I swear on God and my conscience   630
That they are very wrong to abuse such a pleasure.
The Worldly Woman
> Love is a shrewd enemy.
The Shepherdess sings:
>> I love my beloved
>> With a good, steadfast love,
>> For I know well that he loves me,   635
>> And I him as well.[41]
The Wise Woman
> A woman, if she is reasonable,
> Must consider love harmful.
The Shepherdess sings:
>> Love has never, in any season,
>> Been the friend of reason.   640
The Superstitious Woman
> Since she places love outside of reason,
> She feels no concern for her salvation.
The Wise Woman
> She goes from bad to worse.
The Shepherdess sings:
>> Let them talk, let them say,

> Laissez parler qui vouldra.   645
> Médire qui veult mesdire;
> J'aymeray qui m'aymera.

La *Mondainne*
> Elle n'a ny crainte ny honte.

La *Sage*
> Rien que d'amour ne faict son compte.

La *Supersticieuse*
> Elle ne sent melencolye.   650

La *Bergère chante:*
> Petite fleur belle et jollie,
> Je scay bien que vous m'entendez,
> Que vous m'aymez et attendez:
>> En vous me fie,
>> Je vous affie.   655

La *Mondainne*
> Mais qu'est ce donc qui la contente?

La *Bergère chante:*
Une amour seure, gratieuse et plaisante.

La *Supersticieuse*
Qui l'entretient en ceste amour aymée?

La *Bergère chante:*
Doulce memoire en plaisir consommée.

La *Sage*
> Voicy une nouvelle loy: 660
> Comment venez vous si contente?

La *Bergère chante:*
>> Seure et loiale en foy,
>> Jusqu'à la mort amante.

La *Mondainne*
> N'avez vous d'autre vie envie?

La *Bergère chante:*
> Chanter et rire est ma vie,   665
> Quant mon amy est près de moy.

La *Supersticieuse*
> J'oy d'elle ce que croire n'oze.

La *Bergère chante:*
> Helas! il n'est si doulce chose. . .

La *Sage*
En sa fasson ny chant je n'entendz rien.

Let them talk as they want.   645
May he who will speak ill of me do:
I will love the one who will love me.

The Worldly Woman
She has no fear or shame.

The Wise Woman
Nothing but love matters to her.

The Superstitious Woman
She feels no melancholy.   650

The Shepherdess sings:
Beautiful little pretty flower,
I know that you hear me,
That you love me, and that you wait.
    I trust in you,
    I assure you.   655

The Worldly Woman
But what is it that makes her so happy?

The Shepherdess sings:
A steadfast love, gracious and pleasing.

The Superstitious Woman
What sustains her love in this love?

The Shepherdess sings:
Sweet memory consummated in pleasure.

The Wise Woman
This is a novel law.   660
How did you come to be so happy?

The Shepherdess sings:
    Sure and loyal in faith,
    Beloved unto death.

The Worldly Woman
Have you no desire for a different life?

The Shepherdess sings:
To sing and to laugh is my life   665
When my beloved is close to me.

The Superstitious Woman
I dare not believe what I hear her say.

The Shepherdess sings:
Alas! There is no sweeter thing. . .

The Wise Woman
I understand nothing, neither in her manner nor in her song.

La Bergère chante:
Que ne m'entendz! assez je m'entendz bien.　　　　670
La Supersticieuse
　Vous estes folle, par ma foy.
La Mondainne
　Pour telle la doibt on tenir.
La Bergère chante:
　　Amourettes, sauvez moy,
　　Que pourray je devenir?
La Sage
　Je tiens malheureuse la femme,　　　　675
　Dont le cueur est d'amour martir.
La Bergère chante:
　　Heureuse tiens ma flame,
　　Sans poinct m'en repentir.
La Mondainne
　Mieulx vault vostre cueur nous ouvrir
　Et vostre secret descouvrir.　　　　680
La Sage
　La peine amoindrit en parlant
　Et croist quant lon la va cellant.
La Bergère chante:
　　O combien est heureuse
　　La peine de celler
　　Une flame amoureuse　　　　685
　　Qui fayct ung ceur brusler.
La Supersticieuse
　Vous perdez à dissimuler:
　Or, parlez à nous franchement.
La Sage
　Quand vous ne voiez vostre amant,
　Chantez vous par esjouyssance?　　　　690
La Bergère chante:
　　Las! On peult juger clairement
　　Par le desir de la presence,
　　Quelle douleur et quel tourment
　　Peult venir du mal de l'absence.
La Mondainne
　Maintenant qu'il n'est pas ycy,　　　　695
　Vous debvez avoir grand soucy,
　Car vous faillez à vos partances.

The Shepherdess sings:
So be it! I understand myself enough.   670
The Superstitious Woman
   Upon my faith, you are crazy.
The Worldly Woman
   There is no other way to take her.
The Shepherdess sings:
     Love, save me,
     What will become of me?
The Wise Woman
   I think unhappy the woman   675
   Whose heart is a martyr for love.
The Shepherdess sings:
     I am happy to hold this flame
     And do not regret it at all.
The Worldly Woman
   It would be better for you to open your heart to us
   And to reveal your secret.   680
The Wise Woman
   The suffering lessens in the telling
   And increases when you try to hide it.[42]
The Shepherdess sings:
     Oh, how happy is
     The pain of hiding
     A flame of love   685
     That sets a heart aflame.
The Superstitious Woman
   It is your loss to hide the truth,
   So speak to us openly.
The Wise Woman
   When your beloved is not here,
   Do you sing for enjoyment?   690
The Shepherdess sings:
   Alas! One can clearly judge
   By my desire for his presence
   The pain and torment
   That can come from the sorrow of his absence.[43]
The Worldly Woman
   But now that he is not here   695
   You must be greatly distressed
   Because you cannot go to him.

La Bergère chantant:

> Vous qui estes ignorantes
> Que c'est que la ferme foy:
> O combien seriez contantes   700
> Sy vous le saviez comme moy!

La Sage

> Comment vostre cuer tousjours sent
> Cest amour present ou absant?
> Je ne sçay plus que j'en diray.

La Bergère chante:

> Je l'ayme tant, tant, tant,   705
> Tousjours le serviray.

La Supersticieuse

> Pour vous ny pour nostre langage
> Ne change ny chant ny courage,
> Mais en sa voie veult advancer.

La Bergère chante:

> Plustot mourir que changer mon penser.   710

La Mondainne

> La mort rompra vostre accoinctance.

La Sage

> Quant à moy je la laisseray.

La Bergère chante:

> Encores quant morte seray,
> L'esprit en aura souvenance.

La Supersticieuse

> Adieu, ma mie, car je pense   715
> Que vous estes sur toutte folle.

La Mondainne

> Ne direz-vous nulle parolle?
> Au moins pour l'amour de l'amy,
> Dictes nous ung mot ou demy.

La Bergère

> Que voullez-vous que je vous die?   720
> Jugé avez ma maladie,
> Avant que me toucher le poux.

La Sage

> Or, puis qu'elle est en bon propos,
> Devers elle veulx retorner.
> Mais dictes nous, sans sejorner,   725
> Qui est l'amy que tant aimez.

The Shepherdess, singing:
>> You who are ignorant
>> Of what strong faith is,
>> How happy you would be   700
>> If you understood it like me!

The Wise Woman
> How is it that your heart feels
> This love all the time, present or absent?
> I no longer know what to say about it.

The Shepherdess, singing:
>> I love him so, so, so,   705
>> I will always serve him.

The Superstitious Woman
> She won't change either her song or her heart
> For you or for our words;
> She wants to continue on her path.

The Shepherdess sings:
> I would rather die than change my mind.   710

The Worldly Woman
> Death will break off your acquaintance.

The Wise Woman
> As for me, I will leave her behind.

The Shepherdess sings:
>> Still when I am dead,
>> My spirit will remember it.

The Superstitious Woman
> Adieu, my friend, for I think   715
> That you are the craziest of them all.

The Worldly Woman
> Will you say nothing?
> If only for the love of your beloved,
> Say to us a word or two.

The Shepherdess
> What would you like me to say?[44]   720
> You've judged my sickness
> Before even taking my pulse.

The Wise Woman
> Well then, since she is making sense now,
> I want to return to her.
> But tell us without delay,   725
> Who is this beloved you love so much.

La Bergère

> Vous qui sy fort l'amour blasmez,
> De l'amy ne vous fault enquerre,
> Mais tant en dy que ciel et terre
> Sa vertu ne peuvent comprandre.   730

La Mondainne

> Vous l'aimez fort?

La Bergère

>   Je me doy randre
> Coulpable de l'aimer trop peu.

La Sage

> D'amour ne sentez que le feu,
> Si du mal ne vous contantez.   735

La Bergère

> Je ne sçay lequel vous sentez,
> Mais le plus chault et plus cuisant
> M'est le plus doulx et plus plaisant.

La Mondainne

> Helas! m'amie, comme vous
> J'ai gousté de ce feu tant doux,   740
> Mais je m'en repens de bon cœur.

La Bergère

> Si agreable est la licqueur
> De cest amour, que plus bruslant
> Est son feu, plus est exellant.
> Et celluy qui le peult sentir   745
> Ne s'en peult jamais repentir.

La Supersticieuse

> Helas, helas, sans repentance,
> Mutation et penitence,
> Vous estes en ung mauvais train.

La Bergère

> Ceulx qui ont l'amour en la main,   750
> Ou à l'œil, s'en peuvent retraire,
> Laschant la main, ou l'œil distraire
> De regarder, mais qui le sent
> Au fond du cueur, jamais absent
> Estre n'en peult, jour ny moment.   755

La Sage

> Faulte de sens et jugement

The Shepherdess
>You who are so quick to condemn love
>Should not inquire about my beloved.
>But I will say this much:
>The earth and the sky cannot contain his virtue.   730

The Worldly Woman
>You really love him?

The Shepherdess
>I have to say that I am guilty
>Of not loving him enough.

The Wise Woman
>You feel only the fire of love
>If you are not satisfied with the pain.   735

The Shepherdess
>I don't know which one you feel,
>But the hottest and the sharpest
>Is the sweetest and the most pleasing to me.

The Worldly Woman
>Alas! My friend, like you
>I tasted this fire so sweet,   740
>But I regret it with all my heart.

The Shepherdess
>The liqueur of this love is so pleasant
>That the more burning the fire,
>The more excellent it is.
>And the one who can feel it   745
>Can never regret it.

The Superstitious Woman
>Alas, alas, without repentance,
>Contrition, and penance,
>You are in a bad way.

The Shepherdess
>Those who hold love in their hand   750
>Or in their eye can withdraw from it,
>Letting go of the hand or distracting the eye
>From looking, but the one who feels it
>Deep in the heart can never leave it
>For a day or even a moment.   755

The Wise Woman
>A lack of good sense and of judgment

Vous donnent telle passion,
Que vous jugés parfection
Et qui est l'imparfaict sans doubte.

La Bergère

Il est vray que je ne voy goutte,   760
Fors en amour, et n'ay pouvoir
De rien que n'est amy veoir
Et ne le voy pas à demy.

La Mondainne

Voiez vous amour ou amy?

La Bergère

Si fort l'un à l'autre ressemble   765
Que d'un regard les voy ensemble.

La Supersticieuse

Elle rayve ou est idiotte.
Mieulx vous appartient la marotte
Que ne faict pas vostre houlette.

La Bergère

J'ayme mieulx une violette,   770
Par quy me vient le souvenir
De mon amy, que de tenir
En mon guiron ung grand tresor.

La Sage

Vous estimez donc bien peu l'or.

La Bergère

Aultant qu'il vault, ne plus ne moins.   775

La Mondainne

Vous n'en tenez guere en voz mains:
Parquoy ne savez ce qu'il vault.

La Bergère

Qui n'a ny faim, ny froid, ny chault,
Ny faulte de vivre ou vesture,
D'or ny d'argent certe n'a cure.   780

La Mondainne

Vous n'avez donc de rien affaire?

La Bergère

J'ay ce qui me peult satisfaire:
Cherche ailleurs son bien qui vouldra,
Jamais le mien ne me fauldra.
Je n'ay nulle nécessité;   785

Has given this passion to you,
Which you judge as perfection
And which is, without doubt, imperfect.

The Shepherdess

It is true that I see absolutely nothing   760
Except through love and I have no power
To see anything except my beloved,
And I do not see him incompletely.

The Worldly Woman

Do you see love or your beloved?

The Shepherdess

One looks so much like the other   765
That with one look I see them both together.

The Superstitious Woman

She is in rapture or she is an idiot.
A dunce cap is better suited to you
Than your shepherd's crook.

The Shepherdess

I would rather have a violet   770
That reminds me
Of my beloved than hold
At my breast a great treasure.[45]

The Wise Woman

You don't value gold much, then.

The Shepherdess

As much as it's worth, neither more, nor less.   775

The Worldly Woman

You hold so little of it in your hands,
Which is why you don't know what it is worth.

The Shepherdess

The one who is neither hungry nor cold nor hot,
Who lacks neither food nor clothes,
Certainly does not care about gold or silver.   780

The Worldly Woman

So you have no worries at all?

The Shepherdess

I have what satisfies me.
May those who wish look elsewhere for their treasure,
Mine will never be lacking.
I need nothing.   785

En voiant la diversité
Des estoilles, des fleurs, des champs,
En joye, en plaisir et en chants,
Doulcement passe ma journée.

La Sage

M'amie, vous n'estes pas née   790
En ce monde pour rien ne faire:
A la loy il fault satisfaire
Qui commande de travailler.

La Bergère

Qui ne peult dormir ne veiller,
Luy est permis cest belle chose.   795

La Supersticieuse

Mais celle qui tousjours repose,
Nul bien ne luy peult advenir.

La Bergère

Qui atant le bien advenir,
Il ne l'a pas, mais qui le tient,
Et travailler ne luy souvient.   800
Ne dy je pas vray?

La Supersticieuse

              Non, qui l'a
Tout: mais monstrez-moy cestuy-là,
Auquel ne default quelque chose.

La Bergère

Ha! qui l'a, tient la bouche close   805
Et ceste odeur là pas n'esventte.
Garde vous n'avez qu'il s'en vente
Ny que ung seul semblant il en face.

La Sage

Sy juge lon bien par la face
Quant le cueur est bien satisfaict.   810

La Bergère

J'estime que c'est beaulcoup faict
De juger par l'œil le penser.
Vous me voiez chanter, dancer:
Jugez donc que je suis contante.

La Sage

Mais plustost vous juge ignorante,   815
Qui s'esjouict sans savoir quoy.

Seeing the diversity
Of the stars, the flowers, the fields,
I spend my day sweetly
In joy, pleasure, and song.

The Wise Woman

My friend, you were not born 790
In this world to do nothing.
You must fulfill the law
That demands that one work.[46]

The Shepherdess

The one who can neither sleep nor stay awake
Is allowed this wonderful thing. 795

The Superstitious Woman

But no good can ever come
To the one who is always resting.

The Shepherdess

The one who awaits his treasure,
Does not have it. But the one who does have it
Does not need to work to attain it. 800
Do I not speak the truth?

The Superstitious Woman

No. The one who has it
Has all; but show me that person
Who wants for nothing.

The Shepherdess

Ha! The one who has it keeps his mouth shut 805
And does not breathe a word.
Have no fear that he will brag about it
Nor that he will show the least semblance of it.

The Wise Woman

But one judges well by the face
When the heart is well satisfied. 810

The Shepherdess

I think that it is done often,
To judge the thoughts by the eye.
You see me singing and dancing;
You judge then that I am happy.

The Wise Woman

But I would sooner judge you ignorant, 815
Someone who rejoices without knowing why.

La Bergère

>   Vous avez bien jugé de moy,
>   Car ma joye ne congnois pas.
>   Je m'esjouis et prens soulas
>   Et ne congnois pas bien ma joye.   820

La Mondainne

>   Las! J'ay cheminé par sa voye,
>   Mais aultre chemin fault à prendre.

La Bergère

>   Quel chemin vous plaict il m'aprendre?
>   Je vis ycy en passiance.

La Sage

>   C'est ce beau chemin de science,   825
>   Que chascun doibt tant estimer.

La Bergère

>   Je ne sçay rien sinon aimer.
>   Ce sçavoir là est mon estude,
>   C'est mon chemin, sans lacitude
>   Où je courray tant que je vive.   830

La Supersticieuse

>   Elle est bien simple et bien naifve.
>   Rien ne sçait et ne veult sçavoir.

La Bergère

>   Je sçay ce que je veulx avoir:
>   D'autre science n'ay besoing.
>   Tel cuide estre près qui est loing,   835
>   Mais qui est près, sy loing se cuide
>   Que sans cesser crye à l'aïde,
>   De peur qu'il a aymer trop peu.

La Sage

>   Or, allez desnouer ce neu.
>   Croiez qu'amour l'a abuzée,   840
>   Et quelque amy l'a amuzée,
>   Parquoy elle a perdu son sens.

La Bergère

>   Vous en parlez, et je le sens,
>   Mais non pas sy fort que je veulx,
>   Car mes desirs sont tousjours neufz   845
>   Et recommancent par leur fin.

The Shepherdess

    You have judged me well,

    For I do not understand my joy.

    I rejoice and am soothed

    Without clearly understanding my joy.   820

The Worldly Woman

    Alas! I've traveled on her path;

    But it is another path that you must take.

The Shepherdess

    What other path would you like me to take?

    I live here patiently.

The Wise Woman

    It is the beautiful path of knowledge   825

    That everyone should cherish.

The Shepherdess

    I know nothing outside of love.

    This knowledge is my study,

    It is my path where I will run,

    Without tiring, for as long as I live.   830

The Superstitious Woman

    She is truly simple and quite naive.

    She knows nothing and wants to know nothing.

The Shepherdess

    I know what I want to have;

    I don't need any other knowledge.[47]

    Some believe they are near although they are far,   835

    But the one who is near and believes himself to be far

    Cries for help incessantly

    Out of fear that he loves too little.

The Wise Woman

    Well, go ahead and make sense out of that.

    We must believe that love has abused her,   840

    And some lover has amused her,

    And for this she has lost her mind.

The Shepherdess

    You speak of it, but I feel it,

    Although not as strongly as I would like,

    For my desires are always brand new   845

    And begin again where they left off.

La Supersticieuse

    M'amye, celluy est plus fin

    Que bon, qui à soy tant vous tire.

La Bergère

    Je ne vous en veulx contredire,

    Car vous ne mentez d'un seul mot.   850

    Il n'est fol, ny facheulx, ny sot,

    Mais est fin, sage, plus que moy:

    Donc plus que moy aymer le doy,

    Pour sa tresdoulce tromperie.

La Sage

    Mais vous deussiez estre marrie   855

    D'estre aussy trompée et deceue.

La Bergère

    Hellas, telle joye j'ay receue

    D'avoir sens et honneur perdu

    Pour luy, que mon cueur s'est rendu

    Entre ses bras, en sa puissance,   860

    Perdant de soy la congnoissance

    Pour penser en luy nuict et jour.

La Mondainne

    J'ay autrefois porté amour

    A mon corps, à moy mesme seulle,

    Dont maintenant fault que me deulle.   865

La Bergère

    Mon corps ne sens ny n'ayme poinct,

    Car le sien où mon ceur est joinct

    Faict mettre le mien en oubly.

    Le sien de vertu anobly,

    Je le dy mien et le sens tel.   870

La Supersticieuse

    Pas n'ay aimé mon corps mortel,

    Mais l'ay haÿ et tourmenté

    Pour veoir par tourment augmenter

    De mon ame le grand loyer.

La Bergère

    Mon ame perir et noier   875

    O! puisse en ceste doulce mer

    D'amour, où n'y a poinct d'amer.

    Je ne sens corps, ame ne vie,

The Superstitious Woman
>My friend, the one who draws you so to him
>Is more clever than good.

The Shepherdess
>I don't want to contradict you
>For not one word that you speak is a lie.   850
>He is neither foolish, a bore, nor an idiot,
>But he is more clever and wise than I.
>Thus I must love him more than myself
>For his sweet trickery.

The Wise Woman
>But you should be angry   855
>To have been so fooled and deceived.

The Shepherdess
>Alas, I have received such joy
>From having lost reason and honor for him
>That my heart has leapt
>Into his arms through his power,   860
>Losing consciousness of self
>In order to think of only him night and day.

The Worldly Woman
>I have in the past given love
>To my body, only to myself.
>Now I must mourn for it.   865

The Shepherdess
>I do not feel or love my body at all,
>For his body, to which my heart is joined,
>Has made me forget my own.
>His is ennobled in virtue;
>I call it mine and feel it as such.[48]   870

The Superstitious Woman
>I have not loved my mortal body
>But have hated and tormented it
>In order to see my soul's great reward
>Increase through the pain.

The Shepherdess
>Oh! May my soul perish and drown   875
>In this sweet sea of love
>Where nothing is bitter.
>I feel neither body, soul, nor life,

Sinon amour, ny n'ay envye
De Paradis, ny d'enfer crainte;   880
Mais que sans fin je soys est raincte
A mon amy, unie et joincte.

La Sage

Je n'y congnois teste ny poincte,
Bref à elle pour rien parlons
Et nous faisons ce que voulons,   885
Car elle ne nous veult entendre.

La Bergère

Je suis trop sotte pour apprendre;
Parquoy ne veulx faire ne dire
Rien que ce qui me faict tant rire,
N'y les fascheux ne veulx henter.   890

Elle chante:

Dame, qui m'escouttez chanter,
Qui me voiez joieuse et rire,
Je vous veulx mes plaisirs conter:
Contraincte suis de le vous dire.
Ne me doib je pas contanter,   895
Quant j'ay le bien que je desire?

La Sage

Puis qu'à son chanter se remect,
Sa contenance nous promect
Qu'elle ne se veult amander.

La Mondainne

Il ne fault raison demander   900
Où est ung si foible cerveau.

La Supersticieuse

Mais n'est ce pas ung cas nouveau,
Que corps, ame, honneur et richesse,
N'estime auprès de la liesse
D'amour, dont parle si souvent?   905

La Bergère chante:

Autant en emporte le vent.

La Sage

Je m'esbahy comme amour forte
Si fort en joye la conforte,
Que de rien ne se plaing ny deult.

Except love; I do not want
Paradise, nor do I fear hell; 880
But I wish I may be eternally bound
To my beloved, united as one.
The Wise Woman
    I cannot make heads or tails of this.
    In truth we are wasting our time talking to her.
    Let us do as we will, 885
    For she does not want to listen to us.
The Shepherdess
    I am too stupid to learn,
    That is why I wish to do or to say
    Only that which makes me laugh.
    Nor do I want to spend time with bores. 890
She sings:
    Ladies, you who listen to me sing,[49]
    Who see me joyous and laughing,
    I want to tell you about my pleasure.
    I feel a need to explain it to you.
    Should I not be satisfied 895
    That I have the treasure that I desire?
The Wise Woman
    As she's taken up her singing again,
    Her demeanor assures us
    That she does not want to mend her ways.
The Worldly Woman
    One must not ask reason 900
    From such a feeble brain.
The Superstitious Woman
    But is this not new,
    That body, soul, honor, or riches
    She scorns over the happiness
    Of love that she speaks of so often? 905
The Shepherdess sings:
    It is gone with the wind.[50]
The Wise Woman
    I am astounded how such a strong love
    Comforts her, a love strong in joy;
    She neither complains nor moans about anything.

La Bergère chante:

 Il ne faict pas le tour qui veult   910

La Mondainne

 Si son amour estoit divine,

 Bien l'eussions congnu à sa mine:

 Elle en eust dict quelque passage.

La Sage

 L'amour de Dieu faict l'homme saige,

 Prudent, de bonne conscience,   915

 Estudiant en sapiance,

 Jour et nuict et matin et soir.

La Supersticieuse

 Elle sçait ung bien, c'est se seoir,

 Car pour nous ne s'est pas levée.

La Mondainne

 La sottie en est esprouvée;   920

 Jamais plus sotte ne vid on.

La Bergère chante:

 Ho ho y y on on on on.

La Mondainne

 Elle rid et de nous se mocque.

La Supersticieuse

 Sa teste est telle que sa tocque:

 C'est d'une bergere ignorante.   925

La Sage

 Mais (qui pis est) brebis errante,

 Qui au pasteur poinct ne retorne.

La Bergère chante:

 Et je seray sy mignonne,

 Il sera mon grand mignon

La Sage

 Ces motz ne vaillent ung oignons.   930

 Laissons la et nous retirons.

La Mondainne

 Et en vous suivant nous lirons;

 Il me tarde que tant sejurne.

La Supersticieuse

 Mieulx vault que lire je retorne,

 Le temps perdons de plus parler.   935

The Shepherdess sings:
>Not all who desire can succeed.   910
The Worldly Woman
>If her love were divine,
>We would have recognized it in her expression.
>She would have said something of it.
The Wise Woman
>God's love makes man wise,
>Prudent, of good conscience,   915
>A student of wisdom
>Night and day, morning and evening.
The Superstitious Woman
>She knows one thing well: to sit down,
>For she has not risen for us.
The Worldly Woman
>Her foolishness has been proven;   920
>Never has there been such a fool.[51]
The Shepherdess sings:
>Ho ho yo yo on on on.
The Worldly Woman
>She is laughing and making fun of us.
The Superstitious Woman
>Her head is just like her hat:
>It belongs to an ignorant shepherdess.   925
The Wise Woman
>But what is worse, she is a lost sheep
>Who will not return to the shepherd.
The Shepherdess sings:
>>And I will be so adorable,
>>He will be my Prince Charming.
The Wise Woman
>These words are not worth a hill of beans.   930
>Let us leave her and be off.
The Worldly Woman
>And we will read as we follow you.
>I am impatient that we have put it off so.
The Superstitious Woman
>It's better that I return to reading;
>We are wasting more time talking.   935

La Bergère chante:
>   Laissez-moy aller, aller,
>   Laissez-moy aller jouer.

La Supersticieuse
>   Vostre chant ne pouvons louer,
>   Dont par charité j'ay regret.

La Mondainne
>   Et moy je m'en vois mal contante.   940

La Bergère chante:
>   Vostre amour froide et lante. . .
>   N'entend poinct son secret.

La Sage
>   D'une chanson elle ne chante
>   Qu'un mot, et puis ne la poursuit,
>   Sans nul arrest: parquoy s'ensuyt   945
>   Qu'il n'y a grand sens en sa teste.

La Supersticieuse
>   Elle est du tout ou folle ou beste,
>   Ou opiniastre ou glorieuse.

La Bergère chante:
>   J'estime malheureuse
>   Celle qui n'ayme poinct;   950
>   Et celle trop facheuse
>   Qui craint venir au poinct,
>   Ouquel la seureté
>   Est la bienheureté.

La Sage
>   Oyez, malheureuse elle juge   955
>   Celle qui n'est au grand delluge
>   D'amour, ainsy qu'elle, perie.

La Mondainne
>   Elle est digne de moquerie.

La Supersticieuse
>   Mais de pitié voiant ses termes
>   Nous debvons gecter grosses larmes,   960
>   Priant Dieu qu'il luy pardonne.

La Sage
>   Peult estre qu'un jour sera bonne;
>   Pensez que telle avez esté:

The Shepherdess sings:
> Let me go, go,
> Let me go and play.

The Superstitious Woman
> We cannot praise your song,
> Which, with kindness, I regret.

The Worldly Woman
> I, too, am leaving with regret.   940

The Shepherdess sings:
> Your cold, slow love. . .
> Does not hear his secret.

The Wise Woman
> She sings only a few words from each song
> And then goes no further,
> Endlessly; so it seems   945
> That there is not much sense in her head.

The Superstitious Woman
> She is either completely crazy or stupid
> Or opinionated or conceited.

The Shepherdess sings:
> I judge unhappy
> The woman who does not love.   950
> And unfortunate is the woman
> Who fears arriving at the point
> Where certainty
> Is bliss.

The Wise Woman
> Listen! Unhappy she calls   955
> The woman who has not, in the great deluge
> Of love, perished as she.

The Worldly Woman
> She deserves to be mocked.

The Superstitious Woman
> But seeing her limitations, in pity
> We should cry rivers of tears,   960
> Praying to God to forgive her.

The Wise Woman
> Perhaps one day she will be good.
> Just think that once you were like that.

L'iver ne resemble à l'esté.
Retirons-nous, car il est tard.   965

La Bergère

O doux amour! ô doux regard
Qui me transperse de ton dard!
    O l'ignoré!
L'amy de moy tant adoré,
Le vertueulx mal honoré   970
    Et l'incongnu
Pour tout autre qui n'est tenu!
L'un est dict vestu, qui est nud,
    Et l'autre, obscur.
La coriette qui part le mur,   975
Et le caillou sy fort est dure:
    On le dict mol;
Et le saige on nomme fol,
Et qui est Pierre, on nomme Pol.
    Ainsy chacun   980
Parle son langaige commun.
Mais mon ceur qui n'en aime qu'un
    D'un seul caquet,
J'obliant Jaques et Jaquet,
Corps, chemise, cotte et jaquet,   985
    Homme et habis,
Tresor et biens, moutons, brebis,
Boire, manger, pain blanc ou bis,
    Plaisir, sancté,
Pour plaisir ne peult frequenter   990
Plus ami, et tant plus le enter.
    Helas! j'ay peur
De n'aymer poinct d'assez bon cueur,
Ou de faincte amour, quelle orreur!
    Sy j'aimais fort,   995
C'est amour me donroit la mort. . .
Mais puis que suis vivant, au fort,
    Je n'ayme assez.
Bras et gembes seroient lassez,
Si d'amour estoient pourchassez. . .   1000
    Non, mais plus forts,
Car amour par ses grandz effors

Winter does not resemble summer.
Let us withdraw, for it is late. 965
The Shepherdess
   O sweet love! O sweet gaze
   That pierces me with your arrow!
      O the forsaken one!
   My beloved, whom I adore,
   The virtuous one so badly honored 970
      And unrecognized
   By all who are not beholden!
   One who is said to be dressed is naked,
      And another, hidden.
   The sling[52] that divides the wall 975
   And the very strong flint are hard,
      But they are called soft.
   The wise man is called foolish,
   Peter is called Paul.[53]
      Thus everyone speaks 980
   An ordinary language.
   But my heart loves only one.
      I chatter on
   Already forgetting this and that,
   Body, shirt, coat and jacket, 985
      Men and clothes,
   Treasure and wealth, sheep and ewes,
   To drink, to eat, white bread or wheat,
      Pleasure and health.
   For joy, I could have no closer friend, 990
   Nor be more bound to him.
      Alas! I'm afraid
   Of not loving him with enough heart
   Or with false love, what horror!
      If I loved him enough, 995
   This love would bring death to me;
   But since I am living, at best
      I do not love enough.
   My arms and legs would be weary
   If they were chased by love. . . 1000
      No, they would be stronger,
   For love, with its great strength,

Peult bien resuciter les mors.
    Or t'esvertue,
Amour, et tout soudain me tue.   1005
Puis, quant tu m'auras abatue,
    Me feras vivre.
Pour toy veulx estre folle et yvre
Sans jamais en estre delivre
    Mais toy, amour,   1010
S'il te plaict me faire ce tour,
Que tu me brusles sans séjour,
    Ton consummer
Me donra ung estre d'aymer,
Me rellevant pour m'assommer,   1015
    Et ta lumiere,
Qui en moy sera toutte entiere,
Comme toy me fera legiere.

Tu l'as faict et je t'en mercie.
Voila l'estat de la bergère   1020
Qui suivant d'amour la banniere
D'autre chose ne se soucye.

Can bring the dead back to life.
    So, labor, Love,
And bring death to me suddenly.   1005
Then, after having killed me,
    You will give me life.
For you, I want to be foolish and giddy
Without ever being free.
    But if it pleases you, Love,   1010
To come around to me,
May you consume me relentlessly,
    Your fire will make of me
A being of love,
Raising me up to strike me down.   1015
    And your light,
That will fill me completely,
Will make me, like you, weightless.

You have done it and I thank you.[54]
Here is the fate of the Shepherdess   1020
Who, following the banner of love,
Cares for nothing else.

VII

SELECTIONS FROM *THE HEPTAMERON*

EDITOR'S INTRODUCTION

In spite of Montaigne's unappreciative comment about Marguerite's collec-
tion of tales, calling it "nice enough for what it is,"[1] the *Heptameron* is the
single text by her that has continued to be published and admiringly read
throughout the centuries. There are, however, all kinds of mysteries sur-
rounding its composition and publication. At what point did she actually
begin composing it? Did she work on it to the very end? Why was it never
completed? Why was it not published during her own lifetime? And, finally,
who and what were her sources? None of these questions can be answered
definitively, but one can offer some reasonable hypotheses.

While Jourda feels little actually got written much before the 1540s,[2]
that does not by any means preclude the real possibility that Marguerite—
always interested in storytelling—may have made mental notes early on
and perhaps even written down some of the tales which eventually became
a part of her collection. It is likely, moreover, that she worked steadily on
her project until the very end. Novella 66 takes place after the marriage of
her daughter Jeanne to the duke of Vendôme in 1548, only one year before
her death.

The issue of why Marguerite did not finish the work and of why it was
published only posthumously are in fact the same question. Death inter-
rupted her project, and it is reasonable to assume that had time allowed, she
would have turned her seventy-two tales into the anticipated one hundred
and would most probably have added a third volume to the two compila-
tions she had already put out near the close of her life. In one of the most
important of the seventeen manuscript copies available to us from the pe-

---

1. Michel de Montaigne, *Essays*, book 2, chap.2.
2. Jourda, *Marguerite d'Angoulême*, 2: 664–75.

riod of the early 1550s—before the first publication of the *Heptameron*—
Adrien de Thou, who signed and dated this manuscript, not only speaks
of the work as a "decameron" but leaves space for further additions. Did he
believe that he might have the good fortune to uncover somewhere among
the queen's papers, tales she intended to add to her collection? In any event,
there was no doubt in his mind, or anyone else's, that this was supposed to
be a French decameron.

Modern-day strict rules of copyright did not exist, and manuscripts
lying around were often appropriated and even mutilated by ambitious, if
not unscrupulous, editors. In 1557, the humanist writer Pierre Boiastuau had
access to one of these manuscripts, and because he either did not know its
authorship or did not care, put out a volume of sixty-seven stories under the
title *Histoires des amans fortunez*. It was not, however, until 1559 that Claude
Gruget, prompted it would seem by Marguerite's daughter Jeanne d'Albret,
produced a much more accurate edition of the work. He identified its author
as Marguerite and supplied the text with the title by which it is known to
this day, *L'Heptaméron*.

Finally, on the complicated matter of sources, this much can be said.
Storytelling was an integral part of intellectual life at all levels of Renais-
sance society, and Marguerite and her friends no doubt often indulged in
exchanging tales. So in a sense she was always involved in that kind of nar-
ration. But she was also thoroughly familiar with the written tradition of
the novella, or short story, both in her own country and in Italy. Educated
woman that she was, Marguerite had read the anonymous *Cent Nouvelles Nou-
velles* as well as Philippe de Vigneulle's collection of the same name. And as
for the Italian short fiction or *novellieri*, she not only knew that literature but
was capable of reading it in the original. Authors like Poggio Bracciolini,
Matteo Bandello, Salernitano Masuccio, and most especially Giovanni Boc-
caccio were all part of her reading experiences. Indeed, in the 1540s one of
the writers in her own entourage, Antoine Le Maçon, began translating the
Decameron into French for her.

In the prologue to the *Heptameron* Marguerite speaks of how members of
the French royal court thought of putting together a Boccaccio-like collec-
tion of their own. But she was not ready to follow slavishly in the footsteps
of her much-admired predecessor. There are significant differences between
the two collections. Like Boccaccio, she conceives of a frame device in order
to give a general structure to her collection, but her frame is at one and the
same time more elaborate and more psychologically interesting. While Boc-
caccio's narrators are mere storytelling mouthpieces, Marguerite's *devisants*
are persuasively real people who engage in lively and intriguing discussions.

While Boccaccio offers an entertaining selection of scabrous love stories, Marguerite wants to explore the very nature of human love. While Boccaccio makes no claims about the originality of his tales, Marguerite insists that hers are "true" stories.

No two people, faced with making a selection, will come up with quite the same list of texts. But it seemed wise to us to start with the work's justly famous prologue, where readers are elaborately informed about the circumstances of the storytelling project. This richly layered introduction, already bubbling over with narrative inventiveness, not only takes great pains to define the geography and circumstances of the storytelling—in other words, its frame device—but goes much further than any of Marguerite's predecessors had in making the narrators into very real-sounding people, testament, no doubt, to the creator's extraordinary skills as a writer. This has inevitably led commentators like Felix Frank to see in these invented characters historical figures taken from Marguerite's personal entourage.[3] But while she was keen on portraying her storytellers with as much psychological realism as possible, far beyond any narrative written to that date, Marguerite did not set out to write a roman à clef. On the other hand, it is equally unjust to conclude that she created her *devisants* out of whole cloth. There is arguably much of herself, for example, in the quick-witted, exuberant character of Parlamente.[4]

As for the tales themselves, we wanted to provide novice reader with enough of a sampling to indicate some of the collection's most salient narrative themes. Novella 4, likely an autobiographical tale, raises issues of unbalanced sexual privilege among men and women of the period.[5] Novella 11 shows that the queen of Navarre is no prissy prude, self-importantly beyond scatological humor.[6] Novella 69 provides one example among others in which a clever woman makes a mockery of an adulterous, two-timing

3. This important nineteenth-century editor of the *Heptameron* provides in his introductory remarks a suggestion of names of real people who might have inspired each of Marguerite's ten tale tellers (3: lxix ff.).

4. See Jourda, *Marguerite d'Angoulême*, 2: 763.

5. An important source for Marguerite scholarship is the contemporary author Pierre de Bourdeille, seigneur de Brantôme (1540–1614), who wrote extensively about the French aristocracy of the sixteenth century. He specifically identifies the two main characters here as Marguerite and her would-be seducer, Guillaume Gouffier, seigneur de Bonnivet. Patricia Cholakian sees this story as not only autobiographical but the thematic springboard for the many rape tales in the collection (*Rape and Writing in the* Heptameron).

6. For an interesting commentary on scatological humor in Marguerite's collection, see Dora Polacheck, "Scatology, Sexuality, and the Logic of Laughter in Marguerite de Navarre's Heptameron," *Medieval Feminist Forum* 33 (2002): 30–42.

husband.[7] And, finally, novella 72 is illustrative of the anticlericalism which abounded in all the popular literature of the time.[8]

༈

PROLOGUE

On the first of September, when the spring waters of the Pyrenees were at their very best, a group of Spanish and French visitors were at the spa town of Cauterets, some to drink the waters, some to bathe in them, and still others to experience the mud cures.[9] The treatments were viewed as so efficacious that patients whose doctors had long since given up on them went home totally cured. But it is not my objective here to praise either the locale or the value of these waters, but merely to set the stage for the story I wish to tell.

These clients stayed on for over three weeks, until they felt well enough to return to their homes. But in the midst of their preparations to leave, it began to rain so violently that it seemed as if God had forgotten his promise to Noah never to flood the world again. All the buildings at Cauterets, big and small, were so filled with water that they became uninhabitable. The Spanish guests tried to make it over the mountains, the most adept at managing the routes faring better than the others. Meanwhile, the French men and women, thinking they could return to Tarbes as easily as they had come, found the swollen streams impassable. And as for the gorge at Béarn,[10] which upon arrival had been only two feet deep, it was now turned into a raging torrent. So they headed back, hoping to find a passable bridge, but none of these fragile wooden structures had been able to withstand the violent waters. Some, believing that if they moved as a group, they might be able to cope, were quickly swept away. Those poised to follow suit dared not take that chance. Thus, unable to come to any common plan of action, they each parted company in search of other possibilities.

A few crossed the mountains, and passing through Aragon, headed for

---

7. Adulterous relations were one of the time-honored themes in all the so-called bourgeois literature of the Middle Ages, including the fabliau and the novella. For a thorough review of these popular motifs, students might look at Stith Thompson's six-volume study, *Motif-Index of Folk Literature* (Copenhagen: Rosenkilder and Begger, 1955–58).

8. It is worth mentioning that while the queen of Navarre does offer examples of both noble and less noble characters in her stories, there is not one honest cleric in the entire bunch!

9. The translation is based on *L'Heptaméron*, ed. Michel François (Paris: Garnier, 1960).

10. Today's Gave de Pau.

Roussillon, and from there on to Narbonne. Others set their sights on Barcelona, in order to cross the sea to Marseille and to Aigues-Mortes. But one of these, an elderly lady and experienced widow, Oisille, was determined not to be thwarted by the danger. She set out for the abbey of Notre-Dame at Sarrance.[11] Not that she was so superstitious as to believe that the Holy Virgin would quit her place alongside her Son so as to inhabit such an isolated spot,[12] but she simply wished to visit this well-known sacred institution, feeling quite sure that if there were any safety to be found, the monks would find it. She finally came to her destination, but only after making her way through difficult terrain. In spite of her years and her considerable bulk, she was forced to do a great deal of climbing. Worst of all, most of her servants and horses died in the process, so that by the time she made it to Sarrance, there was but one man and one woman still with her. The monks generously took them all in.

There were also two French noblemen who had come to the spa, less because of health reasons and more because of their devotion to two ladies. When they realized that the group was disbanding and that the husbands were leading their wives away, they decided to follow quietly at a distance. One evening, the two couples came upon a house occupied by a man who was more a felon than a peasant. The gentlemen who were following stopped at a nearby farmhouse. Toward midnight, a tremendous noise startled them out of their beds. Waking up their servants, they went to inquire from their host just what the racket was all about. The poor man was himself in a state and said that a band of brigands had come in search of money that their partner-in-crime had hoarded away next door.

Upon hearing this, the two gentlemen quickly grabbed their weapons, and with servants in tow, set out to rescue the women, for whose sake death was preferable to any idea of life without them. When they got to the house, they found the front door broken in and the two other men and their servants already engaged in a valiant fight, but to no avail. They were outnumbered, badly wounded, and most of their servants dead. They were ready to surrender just as the two heroes arrived on the scene. Seeing through the window the sorry state of the women and driven by their

11. All this geographic precision reminds us that Marguerite was personally familiar with this region, having many times been herself a patron at Cauterets. It is also further evidence of how important it was to her as a storyteller to make her narrative seem as real as possible to her readers.

12. This gratuitous aside reeks of irony. Marguerite, the evangelistic reformist, does not lose this opportunity to poke fun at conservative Catholics who, in her mind, exaggeratedly reverenced the Virgin and the saints.

love and compassion, they fell upon the criminals with a mad fury. Like two furious mountain bears they slaughtered so many of the bandits that the remaining few, unwilling to face them any longer, fled to their hideout. The host was among the dead, and the gentlemen, hearing that the hostess was no more likable than her dead husband, with a single blow of the sword sent her along to join him.

In a downstairs room they discovered the two husbands, one breathing his last, the other alive but in tattered clothes, his sword broken. He thanked them for coming to his rescue, gratefully hugged them, and begged that they not abandon them, a request the gentlemen were more than happy to fulfill. And so after seeing to the burial of the one husband, whose wife they comforted as best they could, they all set out again with no specific destination, but trusting in God's protection.

And if you wish to know the names of these characters, the husband was Hircan, his wife Parlamente, and the widow Longarine. The two other gentlemen in question were Dagoucin and Saffredent. At the end of a day's journey on horseback, they glimpsed in the distance a church spire, toward which they painfully groped. It was the abbey of Saint-Savin, where both monks and abbot alike greeted them warmly. The abbot was himself a man of good breeding and offered them accommodations worthy of their station. While showing them to their quarters, he inquired into their travels. Learning of their many trials, he informed them that there were others who had had much the same unfortunate experiences.

Indeed, in another room were two women who had escaped dangers even greater than theirs, for they had had to fend off, not men, but wild animals. Half a league from the town of Pierrefitte[13] they ran into a mountain bear, from which they had fled so fast that their horses had dropped dead right under them while they were entering through the abbey gates. Two of their maids, arriving a bit later, said the bear had killed every one of the male servants in the group. When the three gentlemen and two ladies came into the room and found them weeping, they recognized their friends Nomerfide and Ennasuite. They all embraced and began exchanging news of their separate misfortunes. Only some comforting words from the abbot were able to put them all in a calmer state of mind.

The following morning they listened devotedly to Mass and praised God for their deliverance from all these mountain hazards. While they were still in church, a half-clad man came rushing in as if being chased.

---

13. There are in fact three towns in France with this name. This one is located in today's department of Hautes Pyrénées.

He screamed for help as two armed men came running after him. Seeing so many people around, they turned away, but Hircan and the others tracked them down and slew them all. When Hircan returned, he recognized in the man in his nightshirt yet another companion, Geburon.

Geburon told them how he had been at a farmhouse near Pierrefitte, settling into bed in his nightshirt, when suddenly three men appeared at his door. Jumping up and seizing his sword he succeeded in wounding and rendering one of them immobile. As the other two came to their companion's aid, he concluded that his only hope was to flee, since he was more lightly clad than they, for which he now thanked God and those who came to his rescue.

Having heard Mass and having had their meals, the travelers sent to find out whether it was possible yet to cross the river. Learning that it was not, they became very concerned, in spite of the abbot's repeated generous offer for them to remain so long as the waters were still high. They accepted to stay another day. That same evening, as they were about to retire, an aged monk appeared, who had come from Sarrance, where he had completed his annual September journey to celebrate the Virgin's birth. When asked about the mountain trails, the monk said that he had never seen them so bad and that he had witnessed a very sorry sight.

He had met a gentleman by the name of Simontaut, who, tired of waiting for the flood to subside and trusting in his horse, had made up his mind to attempt a crossing. He surrounded himself with his servants in order to break the force of the water. Halfway, those on less sturdy animals were swept away, never to be seen again. The gentleman, seeing he was alone, started to turn back, but the horse, unable to withstand the rush of water, immediately gave way under him. Thank God, he was near enough the stony embankment that he was able to drag himself out on all fours. He had swallowed a great deal of water, however, and was so done in that he could barely move.

Soaked through and miserable because of the servants he had watched perish before his very eyes, he lay down among the rocks. Fortunately, a shepherd, while leading his flock home for the evening, came upon him thus laid out and quickly understood, from the look of the gentleman and the tale he told, the seriousness of his situation. He took him by the hand and led him to his simple hut, where he built a small fire out of kindling. That same evening, God saw to it that this good monk should also pass by, who told the traveler about Sarrance. He guaranteed him that he would find the best possible lodgings there. He also mentioned that he would meet an old widow by the name of Oisille, who had experienced many of the same misfortunes.

When the gathered group heard mention of the good Lady Oisille and of the noble knight Simontaut, they were overjoyed. They gave heartfelt thanks to their Creator, who had been satisfied to take the servants and had saved the masters and mistresses. This was especially true for Parlamente, since Simontaut had for some time now been her devoted admirer.

They urged the monk to give them instructions on how to get to Sarrance. And although the old man made it sound like a very difficult trip, they nonetheless were determined to undertake it. In fact they set out that very day, and the abbot, seeing to their needs, provided them with wine, food, and competent guides to help them through the mountain passes, where one had more often than not to travel on foot rather than on horseback. Exhausted and perspiring, they finally made it to Notre-Dame de Sarrance, where the abbot in charge, although not noted for his kindness, dared not refuse them lodging for fear of irritating the lord of Béarn, a good friend of theirs. He put a hypocritical smile on his face and then led them to Lady Oisille and the noble Simontaut.

Their joy was so great at being thus so miraculously reunited that the night seemed too short for giving thanks to God in the church for having favored them in this manner. After a brief rest the following morning, they heard Mass and took communion together, the sacred act that unites all Christians. They prayed that he who had reunited them would allow them to finish their journey to the glory of his name.

After dinner, they sent someone to see if the waters had subsided but learned that things were worse than ever and that it would be a long while before they could cross safely. So they decided to construct a bridge joining two rocks that were close to each other. To this very day, one can still see the original boards they laid there for people traveling by foot from Oléron and not wanting to wade through shallow waters. The abbot was happy that they were willing to go to this expense since it would increase tourist trade. So he offered workmen, but in fact, essentially ungenerous, he himself was not willing to fork up a cent. When the workmen announced that it would take a minimum of ten to twelve days, the group grew restless.

But Parlamente, Hircan's wife, unwilling to fall prey to idleness or melancholy, asked him permission to speak. And this is what she said to the elderly Lady Oisille: "Madame," said she, "I am surprised that you, a woman of the world and like a mother to the rest of us, cannot come up with some entertainment to help while away the endless time we're to spend here together. If we do not find some amusing and worthy way to pass the time, we risk falling ill."

The young widow Longarine added to this: "Worse still, we will turn bad-tempered, and that's an incurable sickness. Given what we have all been through, there isn't one of us who isn't prone to give way to deep despair."

Laughing, Ennasuite answered: "Not everyone has, like you, lost a husband, and as for admirers, no need to lose heart on that score. There are plenty enough of those around! Nevertheless, I quite agree that we need some form of amusement to fill the void. Otherwise they'll find us dead by tomorrow."

All the men were of the same opinion; and so they asked Lady Oisille if she would consent to making a suggestion.[14] To which she responded:

"My children, what you ask of me, to find what would undo human despair, is no easy task. I have spent my entire lifetime searching and have found but one solution—the reading of Holy Scriptures. There one finds true and perfect spiritual happiness, itself the basis for bodily repose and health. If you ask what, in all these years, has assured my joy and good health, I can tell you this. The moment I rise in the morning, I pick up the Scriptures and read. I meditate upon the goodness of our God, who for our sake sent his son on earth to bring us the holy word and the good news for the remission of our sins and the payment of our debts. This he does through his gift to us of love, worthiness, and ultimate sacrifice. These thoughts fill me with such joy that I take my psalter and in great humility give enthusiastic voice to the wonderful hymns and canticles that the Holy Spirit inspired in David and the other psalmists. The happiness this brings me is so great that whatever the travails of the day, I see them as so many blessings. For through faith I have him in my heart who has taken these burdens upon himself for my sake.

"Likewise before supper, I withdraw to take in some spiritual nourishment, to think of all that has transpired during the day, so that I might ask for God's forgiveness and give thanks for his many kindnesses. And thus I retire with thoughts of his love, peace, and power, protected thus against all evil. And this, my children, after years of searching in vain for happiness in other places, is the activity I have chosen. I am of the opinion that if every morning you were to give one hour over to reading and to saying your prayers devoutly at Mass, you would find, even here in this barren place, the splendors of any city. For whoever knows God discovers beauty everywhere, and whoever does not finds all things ugly. And so I tell you, follow my counsel if you wish to live in joy."

14. This is a set piece, in which Marguerite puts into the mouth of her character—sometimes believed to be based on her own mother, the formidable Louise of Savoy—some of the major points of the evangelistic agenda.

Then Hircan took the floor: "Madame, anyone who has read the Scriptures, as I believe everyone here has, will surely share your point of view. But take note that we are not so indifferent to our bodily needs that we can manage without some sort of entertainment and physical exercise in order to pass the time. Were we in our homes, the menfolk would have hunting and hawking by which to forget the thousands of unhappy thoughts they are prey to. And as for the women, they would have their house chores, their needlework, and sometimes too their dances as a thoroughly respectable physical outlet. So speaking on behalf of the men here, Madame, I am led to suggest that you, being the oldest among us, read to us every morning of the many wonderful things Jesus Christ has done for us; but that between dinner and vespers we find some other pastime which, while nowise harmful to our souls, will bring some satisfaction to our bodies. In that way our days will be pleasant."

Lady Oisille told them that she had taken so much trouble to forget all the vanities that she was afraid of making an unwelcome choice. She therefore suggested that the issue be arbitrated by means of a general discussion and asked Hircan to give his opinion first.

"As far as I'm concerned," he began, "I know perfectly well what I would choose to do, if a certain lady among us would agree. That being said, for the moment I will keep still and accede to the wishes of others."

Realizing what he meant, his wife Parlamente blushed and, half angry and half amused, responded: "Perhaps, Hircan, the person you think you have upset would be quite able to revenge herself if she wanted. Let us, however, set aside for the moment two-person games and think only of those pleasures in which everyone can participate."

Hircan turned to say to the ladies: "Inasmuch as my wife has correctly interpreted my meaning and rejected any such private amusements, she is in the best position to recommend a common pastime for us all."

Everyone agreed, and Parlamente, seeing that it had fallen to her lot to choose, spoke as follows: "If I were as well versed as the ancients, discoverers of the arts, I would create a game that would fulfill the demands laid upon me. But all too aware of my limitations, I'd be lucky to remember the inventions of others, let alone make up any of my own. I shall be glad enough therefore to follow in the footsteps of my predecessors. Among other things, I suspect you have all read Boccaccio's *Decameron*, recently translated into French and much admired by the king, Francis the First, the Dauphin and Dauphine, and by Lady Marguerite. If Boccaccio could have heard how much these people esteem him, it would have been enough to make him rise up from his current resting place.

"Indeed, the above-mentioned ladies, along with other court personalities, decided to do as Boccaccio had done, with this one proviso: to compose only stories that were true. So with the Dauphin, these ladies set out to assemble ten persons who would compose ten tales each. They would, however, exclude from their party any scholars and writers who might, the Dauphin deemed, falsify the truth with their artful skills and rhetorical devices.

"Alas, a number of important events, however, caused the entire project to be tabled: the peace accord between the French and English kings, the confinement of the Dauphine, and several other distracting issues."[15] Parlamente concluded: "But during this period of ten long days, while we await the completion of our bridge, we can at last realize that ambition. With your consent, we can each day, from noon to four, gather in the lovely field alongside the river, where leaf-laden trees will protect us with their shade and keep us cool from the heat of the burning sun. There, comfortably seated, each of us can tell a story which has either been personally witnessed or told to us by a reliable source. At the end of ten days, we will have heard our one hundred tales, and upon our return, if they turn out to be pleasing to the lords and ladies I have spoken of, we can offer them up as a gift in lieu of the usual religious beads and statuettes. On the other hand, if someone thinks of something better, I will not object."

They all agreed that they were not able to come up with anything preferable and were impatient for the next day, so that they might begin. And all ended on a happy note, as each reminisced about his or her past.

As soon as it was morning, they came to Madame Oisille's room, where she was already saying her prayers. After listening devotedly for a good hour, following Mass, at ten, they sat down together to eat. They then retired to their respective rooms to attend to their personal affairs. As agreed, at midday, they returned to the meadow, which was looking so lovely and appealing that only a Boccaccio could do justice to its description. Suffice it to say here, there was never a more beautiful spot, and when they were all seated on the green grass, so soft and comfortable that no carpet or cushion was called for, Simontaut said: "Which of us will take the lead?"

"Since you were the first to speak," Hircan replied, "it is you who should give the command. In game playing everyone is on equal footing."

15. Marguerite is keen on situating her text in a real and historical setting, and thus she includes references that her readers would probably have remembered: the peace treaty of Ardres, signed in June of 1546, following hostilities between Francis I and Henry VIII; several significant royal births, including that of the future king Francis II; not to mention all the confusion that had surrounded the annulment of the marriage of Marguerite's daughter to the duke of Cleves, a political marriage she had vigorously opposed.

"Would to God," Simontaut said, "that the one power I might have in this world would be authority over this group."

Parlamente, realizing the significance of his remark, began to cough.[16] Hircan, not noticing that she grew red in the face, told Simontaut to start, and he complied.[17]

NOVELLA 4

There once lived in the country of Flanders a woman of such high birth that no higher could ever be imagined. She was the widow of two husbands, though no children had issued from either marriage. Since her widowhood, she had gone to live with a brother who was very fond of her. He was married to the daughter of a king and was a man of high social standing. This young prince was greatly caught up in the pursuit of his pleasures, and like most men of his age, given to hunting, women's company, and other pleasant distractions. He had an unpleasant wife who disapproved of his pastimes. And so wherever he went, along with his wife he took his sister, a most cheerful and pleasant companion, though both wise and sensible.[18]

There was a member of this entourage, a gentlemen who in stature, charm, and physical beauty surpassed all his friends. Seeing his master's sister to be a vivacious and fun-loving person, he decided to see if he might succeed in establishing an affable relationship with her.[19] In approaching her, he learned, however, that she was not likely to be susceptible. Responding with the dignity of a princess and a woman of breeding, she nonetheless saw him to be a handsome gentleman of sophistication, and she readily forgave his boldness.

While making it clear she would not tolerate such behavior, she was not averse to making conversation with him. And he, eager not to lose the opportunity of such an honor and such a delight, gave in to her wishes. But

16. We remember that Simontaut is one of Parlamente's secret admirers or *serviteurs*.

17. Simontaut is thus elected to tell the very first story in the collection and establishes as the day's theme the "foul deeds of women" perpetrated against us "poor men." It is in fact the bloody tale of a procurator's wife who takes on a lover and then, like a black widow spider, proceeds to have him butchered by her own husband.

18. This self-referential remark is important because it shows that Marguerite saw herself as a reasonable and serious person without being a tedious prig, in short, a good model of the ideal Renaissance lady.

19. The original French reads *honneste amityé*, suggesting an acceptable courtly companionship which, according to the rules of the amorous game, would make him her *serviteur* (admirer). However, as we soon learn, discreet familiarity, when fueled by passion, can, and in this case does, turn into something much more erotic in nature.

eventually he was so overcome by desire, he quite forgot his earlier promise. Having already experienced her ability to outwit him, he was not about to go back to his first tactic, but devised rather a quite different plan of action. If only he could find the right time and place, being as yet a young, healthy, good-looking, and spirited widow, she might just surrender to their mutual pleasure.[20]

To execute his strategy, he persuaded his master that there was good hunting near his estate, where, in the month of May, he might enjoy slaying a stag or two. Because the prince appreciated both this gentleman and hunting, he accepted the invitation and set out for his residence, which, consistent with the gentleman's being the richest man in the land, was sumptuous and beautifully maintained.[21] In one part of the house, he put up the prince and his wife, and in another, the woman whom he loved more than himself. Her room was handsomely appointed with full-length tapestries, and the floor was so thickly carpeted that one could not see the trapdoor which lay beside the bed and connected with the room below.

Because the gentleman's old mother, who normally slept below, might awake the princess with her hacking cough, she accepted to exchange rooms with her son. Every evening the elderly lady brought preserves to the princess for a snack, accompanied by the gentleman, who was on such good terms with her brother that he was allowed to be present when she dressed and undressed, greatly increasing thus his love of her.

And so it was that one evening, having kept the princess up till she began to get so sleepy that she asked him to depart to his own room, he went and put on his best and most sweet-smelling nightshirt and the handsomest nightcap imaginable. Looking at himself in his mirror, he concluded no woman could possibly reject so alluring and desirable an object.[22] With thoughts of a happy outcome to his amorous scheme, he retired to his bed, though he had no intention of staying there long. He was devoured by lust and the expectation of soon gaining access to a bed more worthy and more agreeable than his own. As soon as he had dismissed his attendants,

---

20. In the manner of any sexually inspired young man, Bonnivet acts as if he needed only to find the right opportunity in order to cause the object of his affections to surrender to her *own* passion. Love is not only blind but presumptuous.

21. Bonnivet's chateau was so noted for its elegance that it inspired the idealized Abbaye de Thélème that François Rabelais describes in his giant stories (*Gargantua*, chaps. 52–53). For more details on this architectural connection, see Francis Ambrière, *Le favori de François Ier, Gouffier de Bonnivet, amiral de France* (Paris: Hachette, 1936).

22. Marguerite makes much of this male narcissism because it fits in with her idea of a seducer who self-importantly imagines himself utterly irresistible.

he locked the door behind them and listened attentively for noises in the princess's bedchamber above. Assured that all was quiet, and eager to set himself to the pleasant task ahead, he slowly lowered the trapdoor, which was so carefully constructed and so heavily covered with matting that it didn't make a single sound. He hoisted himself up through the opening and entered the room where the princess was on the verge of sleep. In haste, without due regard for either the mistress of the household or this woman's rank and station, with nary a moment's hesitation, he leapt into the bed alongside of her. She, meanwhile, hardly knew what was happening before finding herself locked in his embrace. But, strong as she was, she began attacking with both hands, scratching and biting and demanding his name, so that he, fearing she would call out, stuffed her mouth with the bedding in order to keep her quiet. But it was of no use, for, eager to save her honor, she matched her will against his and shouted with such force that her lady-in-waiting, a reputable old woman who was sleeping next door, came rushing in as fast as she could, still clad in her nightshirt.

When the gentleman realized he was about to be caught, and terrified at the thought that the princess might recognize him, he made a quick dash for the trapdoor, as ready to hide his disgrace as he had earlier been to bring it about. He examined his face in the candle-lit mirror on his bed stand, and saw it streaked with blood from her scratches and bites. It dripped down onto his nightshirt, now more red than gold, and he lamented: "And so, you handsome fellow, you got what you deserved. Your vanity inspired you to attempt the impossible, and now, rather than improving your lot, you have made it worse still. If, despite all my promises to her, she learns that I did such an awful thing, I will squander away the uniquely honest and open contact I had been enjoying in her company. My arrogance has done me in, for if I wanted to win her over with my charm and good looks, I should not have hidden them in the darkness; I should not have tried to conquer chastity by force but should instead have used long service and humble patience. I ought to have waited for love to triumph, for without love, force and aggression are powerless."

And thus he spent the night in tears, pain, and sorrow beyond description. In the morning, looking at his disfigured face, he pretended illness and sensitivity to the light and took to his bed, where he remained until all the guests had departed.

The princess enjoyed her triumph, recognizing that there was no other man in her brother's court capable of such a misdeed than the man who had declared his love to her, and sure it was their host. After unsuccessfully searching her room with her lady-in-waiting for all possible hiding places, she angrily said to her: "Rest assured it could be none other than the master of the household, and I shall see to it that my brother has his head as testimony to my chastity."

The lady-in-waiting, seeing how angry she was, responded: "I am happy to hear speak of the great store you put in your honor and that you chose not to diminish it by saving the life of a man who has risked his own for love of you. But all too often those who wish to increase their honor damage it. I urge you thus to tell me precisely what happened."

When she had told the entire story, the lady-in-waiting asked: "Are you sure that all he got from you were bruises and scratches?"

"I can assure you that that is all he managed to get, and unless he finds a very competent doctor, I think by tomorrow we will see results on his face."

"If that is the case, you have more reason to praise God than to seek revenge, for if, in spite of his boldness to undertake such a thing, he has so miserably failed, then death will seem welcome to him. If revenge is what you want, love and shame can do the job better than you. And if you are worried about your honor, take care not to fall into the same trap as he did. Hoping to find the greatest of pleasures, he experienced the worst imaginable disgrace for a gentleman. Thus you too, in wanting to achieve honor, may lose it. If you protest, you will reveal what no one as yet knows, and you can be sure *he* is certainly not going to tell the truth. And if your brother should do your bidding and put the gentleman to death, people will merely conclude that he had his way with you, and most believe that it is extremely difficult for a man to succeed without encouragement. You are young, attractive, and sociable, and everyone at court knows how you have treated the gentleman you accuse. They will say that if he was guilty, you were as well. Your honor, which until now has allowed you to hold your head up high, will be suspected wherever the story is told."

The princess, hearing the wise comments of her lady-in-waiting, realized she was speaking the truth and that, in view of how encouraging and kind she had been to the gentleman, she no doubt would be found at fault. She therefore asked her what she should do, to which the lady-in-waiting answered: "Since you wish to heed my counsel, seeing how it is given in affection, it seems to me that you should rejoice in your heart, since the handsomest and finest gentleman around was by neither force nor love able to turn you away from the true path of virtue. Thus, Madame, you ought to humble yourself before God, acknowledging that virtue alone has not saved you; for many a woman, more ascetic than you, has been undone by men far less worthy than your seducer. Now more than ever you should be wary of such overtures of love, since goodly numbers of victims have succumbed the second time around, who had been able to escape the first.[23] Keep in mind, Madame, that Love is blind and dupes when one thinks oneself the safest. And it seems to me, Madame, that you ought not to bring up what has happened, either to him or to anyone else. And if he himself should ever say anything, you ought to pretend ignorance. In this manner you can avoid two dangers: glorying in your success and savoring the memory of physical pleasure. Even the most virtuous, despite every effort, have had difficulty in escaping from such sensual thoughts. But also, Madame, lest he should believe you took some delight in his little scheme, I think you ought gradually to give up your pastimes with him and thus make him see how little you appreciate his foolish advances and how great is your goodness, which is content with the victory God has given you without demanding further vengeance. May God give you the grace, Madame, to continue in the path of virtue that he has put into your heart, and may you see that all good comes from him and serve him hereafter better even than before."

The princess, convinced of the truth of her lady-in-waiting's good advice, slept as comfortably as her aggressor did not. And the following morning, when the lord, her brother, wanted to ask permission of his host to take his leave, he was informed that his host was too ill either to come out into the light of day or to talk to anyone. The prince was greatly surprised and wanted to go and see for himself. But realizing he was asleep, he did not wish to awaken him, and thus, along with his wife and sister, he left without saying a word. When his sister heard about their host's desire not to witness the departure of his guests, she quickly understood that it was he who had molested her and therefore dared not appear with his bruised face. And though his lord frequently invited him to court, he chose not to accept until he was cured of all his wounds save those he suffered to his heart and to his pride. When at last he did return and had to face his victorious enemy, he blushed from shame. He who had been the bravest of men could not bear to be in her presence and often fell completely to pieces, which merely confirmed her suspicions. The princess avoided him more and more, but not so unobtrusively that he was not made aware of what she was doing. He dared not breathe a word about it, however, so as not to bring further humiliation

---

23. Again Marguerite may be alluding to her own experiences. Novella 10 defines an earlier attempted rape story probably involving the same original characters. Interestingly, in this tale, it is the heroine who intentionally disfigures herself. For an autobiographical examination of these two stories, see Cholakian and Cholakian, *Marguerite de Navarre*, 1–3, 34–35, 58–61, and passim.

upon himself. Instead he kept his secret love in his heart and endured his justly merited rejection.

"And there you have it, ladies, a tale that should strike terror into the hearts of any man who thinks he can take what is not rightfully his, and give comfort to women because of the virtue of its heroine and the wisdom of her lady-in-waiting. So whoever should be faced with a like problem, you have here your remedy, ready-made."

"It seems to me," said Hircan, "that the wonderful gentleman of your story lacked courage and is not deserving of mention. With such an opportunity at hand, neither old nor young should have steered him from his course. It has to be said that if fear of death and dishonor filled his heart, there was no room for love."[24]

Nomerfide replied: "What choice did he have, seeing there were two against one?"

"He should have killed the old lady, and when the young one saw she was alone, she would have considered herself half defeated."

"Kill? You want to turn your lover into a murderer? If that's what you think, one should be leery of ever falling into *your* hands!"

"If I had gotten that far, I would have thought myself dishonored for not finishing the job."

Then Geburon replied: "If you find it so peculiar that a princess of rank, raised by a fierce code of honor, could not be seduced by a single man, what on earth would you say about a poor unfortunate who escaped from *two* men?"

"Geburon," Ennasuite said, "I select you to tell the fifth story, because it sounds as if you have a good one to tell us about just such a poor unfortunate."

"Since you have chosen me," he answered, "I shall recount a story I personally know, having checked into it on the very site where it took place,[25] and you will see that it is not only princesses who are endowed with good sense and virtue. Furthermore, love and cleverness are not always where you would expect to find them."

---

24. Into the mouth of this character—presumably Marguerite's own second husband, Henry of Navarre, who was noted for his womanizing—the author places the male idea of honor and heroism. In the battlefield as in bed, he is to be valued by his success as a conqueror.

25. Such allusions are intended to remind readers that these are, as promised in the collection's prologue, real events, often personally witnessed by the teller.

NOVELLA 11

In the household of a certain Madame de la Trimoïlle there was a woman named Roncex,[26] who, one day when her mistress had gone off to see the Franciscans at Thouars,[27] suddenly had the urge to visit that place where you cannot send a servant in your stead. She asked a girlfriend called La Mothe to keep her company, but for the sake of privacy and modesty, to remain waiting nearby. She then proceeded alone into the darkened latrine, the same place used by all the Franciscans. It soon became obvious that their bellies had everywhere deposited the gifts of Bacchus and Ceres.[28]

The poor woman, in such a rush that she hardly had time to pick up her skirts, sat down on the filthiest seat in the whole place and became stuck as if attached by glue. Her clothes, her feet, and her rear were so soiled she dared not move lest she make the situation worse. She began to scream as loudly as she could: "La Mothe, dear friend, I am disgraced and dishonored."

The friend, well aware of the long history of Franciscan misbehavior and believing that a few of them, hidden within, were trying to take Roncex by force, ran off shouting everywhere: "Please, please come to the rescue of Madame de Roncex, whom the Franciscans are trying to rape in the latrine."

Everyone hastened to the latrine, only to find the unfortunate woman standing bare-assed, holding up her gown, and bellowing for someone to come and clean her off. The menfolk who responded at the sound of her shouting found no evidence of Franciscans, aside from what was affixed to the rear-end of the lady—a most bewitching sight! Needless to say, they thought it very entertaining, while she in turn blushed with shame. Instead of having other women come to do the job of wiping her clean, here she was surrounded by men, gazing at a woman in the most humiliating posture conceivable.

Seeing them and feeling utterly ashamed, she dropped down her clothes to avoid their glances, thereby further soiling the little that had remained clean. She departed from this disgusting place, but was obliged first to change all her clothes before leaving the monastery altogether. Her immediate reaction was to blame La Mothe for her supposed help, but when

---

26. It doesn't take a great deal of imagination to decipher the obscene pun intended here.

27. Thouars is a town in the department of Sèvres, in western France. Such frequent geographical precisions in the collection supposedly underscore authenticity. Nomerfide claims to have been told this dirty tale the previous evening by "one of the ladies" in the company!

28. Gods of drink and food.

she realized that the poor girl had imagined much worse, she forgot to be angry, and joined the others in laughter.

"I believe, ladies, that this little tale was neither too long nor too sad and gave you what you had hoped for."

This said, her listeners burst into laughter. Oisille noted:[29] "Albeit this is a dirty story, knowing the people involved, one is inclined to be amused. How I would have loved to see La Mothe's face and the face of the woman to whom she had brought such questionable help. In any event, Nomerfide, since your tale was told so quickly, perhaps you would like to choose a new storyteller, someone a bit more serious."

Nomerfide remarked: "If you want to make up for my playful humor, I think my choice would have to be Dagoucin,[30] who even at the threat of death would never allow a single word of ugliness to pass his lips!"

Dagoucin, thanking her for the generous assessment of his good taste, began thus: "The tale I am about to tell will demonstrate how love can blind the best and the most honorable among us, and how kind consideration is of little avail against evil."

NOVELLA 69

There once lived in Bigorre, in the château of Odos, an Italian-born squire who worked for the king and whose name was Charles.[31] He was married to a high-born, worthy lady who had given him several children but who was now getting on in years. He himself was not young either and lived with her as a good friend.[32] From time to time he did, however, carry on with some of her chambermaids. His wife turned a blind eye, dismissing those who seemed to get a bit too chummy.

---

29. This important older character, who early on establishes the religious tone of the gathering, is suggested to be none other than Marguerite's own mother, Louise of Savoy. Inasmuch as she is responsible for lending a more serious atmosphere to the proceedings, it is interesting that even she has to admit that the tale is amusing.

30. It is generally conceded that this character is based on Nicolas Dangu, bishop of Séez and a friend of Marguerite. In the discussions, he often defends the position taken by Parlamente.

31. There is a great deal here to give validity to this sixty-ninth novella. Not only is there a place in southwestern France by the name of Bigorre, but Odos is the very château where Marguerite lived in her later years and where she finally died on December 21, 1549. As for the Charles in question, he has been identified as Charles de Saint-Séverin, originally from Naples and sometime in the 1520s a regular staff member of the French royal stables.

32. Marguerite uses a lovely euphemistic phrase to designate that they no longer were having sexual relations together.

When she hired a well-brought-up young girl, she warned her about her husband's inclinations, telling her that if she misbehaved, she would fire her. The new maid, not wanting to annoy her mistress or lose her job, was determined to act properly. Whenever the husband made advances, she not only ignored him but reported his behavior to her mistress, which made them both laugh at his foolish ways.

One day, the chambermaid, wearing a smocklike hood which went on her head and down upon her shoulders—a style peculiar to that region[33]— was sifting grain in a backroom when along came the husband. Seeing her dressed thus, he was inspired to begin his little routine. Not for the world wanting to give in to him, however, she only pretended to go along by asking his leave to go and make sure first of all that his wife was nowhere to be seen. He agreed.

Then she asked him to put the smock on his own head and continue with the sifting in her absence so as to raise no suspicions about why the noise had suddenly stopped. He was clearly more than happy to be accommodating, in the hopes of finally getting his way with her. The chambermaid, meanwhile, overjoyed, ran to inform her mistress: "Come have a look at this husband of yours; I am teaching him to sift grain just to get rid of him!"

The wife hurried to meet this newest servant girl, who was her husband with a hood on his head and shoulders. She laughed so hard and applauded with so much pleasure that she could hardly spill these words out of her mouth: "Well, young lady, how much a month do you want for your services?"

The husband, recognizing her voice and realizing he had been duped, angrily threw off his hood and turned in a rage against the chambermaid, whom he blasted with every vile name he could think of. If the wife had not intervened, he would most assuredly have handed over her last salary along with her walking papers. However, everyone did eventually calm down, and from that day on they lived happily ever after.

"So what do you make of such a woman, ladies? Wasn't she wise not to take her husband's dalliances too seriously?"

"It was no small matter," said Saffredent, "when his little scheme fell through."

"He would have done better at his age to seek entertainment with his

---

33. The French term in the text is *surot*, more often written *surcot*, and is one of those passing details which assures us that Marguerite was not making the tale up.

wife rather than to go chasing stupidly after her chambermaid," Ennasuite noted.[34]

"I myself would not have wanted to be caught with her hood on *my* head," added Simontaut.[35]

"I have heard tell," said Parlamente, "that in spite of your shrewdness, your wife came very close to catching you as well in such a situation, and that ever since, there has been little peace in your family."[36]

"You'd do well to dwell on your own household without interfering with mine. Though my wife has no cause to complain, even if what you said were true, she would say nothing since she gets what she needs," Simontaut replied.

"Good women require no more than the love of their husbands, and those who seek bestial pleasure find it only through disreputable means," Longarine added.[37]

"Do you consider it 'bestial' when a woman asks of her husband what is rightly hers?" inquired Geburon.

"What I mean," replied Longarine, "is that an honest woman whose heart is filled with tenderness gets more gratification from perfect love than from all other physical pleasures imaginable."

"I am inclined to agree," said Dagoucin, "but our gentlemen are not ready to accept or admit it. If mutual love does not make a woman happy, no husband will ever satisfy her. I mean to say that if she is not satisfied with what for a woman is honorable in love, she is most likely to be tempted by animal behavior."

"What you say reminds me," said Oisille, "of a woman who did not live according to the code of honest and respectable love and became more lustful than a swine, more vicious than a lion."

"Would you, Madame, tell us this tale," Simontaut asked, "and thus bring our day's storytelling to an end?"[38]

---

34. While most agree that the character named Ennasuite refers to Brantôme's grandmother, Louise de Daillon, who, according to her grandson, held the queen's inkwell as she wrote in her carriage, there is less certainty about the identity of Saffredent. Some have suggested that he was Bonnivet, the very man who tried to rape Marguerite.

35. This character would seem to have been inspired by Brantôme's father, François de Bourdeille.

36. These half-serious rivalries and personal digs humanize Marguerite's conversationalists and add enormously to the psychological interest of the discussions.

37. It has been suggested that the inspiration for this pro-feminist *devisante* was most likely Jeanne d'Albret's governess, Aymée Motier de La Fayette.

38. As with Boccaccio's frame, here too Marguerite intended that her storytellers should relate one tale each for a period of ten days. This arbitrary division must be among the least realistic elements in either collection.

"I hesitate for two reasons," she replied. "It is first of all a lengthy narrative, and second, though the tale is told by a reliable author, we have committed ourselves to avoiding written sources and events which are not from our own time."

"That is so," replied Parlamente, "but suspecting which one it is and that the story was composed in such a long-ago style, I imagine that aside from the two of us, no one here will have ever heard of it. So it will seem new."[39]

And with that remark, everyone turned to Oisille, who, they assured her, ought to disregard its length since there was still a full hour before vespers. With their bidding, she began thus.

NOVELLA 72

In one of France's finest cities after Paris, there was a wealthy hospital run by a prioress and fifteen or sixteen nuns, along with a nearby priory with some eight monks who performed the daily services there. Too busy with patients, the nuns recited only their Paternoster and the hours of Notre Dame.

One day, a poor, dying villager came to the nuns, who did all they could to help him, but, in spite of their efforts, they had finally to send for a father confessor as the man's condition continually worsened. They administered the last rites while he slowly lost speech.[40] Since, however, he seemed still to be breathing and able to hear, they spoke comforting words to him, until, growing weary and seeing the lateness of the night, they one by one retired to their rooms, leaving behind a young nun to deal with the body. One of the monks also stayed behind, a man noted for his sobriety and for whom she had more respect than for the prior himself.

They knew the poor man was dead when he did not respond to their several cries of "Jesus" in his ear; and so they promptly covered his body. And while they completed this final act of mercy, the monk spoke of human misery and the blessedness of death, until it was past midnight. The young girl, listening attentively to his pious words, gazed upon him with tear-filled eyes, which pleased the monk no end, so that, speaking of the life to come, he began to embrace her as if he wanted to carry her in his arms to paradise. The poor girl, hearing his words and considering him the most devout of all, did not dare to refuse him. Seeing this, as he spoke of the Almighty, the wicked monk managed to get his arms around her and to execute the evil in-

39. Of course Parlamente (Marguerite) would know in advance. After all, she wrote all the stories.

40. Interestingly, Marguerite herself would lose her faculty of speech just before dying.

tent put into their hearts by none other than the devil, since there had been no thought of it previously.

He assured her that a hidden sin was not a sin before the eyes of God and that two unattached people were guiltless so long as their act remained undiscovered.[41] In order to maintain that secrecy, he urged her to confess only to himself. And so they parted, to go their separate ways. The first to leave, she stopped at the Chapel of Our Lady, where she was accustomed to saying her prayers. As she started to recite the name of the "Virgin Mary," she remembered that she no longer was one, neither through love nor necessity, but quite simply because of her timidity. She wept till she thought she would rend her heart in two.

The monk, hearing her sighs from afar and fearing a conversion that would deprive him of his pleasures, came to advise against it. Finding her prostrate before the statue, he spoke to her in a harsh voice, telling her that if she had guilt feelings, she should confess to him and never sin again; since they were both free agents, she need not act against her will. The foolish girl, thinking she could win God's favor by confessing to the monk, was told, by way of putting her mind at rest, that a bit of holy water would wipe away her offenses and that she would not be committing a sin by making love to him. Putting more store in the monk than in God, she soon returned for a repeat performance. In short order she was with child, and she became so afraid that she pleaded with the prioress to dismiss the monk, knowing that in his cunning ways he would surely seek her out again.

The abbess and the prior, who were the best of friends, made fun of her, telling her that she was old enough to take care of herself, and, what is more, that the fellow in question was an entirely honorable man. Finally, at a loss as to what she should do, and stricken with guilt and remorse, the nun asked to go to Rome, thinking that were she to confess her sin at the feet of the pope, she might regain her virginity. They granted her wish and gave her the necessary travel money, preferring to see her break the rules by leaving than to watch despair cause her to give up the convent life altogether.

As it happened, she arrived at Lyons at the same time that the duchess of Alençon—later to become queen of Navarre—was there.[42] One evening, at vespers, when the duchess and a few friends had discreetly come into

41. We recall that Molière's Tartuffe, in the play of that name, makes much the same argument.

42. This self-referential detail is significant for two reasons. The clarification of her married status proves how much Marguerite wanted to give an authentic aura to her tales. But more importantly, the story underscores how the author wanted to be judged in the eyes of her readers, as the vigilant defender of women's causes.

the Church of St. John to recite a few novenas at the foot of the cross, they heard the footsteps of someone coming up the stairs and, by the light of a lamp, noticed a nun. The duchess withdrew to the side of the alter in order to eavesdrop on her prayers.

The unhappy nun, thinking she was alone, knelt down and with a mea culpa, began weeping so much that it was a pity to listen to her. She cried out, sobbing continuously: "Dear God, have compassion for this poor sinner."

The duchess, eager to learn the cause of such dismay, approached and said: "My dear girl, what grieves you so? Where are you from and what brings you to this place?"

The wretched creature, not recognizing to whom she spoke, said: "Alas, dear lady, my sorrow is so great that it is only to God that I can turn, asking that he find some way that I might speak with the duchess of Alençon, for she alone will be sensitive to my suffering. For if anything can be done, she will do it."

"My dear, you may speak to me as if you were speaking to her, for I am among her closest friends."

"Forgive me for no one but she will ever know my secret."

The duchess told her she could speak frankly for she had found the one she was asking for. And so the poor wretch threw herself at her feet, and weeping and lamenting she told her the dreadful tale you have already heard. The duchess comforted her as best she could. Though she did not relieve her of the need for continued repentance, she did make her give up the idea of a pilgrimage to Rome, and directed her back to her convent with letters to the local bishop asking that the disgraceful monk be sent away.

"The duchess herself has reported this story to me, and it shows, ladies, that Nomerfide's rule does not apply universally.[43] The fact that these characters were preparing a dead man's body did not keep them from giving in to their sexual appetites."

"Now that's a new one: dealing with death while creating life!" said Hircan.

"It is not creating life to sin in that fashion. Everyone knows that the wages of sin is death," Oisille responded.[44]

---

43. In the previous tale's discussion, Nomerfide had said that with death at hand, one is less inclined to think of sinful acts. This is but one example of how well integrated Marguerite's entire narrative is.

44. Oisille, the most conspicuously religious of the lot, cites Paul's famous dictum in Romans 6: 23: "For the wages of sin is death" (NRSV).

"However," said Saffredent, "that fine theological point was far from their thoughts. It was the same with these two as it was with the daughters of Lot, who made their father drunk in order to continue the human race.[45] They wanted to undo the works of death by replacing an old by a new being. The only bad thing here that I see was that the unfortunate nun could not keep herself from lamenting."

"I've seen enough of that kind," commented Hircan. "They weep while enjoying their pleasures."

"I can guess for whom that remark is intended," added Parlamente, "and now that her laughter has lasted long enough, it is time to weep."

"Say no more," retorted Hircan, "for the tragedy that began with laughter is far from over!"

"To change the subject," she continued, "it seems to me that Dagoucin, in telling this sad tale, has strayed from our resolve to relate only amusing ones."

"You said," replied Dagoucin, "that we should deal only with foolishness, and in that sense, I have *not* gone astray. But in order to hear a more amusing story, I cede my place to Nomerfide, trusting that she will make up for my disappointment."

"In fact I do have a tale to tell," Nomerfide responded, "and it fits in perfectly with yours, for it has to do with death and a monk. So listen with care."[46]

45. "To continue the human race" is a comic euphemism. The reference is to the story of incest between Lot and his daughters, related in Genesis 16: 30–38.

46. Here is abundant evidence that not only was Marguerite ready to continue her collection but that she had apparently already chosen the seventy-third tale.

NOTES

7.   Text and translation are based on the text included in *Poésie du roi François Ier, de Louise de Savoie, duchesse d'Angoulême, de Marguerite de Navarre*, ed. Aimé Champollion-Figeac (1847; Reprint, Geneva: Slatkine, 1970).

8.   The convoluted syntax of this opening sentence is some measure of Marguerite's conflicted emotions. On the one hand she is angry not to be with her family; on the other she wishes to please her mother.

9.   This is one of the most interesting revelations of how Marguerite views both the joys and the inadequacies of written expression. In another context she speaks of the special pleasures of putting words to paper, what she lovingly calls her *doulce escripture* (sweet writing). It also gives a good example of overworking a metaphor.

10.   The perfect triangle to which Marguerite alludes is the strong family alliance made up of Louise of Savoy and her two children. The fact that the father, Charles d'Angoulême, had died in 1496, when Marguerite was only four and her brother Francis only two, reinforced the intimacy and interdependence of mother and children.

11.   In this change of focus, in which Marguerite suddenly addresses her brother, Francis, she remembers her distress in finding him gravely ill when she went to negotiate his release after the tragic battle of Pavia (1525).

12.   This second child, a son named Jean, born in July of 1530, lived only five and a half months. The superstitious might argue that Marguerite was punished for her flippancy.

13.   During Francis's second Italian campaign of 1525, Louise of Savoy was named regent, and among her duties was to assure France's southern border against possible invasion by Charles V's imperial forces.

14.   Waterways were heavily trafficked in Europe and the royal family would no doubt return triumphantly up the Loire.

15.   Text and translation are based on the text included in *Œuvres choisies: Marguerite de Navarre*, vol. 1: *Poèmes*, ed. H. P. Clive (New York: Appleton-Century-Crofts, 1968).

16.   The "lesson of obedience" is an allusion to the sacrifice of Isaac (Genesis 22: 1–19). In classical mythology there are countless examples of such theophanies, visits of gods in human disguise. Here it functions as a test of Abraham's inherent connection with the divine. He immediately recognizes the only true God. Genesis 18: 1–33. The passage is also noteworthy because as a serious reformist thinker Marguerite once again shows her thorough knowledge of Hebrew sacred literature.

17.   The reference is to one of Marguerite's favorite hideaways, the chateau at Mont-de Marsan, located in the modern-day region of the Landes. One of her last pieces of writing was a play written there, quite simply bearing the title of *Comédie de Mont-de-Marsan* and included in this anthology.

18.   The allusion is to Guillaume Poyet (1473–1548), an important administrator in the king's court, who was accused of mishandling royal funds, probably falsely. Poyet was little more than a victim of court intrigue, and Marguerite may have had a hand in his disgrace.

19.   In the late 1530s, James V of Scotland began siding with the French against the Holy Roman Empire. Is the "French lady" referred to here Francis's daughter Madeleine, who married the Scottish king in 1537 but died that same year, or Marie of Lorraine, who married him the following year?

20.   This is neither the first nor the last time that Marguerite deifies her brother. We realize how far this reverence would finally lead in the person of a self-centered monarch like Louis XIV.

21.   If the birth of this first grandchild was so enthusiastically celebrated, it was not only because Henry and Catherine de' Medicis had had no children for the first ten years of their marriage, but also because the French Salic Law allowed only male succession to the throne.

22.   The Angoulêmes were proud of that feature, seen as a sign of special distinction. Several centuries later the playwright Edmond Rostand has his character Cyrano de Bergerac, blessed with a prominent proboscis, vaingloriously announce: "A great nose indicates a great man."

23.   He is the third Francis, preceded by his grandfather and his uncle, the Dauphin, who unfortunately died in 1536, under mysterious circumstances.

24.   Like the milkmaid's in La Fontaine's famous fable, Marguerite's imagination moves very rapidly, from birth to conquering hero.

25.   Marguerite is by no means the only person to imagine the Almighty as her nation's defender.

26.   Did Marguerite or a copyist make a mistake? Could this be a reference to the *seven* stars in Revelation 2: 1?

27.   Text and translation are based on the text included in *Les marguerites de la Marguerite des princesses*, ed. Félix Frank (Paris: Cabinet du Bibliophile, 1873).

28.   In a world in which speech was still considered the most reliable form of communication, Marguerite offers the written word as a poor substitute.

29.   It is speculated that her husband, Henri d'Albret, like so many, suffered from gout.

30.   Though Marguerite seems at first to have been genuinely smitten by this young (he was ten years her junior) and dashing Gascon hero, this second marriage was not a match of unremitting joy. Marguerite often accused Henri, and probably with justification, of infidelity and did not always find him a supporter of her reformist views. That makes this letter of tender concern for his health—the only surviving example of any correspondence from her to her husband—that much the more noteworthy.

31.   The *parfait ami* was the usual expression in Neoplatonist writings to define the devoted admirer, who was typically outside of the marriage bond.

32.   Is the pillaging to which she refers the continuing struggle between French and imperial forces in the south of France or religious conflicts between conservatives and reformists? In any event, the king in question is not the deceased and beloved Francis but his son, Henry II. Francis had died on March 31, 1547.

33.   In the Rabelaisian text, Pantagruel hears the barking of his father Gargantua's dog and correctly predicts the king's imminent arrival. See Rabelais, *Tiers Livre*, chap. 35. The literary allusion is proof that Marguerite kept abreast of what was being written during her own lifetime. We remember too that the distinguished author of giant stories dedicated his *Tiers Livre* to the queen of Navarre, whom he half seriously identified as a "ravished, ecstatic, and abstract soul."

34.   Text and translation are based on the text included in Marguerite de Navarre, *Les dernières poésies*, ed. Abel Lefranc (Paris: Colin, 1896).

35.   It is worth noting that conversations with the goddess of love are more frequently carried on when involving a man and woman, and not a mother and daughter, some indication of the depth of feeling here.

36.   On October 20, 1548, in the city of Moulins, Jeanne d'Albret had married Antoine de Bourbon, second duke of Vendôme. The "happy destination" to which her mother alludes would thus have been Jeanne's new home at Vendôme.

37.   This entire romantic scene is strangely similar to the famous love poem *Le lac*, composed by Alphonse Lamartine (1790–1869), in which the poet revisits the place where once he wooed the woman he loved, now dead.

LE MIROIR DE L'ÂME PÉCHERESSE / THE MIRROR OF THE SINFUL SOUL

6.   Text and translation are based on the text in Joseph L. Allaire, *Le miroir de l'âme pécheresse* (Munich: Wilhelm Fink, 1972).

7.   In reformist theology, this term invariably referred to the Mosaic prescriptions of the Pentateuch superseded by Jesus' ultimate and redemptive sacrifice on the cross.

8.   Eventually, a significant part of the Protestant reform would question childhood baptism and advocate adult immersion. Is Marguerite merely speaking metaphorically?

9.   The argument here is not so much that anyone is condemned beyond redemption, but, on the contrary, that it is the grace of God which is the source of a transformative experience and which is available to all alike.

10.   This is one of several places in the text where the narrator changes her perspective and addresses her *savior* directly. A highly personal intimacy with Jesus was to become another salient feature in the new theology.

11.   The mystical discourse is often marked by references to a family relationship between the prayerful Christian and the divinity. Marguerite, as we shall see, overworks this theme.

12.   In the heated discussion over justification (a journey to paradise) through faith (guaranteed passage) versus works (earned passage), Marguerite would never go so far as her contemporary Martin Luther (1483–1546), who argued that even the Catholic Mass was an example of "works."

13.   The reformers believed that the sacred word was not the exclusive domain of priests who alone could interpret God's message. Marguerite was thus an important sponsor of vernacular translations of the Bible.

14.   Marguerite makes reference here to the fall of Adam in the Garden of Eden and to subsequent human redemption through the sacrifice of Christ. She must have many times read the Pauline interpretation on this theme, especially in the letter to the Romans, chapter 5. It is rather startling, however to see that this proto-feminist seems to have bought into the anti-Eve doctrine which makes Eve complicit in the exile from paradise (Genesis 3).

15.   The "rapture" is the eschatological assumption that in the day of the last things, Christians will be "caught up together . . . in the clouds to meet the Lord in the air" (1 Thess. 4: 17).

16.   One of the interpretations of the love song in the Hebrew Bible known as the Song of Songs is to see it in allegorical rather than literal terms. In any event, this is not a direct citation but Marguerite's paraphrase.

17.   This is an allusion to the famous story of the prodigal son (Luke 15: 11–32).

18.   The reference is to the Hebrew Bible (Num. 12: 1–16).

19.   The reference is to the well-known tale recounted in the Hebrew Bible (Kings 3: 16–28).

20.   Moses, a Jew, marries the Midian woman Zipporah (Exodus 2: 16–21).

21.   In ancient Jewish law, skin diseases were looked upon as an outward sign of inward impurity and required extensive ritual cleaning (Lev. 13–14).

22.   Marguerite significantly climaxes her litany of unforgiving people with unforgiving husbands. She was well aware of the injustices in the marriage code and deals harshly with all kinds of infidelity, male and female, in the *Heptameron*. There are, it must be noted, also a few tales about adultery which appear complicitous, such as 3 and 55.

23.   The Neoplatonic *parfait ami* is the amorous ideal favored by writers like Marguerite. Antoine Héroët (1492?–1568), one of Marguerite's protégés, composed an entire work entitled *La parfaicte amye* (1542), in which he defines human love as a prototype of divine love.

24.   Marguerite cites Jesus: "Come to me, all you who are weary and heavy-laden, and I will give you rest" (Matthew 11: 28).

25.   Is this a misspelling or an alternate transliteration from the original Hebrew text? Whatever the case may be, it is more evidence of how well Marguerite knew both the Hebrew and Christian Bibles. The citation is from the Song of Songs: "Come back, come back, O Shulamite / Come back, come back, that we may gaze at you!" (6:13—14).

26.   Jeremiah 3.

27.   This elaborate rhetorical game playing owes much to the earlier poetic movement of the *rhétoriqueurs*, who indeed placed great emphasis on verbal wit and cleverness.

28.   In spite of this abstract acceptance of human mortality, Marguerite struggled all her life with the death of people whom she loved. A good case in point is her poem *Dialogue en forme de vision nocturne*, composed at the time of the death of her young niece Charlotte.

29.   "O Death, where is your victory? O Death, where is your sting" (1 Cor. 15: 55).

30.   The biblical exemplum of this Manichean battle is the story of Job. In the prefatory remarks of the tale, God in fact challenges Satan to turn the head of Job, "a blameless and upright man," whose unflinching resistance causes his Lord to bless "his latter days more than his beginning."

31.   Marguerite makes clear her "Protestant" inclination to favor grace over works as a way of gaining salvation.

32.   Marguerite sees the paradox of her assertion. On the one hand she should be awed into silence. On the other, as a mystic poet, she senses the need to give expression to her sentiments.

33.   The dramatic conversion of Paul on the road to Damascus is related in Acts 9.

34.   There is an unintentional irony in this remark, since it has taken the author nearly fifteen hundred lines of dense verse to arrive at this unexpected conclusion!

35.   The closing "amen" reminds the reader that this is a prayer. The expression in Hebrew verse frequently marked the doxology or praise to God which might conclude a prayer (Psalm 41). In the Christian Bible Jesus frequently prefaced his comments with "truly" (Gk *amen*).

LA COCHE / THE COACH

2.   This is the first of a series of scene-setting descriptions that introduce each section. It is clear that Marguerite intended them to be instructions for the illuminations to give a visual aspect to the text. They are included in all manuscript and print editions that are not illustrated. They are omitted from the illustrated volumes. Robert Marichal rightly notes the importance of these descriptions/illustrations in visualizing Marguerite's landscape in the introduction to his critical edition of *La coche* (Geneva: Droz, 1971), 15—16. Text and translation are based on this edition.

3.   The first lines of the poem make the connection between love and writing that is essential in understanding Marguerite's purpose here. They also introduce the reader to the three-part grouping that Marguerite often uses in her text. The string

of present participles emphasizes the static nature of the suffering felt by the queen as well as the three ladies she will meet.

4.   The pastoral setting is a familiar poetic motif and a conventional way of opening up a debate poem, placing *The Coach* in this tradition. Marichal traces the pastoral framework for the debate poem back to Guillaume de Machaut's *Jugement dou Roy de Behaingne*. Machaut's work is an indirect influence through more recent authors such as Alain Chartier and Christine de Pizan, whom Marguerite would have read. While the debate poem was all the vogue in the fourteenth and fifteenth centuries, the popularity of this poetic form was receding by the beginning of the sixteenth century (*La coche*, ed. Marichal, 4).

5.   The year 1541, in which *The Coach* was probably composed, was a difficult year for Marguerite personally. Scholars have used the state of mind of the protagonist as described here to date the poem in correspondence with the time during which Marguerite struggled with her brother and her husband over negotiations for her daughter's marriage (Jourda, *Marguerite d'Angoulême*, 1: 267; *La coche*, ed. Marichal, 35). Jourda gives a greatly detailed account of this year in Marguerite's life in his *Marguerite d'Angoulême*, 1: 251–74.

6.   The originality of Marguerite's setting stems directly from her own position as older woman and queen. Because she depicts herself as the poet, she must break away from the tradition where the poet/listener is a melancholy young lover, himself searching for solitude in sadness, the model she would have inherited from Chartier. In contrast, Marguerite clearly distances herself from love; her conversation with a local peasant, perfectly in keeping with her responsibilities as queen, draws her even further from thoughts of love (*La coche*, ed. Marichal, 12–13).

7.   In the *Oxford English Dictionary* a shadow is defined as "a woman's head-dress, or a portion of a head-dress, projecting forward so as to shade the face"; a muffler is "a sort of kerchief or scarf worn by women in the sixteenth and seventeenth centuries to cover part of the face and neck, either for partial concealment when in public, or as a protection against the sun or wind." The three women's heads are well covered to hide their sorrow.

8.   Alain Chartier is considered one of the great French lyric poets of the fifteenth century. He is perhaps best known for his *Belle dame sans merci*, whose proud heroine refuses not only love but also the homage of love. There is therefore some irony in Marguerite's choice of this author as the ideal man to write a story which will concern the sad aftermath of love for women.

9.   The debate that ensues is focused on the question of which of the women suffers the most. While Marguerite includes herself in the group with this thought, she does not in fact participate in the debate and presents herself solely as a mediator between the women and the court. It is clear, though, that the women are an extension of Marguerite and their sorrow is an extension of her own.

10.   The physical description of the three ladies is typical of the kind one finds in the traditions of courtly poetry descended from the troubadours. Described through hyperbole and a restricted vocabulary, the three women are not only perfect reflections of each other but also become a kind of allegory of the qualities they possess. The exterior beauty is a reflection of the interior qualities. The familiarity between

the poet and the debaters is unusual in the tradition of debate poems. Marichal surmises that Marguerite was influenced by Christine de Pizan, who also creates a relationship of familiarity between the poet and the debaters in her *Dit de Poissy* (*La coche*, ed. Marichal, 11–12).

11.   The French word used here is *union*. Marguerite begins the description of the three women by emphasizing the oneness of the trio, reflected in the physical. When the women speak for themselves, they speak of the spiritual union that ties them together. The move from the physical to the spiritual signals the Neoplatonism that informs the relationships in this text. Physical beauty is a reflection of the spiritual beauty contained within and is the doorway to a journey toward the spiritual in love. Colette Winn asserts that the word *union* expresses the totality of their friendship. "Aux origines du discours féminin sur l'amitié: Marguerite de Navarre, *La coche* (1541)," *Women in French Studies* 7 (1999): 15.

12.   The trinity plays an important role for Marguerite in both her personal life and her spiritual writings. Her more important relationships, such as that with her mother and brother or with her brother and his wife or his mistress, were often publicly represented as trinities. See Anne-Marie Lecoq, *François Ier imaginaire: symbolique et politique à l'aube de la Renaissance française* (Paris: Macula, 1987), 393–433. The trio of women, then, is both a reflection of Marguerite's life and a projection of a spiritual love that surpasses all courtly love.

13.   In Marguerite's initial words to her three friends one begins to see the elements that will define friendship in her text: compassion and fidelity. Marguerite's interest in the subject led her to request a translation of Plato's work on friendship, the *Lysis*. It was done for her by Bonaventure des Périers in 1541. However, there is little resemblance between Socrates' discussion of friendship and Marguerite's presentation of it here; Socrates subordinates friendship to love, rejecting the idea that a relationship can be formed from mutual feelings. Marguerite comes to the opposite conclusion, subordinating courtly love to female friendship (Skemp, "Reading a Woman's Story" 288; Winn, "Aux origines du discours féminin sur l'amitié," 11). Perhaps of greater importance to Marguerite's poem in terms of ideas is Cicero's *De amicitia* or *Laelius*, translated into French in 1537. Marguerite's interest in the subject may have brought her to this text that echoes *La coche* in places. Cicero also writes that friendship lightens the load of adversity through sharing and taking part in another's suffering. Certainly the central elements in Cicero's understanding of friendship, virtue, and fidelity mirror Marguerite's.

14.   The tricks of Love are displayed most obviously in Marguerite's *Heptameron*, which was not published until 1558, well after Marguerite's death in 1549. However, most scholars, following the argument of Pierre Jourda, date the beginning of the composition of the *nouvelles* to 1542. See the introduction to Renja Salminen's edition of the *Heptameron* (Geneva: Droz, 1999), xli–xlix. If it is indeed the *Heptameron* that she refers to in this passage, then the work must have been under way by 1541 when *The Coach* was written. This passage also underlines the unique quality of Marguerite's debate poem. Marichal articulates the connection between Marguerite's life and her work in this way: "As surprising as this may seem, the "erotic" that is professed in *The Coach* is not at all a literary convention but rather the analysis of feelings that the queen has

experienced or observed or imagined as capable of actually being lived. For this reason *The Coach* is a document whose interest for the psychologist is obvious" (*La coche*, 1).

15. The first lady's monologue begins the debate which is the substance of the poem. The model for her particular situation was probably borrowed from Christine de Pizan's *Trois jugements* (*La coche*, ed. Marichal, 20). The transition to another voice is marked by a change in rhyme scheme. While the queen's discourse is rendered in rhymed couplet, the first lady's monologue follows the pattern of the *terza rime*. Hilda Dale rightly suggests that the rhyme scheme reflects the attitude of the speaker. Marguerite de Navarre, *The Coach, and the Triumph of the Lamb*, trans. Hilda Dale (Exeter: Elm Bank, 1999), 3. In the case of the first lady, the *terze rime*, with its constant change in rhyme, mirrors the constant movement between hope and despair contained within her story. With the exception of the second lady's discourse, the whole of the poem is written in decasyllabic lines.

16. *The Coach* is built on an intertwining of relationships based on traditional courtly love, Neoplatonic principles, and *amitié d'alliance*. While each of the courtly relationships is described in conventional terms of courtly love and the principles of Neoplatonic love are most evident in the third monologue, the description of the women's relationship uses language from all three traditions. The preceding stanza is the first description of the friendship among the three women at the center of the poem. One can discern some of the qualities of that friendship here, including complete equality, reciprocity, and the union of hearts. See Winn, "Aux origines du discours féminin sur l'amitié," 14. These ideas can also be found in Cicero's *De amicitia* 14.50, 13.49, 21.80.

17. The lady uses the verbs *doit choysir* demonstrating that the relationships that the three ladies have entered into are typical of courtly love; the lover chooses the lady he pursues and the lady then chooses whether or not to accept this *soupirant*.

18. *Ferme amour*, a term used also by Clément Marot when referring to an "authentic" or Neoplatonic love.

19. Marichal points out that the union of hearts was the sole goal of the courtly love not only in Marguerite's text but in those examples that most immediately preceded hers in the fifteenth century. Marguerite was especially concerned about the loosening of mores at court, and in her own works she strove to give examples of a chaste love the articulation of which is influenced by the Neoplatonism in vogue at the beginning of the sixteenth century in France.

20. Throughout her monologue, the first lady often refers to her heart and those of the other ladies in the third person. She will ask her heart to speak later in her speech.

21. The voice of the woman who suffers in love is not typical of the courtly tradition. Women were objects of veneration in courtly poetry rather than victims of passion, and it is rare that they share in the passion voiced by the lover. The suffering female voices contribute to the originality of Marguerite's text, again influenced by Christine de Pizan (*La coche*, ed. Marichal, 24).

22. The lady's fidelity is required by the laws of courtly love; she follows them closely.

23. Here the reader is introduced to the situation that links the first two ladies. Marichal rightly points out that Marguerite innovatively connects the fate of the three ladies not only by making them friends but also by entwining their stories. In weaving together the different parts of her debate she is moving toward the kind of narrative that is found in the *Heptameron*. Marichal is equally accurate in asserting that Marguerite does not, however, succeed in individualizing the personalities of the three *devisants* as she does in the *Heptameron* (*La coche*, 20).

24. With the start of the second lady's monologue, the rhyme scheme changes as well as the meter. The first line as well as every third line following is four syllables long; each tercet, composed of the four-syllable line followed by two decasyllabic lines, contains one rhyme. As the only truly betrayed lady of the three, her staccato voice reflects her unique pain.

25. With the third lady's monologue, the meter returns to decasyllables. Her discourse is organized, however, in quatrains, each of which contains a *rime embrassée*. Again, the change in form reflects a change in voice; the third lady is the most reasoned of the three. In her relationship with her lover, as we shall see, she also represents the ideal of Platonic love; the *rime embrassée* reflects the one heart contained within the other.

26. Although this recalls the famous passage from Plato's *Phaedrus*, it is likely that Marguerite would have been familiar with this image through Castiglione's *Courtegiano*.

27. Here the third lady articulates another quality of friendship that defines the relationship among the three. Friendship must be a choice entered into freely; the third lady emphasizes the sacrifice she has made in choosing to abandon her lover in order to suffer completely with her friends. See Winn, "Aux origines du discours féminin sur l'amitié," 15; and Cicero 8.26: "quidquid est, id est uerum et uoluntarium."

28. The word used here is *serviteur*, literally "servant." It is a common word in courtly love, used to refer to the lover who serves the lady in order to win her love.

29. The third lady is the only one of the three whose love follows the rules of Neoplatonism as articulated by Marsilio Ficino in his *Commentary on Plato's Symposium on Love*. Ficino's model for love was much in fashion during Marguerite's life and served her well in her efforts to improve the moral quality of relations between the sexes. However, Marguerite did not uncritically accept the Ficinian doctrine. See *La coche*, ed. Marichal, 31, and Emile Telle, *L'oeuvre de Marguerite d'Angoulême, reine de Navarre et la querelle des femmes* (Toulouse: Toulousaine Lion et Fils, 1937), 296: "Obsessed by the idea that man is Nothing, God Everything, she is unable to idealize human love as the Neoplatonists do in order to arrive at divine ecstasy." Although it is sometimes difficult to distinguish between courtly love and Platonic love, Platonism defined itself as a philosophical system in contrast to the simple manners of *amour courtois* that developed throughout the Middle Ages. Platonic love took form exclusively through *veoir, ouyr, penser,* and *parler* and was by definition reciprocal (see Telle, 235). J. Festugière, *La philosophie de l'amour de Marsile Ficin et son influence sur la littérature française* (Paris: J. Vrin, 1941), gives a complete overview of how Platonic love was understood in the French Renaissance. Marichal suggests that *La coche* is in part a rallying cry from Marguerite in favor of Ficinian philosophy. While it is certain that Neoplatonism

plays a central role in defining love in the text, the third lady's love is overshadowed, as all else, by the friendship among the women. In fact, female friendship in the text shows itself to be the most perfect relationship represented.

30.   The third lady represents again the central drama of the poem which juxtaposes courtly love and friendship. Love between a man and a woman is shown to be fallible, whereas the love shared by the women will sustain them always. Marguerite privileges female friendship over male/female relationships, and this reflects the originality of her arguments in the poem. The incredulity that some scholars have expressed over the choice of the third lady to abandon her lover is misplaced (See Jourda, *Marguerite d'Angoulême*, 1: 545).

31.   The vocabulary used in this passage recalls a feudal relationship that characterizes some of the language used in describing the relationship among the three women (see lines 675–77). The queen will also evoke a feudal *promesse* when she leaves the woman to fulfill her *serment* (l. 1323). The presence of the feudal language in *The Coach* is an example of the shifting of minds that is taking place at the beginning of the sixteenth century in France. Winn articulates the transition in this way: "In its search for a definition of friendship, *The Coach* is witness to a change in mentality that is seen to be at work during the Renaissance. This evolution is made manifest in different areas of social life, especially in interpersonal relations and the experience of friendship, through a radical break with the feudal regime in favor of classical models." "Aux origines du discourse féminin sur l'amitié," 15. Thus, the presence also of the Neoplatonic love that is used to define the ideal relationship, be it between women or men.

32.   Fidelity is an essential quality of friendship according to Cicero (*De amicitia* 17.64). In the evocation of it here, the first lady underscores the centrality of the concept to friendship among the women. Although the question of faithfulness is not debated, it is certainly the center of the debate, as each lady comes back to her relationship with her friends as the foundation from which she is able to sustain herself and tell her story.

33.   It is clear that the sacrifice she makes for her friends is another essential quality of their friendship. See Winn, "Aux origines du discours féminin sur l'amitié," 15.

34.   Cicero, *De amicitia* 8.26.

35.   Finally the coach which gives the poem its name appears. The women spend the time riding back to the court discussing who would be the best judge of their debate. In the coach they come to a consensus and, thus, end their debate, giving it over to Marguerite. The coach functions as a metaphor for Marguerite's written version of their argument; it will move them away from the debate that was becoming more and more fractious and toward a resolution. It ultimately brings them back to the court from which they are alienated through their suffering.

36.   Cicero defines friendship in *De Amicitia* as "nothing else than an accord in all things, human and divine, conjoined with mutual goodwill and affection" (6.20). Could Marguerite also be thinking of his statement that "nothing was harder than for a friendship to continue to the very end of life" (10.33). The translations are from *Cicero: De Senectute, De amicitia, De divinatione*, trans. William A. Falconer (Cambridge: Harvard University Press, 1964), 131, 145.

37.   If the king is being called upon as the ultimate example of virtue in love, there must also be echoes here of the virtue that repeats itself in *De amicitia*. Cicero repeatedly states that there can be no friendship without virtue (6.20, 8.27, 27.100).

38.   1 Kings 3: 16–28.

39.   The duchess of Étampes was the king's favorite from 1526 upon his return from Spain to the end of his reign at his death in 1547. She garnered considerable political influence during this time, most notably maneuvering against the conné-table of Montmorency. Her aversion to the latter was shared by Marguerite and united them right at the time that Marguerite was caught in negotiations over Jeanne d'Albret's marriage. The duchess showed herself to be Marguerite's friend in these negotiations, as she also argued against the marriage of Jeanne to the duke of Clèves, the king's choice. Marichal (39) mentions other common interests that would have united the two women, such as their shared interest in the new humanist ideas, including Neoplatonist thought.

40.   The word "cousin" did not connote necessarily a family relationship; it is used here to indicate equality of status and friendship. "Mistress" seems to be used to honor the duchess, emphasizing her power and Marguerite's willingness to submit to it.

41.   The verb used here is *veoir*. This word is in a semantic transition in the sixteenth century, moving from the sense of "to study" or "to read" to the modern sense of "to see." In the context of Marguerite's plea, it seems that she wants the duchess to read the book aloud to him rather than let him read it alone. In this way she can guide his reading.

42.   Marguerite uses the word *union* to characterize the community of the three. See Cicero, *De amicitia* 4.15, 17.61, 21.80.

LA FABLE DU FAUX CUYDER / THE FABLE OF FALSE PRIDE

5.   Text and translation are based on the text included in *Les marguerites de la Marguerite des princesses*, ed. Félix Frank (Paris: Cabinet du Bibliophile, 1873).

6.   It was common practice in those days, before mass distribution of printed matter, to exchange manuscripts and even to read them aloud.

7.   The god in this instance is the Roman goddess Diana (Gk Artemis), who is associated with the moon, forests, animals, and women in childbirth. It is curious that while she is favored by pregnant women, she is also known as the goddess of virgins.

8.   It would be some time before extensive descriptions of nature would be a part of the poetic language. Marguerite's inspiration is more of the pastoral type.

9.   In Greek mythology the Sileni were older Satyrs and members of Dionysus's entourage. They had the ears of a horse and were known for their drunken pranks. In some legends there was but one Silenus, child of either Hermes or Pan, and represented as Dionysus's tutor.

10.   A reference no doubt to the fact that Satyrs were often represented as winding ivy around their horns.

11.   In traditional Christian theology, one speaks of seven "deadly" (mortal) sins: pride, covetousness, lust, anger, gluttony, envy, and sloth. Modern Protestantism tends to emphasize lust over all the others.

12.   It is the reformist Christian speaking here. Love and redemption supersede sin and punishment

13.   In her dialogical bent of mind, Marguerite wants to convey the real complexity of the events. Perhaps the virgins were too hasty and too naive, but they were also victims. They were taken advantage of, and that fact militates in their favor. No doubt the queen of Navarre wishes to situate her plot in the larger social context of her times, when men were to be admired for their amorous conquests in much the same way that they were praised for their heroism in the battlefield.

14.   Marguerite is contrasting two different concepts of love, erotic love (*eros*) and unselfish love (*agape*). It is this return to Christian ethics which no doubt led Jourda to see this essentially as a religious rather than a social moral.

15.   The poet could as easily have not given a final voice to the accused. But she does so with the specific purpose of having them accuse themselves. Their closing remarks merely reinforce the overall theme of the moralizing tale and underscore male culpability.

16.   This technique of pretending to be only the messenger and not the inventor will, in the hands of an Enlightenment author like Voltaire, serve an altogether different objective. Here the distancing from authorship is merely a clever trick to give the text an aura of legendary significance. Two centuries later, writers denied authorship in order to escape the critical eyes of the censors. Pierre Jourda might argue otherwise since he sees the tale as a religious text and therefore subject to disapproval by the church authorities, who did not wish writers—especially women writers—to undertake anything that smacked of theology, even disguised theology (*Marguerite d'Angoulême*, 1: 414–19).

CHANSONS SPIRITUELLES / SPIRITUAL SONGS

3.   Texts and translations based on George Dottin, *Chansons spirituelles: Marguerite de Navarre* (Geneva: Droz, 1971).

LA COMÉDIE DE MONT-DE-MARSAN / THE COMEDY OF MONT-DE-MARSAN

12.   The three days before Ash Wednesday: Shrove Sunday, Shrove Monday, and Shrove Tuesday. Saulnier identifies the play as a "mascarade du mardi-gras" (*Théâtre profane*, 241). Régine Reynolds-Cornell thus identifies the date that the play was performed as Shrove Tuesday, February 13, 1548 (new style) (Trans. *Théâtre profane*, 220). Saulnier's critical edition is the basis of this text and translation. I am greatly indebted to the work of both Saulnier and Reynolds-Cornell.

13.   The play is written in a mixture of decasyllabic ten-line stanzas, octosyllabic eight-line stanzas, as well as heptasyllabic, hexasyllabic, and pentasyllabic sizains. The rhyme scheme varies.

14.   The Worldly Woman is often compared to *L'Amye de cour* of Bertrand de La Borderie, a work written in response to Antoine Héroët's *La Parfaicte amye* (1542), in which he imagines a purely spiritual love inspired by the Italian Neoplatonists. La Borderie's work also sparked a response in the form of Charles Fontaine's *Contr'amye de cour.*

15.   The word used here is *saultier.* Both Saulnier and Reynolds-Cornell read this word as a metaphor for "rosary," which makes sense given the number of Hail Marys the pilgrim recites; a rosary is made up of five decades of beads each divided by one bead. The Hail Mary is recited on each of the fifty grouped beads.

16.   Abel Lefranc identifies this as either Mount Carmel or Our Lady of the Hermits at Einsiedeln. *Dernières poésies*, quoted from *Théâtre profane*, ed. Saulnier, 276 n. 55.

17.   Saint Bridget of Sweden, 1303–73. Founder of the Brigittine order, she believed that Christ appeared to her in visions throughout her life, and she authored an account of the revelations she received. Saint Bridget made many pilgrimages herself.

18.   Saulnier rightly notes that this last sentence is a reference to the cult of the saints, one of the Catholic practices that reform-minded Marguerite questions in this work through the character of the Superstitious Woman.

19.   These are the first two lines of a popular song included in a collection printed in Paris in 1530. V. L. Saulnier, "Etudes critiques sur les comédies profanes de Marguerite de Navarre," *Bibliotheque d'humanisme et Renaissance* 9 (1949): 65. Popular song plays an important role in this play, as many of the lines of the Shepherdess are taken directly from popular or courtly songs. Much of the dialogue among the first three women is filled with proverbs.

20.   Saulnier calls this theme a "proverbial motif of learned poetry." Cf. Ovid's "he gave to man an uplifted face" in the *Metamorphoses* (1.85), as well as Marot's translation of the same given by Saulnier in his text: "And regardless of the fact that every other animal casts its primary gaze down, God has given to man a sublime face and has ordered him to look at the excellence of the heavens and to raise his eyes to the stars." In his *Microcosme* Maurice Scève repeats the same, "la teste en haut," 1.42. See Saulnier, "Etudes critiques," 62.

21.   Matthew 22: 37–40: "He said to him, 'You shall love the Lord your God with all your heart, and with all your soul, and with all your mind.' This is the greatest and the first commandment. And a second is like it: 'You shall love you neighbor as yourself.' On these two commandments hang all the law and the prophets" (NRSV).

22.   Marguerite often uses "sans si" to refer to the one without whom there is nothing, the *Tout* (Everything) as opposed to the *Rien* (Nothing) that is the human condition.

23.   The Superstitious Woman demonstrates the attitude of the Pharisee condemned by Jesus in Luke 18: 9–14, "O God I thank you that I am not like the rest of humanity—greedy, dishonest, adulterous—or even like this tax collector." She also reflects an attitude condemned by the spiritual libertines who refuse to judge the acts of their neighbors because they understand them to be produced by the will of God.

24.   Marguerite makes allusion here to religious practices taken to the extreme. The first refers perhaps to the idea that one cannot lift a finger even to remove a fly from a glass during the Sabbath; the second may be a reference to Calvin who prohibited certain games. Clément Marot, a protégé of Marguerite, was chased out of Geneva for having gambled too much. *Théâtre profane*, ed. Saulnier, 285.

25.   The coupling of the body and the soul is characteristic of Renaissance and evangelistic thinking. *Théâtre profane*, ed. Saulnier, 285.

26.   The Wise Woman is very clever in her choice of arguments to persuade the Worldly Woman of her faults. She focuses on that thing that is most precious to the Worldly Woman, i.e., her beauty, by first arguing that while the body will die and fade away, the soul will always be beautiful. She then points out how the beauty of the soul has an effect on the beauty of the body, before reminding her of the suffering one can look forward to after death "down below."

27.   She has given her a copy of the Bible: the Old and the New Testaments.

28.   Seven prayers recited over the course of the day: Laud and Matins, said together at dawn, Prime at 6:00 a.m., Tierce at 9:00 a.m., Sext at noon, None at 3:00 p.m., Vespers at 6:00 p.m., and Compline just before sleep.

29.   The attitude of indifference toward the sin of others is characteristic of the spiritual libertines.

30.   John 8: 7: "Let anyone among you who is without sin be the first to throw a stone at her" (NRSV).

31.   A critique of pilgrimages, which Marguerite often represents as futile.

32.   Matthew 5: 8: "Blessed are the pure in heart, for they will see God" (NRSV).

33.   Marguerite mocks those who are so entrenched in their thinking that they do not understand even the most transparent reference to divine love.

34.   The reference to God as master and spouse comes directly from Marguerite's spiritual advisor, Guillaume Briçonnet, bishop of Meaux, with whom Marguerite was in regular correspondence for four years, 1521–24. His teaching in his letters to her inform much of her own articulation of faith. See *Guillaume Briçonnet/Marguerite d'Angoulême: Correspondance.*

35.   Luke 11: 9, Matthew 5: 8: "So I say to you, Ask, and it will be given you; search, and you will find; knock, and the door will be opened for you" (NRSV).

36.   The Wise Woman has given the Superstitious Woman her Bible, which she hesitates to read. Reynolds-Cornell rightly points out what a daring act it is for these women to read the Bible. Despite the lack of education professed by the Superstitious Woman, she has surely been given a French translation of the Bible. Translations of Scripture into French were forbidden by an edict of February 3, 1526, a law that was enforced by the Parlement of Paris. *Théâtre profane*, trans. Régine Reynolds-Cornell, 221.

37.   The metaphor "illness" is another borrowing from the writings of Briçonnet.

38.   The appearance of the Shepherdess completes the progress of grace in the sinful soul according to the theology of Briçonnet that so informs Marguerite's thoughts. Sensuality, superstition, reason, and rapture are allegorized here. See Jelle

Koopmans, "L'allégorie théâtrale au début du XVIe siècle: Le cas des pièces 'profanes' de Marguerite de Navarre," *Renaissance and Reformation/Renaissance et Réforme* 26, no. 4 (2002): 65–89. Koopmans disputes the assumption that Marguerite uses a medieval genre in writing her theater and suggests that allegorical drama was a new form at the end of the Middle Ages and the beginning of the Renaissance. Marguerite's innovations come more from content than from form.

39.   The first line of a *chanson galante* used also by Marguerite in one of her *Chansons spirituelles* (Saulnier, "Études critiques," 66). The songs of the Shepherdess are sprinkled with references to popular songs of the period. Too numerous to note here, Saulnier's "Études critiques" includes a study of these allusions. Saulnier argues that the use of popular song that everyone would recognize and understand is a response to Calvin's critique of the language used by the spiritual libertines which he qualifies as purposefully opaque and difficult.

40.   I.e., love. The encounter between the first three ladies and the Shepherdess is built upon the basic misunderstanding of the word *love*. Whereas the Shepherdess speaks of divine love, the three others understand worldly love. Marguerite's conceptualization of love lends itself to this confusion, for she infuses her discourse on love with Platonic nuance. Saulnier summarizes the result: "A love pure, mutual, and serene: it is a mixture of Christianity and Platonism (a mixture of Eros and Agape), an ideal at once both earthly and heavenly." *Théâtre profane*, xvi.

41.   "Et aussi fay je luy." Saulnier calls this expression "one of the most banal cliches of the poem" ("Études critiques," 63).

42.   Marguerite gives the same advise to the three ladies in *La coche*.

43.   This formula is taken from the Petrarchan tradition where the beloved is always absent and the poetry inspired by the love is nourished by the sorrow of this absence.

44.   This line marks the transition into the conversation between the three women and the Shepherdess, who has finally agreed "for the love of the beloved" to talk.

45.   Psalm 119: 72: "The Law of your mouth is better to me than thousands of gold and silver pieces" (NRSV).

46.   Genesis 3: 19: "By the sweat of your face you shall eat bread" (NRSV).

47.   The Shepherdess articulates here one of the principal ideas behind the doctrine of the spiritual libertines. For the person who is full of the spirit, book knowledge is as unnecessary as good works. Ignorance is not considered a vice.

48.   Another reference to the doctrine of the spiritual libertines. The true believer is assimilated into the person of Christ and thus resembles him exactly.

49.   The Shepherdess takes up singing again, signaling an end to all communication with the three other women.

50.   "Autant en emporte le vent": A very popular refrain in the fifteenth century. Villon uses it in his "Balade en vieil langage françois."

51.   Calvin uses similar terms to refer to the spiritual libertines, who believed that one did not need to be well educated in order to speak reasonably about God.

52.   Saulnier put two question marks after his definition of this word *coriette* in his

glossary, "ceinture d'échafaudages entourant une construction en cours d'oeuvre." He arrived at this unsatisfactory solution to a problem unsolved by earlier editors through a citation in Godefroy in which the term itself is not defined. His interpretation of these lines is interesting but does not seem to correspond well to the text itself or its grammar; "une fois débarassé de ses bandages (quittant la coriette) le mur se tient vaillamment debout (est dur) comme roc (et le caillou sy fort): ce qui n'empêche pas qu'on le dise chancelant" ("Etudes critiques, " 74). Reynolds-Cornell proposes an alternate interpretation where the *coriette* is a sling strong enough to split the wall (*part le mur*). Because her definition seems to fit better the grammar of Marguerite's text, I have chosen to follow her lead in translation.

53. The upside-down world that the Shepherdess describes here is a reflection of the play itself, where expectations are foiled more than once. The Worldly Woman is converted much more quickly than the Superstitious Woman, contrary to what one would think; and it is the Wise Woman who most quickly tires of the Shepherdess, while the patience of the Worldly Woman finally succeeds at getting the Shepherdess to talk.

54. This moment of silence marks the assimilation of the Shepherdess into the person of Christ.

SERIES EDITORS' BIBLIOGRAPHY

PRIMARY SOURCES

Alberti, Leon Battista (1404–72). *The Family in Renaissance Florence*. Trans. Renée Neu Watkins. Columbia, SC: University of South Carolina Press, 1969.

Arenal, Electa, and Stacey Schlau, eds. *Untold Sisters: Hispanic Nuns in Their Own Works*. Trans. Amanda Powell. Albuquerque, NM: University of New Mexico Press, 1989.

Astell, Mary (1666–1731). *The First English Feminist: Reflections on Marriage and Other Writings*. Ed. and Introd. Bridget Hill. New York: St. Martin's Press, 1986.

Atherton, Margaret, ed. *Women Philosophers of the Early Modern Period*. Indianapolis, IN: Hackett Publishing Co., 1994.

Aughterson, Kate, ed. *Renaissance Woman: Constructions of Femininity in England: A Source Book*. London and New York: Routledge, 1995.

Barbaro, Francesco (1390–1454). *On Wifely Duties*. Trans. Benjamin Kohl in Kohl and R. G. Witt, eds., *The Earthly Republic*. Philadelphia: University of Pennsylvania Press, 1978, 179–228. Translation of the preface and book 2.

Behn, Aphra. *The Works of Aphra Behn*. 7 vols. Ed. Janet Todd. Columbus, OH: Ohio State University Press, 1992–96.

Blamires, Alcuin, ed. *Woman Defamed and Woman Defended: An Anthology of Medieval Texts*. Oxford: Clarendon Press, 1992.

Boccaccio, Giovanni (1313–75). *Famous Women*. Ed. and trans. Virginia Brown. The I Tatti Renaissance Library. Cambridge, MA: Harvard University Press, 2001.

———. *Corbaccio or the Labyrinth of Love*. Trans. Anthony K. Cassell. Second revised edition. Binghamton, NY: Medieval and Renaissance Texts and Studies, 1993.

Booy, David, ed. *Autobiographical Writings by Early Quaker Women*. Aldershot and Brookfield: Ashgate Publishing Co., 2004.

Brown, Sylvia. *Women's Writing in Stuart England: The Mother's Legacies of Dorothy Leigh, Elizabeth Joscelin and Elizabeth Richardson*. Thrupp, Stroud, Gloceter: Sutton, 1999.

Bruni, Leonardo (1370–1444). "On the Study of Literature (1405) to Lady Battista Malatesta of Moltefeltro." In *The Humanism of Leonardo Bruni: Selected Texts*. Trans. and Introd. Gordon Griffiths, James Hankins, and David Thompson. Binghamton, NY: Medieval and Renaissance Studies and Texts, 1987, 240–51.

Castiglione, Baldassare (1478–1529). *The Book of the Courtier*. Trans. George Bull. New

York: Penguin, 1967; *The Book of the Courtier*. Ed. Daniel Javitch. New York: W. W. Norton & Co., 2002.

Christine de Pizan (1365–1431). *The Book of the City of Ladies*. Trans. Earl Jeffrey Richards. Foreward Marina Warner. New York: Persea Books, 1982.

———. *The Treasure of the City of Ladies*. Trans. Sarah Lawson. New York: Viking Penguin, 1985. Also trans. and introd. Charity Cannon Willard. Ed. and introd. Madeleine P. Cosman. New York: Persea Books, 1989.

Clarke, Danielle, ed. *Isabella Whitney, Mary Sidney and Aemilia Lanyer: Renaissance Women Poets*. New York: Penguin Books, 2000.

Couchman, Jane, and Ann Crabb, eds. *Women's Letters Across Europe, 1400–1700*. Aldershot and Brookfield: Ashgate Publishing Co., 2005.

Crawford, Patricia and Laura Gowing, eds. *Women's Worlds in Seventeenth-Century England: A Source Book*. London and New York: Routledge, 2000.

"Custome Is an Idiot": Jcobean Pamphlet Literature on Women. Ed. Susan Gushee O'Malley. Afterword Ann Rosalind Jones. Chicago and Urbana: University of Illinois Press, 2004.

Daybell, James, ed. *Early Modern Women's Letter Writing, 1450–1700*. Houndmills, England and New York: Palgrave, 2001.

De Erauso, Catalina. *Lieutenant Nun: Memoir of a Basque Transvestite in the New World*. Trans. Michele Ttepto and Gabriel Stepto; foreword by Marjorie Garber. Boston: Beacon Press, 1995.

Elizabeth I: Collected Works. Ed. Leah S. Marcus, Janel Mueller, and Mary Beth Rose. Chicago: University of Chicago Press, 2000.

Elyot, Thomas (1490–1546). *Defence of Good Women: The Feminist Controversy of the Renaissance*. Facsimile Reproductions. Ed. Diane Bornstein. New York: Delmar, 1980.

Erasmus, Desiderius (1467–1536). *Erasmus on Women*. Ed. Erika Rummel. Toronto: University of Toronto Press, 1996.

Female and Male Voices in Early Modern England: An Anthology of Renaissance Writing. Ed. Betty S. Travitsky and Anne Lake Prescott. New York: Columbia University Press, 2000.

Ferguson, Moira, ed. *First Feminists: British Women Writers 1578–1799*. Bloomington, IN: Indiana University Press, 1985.

Galilei, Maria Celeste. *Sister Maria Celeste's Letters to her father, Galileo*. Ed. and trans. Rinaldina Russell. Lincoln, NE, and New York: Writers Club Press of Universe .com, 2000; *To Father: The Letters of Sister Maria Celeste to Galileo, 1623–1633*. Trans. Dava Sobel. London: Fourth Estate, 2001.

Gethner, Perry, ed. *The Lunatic Lover and Other Plays by French Women of the 17th and 18th Centuries*. Portsmouth, NH: Heinemann, 1994.

Glückel of Hameln (1646–1724). *The Memoirs of Glückel of Hameln*. Trans. Marvin Lowenthal. New Introd. Robert Rosen. New York: Schocken Books, 1977.

Harline, Craig, ed. *The Burdens of Sister Margaret: Inside a Seventeenth-Century Convent*. Abridged ed. New Haven: Yale University Press, 2000.

Henderson, Katherine Usher, and Barbara F. McManus, eds. *Half Humankind: Contexts and Texts of the Controversy about Women in England, 1540–1640*. Urbana: University of Illinois Press, 1985.

Hoby, Margaret. *The Private Life of an Elizabethan Lady: The Diary of Lady Margaret Hoby 1599–1605*. Phoenix Mill: Sutton Publishing, 1998.

Humanist Educational Treatises. Ed. and trans. Craig W. Kallendorf. The I Tatti Renaissance Library. Cambridge, MA: Harvard University Press, 2002.

Hunter, Lynette, ed. *The Letters of Dorothy Moore, 1612–64.* Aldershot and Brookfield: Ashgate Publishing Co., 2004.

Joscelin, Elizabeth. *The Mothers Legacy to her Unborn Childe.* Ed. Jean leDrew Metcalfe. Toronto: University of Toronto Press, 2000.

Kaminsky, Amy Katz, ed. *Water Lilies, Flores del agua: An Anthology of Spanish Women Writers from the Fifteenth Through the Nineteenth Century.* Minneapolis: University of Minnesota Press, 1996.

Kempe, Margery (1373–1439). *The Book of Margery Kempe.* Trans. and ed. Lynn Staley. A Norton Critical Edition. New York: W. W. Norton, 2001.

King, Margaret L., and Albert Rabil, Jr., eds. *Her Immaculate Hand: Selected Works by and about the Women Humanists of Quattrocento Italy.* Binghamton, NY: Medieval and Renaissance Texts and Studies, 1983; second revised paperback edition, 1991.

Klein, Joan Larsen, ed. *Daughters, Wives, and Widows: Writings by Men about Women and Marriage in England, 1500–1640.* Urbana, IL: University of Illinois Press, 1992.

Knox, John (1505–72). *The Political Writings of John Knox: The First Blast of the Trumpet against the Monstrous Regiment of Women and Other Selected Works.* Ed. Marvin A. Breslow. Washington: Folger Shakespeare Library, 1985.

Kors, Alan C., and Edward Peters, eds. *Witchcraft in Europe, 400–1700: A Documentary History.* Philadelphia: University of Pennsylvania Press, 2000.

Krämer, Heinrich, and Jacob Sprenger. *Malleus Maleficarum* (ca. 1487). Trans. Montague Summers. London: Pushkin Press, 1928; reprinted New York: Dover, 1971.

Larsen, Anne R., and Colette H. Winn, eds. *Writings by Pre-Revolutionary French Women: From Marie de France to Elizabeth Vigée-Le Brun.* New York and London: Garland Publishing Co., 2000.

de Lorris, William, and Jean de Meun. *The Romance of the Rose.* Trans. Charles Dahlbert. Princeton: Princeton University Press, 1971; reprinted University Press of New England, 1983.

Marcus, Leah S., Janel Mueller, and Mary Beth Rose, eds. *Elizabeth I: Collected Works.* Chicago: University of Chicago Press, 2000.

Marguerite d'Angoulême, Queen of Navarre (1492–1549). *The Heptameron.* Trans. P. A. Chilton. New York: Viking Penguin, 1984.

Mary of Agreda. *The Divine Life of the Most Holy Virgin.* Abridgment of *The Mystical City of God.* Abr. by Fr. Bonaventure Amedeo de Caesarea, M.C. Trans. from French by Abbé Joseph A. Boullan. Rockford, IL: Tan Books, 1997.

Mullan, David George. *Women's Life Writing in Early Modern Scotland: Writing the Evangelical Self, c. 1670–c. 1730.* Aldershot and Brookfield: Ashgate Publishing Co., 2003.

Myers, Kathleen A., and Amanda Powell, eds. *A Wild Country Out in the Garden: The Spiritual Journals of a Colonial Mexican Nun.* Bloomington: Indiana University Press, 1999.

Russell, Rinaldina, ed. *Sister Maria Celeste's Letters to Her Father, Galileo.* San Jose and New York: Writers Club Press, 2000.

Teresa of Avila, Saint (1515–82). *The Life of Saint Teresa of Avila by Herself.* Trans. J. M. Cohen. New York: Viking Penguin, 1957.

———. *The Collected Letters of St. Teresa of Avila. Volume One: 1546–1577,* trans. Kieran Kavanaugh. Washington, DC: Institute of Carmelite Studies, 2001.

Travitsky, Betty, ed. *The Paradise of Women: Writings by Entlishwomen of the Renaissance*. Westport, CT: Greenwood Press, 1981.

Weyer, Johann (1515–88). *Witches, Devils, and Doctors in the Renaissance: Johann Weyer, De praestigiis daemonum*. Ed. George Mora with Benjamin G. Kohl, Erik Midelfort, and Helen Bacon. Trans. John Shea. Binghamton, NY: Medieval and Renaissance Texts and Studies, 1991.

Wilson, Katharina M., ed. *Medieval Women Writers*. Athens: University of Georgia Press, 1984.

———, ed. *Women Writers of the Renaissance and Reformation*. Athens: University of Georgia Press, 1987.

———, and Frank J. Warnke, eds. *Women Writers of the Seventeenth Century*. Athens: University of Georgia Press, 1989.

Wollstonecraft, Mary. *A Vindication of the Rights of Men and a Vindication of the Rights of Women*. Ed. Sylvana Tomaselli. Cambridge: Cambridge University Press, 1995. Also *The Vindications of the Rights of Men, The Rights of Women*. Ed. D. L. Macdonald and Kathleen Scherf. Peterborough, Ontario, Canada: Broadview Press, 1997.

Woman Defamed and Woman Defended: An Anthology of Medieval Texts. Ed. Alcuin Blamires. Oxford: Clarendon Press, 1992.

Women Critics 1660–1820: An Anthology. Edited by the Folger Collective on Early Women Critics. Bloomington, IN: Indiana University Press, 1995.

Women Writers in English 1350–1850: 15 published through 1999 (projected 30-volume series suspended). Oxford University Press.

Women's Letters Across Europe, 1400–1700. Ed. Jane Couchman and Ann Crabb. Aldershot and Brookfield: Ashgate Publishing Co., 2005.

Wroth, Lady Mary. *The Countess of Montgomery's Urania*. 2 parts. Ed. Josephine A. Roberts. Tempe, AZ: MRTS, 1995, 1999.

———. *Lady Mary Wroth's "Love's Victory": The Penshurst Manuscript*. Ed. Michael G. Brennan. London: The Roxburghe Club, 1988.

———. *The Poems of Lady Mary Wroth*. Ed. Josephine A. Roberts. Baton Rouge: Louisiana State University Press, 1983.

de Zayas Maria. *The Disenchantments of Love*. Trans. H. Patsy Boyer. Albany: State University of New York Press, 1997.

———. *The Enchantments of Love: Amorous and Exemplary Novels*. Trans. H. Patsy Boyer. Berkeley: University of California Press, 1990.

SECONDARY SOURCES

Abate, Corinne S., ed. *Privacy, Domesticity, and Women in Early Modern England*. Aldershot and Brookfield: Ashgate Publishing Co., 2003.

Ahlgren, Gillian. *Teresa of Avila and the Politics of Sanctity*. Ithaca: Cornell University Press, 1996.

Akkerman, Tjitske, and Siep Sturman, eds. *Feminist Thought in European History, 1400–2000*. London and New York: Routledge, 1997.

Allen, Sister Prudence, R.S.M. *The Concept of Woman: The Aristotelian Revolution, 750 B.C. – A.D. 1250*. Grand Rapids, MI: William B. Eerdmans Publishing Company, 1997.

———. *The Concept of Woman: Volume II: The early Humanist Reformation, 1250–1500*. Grand Rapids, MI: William B. Eerdmans Publishing Company, 2002.

Altmann, Barbara K., and Deborah L. McGrady, eds. *Christine de Pizan: A Casebook.* New York: Routledge, 2003.

Ambiguous Realities: Women in the Middle Ages and Renaissance. Ed. Carole Levin and Jeanie Watson. Detroit: Wayne State University Press, 1987.

Amussen, Susan D, and Adele Seeff, eds. *Attending to Early Modern Women.* Newark: University of Delaware Press, 1998.

Andreadis, Harriette. *Sappho in Early Modern England: Female Same-Sex Literary Erotics 1550–1714.* Chicago: University of Chicago Press, 2001.

Architecture and the Politics of Gender in Early Modern Europe. Ed. Helen Hills. Aldershot and Brookfield: Ashgate Publishing Co., 2003.

Armon, Shifra. *Picking Wedlock: Women and the Courtship Novel in Spain.* New York: Rowman and Littlefield Publishers, Inc., 2002.

Attending to Early Modern Women. Ed. Susan D. Amussen and Adele Seeff. Newark: University of Delaware Press, 1998.

Backer, Anne Liot. *Precious Women.* New York: Basic Books, 1974.

Ballaster, Ros. *Seductive Forms.* New York: Oxford University Press, 1992.

Barash, Carol. *English Women's Poetry, 1649–1714: Politics, Community, and Linguistic Authority.* New York and Oxford: Oxford University Press, 1996.

Barker, Alele Marie, and Jehanne M. Gheith, eds. *A History of Women's Writing in Russia.* Cambridge: Cambridge University Press, 2002.

Battigelli, Anna. *Margaret Cavendish and the Exiles of the Mind.* Lexington: University of Kentucky Press, 1998.

Beasley, Faith. *Revising Memory: Women's Fiction and Memoirs in Seventeenth-Century France.* New Brunswick: Rutgers University Press, 1990.

———. *Salons, History, and the Creation of Seventeenth-Century France.* Aldershot and Brookfield: Ashgate Publishing Co., 2006.

Becker, Lucinda M. *Death and the Early Modern Englishwoman.* Aldershot and Brookfield: Ashgate Publishing Co., 2003.

Beilin, Elaine V. *Redeeming Eve: Women Writers of the English Renaissance.* Princeton: Princeton University Press, 1987.

Bennett, Lyn. *Women Writing of Divinest Things: Rhetoric and the Poetry of Pembroke, Wroth, and Lanyer.* Pittsburgh: Duquesne University Press, 2004.

Benson, Pamela Joseph. *The Invention of Renaissance Woman: The Challenge of Female Independence in the Literature and Thought of Italy and England.* University Park: Pennsylvania State University Press, 1992.

——— and Victoria Kirkham, eds. *Strong Voices, Weak History? Medieval and Renaissance Women in their Literary Canons: England, France, Italy.* Ann Arbor: University of Michigan Press, 2003.

Berry, Helen. *Gender, Society and Print Culture in Late-Stuart England.* Aldershot and Brookfield: Ashgate Publishing Co., 2003.

Beyond Isabella: Secular Women Patrons of Art in Renaissance Italy. Ed. Sheryl E. Reiss and David G. Wilkins. Kirksville, MO: Turman State University Press, 2001.

Beyond Their Sex: Learned Women of the European Past. Ed. Patricia A. Labalme. New York: New York University Press, 1980.

Bicks, Caroline. *Midwiving Subjects in Shakespeare's England.* Aldershot and Brookfield: Ashgate Publishing Co., 2003.

Bilinkoff, Jodi. *The Avila of Saint Teresa: Religious Reform in a Sixteenth-Century City.* Ithaca: Cornell University Press, 1989.

————. *Related Lives: Confessors and Their Female Penitents, 1450–1750.* Ithaca, NY: Cornell University Press, 2005.

Bissell, R. Ward. *Artemisia Gentileschi and the Authority of Art.* University Park: Pennsylvania State University Press, 2000.

Blain, Virginia, Isobel Grundy, and Patricia Clements, eds. *The Feminist Companion to Literature in English: Women Writers from the Middle Ages to the Present.* New Haven: Yale University Press, 1990.

Blamires, Alcuin. *The Case for Women in Medieval Culture.* Oxford: Clarendon Press, 1997.

Bloch, R. Howard. *Medieval Misogyny and the Invention of Western Romantic Love.* Chicago: University of Chicago Press, 1991.

Bogucka, Maria. *Women in Early Modern Polish Society, Against the European Background.* Aldershot and Brookfield: Ashgate Publishing Co., 2004.

Bornstein, Daniel, and Roberto Rusconi, eds. *Women and Religion in Medieval and Renaissance Italy.* Trans. Margery J. Schneider. Chicago: University of Chicago Press, 1996.

Brant, Clare, and Diane Purkiss, eds. *Women, Texts and Histories, 1575–1760.* London and New York: Routledge, 1992.

Briggs, Robin. *Witches and Neighbours: The Social and Cultural Context of European Witchcraft.* New York: HarperCollins, 1995; Viking Penguin, 1996.

Brink, Jean R., ed. *Female Scholars: A Traditioin of Learned Women before 1800.* Montréal: Eden Press Women's Publications, 1980.

————, Allison Coudert, and Maryanne Cline Horowitz. *The Politics of Gender in Early Modern Europe.* Sixteenth Century Essays and Studies, 12. Kirksville, MO: Sixteenth Century Journal Publishers, 1989.

Broude, Norma, and Mary D. Garrard, eds. *The Expanding Discourse: Feminism and Art History.* New York: HarperCollins, 1992.

Brown, Judith C. *Immodest Acts: The Life of a Lesbian Nun in Renaissance Italy.* New York: Oxford University Press, 1986.

———— and Robert C. Davis, eds. *Gender and Society in Renaisance Italy.* London: Addison Wesley Longman, 1998.

Burke, Victoria E. Burke, ed. *Early Modern Women's Manuscript Writing.* Aldershot and Brookfield: Ashgate Publishing Co., 2004.

Burns, Jane E., ed. *Medieval Fabrications: Dress, Textiles, Cloth Work, and Other Cultural Imaginings.* New York: Palgrave Macmillan, 2004.

Bynum, Carolyn Walker. *Fragmentation and Redemption: Essays on Gender and the Human Body in Medieval Religion.* New York: Zone Books, 1992.

————. *Holy Feast and Holy Fast: The Religious Significance of Food to Medieval Women.* Berkeley: University of California Press, 1987.

Campbell, Julie DeLynn. "Renaissance Women Writers: The Beloved Speaks her Part." Ph.D diss., Texas A&M University, 1997.

Catling, Jo, ed. *A History of Women's Writing in Germany, Austria and Switzerland.* Cambridge: Cambridge University Press, 2000.

Cavallo, Sandra, and Lyndan Warner. *Widowhood in Medieval and Early Modern Europe.* New York: Longman, 1999.

Cavanagh, Sheila T. *Cherished Torment: The Emotional Geography of Lady Mary Wroth's Urania.* Pittsburgh: Duquesne University Press, 2001.

Cerasano, S. P., and Marion Wynne-Davies, eds. *Readings in Renaissance Women's Drama: Criticism, History, and Performance 1594–1998.* London and New York: Routledge, 1998.

Cervigni, Dino S., ed. *Women Mystic Writers. Annali d'Italianistica* 13 (1995) (entire issue).

———— and Rebecca West, eds. *Women's Voices in Italian Literature.* Special issue. *Annali d'Italianistica* 7 (1989).

Charlton, Kenneth. *Women, Religion and Education in Early Modern England.* London and New York: Routledge, 1999.

Chojnacka, Monica. *Working Women in Early Modern Venice.* Baltimore: Johns Hopkins University Press, 2001.

Chojnacki, Stanley. *Women and Men in Renaissance Venice: Twelve Essays on Patrician Society.* Baltimore: Johns Hopkins University Press, 2000.

Cholakian, Patricia Francis. *Rape and Writing in the* Heptameron *of Marguerite de Navarre.* Carbondale and Edwardsville: Southern Illinois University Press, 1991.

————. *Women and the Politics of Self-Representation in Seventeenth-Century France.* Newark: University of Delaware Press, 2000.

Christine de Pizan: A Casebook. Ed. Barbara K. Altmann and Deborah L. McGrady. New York: Routledge, 2003.

Clogan, Paul Maruice, ed. *Medievali et Humanistica: Literacy and the Lay Reader.* Lanham, MD: Rowman & Littlefield, 2000.

Clubb, Louise George (1989). *Italian Drama in Shakespeare's Time.* New Haven: Yale University Press

Clucas, Stephen, ed. *A Princely Brave Woman: Essays on Margaret Cavendish, Duchess of Newcastle.* Aldershot and Brookfield: Ashgate Publishing Co., 2003.

Conley, John J., S.J. *The Suspicion of Virtue: Women Philosophers in Neoclassical France.* Ithaca, NY: Cornell University Press, 2002.

Crabb, Ann. *The Strozzi of Florence: Widowhood and Family Solidarity in the Renaissance.* Ann Arbor: University of Michigan Press, 2000.

The Crannied Wall: Women, Religion, and the Arts in Early Modern Europe. Ed. Craig A. Monson. Ann Arbor: University of Michigan Press, 1992.

Creative Women in Medieval and Early Modern Italy. Ed. E. Ann Matter and John Coakley. Philadelphia: University of Pennsylvania Press, 1994.

Crowston, Clare Haru. *Fabricating Women: The Seamstresses of Old Regime France, 1675–1791.* Durham, NC: Duke University Press, 2001.

Cruz, Anne J. and Mary Elizabeth Perry, eds. *Culture and Control in Counter-Reformation Spain.* Minneapolis: University of Minnesota Press, 1992.

Datta, Satya. *Women and Men in Early Modern Venice.* Aldershot and Brookfield: Ashgate Publishing Co., 2003.

Davis, Natalie Zemon. *Society and Culture in Early Modern France.* Stanford: Stanford University Press, 1975.

————. *Women on the Margins: Three Seventeenth-Century Lives.* Cambridge, MA: Harvard University Press, 1995.

DeJean, Joan. *Ancients against Moderns: Culture Wars and the Making of a Fin de Siècle.* Chicago: University of Chicago Press, 1997.

————. *Fictions of Sappho, 1546–1937.* Chicago: University of Chicago Press, 1989.

————. *The Reinvention of Obscenity: Sex, Lies, and Tabloids in Early Modern France.* Chicago: University of Chicago Press, 2002.

————. *Tender Geographies: Women and the Origins of the Novel in France.* New York: Columbia University Press, 1991.

————. *The Reinvention of Obscenity: Sex, Lies, and Tabloids in Early Modern France.* Chicago: University of Chicago Press, 2002.

D'Elia, Anthony F. *The Renaissance of Marriage in Fifteenth-Century Italy.* Cambridge, MA: Harvard University Press, 2004.

Dictionary of Russian Women Writers. Ed. Marina Ledkovsky, Charlotte Rosenthal, and Mary Zirin. Westport, CT: Greenwood Press, 1994.

Dixon, Laurinda S. *Perilous Chastity: Women and Illness in Pre-Enlightenment Art and Medicine.* Ithaca: Cornell University Press, 1995.

Dolan, Frances, E. *Whores of Babylon: Catholicism, Gender and Seventeenth-Century Print Culture.* Ithaca: Cornell University Press, 1999.

Donovan, Josephine. *Women and the Rise of the Novel, 1405–1726.* New York: St. Martin's Press, 1999.

Early [English] Women Writers: 1600–1720. Ed. Anita Pacheco. New York and London: Longman, 1998.

Eigler, Friederike and Susanne Kord, eds. *The Feminist Encyclopedia of German Literature.* Westport, CT: Greenwood Press, 1997.

Engendering the Early Modern Stage: Women Playwrights in the Spanish Empire. Ed. Valeria (Oakey) Hegstrom and Amy R. Williamsen. New Orleans: University Press of the South, 1999.

Erdmann, Axel. *My Gracious Silence: Women in the Mirror of Sixteenth-Century Printing in Western Europe.* Luzern: Gilhofer and Rauschberg, 1999.

Erickson, Amy Louise. *Women and Property in Early Modern England.* London and New York: Routledge, 1993.

Extraordinary Women of the Medieval and Renaissance World: A Biographical Dictionary. Ed. Carole Levin, et al. Westport, CT: Greenwood Press, 2000.

Ezell, Margaret J. M. *The Patriarch's Wife: Literary Evidence and the History of the Family.* Chapel Hill: University of North Carolina Press, 1987.

————. *Social Authorship and the Advent of Print.* Baltimore: Johns Hopkins University Press, 1999.

————. *Writing Women's Literary History.* Baltimore: Johns Hopkins University Press, 1993.

Farrell, Michèle Longino. *Performing Motherhood: The Sévigné Correspondence.* Hanover, NH and London: University Press of New England, 1991.

Feminism and Renaissance Studies. Ed. Lorna Hutson. New York: Oxford University Press, 1999.

The Feminist Companion to Literature in English: Women Writers from the Middle Ages to the Present. Ed. Virginia Blain, Isobel Grundy, and Patricia Clements. New Haven: Yale University Press, 1990.

Feminist Encyclopedia of Italian Literature. Edited by Rinaldina Russell. Westport, CT: Greenwood Press, 1997.

Feminist Thought in European History, 1400–2000. Ed. Tjitske Akkerman and Siep Sturman. London and New York: Routledge, 1997.

Ferguson, Margaret W. *Dido's Daughters: Literacy, Gender, and Empire in Early Modern England and France.* Chicago: University of Chicago Press, 2003.

———, Maureen Quilligan, and Nancy J. Vickers, eds. *Rewriting the Renaissance: The Discourses of Sexual Difference in Early Modern Europe.* Chicago: University of Chicago Press, 1987.

Ferraro, Joanne M. *Marriage Wars in Late Renaissance Venice.* Oxford: Oxford University Press, 2001.

Fletcher, Anthony. *Gender, Sex and Subordination in England 1500–1800.* New Haven: Yale University Press, 1995.

Franklin, Margaret. *Boccaccio's Heroines.* Aldershot and Brookfield: Ashgate Publishing Co., 2006.

French Women Writers: A Bio-Bibliographical Source Book. Ed. Eva Martin Sartori and Dorothy Wynne Zimmerman. Westport, CT: Greenwood Press, 1991.

Frye, Susan and Karen Robertson, eds. *Maids and Mistresses, Cousins and Queens: Women's Alliances in Early Modern England.* Oxford: Oxford University Press, 1999.

Gallagher, Catherine. *Nobody's Story: The Vanishing Acts of Women Writers in the Marketplace, 1670–1820.* Berkeley: University of California Press, 1994.

Garrard, Mary D. *Artemisia Gentileschi: The Image of the Female Hero in Italian Baroque Art.* Princeton: Princeton University Press, 1989.

Gelbart, Nina Rattner. *The King's Midwife: A History and Mystery of Madame du Coudray.* Berkeley: University of California Press, 1998.

Giles, Mary E., ed. *Women in the Inquisition: Spain and the New World.* Baltimore: Johns Hopkins University Press, 1999.

Gill, Catie. *Somen in the Seventeenth-Century Quaker Community.* Aldershot and Brookfield: Ashgate Publishing Co., 2005.

Glenn, Cheryl. *Rhetoric Retold: Regendering the Tradition from Antiquity Through the Renaissance.* Carbondale and Edwardsville, IL: Southern Illinois University Press, 1997.

Goffen, Rona. *Titian's Women.* New Haven: Yale University Press, 1997.

Going Public: Women and Publishing in Early Modern France. Ed. Elizabeth C. Goldsmith and Dena Goodman. Ithaca: Cornell University Press, 1995.

Goldberg, Jonathan. *Desiring Women Writing: English Renaissance Examples.* Stanford: Stanford University Press, 1997.

Goldsmith, Elizabeth C. *Exclusive Conversations: The Art of Interaction in Seventeenth-Century France.* Philadelphia: University of Pennsylvania Press, 1988.

———, ed. *Writing the Female Voice.* Boston: Northeastern University Press, 1989.

——— and Dena Goodman, eds. *Going Public: Women and Publishing in Early Modern France.* Ithaca: Cornell University Press, 1995.

Grafton, Anthony, and Lisa Jardine. *From Humanism to the Humanities: Education and the Liberal Arts in Fifteenth-and Sixteenth-Century Europe.* London: Duckworth, 1986.

The Graph of Sex and the German Text: Gendered Culture in Early Modern Germany 1500–1700. Ed. Lynne Tatlock and Christiane Bohnert. Amsterdam and Atlanta: Rodolphi, 1994.

Grassby, Richard. *Kinship and Capitalism: Marriage, Family, and Business in the English-Speaking World, 1580–1740.* Cambridge: Cambridge University Press, 2001.

Greer, Margaret Rich. *Maria de Zayas Tells Baroque Tales of Love and the Cruelty of Men.* University Park: Pennsylvania State University Press, 2000.

Grossman, Avraham. *Pious and Rebellious: Jewish Women in Medieval Europe.* Trans. Jonathan Chipman. Brandeis/University Press of New England, 2004.

Gutierrez, Nancy A. *"Shall She Famish Then?" Female Food Refusal in Early Modern England*. Aldershot and Brookfield: Ashgate Publishing Co., 2003.

Habermann, Ina. *Staging Slander and Gender in Early Modern England*. Aldershot and Brookfield: Ashgate Publishing Co., 2003.

Hacke, Daniela. *Women Sex and Marriage in Early Modern Venice*. Aldershot and Brookfield: Ashgate Publishing Co., 2004.

Hackel, Heidi Brayman. *Reading Material in Early Modern England: Print, Gender, Literacy*. Cambridge: Cambridge University Press, 2005.

Hackett, Helen. *Women and Romance Fiction in the English Renaissance*. Cambridge: Cambridge University Press, 2000.

Hall, Kim F. *Things of Darkness: Economies of Race and Gender in Early Modern England*. Ithaca, NY: Cornell University Press, 1995.

Hamburger, Jeffrey. *The Visual and the Visionary: Art and Female Spirituality in Late Medieval Germany*. New York: Zone Books, 1998.

Hampton, Timothy. *Literature and the Nation in the Sixteenth Century: Inventing Renaissance France*. Ithaca, NY: Cornell University Press, 2001.

Hannay, Margaret, ed. *Silent But for the Word*. Kent, OH: Kent State University Press, 1985.

Hardwick, Julie. *The Practice of Patriarchy: Gender and the Politics of Household Authority in Early Modern France*. University Park: Pennsylvania State University Press, 1998.

Harris, Barbara J. *English Aristocratic Women, 1450–1550: Marriage and Family, Property and Careers*. New York: Oxford University Press, 2002.

Harth, Erica. *Ideology and Culture in Seventeenth-Century France*. Ithaca: Cornell University Press, 1983.

———. *Cartesian Women. Versions and Subversions of Rational Discourse in the Old Regime*. Ithaca: Cornell University Press, 1992.

Harvey, Elizabeth D. *Ventriloquized Voices: Feminist Theory and English Renaissance Texts*. London and New York: Routledge, 1992.

Haselkorn, Anne M., and Betty Travitsky, eds. *The Renaissance Englishwoman in Print: Counterbalancing the Canon*. Amherst: University of Massachusetts Press, 1990.

Hawkesworth, Celia, ed. *A History of Central European Women's Writing*. New York: Palgrave Press, 2001.

Hegstrom (Oakey), Valerie, and Amy R. Williamsen, eds. *Engendering the Early Modern Stage: Women Playwrights in the Spanish Empire*. New Orleans: University Press of the South, 1999.

Hendricks, Margo, and Patricia Parker, eds. *Women, "Race," and Writing in the Early Modern Period*. London and New York: Routledge, 1994.

Herlihy, David. "Did Women Have a Renaissance? A Reconsideration." *Medievalia et Humanistica* 13 n.s. (1985): 1–22.

Hill, Bridget. *The Republican Virago: The Life and Times of Catharine Macaulay, Historian*. New York: Oxford University Press, 1992.

Hills, Helen, ed. *Architecture and the Politics of Gender in Early Modern Europe*. Aldershot and Brookfield: Ashgate Publishing Co., 2003.

A History of Central European Women's Writing. Ed. Celia Hawkesworth. New York: Palgrave Press, 2001.

A History of Women in the West.
> Volume 1: *From Ancient Goddesses to Christian Saints.* Ed. Pauline Schmitt Pantel. Cambridge, MA: Harvard University Press, 1992.
> Volume 2: *Silences of the Middle Ages.* Ed. Christiane Klapisch-Zuber. Cambridge, MA: Harvard University Press, 1992.
> Volume 3: *Renaissance and Enlightenment Paradoxes.* Ed. Natalie Zemon Davis and Arlette Farge. Cambridge, MA: Harvard University Press, 1993.

A History of Women Philosophers. Ed. Mary Ellen Waithe. 3 vols. Dordrecht: Martinus Nijhoff, 1987.

A History of Women's Writing in France. Ed. Sonya Stephens. Cambridge: Cambridge University Press, 2000.

A History of Women's Writing in Germany, Austria and Switzerland. Ed. Jo Catling. Cambridge: Cambridge University Press, 2000.

A History of Women's Writing in Italy. Ed. Letizia Panizza and Sharon Wood. Cambridge: University Press, 2000.

A History of Women's Writing in Russia. Edited by Alele Marie Barker and Jehanne M. Gheith. Cambridge: Cambridge University Press, 2002.

Hobby, Elaine. *Virtue of Necessity: English Women's Writing, 1646–1688.* London: Virago Press, 1988.

Horowitz, Maryanne Cline. "Aristotle and Women." *Journal of the History of Biology* 9 (1976): 183–213.

Howell, Martha. *The Marriage Exchange: Property, Social Place, and Gender in Cities of the Low Countries, 1300–1550.* Chicago: University of Chicago Press, 1998.

Hufton, Olwen H. *The Prospect defore Her: A History of Women in Western Europe, 1: 1500–1800.* New York: HarperCollins, 1996.

Hull, Suzanne W. *Chaste, Silent, and Obedient: English Books for Women, 1475–1640.* San Marino, CA: Huntington Library, 1982.

Hunt, Lynn, ed. *The Invention of Pornography: Obscenity and the Origins of Modernity, 1500–1800.* New York: Zone Books, 1996.

Hutner, Heidi, ed. *Rereading Aphra Behn: History, Theory, and Criticism.* Charlottesville: University Press of Virginia, 1993.

Hutson, Lorna, ed. *Feminism and Renaissance Studies.* New York: Oxford University Press, 1999.

The Invention of Pornography: Obscenity and the Origins of Modernity, 1500–1800. Ed. Lynn Hunt. New York: Zone Books, 1996.

Italian Women Writers: A Bio-Bibliographical Sourcebook. Edited by Rinaldina Russell. Westport, CT: Greenwood Press, 1994.

Jaffe, Irma B., with Gernando Colombardo. *Shining Eyes, Cruel Fortune: The Lives and Loves of Italian Renaissance Women Poets.* New York: Fordham University Press, 2002.

James, Susan E. *Kateryn Parr: The Making of a Queen.* Aldershot and Brookfield: Ashgate Publishing Co., 1999.

Jankowski, Theodora A. *Women in Power in the Early Modern Drama.* Urbana, IL: University of Illinois Press, 1992.

Jansen, Katherine Ludwig. *The Making of the Magdalen: Preaching and Popular Devotion in the Later Middle Ages.* Princeton: Princeton University Press, 2000.

Jed, Stephanie H. *Chaste Thinking: The Rape of Lucretia and the Birth of Humanism*. Bloomington: Indiana University Press, 1989.

Jones, Ann Rosalind and Peter Stallybrass. *Renaissance Clothing and the Materials of Memory*. Cambridge: Cambridge University Press, 2000.

Jordan, Constance. *Renaissance Feminism: Literary Texts and Political Models*. Ithaca: Cornell University Press, 1990.

Kagan, Richard L. *Lucrecia's Dreams: Politics and Prophecy in Sixteenth-Century Spain*. Berkeley: University of California Press, 1990.

Kehler, Dorothea and Laurel Amtower, eds. *The Single Woman in Medieval and Early Modern England: Her Life and Representation*. Tempe, AZ: MRTS, 2002.

Kelly, Joan. "Did Women Have a Renaissance?" In her *Women, History, and Theory*. Chicago: University of Chicago Press, 1984. Also in Renate Bridenthal, Claudia Koonz, and Susan M. Stuard, eds., *Becoming Visible: Women in European History*. Third edition. Boston: Houghton Mifflin, 1998.

———. "Early Feminist Theory and the *Querelle des Femmes*." In *Women, History, and Theory*.

Kelso, Ruth. *Doctrine for the Lady of the Renaissance*. Foreword by Katharine M. Rogers. Urbana: University of Illinois Press, 1956, 1978.

Kendrick, Robert L. *Celestical Sirens: Nuns and their Music in Early Modern Milan*. New York: Oxford University Press, 1996.

Kermode, Jenny, and Garthine Walker, eds. *Women, Crime and the Courts in Early Modern England*. Chapel Hill: University of North Carolina Press, 1994.

King, Catherine E. *Renaissance Women Patrons: Wives and Widows in Italy, c. 1300–1550*. New York and Manchester: Manchester University Press (distributed in the U.S. by St. Martin's Press), 1998.

King, Margaret L. *Women of the Renaissance*. Foreword by Catharine R. Stimpson. Chicago: University of Chicago Press, 1991.

Krontiris, Tina. *Oppositional Voices: Women as Writers and Translators of Literature in the English Renaissance*. London and New York: Routledge, 1992.

Kuehn, Thomas. *Law, Family, and Women: Toward a Legal Anthropology of Renaissance Italy*. Chicago: University of Chicago Press, 1991.

Kunze, Bonnelyn Young. *Margaret Fell and the Rise of Quakerism*. Stanford: Stanford University Press, 1994.

Labalme, Patricia A., ed. *Beyond Their Sex: Learned Women of the European Past*. New York: New York University Press, 1980.

Lalande, Roxanne Decker, ed. *A Labor of Love: Critical Reflections on the Writings of Marie-Catherine Desjardina (Mme de Villedieu)*. Madison, NJ: Fairleigh Dickinson University Press, 2000.

Lamb, Mary Ellen. *Gender and Authorship in the Sidney Circle*. Madison: University of Wisconsin Press, 1990.

Laqueur, Thomas. *Making Sex: Body and Gender from the Greeks to Freud*. Cambridge, MA: Harvard University Press, 1990.

Larsen, Anne R., and Colette H. Winn, eds. *Renaissance Women Writers: French Texts/American Contexts*. Detroit, MI: Wayne State University Press, 1994.

Laven, Mary. *Virgins of Venice: Enclosed Lives and Broken Vows in the Renaissance Convent*. London: Viking, 2002.

Ledkovsky, Marina, Charlotte Rosenthal, and Mary Zirin, eds. *Dictionary of Russian Women Writers*. Westport, CT: Greenwood Press, 1994.

Lehfeldt, Elizabeth A. *Religious Women in Golden Age Spain: The Permeable Cloister*. Aldershot and Brookfield: Ashgate Publishing Co., 2005.

Lerner, Gerda. *The Creation of Patriarchy* and *Creation of Feminist Consciousness, 1000–1870*. Two vols. New York: Oxford University Press, 1986, 1994.

Levack, Brian P. *The Witch Hunt in Early Modern Europe*. London: Longman, 1987.

Levin, Carole, and Jeanie Watson, eds. *Ambiguous Realities: Women in the Middle Ages and Renaissance*. Detroit: Wayne State University Press, 1987.

Levin, Carole, Jo Eldridge Carney, and Debra Barrett-Graves. *Elizabeth I: Always Her Own Free Woman*. Aldershot and Brookfield: Ashgate Publishing Co., 2003.

Levin, Carole, et al. *Extraordinary Women of the Medieval and Renaissance World: A Biographical Dictionary*. Westport, CT: Greenwood Press, 2000.

Levy, Allison, ed. *Widowhood and Visual Culture in Early Modern Europe*. Aldershot and Brookfield: Ashgate Publishing Co., 2003.

Lewalsky, Barbara Kiefer. *Writing Women in Jacobean England*. Cambridge, MA: Harvard University Press, 1993.

Lewis, Gertrud Jaron. *By Women for Women about Women: The Sister-Books of Fourteenth-Century Germany*. Toronto: University of Toronto Press, 1996.

Lewis, Jayne Elizabeth. *Mary Queen of Scots: Romance and Nation*. London: Routledge, 1998.

Lindenauer, Leslie J. *Piety and Power: Gender and Religious Culture in the American Colonies, 1630–1700*. London and New York: Routledge, 2002.

Lindsey, Karen. *Divorced Beheaded Survived: A Feminist Reinterpretation of the Wives of Henry VIII*. Reading, MA: Addison-Wesley Publishing Co., 1995.

Lochrie, Karma. *Margery Kempe and Translations of the Flesh*. Philadelphia: University of Pennsylvania Press, 1992.

Longino Farrell, Michèle. *Performing Motherhood: The Sévigné Correspondence*. Hanover, NH: University Press of New England, 1991.

Lougee, Carolyn C. *Le Paradis des Femmes: Women, Salons, and Social Stratification in Seventeenth-Century France*. Princeton: Princeton University Press, 1976.

Love, Harold. *The Culture and Commerce of Texts: Scribal Publication in Seventeenth-Century England*. Amherst: University of Massachusetts Press, 1993.

Lowe, K. J. P. *Nuns' Chronicles and Convent Culture in Renaissance and Counter-Reformation Italy*. Cambridge: Cambridge University Press, 2003.

Lux-Sterritt, Laurence. *Redefining Female Religious Life: French Ursulines and English Ladies in Seventeenth-Century Catholicism*. Aldershot and Brookfield: Ashgate Publishing Co., 2005.

MacCarthy, Bridget G. *The Female Pen: Women Writers and Novelists 1621–1818*. Preface by Janet Todd. New York: New York University Press, 1994. (Originally published by Cork University Press, 1946–47).

Mack, Phyllis. *Visionary Women: Ecstatic Prophecy in Seventeenth-Century England*. Berkeley: University of California Pres, 1992.

Maclean, Ian. *Woman Triumphant: Feminism in French Literature, 1610–1652*. Oxford: Clarendon Press, 1977.

———. *The Renaissance Notion of Woman: A Study of the Fortunes of Scholasticism and*

Medical Science in European Intellectual Life. Cambridge: Cambridge University Press, 1980.

MacNeil, Anne. *Music and Women of the Commedia dell'Arte in the Late Sixteenth Century*. New York: Oxford University Press, 2003.

Maggi, Armando. *Uttering the Word: The Mystical Performances of Maria Maddalena de' Pazzi, a Renaissance Visionary*. Albany: State University of New York Press, 1998.

Maids and Mistresses, Cousins and Queens: Women's Alliances in Early Modern England. Ed. Susan Frye and Karen Robertson. Oxford: Oxford University Press, 1999.

Marshall, Sherrin, ed. *Women in Reformation and Counter-Reformation Europe: Public and Private Worlds*. Bloomington: Indiana University Press, 1989.

Masten, Jeffrey. *Textual Intercourse: Collaboration, Authorship, and Sexualities in Renaissance Drama*. Cambridge: Cambridge University Press, 1997.

Matter, E. Ann, and John Coakley, eds. *Creative Women in Medieval and Early Modern Italy*. Philadelphia: University of Pennsylvania Press, 1994.

McGrath, Lynette. *Subjectivity and Women's Poetry in Early Modern England*. Aldershot and Brookfield: Ashgate Publishing Co., 2002.

McIver, Katherine A. *Women, Art, and Architecture in Northern Italy, 1520–1580*. Aldershot and Brookfield: Ashgate Publishing Co., 2006.

McLeod, Glenda. *Virtue and Venom: Catalogs of Women from Antiquity to the Renaissance*. Ann Arbor: University of Michigan Press, 1991.

McTavish, Lianne. *Childbirth and the Display of Authority in Early Modern France*. Aldershot and Brookfield: Ashgate Publishing Co., 2005.

Medieval Women's Visionary Literature. Ed. Elizabeth A. Petroff. New York: Oxford University Press, 1986.

Medwick, Cathleen. *Teresa of Avila: The Progress of a Soul*. New York: Doubleday, 1999.

Meek, Christine, ed. *Women in Renaissance and Early Modern Europe*. Dublin and Portland: Four Courts Press, 2000.

Mendelson, Sara, and Patricia Crawford. *Women in Early Modern England, 1550–1720*. Oxford: Clarendon Press, 1998.

Merchant, Carolyn. *The Death of Nature: Women, Ecology and the Scientific Revolution*. New York: HarperCollins, 1980.

Merrim, Stephanie. *Early Modern Women's Writing and Sor Juana Inés de la Cruz*. Nashville, TN: Vanderbilt University Press, 1999.

Messbarger, Rebecca. *The Century of Women: The Representations of Women in Eighteenth-Century Italian Public Discourse*. Toronto: University of Toronto Press, 2002.

Miller, Nancy K. *The Heroine's Text: Readings in the French and English Novel, 1722–1782*. New York: Columbia University Press, 1980.

Miller, Naomi J. *Changing the Subject: Mary Wroth and Figurations of Gender in Early Modern England*. Lexington: University Press of Kentucky, 1996.

——— and Gary Waller, eds. *Reading Mary Wroth: Representing Alternatives in Early Modern England*. Knoxville: University of Tennessee Press, 1991.

Monson, Craig A. *Disembodied Voices: Music and Culture in an Early Modern Italian Convent*. Berkeley: University of California Press, 1995.

———., ed. *The Crannied Wall: Women, Religion, and the Arts in Early Modern Europe*. Ann Arbor: University of Michigan Press, 1992.

Moore, Cornelia Niekus. *The Maiden's Mirror: Reading Material for German Girls in the Sixteenth and Seventeenth Centuries*. Wiesbaden: Otto Harrassowitz, 1987.

Moore, Mary B. *Desiring Voices: Women Sonneteers and Petrarchism*. Carbondale: Southern Illinois University Press, 2000.

Mujica, Bárbara. *Women Writers of Early Modern Spain*. New Haven: Yale University Press, 2004.

Musacchio, Jacqueline Marie. *The Art and Ritual of Childbirth in Renaissance Italy*. New Haven: Yale University Press, 1999.

Newman, Barbara. *God and the Goddesses: Vision, Poetry, and Belief in the Middle Ages*. Philadelphia: University of Pennsylvania Press, 2003.

Newman, Karen. *Fashioning Femininity and English Renaissance Drama*. Chicago: University of Chicago Press, 1991.

O'Donnell, Mary Ann. *Aphra Behn: An Annotated Bibliography of Primary and Secondary Sources*. Aldershot and Brookfield: Ashgate Publishing Co., 2nd ed., 2004.

Okin, Susan Moller. *Women in Western Political Thought*. Princeton: Princeton University Press, 1979.

Ozment, Steven. *The Bürgermeister's Daughter: Scandal in a Sixteenth-Century German Town*. New York: St. Martin's Press, 1995.

———. *Flesh and Spirit: Private Life in Early Modern Germany*. New York: Penguin Putnam, 1999.

———. *When Fathers Ruled: Family Life in Reformation Europe*. Cambridge, MA: Harvard University Press, 1983.

Pacheco, Anita, ed. *Early [English] Women Writers: 1600–1720*. New York and London: Longman, 1998.

Pagels, Elaine. *Adam, Eve, and the Serpent*. New York: Harper Collins, 1988.

Panizza, Letizia, and Sharon Wood, eds. *A History of Women's Writing in Italy*. Cambridge: University Press, 2000.

Panizza, Letizia, ed. *Women in Italian Renaissance Culture and Society*. Oxford: European Humanities Research Centre, 2000.

Parker, Patricia. *Literary Fat Ladies: Rhetoric, Gender and Property*. London and New York: Methuen, 1987.

Pernoud, Regine, and Marie-Veronique Clin. *Joan of Arc: Her Story*. Rev. and trans. Jeremy DuQuesnay Adams. New York: St. Martin's Press, 1998.

Perry, Mary Elizabeth. *Crime and Society in Early Modern Seville*. Hanover, NH: University Press of New England, 1980.

———. *Gender and Disorder in Early Modern Seville*. Princeton: Princeton University Press, 1990.

———. *The Handless Maiden: Moriscos and the Politics of Religion in Early Modern Spain*. Princeton: Princeton University Press, 2005.

Petroff, Elizabeth A., ed. *Medieval Women's Visionary Literature*. New York: Oxford University Press, 1986.

Perry, Ruth. *The Celebrated Mary Astell: An Early English Feminist*. Chicago: University of Chicago Press, 1986.

The Practice and Representation of Reading in England. Ed. James Raven, Helen Small, and Naomi Tadmor. Cambridge: University Press, 1996.

Quilligan, Maureen. *Incest and Agency in Elizabeth's England*. Philadelphia: University of Pennsylvania Press, 2005.

Rabil, Albert. *Laura Cereta: Quattrocento Humanist*. Binghamton, NY: MRTS, 1981.

Ranft, Patricia. *Women in Western Intellectual Culture, 600–1500*. New York: Palgrave, 2002.

Rapley, Elizabeth. *A Social History of the Cloister: Daily Life in the Teaching Monasteries of the Old Regime.* Montreal: McGill-Queen's University Press, 2001.

———. *The Dévotés: Women and Church in Seventeenth-Century France.* Kingston, Ontario: Mc-Gill-Queen's University Press, 1989.

Raven, James, Helen Small, and Naomi Tadmor, eds. *The Practice and Representation of Reading in England.* Cambridge: University Press, 1996.

Reading Mary Wroth: Representing Alternatives in Early Modern England. Ed. Naomi Miller and Gary Waller. Knoxville: University of Tennessee Press, 1991.

Reardon, Colleen. *Holy Concord within Sacred Walls: Nuns and Music in Siena, 1575–1700.* Oxford: Oxford University Press, 2001.

Recovering Spain's Feminist Tradition. Ed. Lisa Vollendorf. New York: MLA, 2001.

Reid, Jonathan Andrew. "King's Sister—Queen of Dissent: Marguerite of Navarre (1492–1549) and Her Evangelical Network." Ph.D diss., University of Arizona, 2001.

Reiss, Sheryl E,. and David G. Wilkins, ed. *Beyond Isabella: Secular Women Patrons of Art in Renaissance Italy.* Kirksville, MO: Turman State University Press, 2001.

The Renaissance Englishwoman in Print: Counterbalancing the Canon. Ed. Anne M. Haselkorn and Betty Travitsky. Amherst: University of Massachusetts Press, 1990.

Renaissance Women Writers: French Texts/American Contexts. Ed. Anne R. Larsen and Colette H. Winn. Detroit, MI: Wayne State University Press, 1994.

Rereading Aphra Behn: History, Theory, and Criticism. Ed. Heidi Hutner. Charlottesville: University Press of Virginia, 1993.

Rheubottom, David. *Age, Marriage, and Politics in Fifteenth-Century Ragusa.* Oxford: Oxford University Press, 2000.

Richardson, Brian. *Printing, Writers and Readers in Renaissance Italy.* Cambridge: University Press, 1999.

Riddle, John M. *Contraception and Abortion from the Ancient World to the Renaissance.* Cambridge, MA: Harvard University Press, 1992.

———. *Eve's Herbs: A History of Contraception and Abortion in the West.* Cambridge, MA: Harvard University Press, 1997.

Roper, Lyndal. *The Holy Household: Women and Morals in Reformation Augsburg.* New York: Oxford University Press, 1989.

Rose, Mary Beth. *The Expense of Spirit: Love and Sexuality in English Renaissance Drama.* Ithaca, NY: Cornell University Press, 1988.

———. *Gender and Heroism in Early Modern English Literature.* Chicago: University of Chicago Press, 2002.

———, ed. *Women in the Middle Ages and the Renaissance: Literary and Historical Perspectives.* Syracuse: Syracuse University Press, 1986.

Rosenthal, Margaret F. *The Honest Courtesan: Veronica Franco, Citizen and Writer in Sixteenth-Century Venice.* Foreword by Catharine R. Stimpson. Chicago: University of Chicago Press, 1992.

Rublack, Ulinka, ed. *Gender in Early Modern German History.* Cambridge: Cambridge University Press, 2002.

Russell, Rinaldina, ed. *Feminist Encyclopedia of Italian Literature.* Westport, CT: Greenwood Press, 1997.

———. *Italian Women Writers: A Bio-Bibliographical Sourcebook.* Westport, CT: Greenwood Press, 1994.

Sackville-West, Vita. *Daughter of France: The Life of La Grande Mademoiselle.* Garden City, NY: Doubleday, 1959.

Sage, Lorna, ed. *Cambridge Guide to Women's Writing in English.* Cambridge: University Press, 1999.

Sánchez, Magdalena S. *The Empress, the Queen, and the Nun: Women and Power at the Court of Philip III of Spain.* Baltimore: Johns Hopkins University Press, 1998.

Sartori, Eva Martin, and Dorothy Wynne Zimmerman, eds. *French Women Writers: A Bio-Bibliographical Source Book.* Westport, CT: Greenwood Press, 1991.

Scaraffia, Lucetta, and Gabriella Zarri. *Women and Faith: Catholic Religious Life in Italy from Late Antiquity to the Present.* Cambridge, MA: Harvard University Press, 1999.

Scheepsma, Wybren. *Medieval Religious Women in the Low Countries: The 'Modern Devotion', the Canonesses of Windesheim, and Their Writings.* Rochester, NY: Boydell Press, 2004.

Schiebinger, Londa. *The Mind has no sex?: Women in the Origins of Modern Science.* Cambridge, MA: Harvard University Press, 1991.

———. *Nature's Body: Gender in the Making of Modern Science.* Boston: Beacon Press, 1993.

Schutte, Anne Jacobson, Thomas Kuehn, and Silvana Seidel Menchi, eds. *Time, Space, and Women's Lives in Early Modern Europe.* Kirksville, MO: Truman State University Press, 2001.

Schofield, Mary Anne, and Cecilia Macheski, eds. *Fetter'd or Free? British Women Novelists, 1670–1815.* Athens: Ohio University Press, 1986.

Schutte, Anne Jacobson. *Aspiring Saints: pretense of Holiness, Inquisition, and Gender in the Republic of Venice, 1618–1750.* Baltimore: Johns Hopkins University Press, 2001.

———, Thomas Kuehn, and Silvana Seidel Menchi, eds. *Time, Space, and Women's Lives in Early Modern Europe.* Kirksville, MO: Truman State University Press, 2001.

Seifert, Lewis C. *Fairy Tales, Sexuality and Gender in France 1690–1715: Nostalgic Utopias.* Cambridge, UK: Cambridge University Press, 1996.

Shannon, Laurie. *Sovereign Amity: Figures of Friendship in Shakespearean Contexts.* Chicago: University of Chicago Press, 2002.

Shemek, Deanna. *Ladies Errant: Wayward Women and Social Order in Early Modern Italy.* Durham, NC: Duke University Press, 1998.

Silent But for the Word. Ed. Margaret Hannay. Kent, OH: Kent State University Press, 1985.

The Single Woman in Medieval and Early Modern England: Her Life and Representation. Ed. Dorothea Kehler and Laurel Amtower. Tempe, AZ: MRTS, 2002.

Smarr, Janet L. *Joining the Conversation: Dialogues by Renaissance Women.* Ann Arbor: University of Michigan Press, 2005.

Smith, Hilda L. *Reason's Disciples: Seventeenth-Century English Feminists.* Urbana: University of Illinois Press, 1982.

———. *Women Writers and the Early Modern British Political Tradition.* Cambridge: Cambridge University Press, 1998.

Snook, Edith. *Women, Reading, and the Cultural Politics of Early Modern England.* Aldershot and Brookfield: Ashgate Publishing Co., 2005.

Sobel, Dava. *Galileo's Daughter: A Historical Memoir of Science, Faith, and Love.* New York: Penguin Books, 2000.

Sommerville, Margaret R. *Sex and Subjection: Attitudes to Women in Early-Modern Society.* London: Arnold, 1995.

Soufas, Teresa Scott. *Dramas of Distinction: A Study of Plays by Golden Age Women*. Lexington: The University Press of Kentucky, 1997.

Spencer, Jane. *The Rise of the Woman Novelist: From Aphra Behn to Jane Austen*. Oxford: Basil Blackwell, 1986.

Spender, Dale. *Mothers of the Novel: 100 Good Women Writers Before Jane Austen*. London and New York: Routledge, 1986.

Sperling, Jutta Gisela. *Convents and the Body Politic in Late Renaissance Venice*. Foreword by Catharine R. Stimpson. Chicago: University of Chicago Press, 1999.

Steinbrügge, Lieselotte. *The Moral Sex: Woman's Nature in the French Enlightenment*. Trans. Pamela E. Selwyn. New York: Oxford University Press, 1995.

Stephens, Sonya, ed. *A History of Women's Writing in France*. Cambridge: Cambridge University Press, 2000.

Stephenson, Barbara. *The Power and Patronage of Marguerite de Navarre*. Aldershot and Brookfield: Ashgate Publishing Co., 2004.

Stocker, Margarita. *Judith, Sexual Warrior: Women and Power in Western Culture*. New Haven: Yale University Press, 1998.

Straznacky, Marta. *Privacy, Playreading, and Women's Closet Drama, 1550–1700*. Cambridge: Cambridge University Press, 2004.

Stretton, Timothy. *Women Waging Law in Elizabethan England*. Cambridge: Cambridge University Press, 1998.

Strong Voices, Weak History: Early Women Writers and Canons in England, France, and Italy. Ed. Pamela J. Benson and Victoria Kirkham. Ann Arbor: University of Michigan Press, 2005.

Stuard, Susan M. "The Dominion of Gender: Women's Fortunes in the High Middle Ages." In Renate Bridenthal, Claudia Koonz, and Susan M. Stuard, eds. *Becoming Visible: Women in European History*. Third edition. Boston: Houghton Mifflin, 1998.

Summit, Jennifer. *Lost Property: The Woman Writer and English Literary History, 1380–1589*. Chicago: University of Chicago Press, 2000.

Surtz, Ronald E. *The Guitar of God: Gender, Power, and Authority in the Visionary World of Mother Juana de la Cruz (1481–1534)*. Philadelphia: University of Pennsylvania Press, 1991.

———. *Writing Women in Late Medieval and Early Modern Spain: The Mothers of Saint Teresa of Avila*. Philadelphia: University of Pennsylvania Press, 1995.

Suzuki, Mihoko. *Subordinate Subjects: Gender, the Political Nation, and Literary Form in England, 1588–1688*. Aldershot and Brookfield: Ashgate Publishing Co., 2003.

Tatlock, Lynne, and Christiane Bohnert, eds. *The Graph of Sex* (q.v.).

Teaching Tudor and Stuart Women Writers. Ed. Susanne Woods and Margaret P. Hannay. New York: MLA, 2000.

Teague, Frances. *Bathsua Makin, Woman of Learning*. Lewisburg, PA: Bucknell University Press, 1999.

Thomas, Anabel. *Art and Piety in the Female Religious Communities of Renaissance Italy: Iconography, Space, and the Religious Woman's Perspective*. New York: Cambridge University Press, 2003.

Tinagli, Paola. *Women in Italian Renaissance Art: Gender, Representation, Identity*. Manchester: Manchester University Press, 1997.

Todd, Janet. *The Secret Life of Aphra Behn*. London, New York, and Sydney: Pandora, 2000.

————. *The Sign of Angelica: Women, Writing and Fiction, 1660–1800*. New York: Columbia University Press, 1989.

Tomas, Natalie R. *The Medici Women: Gender and Power in Renaissance Florence*. Aldershot and Brookfield: Ashgate Publishing Co., 2004.

Traub, Valerie. *The Renaissance of Lesbianism in Early Modern England*. Cambridge: Cambridge University Press, 2002.

Valenze, Deborah. *The First Industrial Woman*. New York: Oxford University Press, 1995.

Van Dijk, Susan, Lia van Gemert, and Sheila Ottway, eds. *Writing the History of Women's Writing: Toward an International Approach*. Proceedings of the Colloquium, Amsterdam, 9–11 September. Amsterdam: Royal Netherlands Academy of Arts and Sciences, 2001.

Vickery, Amanda. *The Gentleman's Daughter: Women's Lives in Georgian England*. New Haven: Yale University Press, 1998.

Vollendorf, Lisa. *The Lives of Women: A New History of Inquisitional Spain*. Nashville, TN: Vanderbilt University Press, 2005.

Walker, Claire. *Gender and Politics in Early Modern Europe: English Convents in France and the Low Countries*. New York: Palgrave, 2003.

Wall, Wendy. *The Imprint of Gender: Authorship and Publication in the English Renaissance*. Ithaca, NY: Cornell University Press, 1993.

Walsh, William T. *St. Teresa of Avila: A Biography*. Rockford, IL: TAN Books & Publications, 1987.

Warner, Marina. *Alone of All Her Sex: The Myth and Cult of the Virgin Mary*. New York: Knopf, 1976.

Warnicke, Retha M. *The Marrying of Anne of Cleves: Royal Protocol in Tudor England*. Cambridge: Cambridge University Press, 2000.

Watt, Diane. *Secretaries of God: Women Prophets in Late Medieval and Early Modern England*. Cambridge, England: D. S. Brewer, 1997.

Weaver, Elissa. *Convent Theatre in Early Modern Italy: Spiritual Fun and Learning for Women*. New York: Cambridge University Press, 2002.

Weber, Alison. *Teresa of Avila and the Rhetoric of Femininity*. Princeton: Princeton University Press, 1990.

Welles, Marcia L. *Persephone's Girdle: Narratives of Rape in Seventeenth-Century Spanish Literature*. Nashville: Vanderbilt University Press, 2000.

Whitehead, Barbara J., ed. *Women's Education in Early Modern Europe: A History, 1500–1800*. New York and London: Garland Publishing Co., 1999.

Widowhood and Visual Culture in Early Modern Europe. Ed. Allison Levy. Aldershot and Brookfield: Ashgate Publishing Co., 2003.

Widowhood in Medieval and Early Modern Europe. Ed. Sandra Cavallo and Lydan Warner. New York: Longman, 1999.

Wiesner, Merry E. *Working Women in Renaissance Germany*. New Brunswick, NJ: Rutgers University Press, 1986.

Wiesner-Hanks, Merry E. *Christianity and Sexuality in the Early Modern World: Regulating Desire, Reforming Practice*. New York: Routledge, 2000.

————. *Gender, Church, and State in Early Modern Germany: Essays*. New York: Longman, 1998.

————. *Gender in History*. Malden, MA: Blackwell, 2001.

———. *Women and Gender in Early Modern Europe*. Cambridge: Cambridge University Press, 1993.

———. *Working Women in Renaissance Germany*. New Brunswick, NJ: Rutgers University Press, 1986.

Willard, Charity Cannon. *Christine de Pizan: Her Life and Works*. New York: Persea Books, 1984.

Wilson, Katharina, ed. *Encyclopedia of Continental Women Writers*. 2 vols. New York: Garland, 1991.

Winn, Colette, and Donna Kuizenga, eds. *Women Writers in Pre-Revolutionary France*. New York: Garland Publishing, 1997.

Winston-Allen, Anne. *Convent Chronicles: Women Writing about Women and Reform in the Late Middle Ages*. University Park: Pennsylvania State University Press, 2004.

Women and Monasticism in Medieval Europe: Sisters and Patrons of the Cistercian Reform, ed. Constance H. Berman. Kalamazoo: Western Michigan University Press, 2002.

Women, Crime and the Courts in Early Modern England. Ed. Jenny Kermode and Garthine Walker. Chapel Hill: University of North Carolina Press, 1994.

Women in Italian Renaissance Culture and Society. Ed. Letizia Panizza. Oxford: European Humanities Research Centre, 2000.

Women in Reformation and Counter-Reformation Europe: Public and Private Worlds. Ed. Sherrin Marshall. Bloomington, IN: Indiana University Press, 1989.

Women in Renaissance and Early Modern Europe. Ed. Christine Meek. Dublin-Portland: Four Courts Press, 2000.

Women in the Inquisition: Spain and the New World. Ed. Mary E. Giles. Baltimore: Johns Hopkins University Press, 1999.

Women in the Middle Ages and the Renaissance: Literary and Historical Perspectives. Ed. Mary Beth Rose. Syracuse: Syracuse University Press, 1986.

Women Players in England, 1500–1660: Beyond the All-Male Stage. Ed. Pamela Allen Brown and Peter Parolin. Aldershot and Brookfield: Ashgate Publishing Co., 2005.

Women, "Race," and Writing in the Early Modern Period. Ed. Margo Hendricks and Patricia Parker. London and New York: Routledge, 1994.

Woodbridge, Linda. *Women and the English Renaissance: Literature and the Nature of Womankind, 1540–1620*. Urbana: University of Illinois Press, 1984.

Woodford, Charlotte. *Nuns as Historians in Early Modern Germany*. Oxford: Clarendon Press, 2002.

Woods, Susanne. *Lanyer: A Renaissance Woman Poet*. New York: Oxford University Press, 1999.

——— and Margaret P. Hannay, eds. *Teaching Tudor and Stuart Women Writers*. New York: MLA, 2000.

Writing the Female Voice. Ed. Elizabeth C. Goldsmith. Boston: Northeastern University Press, 1989.

Writing the History of Women's Writing: Toward an International Approach. Ed. Susan Van Dijk, Lia van Gemert and Sheila Ottway Proceedings of the Colloquium, Amsterdam, 9–11 September. Amsterdam: Royal Netherlands Academy of Arts and Sciences, 2001.

INDEX